Fundamentals of Statistics in Health Administration

Robert W. Broyles, PhD
Director, MHA Program
Department of Health Administration and Policy
College of Public Health
University of Oklahoma
Oklahoma City, OK

JONES AND BARTLETT PUBLISHERS
Sudbury, Massachusetts
BOSTON TORONTO LONDON SINGAPORE

World Headquarters
Jones and Bartlett Publishers
40 Tall Pine Drive
Sudbury, MA 01776
978-443-5000
info@jbpub.com
www.jbpub.com

Jones and Bartlett Publishers
Canada
6339 Ormindale Way
Mississauga, Ontario L5V 1J2
CANADA

Jones and Bartlett Publishers
International
Barb House, Barb Mews
London W6 7PA
UK

Jones and Bartlett's books and products are available through most bookstores and online booksellers. To contact Jones and Bartlett Publishers directly, call 800-832-0034, fax 978-443-8000, or visit our website www.jbpub.com.

Substantial discounts on bulk quantities of Jones and Bartlett's publications are available to corporations, professional associations, and other qualified organizations. For details and specific discount information, contact the special sales department at Jones and Bartlett via the above contact information or send an email to specialsales@jbpub.com.

Production Credits
Publisher: Michael Brown
Production Director: Amy Rose
Associate Production Editor: Daniel Stone
Editorial Assistant: Kylah McNeill
Associate Marketing Manager: Marissa Hederson
Composition: Auburn Associates, Inc.
Cover Design: Kristin E. Ohlin
Manufacturing and Inventory Control: Therese Connell
Photo Research: Kimberly Potvin
Cover Image: © Photos.com
Printing and Binding: Malloy Incorporated
Cover Printing: Malloy Incorporated

Library of Congress Cataloging-in-Publication Data
Broyles, Robert W.
Fundamentals of statistics in health administration / by Robert W. Broyles.
p. ; cm.
Includes bibliographical references and index.
ISBN-13: 978-0-7637-4556-1 (pbk : alk. paper)
1. Medical statistics. 2. Health services administration—Statistical methods. 3. Microsoft Excel (Computer file) I. Broyles, Robert W. II. Title.
[DNLM: 1. Public Health Administration. 2. Statistics. WA 950 B885f 2006]
RA409.B847 2006
361.1'072'7—dc22

Printed in the United States of America
09 08 07 06 05 10 9 8 7 6 5 4 3 2 1

Contents

[R] – Indicates required material that all readers should review.
[O] – Indicates optional material for readers who are interested in more advanced topics.
[R,O] – Indicates both required and optional material.

[R] – Indicates required material that all readers should review.
[O] – Indicates optional material for readers who are interested in more advanced topics.
[R,O] – Indicates both required and optional material.

[R] – Indicates required material that all readers should review.
[O] – Indicates optional material for readers who are interested in more advanced topics.
[R,O] – Indicates both required and optional material.

Preface

This text has three objectives. The first is to present a unified and thorough examination of basic statistics. The second is to illustrate the applicability of statistical analysis to the problems that arise in a typical health service organization. The third is to ensure that the health administrator, or the student, of health administration is able to use Excel when performing the calculations related to the techniques described here. Thus, this book enhances the administrator's understanding of statistical concepts, the use of the computer to perform required calculations, and the application of statistical techniques to health administration.

Most elementary statistics texts rely on simple examples to illustrate the principles of basic concepts. In this book, simplified examples from the health field are used to illustrate statistical techniques and their usefulness to the health administrator. In addition, a set of learning objectives and a set of problems for solution accompany each chapter. These features allow the reader to assess his or her mastery of the statistical methods described in the chapter and to emphasize the problems or issues for which the statistical methods are useful. Solutions to selected problems appear in Appendix C.

Essentially, three approaches are used to illustrate statistical applications to health-related problems. First, each technique is described in detail so that the reader can perform the computations using a hand-held calculator. Second, statistical techniques are demonstrated by using an Excel spreadsheet to perform the computations. Finally, Excel's statistical functions are used to demonstrate most of the statistical concepts and techniques. Excel's statistical functions are surprisingly easy to use and immediately report results to the analyst. In this text, Excel spreadsheets or applications are presented as exhibits. Tables present basic data or mathematical operations that might be performed with a hand-held calculator.

The reliance on Excel and a computer to perform the calculations that accompany most statistical analyses is based on several considerations. First, most statistical applications that the health administrator performs require an analysis of large amounts of data. To accommodate these needs, an Excel spreadsheet or the statistical functions that are available in Excel allow the analyst to process large amounts of data with ease and precision. Second, Excel is extremely user friendly. After mastering the basics, the administrator or student of health administration can transfer those skills to other programs, such as SPSS or SAS. For those readers who are unfamiliar with Excel, Appendix B provides an introduction to spreadsheet basics. Finally, Excel is available in most health care institutions, thus supporting the decision to use Excel to illustrate statistical analyses.

Sections and chapters have been subdivided into several groups. Chapters or sections with a superscript "R" contain required material that all readers should review. Chapters or sections with a superscript "O" contain optional material for readers who are interested in slightly more advanced topics. Finally, chapters or sections with the superscript "R,O" contain both required and optional material.

Health administrators, students of health administration, and instructors who teach a one-semester course in basic statistics should be interested in this book. Thus, a few comments about this text's usefulness are now directed to each of these groups.

Because of the reliance on prospective payment systems, the typical administrator is required to control risk, to monitor the use of service, to control resource consumption, to improve the efficiency of operations, and to contain costs. In addition, he or she also must prepare forecasts that enable the organization to negotiate prices or fixed rates of payment that are based on an individual member of an insured population, the typical discharge, or the day of care. Because of the increased importance of strategic management and strategic planning, the administrator of the health facility must also identify internal strengths and weaknesses, organizational attributes that enhance or impede the ability of the organization to exploit opportunities or increase the adverse effects of threats that exist in the external environment. Because of these responsibilities, the administrator is increasingly forced to rely on a scientific approach to identify problems, to develop policies that are designed to reduce or eliminate undesired outcomes, and to evaluate the results of remedial actions or policies. Such an approach, however, requires a fundamental understanding of descriptive and inferential techniques. This text familiarizes the administrator with the fundamentals of statistical methods and their application to practical problems or issues within a typical health service organization.

Most students approach the study of statistics with anxiety because of difficulties that were previously encountered in their study of mathematics. On the other hand, most students recognize that an understanding of statistical methods is essential to a successful career in health administration. Because fear sometimes accompanies the study of statistics, presented are mathematical derivations and proofs at the lowest level necessary for understanding statistics. As discussed in this text, the presentation of statistics requires nothing more complicated than an understanding of a ratio.

This text is also tailored for an instructor who teaches a one-semester course in elementary statistics. The chapters or sections contain material that cover a full course for beginning students. Specifically, such a course might consist of the presentation of data in table or graph form; distributional properties (i.e., measures of location, dispersion, and skewness); the fundamentals of probability; theoretical probability distributions, to include the binomial probability distribution; the Poisson probability distribution and the normal distribution; the t distribution; the χ^2 distribution and the F distribution; inferences concerning the mean; inferences concerning the proportion; analysis of variance, excluding two-factor analysis of variance with replication; and an introduction to simple regression analysis. Depending on the skills or prior training of the students, the text also includes an introduction to multiple regression and forecasting methods.

Finally, introductory chapters are devoted to the simplest dimensions of statistics and form the foundation for an understanding of slightly more complicated statistical methods that are presented in later chapters. Thus, each chapter's content presents material that is necessary for the next. This approach will hopefully enhance the reader's understanding of the appropriate application of statistical techniques to the administration of the health service organization.

Robert W. Broyles, PhD

Acknowledgments

A work of this magnitude is impossible without the assistance of many contributors. A special word of gratitude is expressed to Mike Brown who guided this text from inception to fruition. Jennifer Allred edited the manuscript with precision and thoroughness. The clarity of the presentation is attributable, in large measure, to her diligence and skill. A special word of gratitude is expressed to Kylah McNeill, editorial assistant, for her patience and diligence in the editorial preparation of this text. The author is indebted to Daniel Stone who guided the text throughout the production phase. His suggestions resulted in an improved presentation and a more comprehensive exploration of statistical methods and their application to health services administration. To the graduate students in the Master of Health Administration Program offered by the Department of Health Administration and Policy who used early drafts, the author is also grateful.

Finally for her encouragement and patience, a special word of gratitude is expressed to my wife Rita. Without her understanding, this effort would not have been possible.

Although many contributed to this book, the author accepts responsibility for errors and omissions.

CHAPTER 1 Introduction to Statistics[R]

OBJECTIVES

1. Describe the importance of statistics in health administration.
2. Distinguish between a sample and a population or a universe.
3. Differentiate between a finite and an infinite population.
4. Describe the differences between descriptive and inferential statistics.
5. Differentiate between a statistic and a parameter.
6. Describe the sources of information that are available to the health administrator.

The Role of Statistics in Health Administration

Statistics is a valuable area of applied mathematics for administrators who are developing strategic plans, assessing alternate plans, and evaluating the operation of the health service organization under conditions of uncertainty. Here *statistics* is referred to as the assembly of information, the analysis of data, and the interpretation of results within an administrative or managerial setting. It emphasizes the application of statistical analyses to problems or issues that exist in health service organizations. Specifically, the focus is on the usefulness of statistical analysis in evaluating the internal environment, identifying or solving problems, reducing deficiencies in performance, developing institutional policies, and making decisions that influence not only daily operations but also the strategic position of the health organization.

The importance of statistics in health administration is demonstrated by first considering the problem of monitoring, evaluating, and controlling internal operations. Figure 1.1 is based on the idea that unidentified problems are unlikely to be resolved. It assumes that comparing or contrasting the actual results of activity with a standard of performance identifies the problem. An unfavorable or undesirable difference suggests that a problem exists and that a remedial plan needs to be applied. After initiating the plan, measuring its effects, and assessing the results, the administrator may decide that the problem is resolved and that no further action is required. In contrast, the comparison or contrast may indicate that the remedial plan was only partially successful or that it created additional problems.

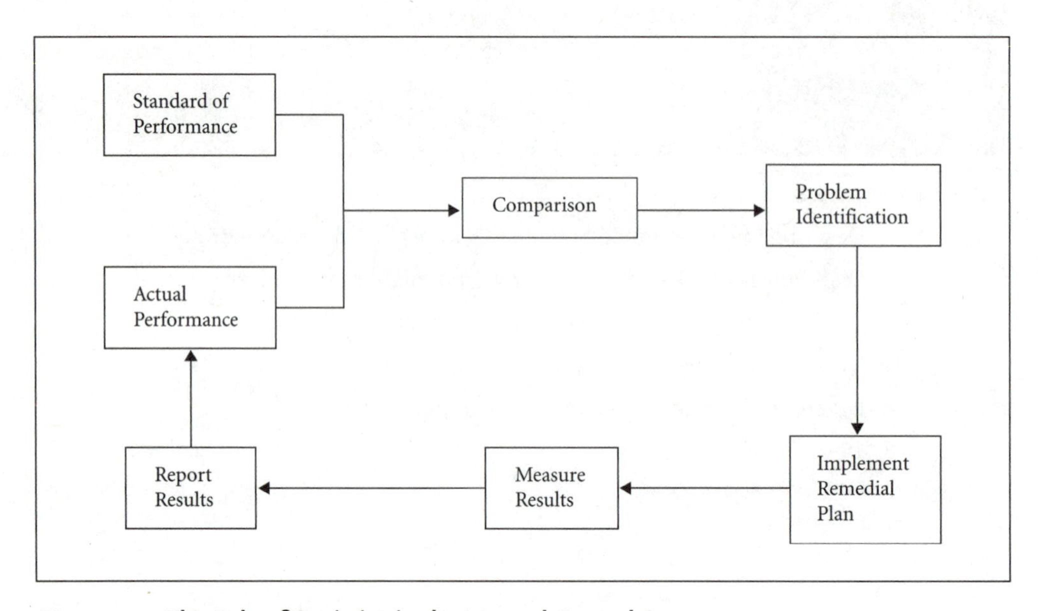

Figure 1.1 **The Role of Statistics in the Internal Control System**

Statistical analyses help to identify problems. Specifically, the standard of performance frequently represents a projection of desired results and might be developed using standard statistical techniques that describe the distributional properties of data that depict the clinical, operational, or financial performance of the organization. For example, the standard of performance might be expressed as the average length of stay or the use of ancillary care by the typical patient assigned to a given diagnostic group or risk category. Obviously, the development of treatment protocols is valuable when evaluating the quality of care, resource use, and related costs. Health organizations must monitor and control costs. A statistical estimate of the relationship between cost and volume enables the institution to set limits on acceptable expenses, to identify situations in which excessive costs were incurred, to isolate the causes, or to implement a remedial plan. Furthermore, simple contrasts between the actual performance and the standard of performance might identify the excessive use of service or resources, outcomes that might compromise the fiscal well-being of the health service organization.

In addition to problem identification and resolution, statistical analyses might be applied to the process of strategic management. Specifically, the situational analysis focuses on the internal and external environment of the health service organization. Evaluating the external environment identifies threats and opportunities. In contrast, when evaluating the internal environment, strengths and weaknesses of the organization should be identified. Focusing on human resources, the clinical function, the administrative function, and information technology, a weakness is an organizational attribute that increases the adverse effects of an external threat or prevents the organization from taking advantage of an opportunity. A strength is a characteristic that insulates the organization from the effects of threats or enhances the organization's ability to take advantage of opportunities that exist or are emerging in the external environment. Accordingly, statistical analysis might be used to

1. Assure the flow of resources, such as labor, supplies, and technology, that are required to provide care
2. Evaluate alternate plans that the administrator might adopt
3. Evaluate new methods of delivering health services or the need to alter the organization's structure
4. Assess the efficiency and effectiveness of the organization in its operating activity
5. Assure the quality of care
6. Ensure the fiscal well-being of the facility in the short term and the adequacy of resources in the long term

This text is intended to explore those statistical techniques that play an increasingly important role in monitoring, evaluating, controlling, and improving the performance of the health service organization.

Basic Definitions

Statistics is used in a variety of contexts, with each having a specific meaning. First, when used in its commonly accepted sense, statistics refers to numeric information and is used when referring to any area that might be expressed numerically. For example, the attributes of an enrolled population, a population at risk, or the daily census might be expressed numerically and might represent the common interpretation of the term statistics. Second, statistics also is used when referring to a body of techniques that are applied in the process of collecting, analyzing, interpreting, and presenting numeric information.

Finally, *statistic* refers to a single value that is derived from a sample selected from a universe or population of interest. A *universe* or *population* is defined as all observations or all theoretically conceivable observations concerning a phenomenon of interest. Populations or universes are further described as finite or infinite. A *finite population* is a universe for which it is possible to list all elements. For example, suppose an inpatient census for a given day represents the population of interest. In this case, it is possible to list all elements or patients that comprise the universe. In contrast, an *infinite population* is unbounded and usually results from the operation of a process under constant conditions. For example, the population of interest might consist of all previous emergency room visits and all of those that might occur in the future. It is not possible to list the elements of an infinite population, and as a result, data derived from a sample of the universe are required to examine the issue of administrative interest.

A *sample* is a subset of the population or universe of interest and conveys information that is of administrative usefulness. Based on the data derived from a sample, we might calculate a statistic that is valuable to the administrator. For example, based on a subset of the appropriate population, the administrator frequently is interested in a statistic such as the average length of stay, the average number of admissions, the average number of visits to the emergency room, or the average number of ancillary services used by patients who are grouped by diagnostic or risk category.

In this text, a sample is differentiated from a population in several ways. First, *parameter* is used when referring to a population, and *statistic* is used when referring to a sample. Furthermore, Greek letters, such as β, μ or σ, are used to identify the parameters of the population. Conversely, statistics derived from samples are represented by letters such as S, r, or b and are used as estimates of their corresponding parameters.

An application of statistical methods requires an understanding of the term *variable.* As indicated previously here, the phenomenon that is of interest to the health administrator exhibits variability or variation. For example, suppose the organization selected a sample of 10 adult discharges and recorded their ages as 23, 45, 34, 35, 67, 54, 64, 43, 32, and 60 years old. In this case, the variable age exhibits variation among the observations. A factor that exhibits variability or volatility or assumes different values is called a variable.

Variables might be classified in terms of their quantitative or qualitative attributes. A *quantitative variable* measures outcomes that are expressed numerically. Examples of quantitative variables include the patient's age, the percentage of outstanding receivables that are recognized as a bad debt, and the days of care the organization provided during a well-specified period. A *qualitative variable* consists of outcomes that without modification are not expressed numerically. Patient satisfaction, represented by very satisfied, satisfied, dissatisfied, and very dissatisfied, and an evaluation of departmental performance, measured by good, fair, or poor, are examples of a qualitative variable. When the administrator applies statistical methods or techniques, the focus of the analysis is on one or more variables.

We frequently apply statistical analyses to problems that involve components of direct patient care, namely, stay-specific and ancillary services. Stay-specific services are components of care that are measured by the number of days of service provided to a patient, to a group of patients, or during a given period. Similarly, we define ancillary services as components of care that are measured by the number of procedures provided to a patient, to a group of patients, or during a specific period. Accordingly, ancillary services are represented by the set of procedures that is provided by the laboratory or radiology and are measured in units of service.

Descriptive and Inferential Statistics

Figure 1.2 presents an overview of statistics, which consists of two distinct branches: descriptive and inferential. The descriptive branch of statistics consists of methods or techniques that are used to rearrange data into a more useful form and methods that are used to measure the properties of a distribution that depicts a set of data. In contrast, the inferential branch of statistics consists of methods that enable the administrator to develop generalizations, estimations, or predictions concerning the phenomenon of managerial interest.

Descriptive Statistics: An Introduction

Descriptive statistics is occasionally limited to methods that might be adopted to describe or present data in a table or as a graph. To illustrate the usefulness of descriptive statistics, consider a set of data that depicts the use of stay-specific services as indicated by the length of stay experienced by 100 patients. In this case, we could present the length of stay for each of the 100 patients in a more useful form.

Assume that the administrator is interested in grouping patients in terms of hospital episodes that extended from 1 to 5 days, 6 to 10 days, 11 to 15 days, and more than 15 days. Adopting these categories, the data depicting the hospital stays of the 100 patients might be presented as the frequency distribution (Table 1.1).

The first column of the table shows the categories that define the frequency distribution. The frequencies in the second column correspond to the number of patients assigned to each group. The distribution indicates that 32 of the 100 patients experienced a 1- to 5-day length of stay.

The relative frequency distribution appears in the final column and indicates the proportion or percentage of patients assigned to each of the categories. These data indicate that 32% of the patients experienced a 1- to 5-day hospital stay. Rather than presenting a list of 100 patients and their corresponding lengths of stay, the frequency distribution is a convenient device that summarizes data and presents numeric information in more useable form.

In addition to presenting information as a graph or table, descriptive statistics, as presented in this text, also includes any treatment of data that does not involve generalizations, predictions, or estimations. Once generalizations, estimations, or predictions are involved, the analysis is inferential rather than descriptive. Hence, inferential statistics allows the administrator to rely on predictions, estimations, and generalizations when developing, implementing, or evaluating decisions.

The distinction between descriptive and inferential statistics might be shown with this simple example. Suppose the administrator is interested in the use of stay-specific services, measured by the length of stay, by patients presenting with diseases of the digestive system, and by patients presenting with diseases of the circulatory system. Five medical records were selected from individuals who were diagnosed with a digestive system disease. The lengths of stay were 4, 6, 7, 10, and

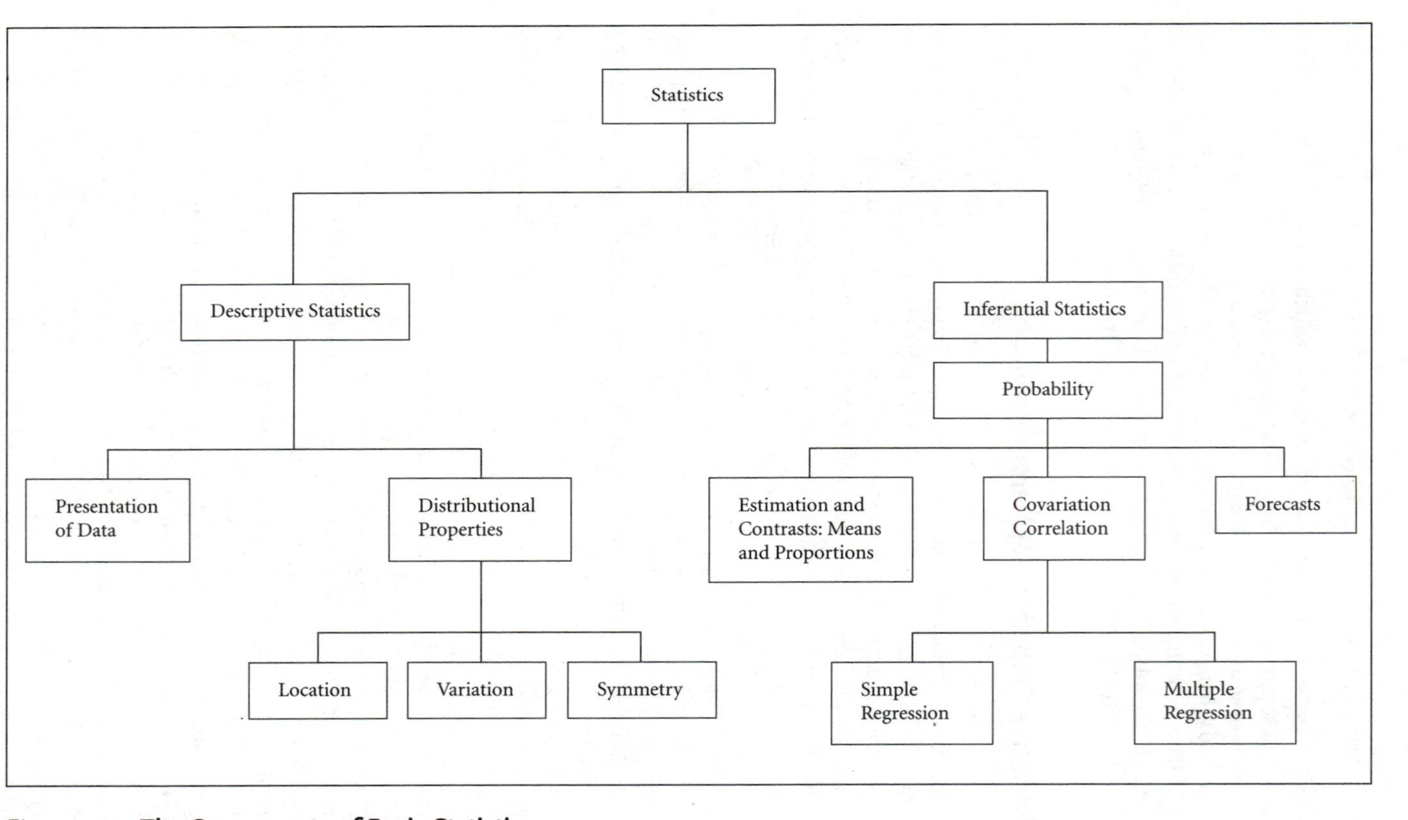

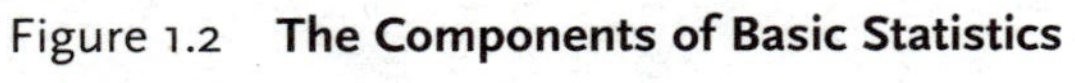

Figure 1.2 **The Components of Basic Statistics**

Table 1.1 **Frequency and Relative Frequency Distribution of 100 Patients**

Length of Stay	Frequency	Relative Frequency
1 to 5	32	0.32
6 to 10	43	0.43
11 to 15	15	0.15
More than 15	10	0.10
Total	100	1.00

13 days. The medical records for five patients presenting with a circulatory system disease were also chosen. Their corresponding lengths of stay were 5, 7, 9, 10, and 14 days. Based on these data, patients with a digestive system disease experienced an average stay of

$$(4 + 6 + 7 + 10 + 13)/5$$

or 8 days. Similarly, the average stay for patients with a disease of the circulatory system was

$$(5 + 7 + 9 + 10 + 14)/5$$

or 9 days.

Thus far, we used simple arithmetic rules to calculate a single value for each set of data. The resulting averages are descriptive of the data and contribute nothing to the original information. Rather, the calculations simply rearranged the data and enabled us to present the information in a more useable form. Accordingly, the mathematical operations described thus far are descriptive rather than inferential statistics.

Inferential Statistics: Their Role in Health Administration

Based on the previous calculations, suppose that the analyst concluded that patients with a circulatory system disease remained in the hospital longer than individuals diagnosed with a digestive system disease. In this case, the analysis and related conclusion far exceed the information originally provided. When we conclude that one group of patients experienced a longer length of stay than another, we move from descriptive statistics to inferential statistics.

Referring to the example, the difference between the two averages does not necessarily imply that patients with a circulatory system disease remain in the hospital longer than individuals with a digestive system disease. The original data reveal that several patients with a digestive system disease experienced a longer stay than those who were diagnosed with a circulatory system disease. In addition, considerable differences exist among the hospital episodes experienced by patients assigned to the same diagnostic category. It also is possible that a second sample might have results that are reversed. The observed difference between the two averages, given by 9 – 8 (or 1 day), might be attributable to chance and chance alone.

Before concluding that the observed difference implies that one group remained longer than another, several issues must be resolved. First, if the observed difference was very large and without a detailed statistical analysis, we are tempted to conclude that patients with a circulatory system disease experienced a longer length of stay than those with a digestive system disease. In contrast, if the difference is very small, we are tempted to conclude that the two groups experienced the same length of stay. Unfortunately, when expressed in natural or epidemiologic units, the terms *very small* and *very large* lack precision and may vary. Before concluding that one average is larger or smaller than another, it is necessary to develop the criteria that enable us to conclude that a difference is very large or small.

A second and related issue that influences the conclusion concerning the comparison or contrast involves the controls that were applied when the data were selected. It is possible that the process of selecting the data may prevent a meaningful conclusion regarding the observed difference. For example, it is possible that patients with a circulatory system disease presented more secondary conditions than those with a digestive system disease. Suppose further that the sample of patients with a circulatory system disease consisted of older individuals, whereas those in the other group were relatively young. However, advancing age is frequently accompanied by a decline in the individual's health and ability to recuperate. In this situation, the observed difference may be related more to the age distribution of the two samples than to the presenting diagnosis. The discharge status of the patients included in the two samples is of importance to inferences regarding the difference between the two averages. Assume, for example, that several of the patients with a digestive system disease died during the hospital episode, whereas all individuals with a circulatory system disease were discharged alive. Thus, the observed difference between the two averages may be attributable more to the patients' discharge status than to the individuals' diagnosis.

The discussion implies that the statistical treatment of data requires more than collecting data, performing calculations, observing differences, and reaching a conclusion. Rather, the method of assembling information and the application of an appropriate research design are of primary importance when analyzing data and reaching valid conclusions or deriving generalizations. An appropriate application of inferential statistics is only one of several essential ingredients in assessing numerical information, reaching valid conclusions, and implementing policies that are designed to improve the performance of the health service organization.

A Statistical Overview

Figure 1.2 shows that statistics consists of two branches: descriptive and inferential. The descriptive branch consists of two main components. As described by the length of stay example, the first consists of techniques that enable the administrator to rearrange data and present numeric information in a table or graph. The second focuses on the methods that are used to measure or describe a distribution. This text focuses on measures that are used to describe the location, scatter or dispersion, skewness, or lack of symmetry associated with a set of data.

The second branch, inferential statistics, enables the administrator to evaluate numerical data, interpret results under conditions of uncertainty, and develop generalizations, predictions, and estimations. The concept of probability forms the foundation for understanding inferential statistics (Figure 1.2). Before exploring inferential statistics, we examine the basic concepts of probability, several theoretical probability distributions, and the sampling distribution of the mean. A major objective of inferential statistics is to use data assembled from a sample to derive generalizations concerning a parameter of the corresponding population or universe. The focus on probability provides the foundation for not only the development of generalizations under conditions of uncertainty but also the interpretation of theoretical sampling distributions and theoretical probability distributions. Theoretical probability distributions such as the standard normal and the t-distribution enable us to develop inferences concerning the mean, the proportion, and statistics derived by regression analysis (Chapter 5). Similarly, Chapters 7 and 8 indicate that an assessment of differences among multiple proportions and means requires an understanding of the χ^2 and F distributions, respectively.

Figure 1.2 also indicates that covariation and correlation analysis are used to examine the direction of association or relationship in a *bivariate analysis*, defined as one that focuses on only two variables. Covariation indicates the direction of association between two variables and is used to identify a direct or inverse relationship. A direct or positive relationship occurs if the value of one variable increases as the value of the other grows. In contrast, in an inverse or negative relationship, the value of one variable grows while the value of the other declines. Correlation analysis enables us to identify not only the direction of relationship but also the strength of the association that exists in a bivariate analysis.

In turn, covariation and correlation form the basis for understanding and using regression analysis to identify or resolve problems or issues that occur in the health service organization. The purpose of simple regression analysis is to establish the relationship between the dependent variable, representing the administrative interest, and a single independent variable, a factor that is believed to influence the value of the dependent variable. For example, the cost of care is of primary concern to the health administrator and, therefore, might represent the item of interest or the dependent variable. In the short term, it is possible to argue that the volume of service is a primary factor that influences cost, and as measured by days of care or the number of visits, volume might represent the independent variable. In the simplified example, simple regression analysis is an approach that allows the administrator to capture the relationship between cost and the volume of service.

Multiple regression analysis is an extension of its simple counterpart. When multiple regression is performed, the number of independent variables is two or more, enabling us to incorporate several factors in an examination of an administrative phenomenon requiring explanation or prediction. For example, the use of care is obviously important to the typical health service organization. In this case, however, the factors that influence the use of care include the patient's age, gender, insurance status, health status, exposure to lifestyle, occupational or environmental risks, social or racial status, and income. Hence, the inclusion of several independent variables in the analysis allows the administrator to explain the phenomenon of interest or to derive predictions with greater precision.

The text concludes with a discussion of methods that might be used to develop projections or forecasts (Figure 1.2). The development of accurate predictions is fundamentally important to the preparation of the organization's budget and the development of operating plans. The development of projections frequently requires a reliance on *time series data*, defined as information that is recorded and reported at equal intervals. The hospital's daily census, financial statements, and monthly operating reports are examples of time series data. Time series data that are recorded annually may exhibit an increasing or decreasing trend, represented by a long-term rise or fall, respectively. Simple regression analysis might be adopted to estimate trend values or the value of the dependent variable for a given year. Similarly, the time series might exhibit seasonal variation. Seasonal factors result in recurring patterns of variation that occur during the span of 1 year. In such a situation, the method of seasonal decomposition might be applied to the general problem of projecting trend and adjusting estimates for seasonal effects. However, an application of seasonal decomposition to the general problem of developing forecasts requires the use of multiple regression analysis.

In summary, statistics consists of two branches: descriptive and inferential statistics. The primary objective of descriptive statistics is to rearrange one or more sets of numeric information into a more useable form and to describe the properties of the distribution. Inferential statistics is based on theoretical probability and sampling distributions. The primary purpose of inferential statistics is to develop generalizations or estimates concerning the mean or the proportion and to develop indicators of relationship between a dependent variable and one or more independent variables.

Sources of Information

As indicated previously here, numeric information is an essential ingredient in any statistical analysis. Thus, before an application of statistical methods, the analyst must evaluate the relevance, reliability, and validity of data. This section reviews various sources of information that are available to the administrator.

The Internal Information System

The information system that the typical health service organization maintains is an invaluable source of data. In general, the data derived from the information system portray financial, clinical, and operational activity. As such, the information assembled and maintained by the organization is an essential ingredient in the process of planning, monitoring, evaluating, and controlling internal affairs.

For example, the financial reporting system of the organization assembles the fiscal data that are communicated to those who use the information to evaluate the organization and to develop or implement decisions that influence operational activity. The two most important types of financial statements are as follows: The first, represented by the income statement or statement of changes in financial position, summarizes the revenues, expenses, and the net surplus or loss for the period. The income statement is a summary of the resources that the health service organization generates internally. The second report is the balance sheet or the statement of financial position. The balance sheet summarizes the assets or resources of the organization, the obligations of the organization to external entities, and residual ownership or equity at the end of the accounting period. In addition, the typical health service organization also generates reports that show the receipt of supplies, payments to those who provide the resources that are required in operations, and reports that depict outstanding receivables, accounts payable, and capital expenses.

The financial statements are particularly valuable when evaluating periodic changes in four domains of fiscal performance. In particular, the income statement allows the administrator to assess changes in profitability, which refers to the organization's ability to earn revenues in excess of expenses and thereby contribute to internally generated funds that are required to acquire necessary resources. The second domain is debt structure, which measures the organization's relative dependence on external credit sources to acquire assets or resources. The third is liquidity, which is the ability of the organization to honor its currently maturing obligations to outside sources. Finally, the fiscal statements might be used to evaluate the intensity of asset use, which is the amount of revenue earned by providing care relative to the assets of the organization.

In addition to the financial reporting system, the typical health service organization also maintains data that measure clinical and operating activity. The clinical information system assembles data that depict the organization's provision of stay-specific and ancillary care, grouped by patient, diagnostic category, risk group, or departmental unit. For example, the days of care provided to a given patient or patients assigned to a diagnostic group or risk category might enable the analyst to assess the effectiveness or quality of service. Similarly, data that measure the intensity of providing outpatient care or laboratory, radiologic, and rehabilitative services are also of value when assessing the effectiveness of clinical activity.

Information systems that measure operating activity routinely assemble data that depict resource use, measured in real or physical terms. Data depicting the use of resources (such as labor and supplies) that are consumed in the provision of stay-specific or ancillary care are valuable. For example, the use of labor, grouped by occupational category, and consumable supplies, classified by the type of item, to provide each service in the set of procedures offered by the laboratory forms the basis for assessing the efficiency of the unit. When combined with the volume of each procedure, data that measure operating activity allow the administrator to monitor, evaluate, and control the efficiency of operations, as indicated by the consumption of resources per unit of service provided.

Recurrent reports and related statistical analyses may identify a problem or weakness that requires the implementation of a remedial action or policy (Figure 1.1). When a problem or weakness is identified, information may need to be assembled, and after appropriate analysis, a special or nonrecurrent report may need to be prepared so that the organization can address the issue. As a consequence, the data derived from the recurrent reporting system are supplemented by numeric information that enables the administrator to assess the specific problem in detail.

External Sources of Data

In addition to the information that the health service organization gathers, data from external entities may be required to resolve specific problems or to develop policies that are designed to reduce or eliminate weaknesses. For example, data files available to the public assemble information that depicts the prevalence or incidence of mortality and morbidity in a well-defined geographic area such as the county. Public entities, such as state departments of health, publish data that describe the use of inpatient and ambulatory care, grouped by diagnostic classification. Data depicting charges, measures of case complexity or severity, and patient attributes also are frequently available in these sources. Data assembled by external sources might be applied in a comparative analysis that is designed to assess the performance of the organization relative to similar facilities.

Before adopting data derived from external entities, the validity, reliability, applicability, and continuity of the information need to be assessed, a process that requires a distinction between primary and secondary sources. A *primary source* is an organization or entity that not only collects information but also publishes related data. A *secondary source* is an organization or entity that publishes data that another agency or institution collects.

Data obtained from primary sources may be more reliable than information available from secondary sources. In addition, data derived from primary sources also are more complete than the data from secondary sources. In particular, detailed or disaggregated data appearing in a primary source may be eliminated when presented in a secondary source. Similarly, details regarding variable descriptions, definitions, and methods of collection that appear in a primary source may be omitted or presented in condensed format when the information is presented in a secondary source. Finally, it is possible that data presented in a primary source may be subject to clerical error when the information is transcribed. Hence, information available from primary sources is likely to be more accurate or reliable than similar data appearing in a secondary source.

Occasionally, the health administrator may require data that are not available from internal or external sources. In such a situation, the administrator might rely on a survey or an experiment to obtain needed information.

Surveys

A survey is a process of collecting information without effective control over factors or variables that might influence population characteristics or measures of the item of interest. Most are familiar with surveys and the process of completing a questionnaire or responding to the questions of an interviewer. Suppose the director of human resources is interested in obtaining information concerning the salaries of 2,000 registered nurses in a given market area. In this case, the characteristic of interest, salaries, may be influenced by age, gender, and years of experience. When collecting the information, however, the administrator has no control over the age, gender, or years of experience of respondents because these are individual attributes.

Surveys are frequently used to collect or assemble data. For example, the health service organization might require information that depicts the health status of families residing in the service area or the perception of potential patients regarding the prestige of the facility. A survey may be self-administered, implying that the respondent completes the survey by addressing each item appearing on a prearranged questionnaire. In contrast, a trained interviewer may administer the survey, ask a series of questions that appears on the interview schedule, and record the respondent's answers. Generally, the interview schedule contains instructions that designate the question order, the interpretation of responses, and the method of recording the respondent's answers. The reliance on a trained interviewer usually increases the proportion of surveys that are usable and lowers the tendency of respondents to misinterpret questions. On the other hand, the interviewer may distort responses to the survey. For example, the interviewer may ignore directions for selecting respondents, an outcome that may bias statistical analyses and related results. In addition, the interviewer may influence responses by the method of asking questions or an inadvertent gesture.

Surveys frequently generate required information that is unavailable from internal sources. In these circumstances, the survey may assemble data based on a census or a sample. As previously mentioned, the totality of the phenomenon is referred to as the population or universe. A *sampling frame* lists all of the elements or members of the population. For example, suppose that the director of human relations is interested in the morale of employees who provide outpatient care and develops a survey that is designed to assess their satisfaction with working conditions. In this case, the sampling frame consists of those employed in the emergency room or in ambulatory clinics. In turn, employees who are included in the survey might be selected from the sampling frame.

A survey that includes all members of the population is called a census. In general, the reliance on a census to collect information is expensive and time consuming, features that reduce the desirability of including all members of the population in a survey. For example, the administrator might be interested in the risks present in an insured population. In such a situation, it may not be possible to contact all individuals and assess their health status. Instead, a sample of the insured population might be selected, and based on related data, the administrator is able to develop inferences concerning the health status of those included in the insured population.

A sample is frequently preferred to a census for several reasons. First, a sample can provide valid and reliable data at less cost than a census. In addition, a sample is likely to provide data on a timelier basis than a census because a smaller amount of information must be collected and analyzed. Furthermore, interviewer bias, typographic errors, and clerical errors are typically lower in a sample than in a census. A sample is a smaller undertaking than a census, and the opportunity to ensure the accuracy of data is correspondingly greater.

Although several advantages accompany the decision to administer a survey to a sample of the population, a complete census may be necessary and desirable. Specifically, if the finite population is small and complete information is required, a census is preferred. Thus, the relative advantage of a sample or a census depends on the size of the population and the nature of the administrative issue or problem.

Experiments

Unlike a survey, an experiment collects information when control is exercised over some or all of the variables that might influence the population characteristic or item of interest. For example, the administrator might be interested in examining whether training in dental hygiene reduces the incidence of caries, gingivitis, or periodontal disease. In this case, we might divide patients into two groups that are similar in terms of age, gender, education, and other factors that might influence the effectiveness of the program. We then provide training to one of the groups (called the experimental group) and let the other group (called the control group) continue without training. Because the two groups are similar in terms of age, gender, education, and so forth, differences in the presence of dental disease might be attributed to the training program.

CHAPTER 2 THE PRESENTATION OF DATA[R]

OBJECTIVES

1. Describe the importance of constructing a frequency distribution.
2. Define the terms class frequency, the class interval, the lower class limit, the upper class limit, and the midpoint or the class mark.
3. Distinguish between a quantitative and a qualitative distribution.
4. Use Excel to construct a frequency, a cumulative frequency, and a relative frequency distribution.
5. Use Excel to construct a bar chart, a pie chart, a radar chart, and a line chart.

As described in Chapter 1, descriptive statistics consists of essentially two components. The first is on methods that are used to present information in a more useable format. The second consists of methods that are used to calculate indicators that measure the properties of a distribution. This chapter and Chapter 3 focus on descriptive statistics. The remaining chapters emphasize inferential statistics.

FREQUENCY DISTRIBUTIONS

A typical health administrator is required to review streams of data that depict clinical, financial, and operating activity. When confronted with a large amount of data, the analyst can conveniently and usefully summarize or rearrange information by using one of several methods. However, when information is summarized, the analyst may describe too much or too little detail. Too much detail may prevent the administrator from identifying essential relationships or interpreting the information appropriately. Too little detail may reduce the usefulness of the data. Obviously, both of these situations should be avoided.

For example, suppose that we are interested in the volume of ancillary services, measured in units, consumed by 1,000 patients treated recently in ambulatory clinics operated by a multi-institutional arrangement. In this situation, it is possible to list the volume of service that each of the 1,000 patients consumes. However, such an approach generates too much detail and may prevent the administrator from developing an appropriate impression of the situation. In contrast, if only the average number of units per patient is presented, the administrator may have too little information.

It is convenient when assessing the use of service by a large number of patients to sort the observations into groups or categories, thus preventing too much or too little detail. For example, the volume of ancillary service consumed by each of the 1,000 patients might have been grouped by using the categories 1–5, 6–10, 11–15, and 16–20 units per person. In this case, the resulting frequency distribution might appear as shown in Table 2.1. A frequency distribution indicates the number of observations or items assigned to each of the categories. In terms of the example, the distribution indicates that 450 of the patients used between 1 and 5 units of ancillary care and that 150 of the individuals required between 16 and 20 units of service.

As indicated, the frequency distribution merely rearranges information into a more useable and understandable form. However, the details appearing in the original set of information are omitted. For example, the distribution appearing in Table 2.1 does not permit us to determine the minimum or maximum number of services per person. Also, the distribution does not indicate the number of services that each of the 450 individuals who required between 1 and 5 units of care consumed.

Table 2.1 also helps to construct a relative frequency distribution that indicates the proportion of items or observations assigned to each category. Let f_i represent the number of observations associated with a given category and T correspond to the total number of observations or items. Expressed as a proportion, the relative frequency distribution is given by the ratio:

$$f_i/T$$

Referring to the example, 210 patients consumed 6 to 10 units per person, implying that the relative frequency is simply 210/1,000 or 0.21. When multiplied by 100, these results indicate that 21% of the observations were assigned to the category.

Before discussing the process of constructing a frequency distribution, a *quantitative frequency distribution* and a *qualitative frequency distribution* should be differentiated. A quantitative frequency distribution is one in which the cate-

Table 2.1 **Outpatients' Use of Ancillary Services**

Units per Patient (1)	Number of Patients (2)	Relative Frequency (3)
1 to 5	450	0.45
6 to 10	210	0.21
11 to 15	190	0.19
16 to 20	150	0.15
Total	1,000	1.00

gories that are used to group the patients are expressed numerically. Table 2.1 is an example of a quantitative frequency distribution. In contrast, the groups that comprise a qualitative frequency distribution are defined by categories. For example, the administrator might require a distribution of the 1,000 patients, grouped by diagnostic name or the primary symptom that brought about the visit to one of several clinics. In such a situation, a distribution defined in terms of diagnosis or primary symptom is an example of a categorical or qualitative frequency distribution.

For example, suppose that the administrator is interested in the distribution of the 1,000 patients, grouped by diagnostic nomenclature. Table 2.2 shows that the categories comprising the distribution are defined in qualitative terms, represented by the diagnostic categories. These data indicate that 150 of the patients presented an eye disorder, whereas 250 of the patients were treated for a digestive system disorder. The distribution of relative frequencies indicates that 20% of the patients were treated for a respiratory system disorder and that 40% of the 1,000 patients had a nervous system disorder.

The construction of a frequency distribution consists of three steps. The first is to select the categories that will characterize the distribution. The second is to sort the data into selected categories, and the third requires the analyst to count the items assigned to each group. Because computer software should be used to complete the second and third steps, only the first is considered in this chapter.

The selection of categories requires two decisions. The first is the number of classes that will characterize the distribution. The number of categories used in a given situation depends on the purpose the distribution is intended to serve and the number of observations available to the analyst. For example, if the data consist of 25 observations, little is accomplished by employing 20 categories because it is likely that many groups would contain no observations. On the other hand, the adoption of only two categories is not likely to provide enough information.

As indicated, the number of categories in a distribution is a matter of judgment. However, it is common to use no fewer than 5 groups or more than 20 groups. Furthermore, the categories must be selected so that the classes are col-

Table 2.2 **Distribution of Patients, Grouped by Diagnosis**

Category	Frequency	Relative Frequency
Digestive Disorders	250	0.25
Eye Disorders	150	0.15
Respiratory Disorders	200	0.20
Nervous System Disorders	400	0.40
Total	1,000	1.00

lectively exhaustive and mutually exclusive. *Collectively exhaustive* means that the distribution will accommodate all observations, ranging from the smallest to the largest value in the set of data. *Mutual exclusion* simply means that an observation is assigned to one and only one category.

The second decision requires a specification of the *class interval,* which indicates the range of values contained in a given category of a frequency distribution. In general, class intervals of equal length should be selected for each category in the distribution.

Referring to the use of ancillary services per patient, suppose that an inspection of the original data revealed that no patient required fewer than 2 units or more than 13 procedures. The classes selected for the distribution are collectively exhaustive (i.e., the categories accommodate all of the patients). In addition, overlapping class intervals were avoided in the construction of the distribution, implying that the categories are also mutually exclusive (i.e., a patient is assigned to one and only one of the groups).

In addition to those described previously here, the effective use of frequency distributions requires an understanding of several terms. First, *class frequency* refers to the number of observations or items assigned to a given category. Referring to the distribution depicting the use of ancillary care per patient, the class frequency of 450 indicates the number of individuals who required between 1 and 5 units of service. The construction and interpretation of frequency distributions also require an understanding of class limits and class boundaries. The *upper class limit* identifies the maximum value that appears in a given category, whereas the *lower class limit* corresponds to the minimum value in a given group. Table 2.1 shows that the lower class limit of the second category is 6 units of service per patient, whereas the upper class limit is 10 units of service per patient.

The class boundaries of a given category are closely related to the class limits. The *class boundary* is the midpoint between successive classes. For example, the lower class boundary of the second category is the midpoint between the upper class boundary of the first category and the lower class boundary of the second category. The upper class boundary of the first category is given by the ratio (5 + 6)/2 or 5.5 units, whereas the upper class boundary of the second class is given by (10 + 11)/2 or 10.5 units. In addition, the upper class boundary of the second group serves as the lower class boundary of the third category. Finally, the *midpoint* or *class mark* is the midpoint between the upper and lower class interval of a given category. The midpoint or class mark is obtained by adding one half of the class interval to the lower boundary of the category.

As indicated, the length of a class or the class interval is given by the difference between the upper and lower class boundary. Table 2.1 shows that the class interval of the first category can be easily verified and is given by the difference between 5.5 and 0.5, whereas the class interval of the second is given by the difference between 10.5 and 5.5 units. As can be easily verified, the class interval of each of the categories in the table is equal to 5 units of service per patient.

Cumulative Distributions

A number of administrative situations require the construction of a cumulative distribution. For example, holding a diagnostic category or risk group constant, an administrator may wish to know the number of number of inpatients who were more than 10, 20, 30, 40, 50, 60, or 70 years old. An assessment of the inpatient mix might require numeric data that indicate the diagnostic or risk groups that comprise 80% of the typical daily census. Similarly, the administrator of a laboratory department that uses multiple items of inventory might require a list of those supplies that comprises 80% or more of the unit's expenses. In these situations, it is convenient to construct a cumulative frequency distribution and related proportions.

To illustrate the usefulness of a cumulative distribution, consider the ages of inpatients that were diagnosed with a disease of the respiratory system during the past year. In this case, it is presumed that as the patient ages, his or her health and power to recover decline. Furthermore, with advancing age, it is likely that case severity or complexity increases, resulting in the use of more service, the consumption of additional resources, and higher costs. The distribution of patients with respect to age is useful for the administrator.

Next consider the development of a cumulative distribution based on the ages of the 2,355 patients who were diagnosed with a respiratory system disease. Based on the age of each patient, assume further that the administrator constructed the frequency distribution that appears in columns 1 and 2 of Table 2.3. Table 2.3 represents a cumulative "or less" distribution. In particular, the first value appearing in the column titled "Cumulative Frequency" indicates that 150 of the patients were 29 years old or less, whereas the second value suggests that 150 + 235 (or 385) patients were 39 years old or younger. The remaining values appearing in the column were calculated similarly.

Table 2.3 **Cumulative Less Than Distribution of Inpatients, Grouped by Age, Presenting Diseases of the Respiratory System**

Age	Number of Patients	Years or Less	Cumulative Frequency	Relative Frequency
20–29	150	29	150	0.06
30–39	235	39	385	0.16
40–49	270	49	655	0.28
50–59	340	59	995	0.42
60–69	400	69	1,395	0.59
70–79	450	79	1,845	0.78
80–89	510	89	2,355	1.00
Total	2,355			

The relative frequencies in the final column were derived from the set of cumulative frequencies. These values were obtained by using the ratio:

$$CF_i/T$$

where CF_i is the cumulative frequency associated with category i and T is the total number of observations. Specifically, the division of each cumulative frequency by the total number of patients, 2,355, yields the values appearing in the final column. For example, the distribution of cumulative frequencies indicates that 1,845 patients were 79 years old or less, implying that the corresponding relative frequency is simply the ratio of 1,845 to 2,355 or 0.78. As a result, the calculations indicate that 78% of the patients were 79 years old or less. The other values appearing in Table 2.3 were computed and are interpreted in a similar fashion.

The original data also illustrate a cumulative "more than" distribution. Table 2.4 shows that the cumulative frequencies indicate the number of patients whose ages were equal to or greater than the lower class limit of each category. Specifically, the results indicate that all of the patients were 20 years of age or more, whereas 2,205 of them were 30 years old or more. As can be easily verified, only 510 patients were 80 years of age or older. Similar to Table 2.3, the relative frequencies are calculated by a ratio in which the numerator is the cumulative frequency and the denominator is the total number of patients. The results in the final column of Table 2.4 indicate, for example, that 0.94 (94%) of the patients were 30 years old or more and that 0.41 (41%) of the patients were 70 years old or more. The cumulative frequency distribution is simply an extension of a quantitative or qualitative frequency distribution and provides the analyst with another interpretation of the data.

Table 2.4 **Cumulative More Than Distribution of Inpatients, Grouped by Age, Presenting Diseases of the Respiratory System**

Age	Number of Patients	Years or More	Cumulative Frequency	Relative Frequency
20–29	150	20	2,355	1.00
30–39	235	30	2,205	0.94
40–49	270	40	1,970	0.84
50–59	340	50	1,700	0.72
60–69	400	60	1,360	0.58
70–79	450	70	960	0.41
80–89	510	80	510	0.22
Total	2,355			

Frequency Distributions and the Use of Excel

The process of constructing a frequency distribution requires the analyst to sort observations into categories and to count the number of items assigned to each. Depending on the amount of information, the task of sorting and counting observations is time consuming and possibly error prone. Fortunately, when Excel is used, these tasks are performed quickly, accurately, and easily.

For example, suppose that we are interested in the number of secondary diagnoses presented by 20 recent discharges. After selecting the classes that make up the distribution, the observations need to be sorted, and the number in each category needs to be counted. Assume that all patients presented at least one secondary diagnosis and that no patient presented more than 15 secondary conditions. The distribution is collectively exhaustive if the categories accommodate 1 to 15 secondary diagnoses. Based on the original inspection of the data, the frequency distribution might consist of four categories defined as 1 to 4, 5 to 8, 9 to 12, and 13 to 16 secondary diagnoses per patient.

The process of sorting and counting class frequencies is relatively simple when Excel is used to make the distribution. The analyst must first enter the patient's identification number and the related number of secondary diagnoses (Exhibit 2.1). In this case, the identification numbers are listed in cells A6 to A25, whereas the number of secondary diagnoses appear in cells B6 to B25 of the spreadsheet.

Second, consider next the process of identifying the receptacles into which the observations are sorted. Specifically, the values 4, 8, 12, and 16 that appear in the column by "BIN" enable us to define the categories that make up the distribution. Listed in cells C6 to C9, the BIN identifiers specify the maximum value that will be included in a given category. For example, the BIN number 4 identifies the maximum value that will be included in the first category and indicates that patients with one to four secondary diagnoses will be included in the first class. Similarly, the BIN identifier 8 indicates the maximum number of secondary conditions for the second category, a class that contains only those patients with five to eight secondary diagnoses. The other values appearing in cells C6 to C9 are interpreted similarly. After the limits of each category have been specified, the analyst should describe the categories that form the frequency distribution. The categories that comprise the distribution are listed in cells E6 to E9 of the spreadsheet (Exhibit 2.1).

The frequency distribution is constructed as follows:

1. Highlight the field in which the class frequencies will appear.
2. Place the cursor on cell F6, and depress the shift key and highlight cells F7 to F9.
3. In cell F6, enter =frequency(.

Exhibit 2.1 **The Use of Excel to Construct Frequency Distributions**

Patient	Number of Secondary Diagnoses	BIN	Secondary Diagnoses	Number of Patients	Relative Frequency
1	1	4	1 to 4	7	0.35
2	4	8	5 to 8	7	0.35
3	7	12	9 to 12	4	0.20
4	10	16	13 to 16	2	0.10
5	3		Total	20	1.00
6	2				
7	3				
8	1				
9	5				
10	6				
11	7				
12	9				
13	11				
14	12				
15	13				
16	14				
17	4				
18	5				
19	7				
20	8				

4. Highlight the field in which the number of secondary diagnoses appear (i.e., B6 to B25), followed by a comma.
5. Highlight the field in which the BIN identifiers appear (i.e., C6 to C9).
6. Enter a right parenthesis.
7. Simultaneously press control, shift, and enter.

The frequency function in Excel automatically sorts the data and calculates the class frequencies as shown in Exhibit 2.1. The results indicate that 7 of 20 patients had between 1 and 4 secondary diagnoses and that 4 of the patients had between 9 and 12 diagnoses.

The distribution of relative frequencies that appears in the exhibit is easily calculated and requires little time. Specifically, the "AutoSum" function was used to calculate the total number of observations that appear in cell F10. The relative frequency distribution is constructed as follows:

1. In cell G6, enter = G6/$F$10 and press enter.
2. Locate the cursor on the cell in which the equation resides, and enter "Copy."
3. Highlight the remaining cells of the relative frequency distribution.

These results indicate that 4 or 0.20 of the patients presented 9 to 12 secondary diagnoses, whereas 7 or 0.35 of the patients reported 5 to 8 secondary conditions.

Excel also might be used to construct a cumulative frequency distribution. Exhibit 2.2 shows the cumulative frequency distribution that was introduced previously in this chapter and portrayed the age distribution of patients diagnosed with diseases of the respiratory system. An inspection of the exhibit reveals that the data have been rearranged to form a "less than" cumulative frequency distribution. As indicated, 150 of the 2,355 patients were 29 years old or less, whereas 385, given by the sum 150 + 235, were 39 years old or less.

The calculations required to construct the cumulative frequency distribution are easily performed when Excel is used. The categories are listed in cells A5 to A11, and the class frequencies appear in cells B5 to B11. The next column identifies key values in the cumulative distribution. For example, the distribution indicates the number of patients who were 29 years old or less and 39 years old or less. The remaining values appearing in the column are interpreted in a similar fashion. The entry in cell B5 indicates that 150 patients were 29 years old or less. Hence, the first step when constructing the distribution is to enter = B5 or 150 in cell D5. Second, 150 + 235 (or 385) patients were 39 years old or less, suggesting that the value appearing in the second row of the cumulative distribution is obtained by the sum of the entries appearing in cells D5 and B6. Hence, the expression = D5 + B6 should appear in cell D6. It also should be noted that the number

Exhibit 2.2 **Cumulative Less Than Distribution of Inpatients, Grouped by Age, Presenting Diseases of the Respiratory System**

Age	Number of Patients	Years or Less	Cumulative Frequency	Relative Frequency
20–29	150	29	150	0.06
30–39	235	39	385	0.16
40–49	270	49	655	0.28
50–59	340	59	995	0.42
60–69	400	69	1,395	0.59
70–79	450	79	1,845	0.78
80–89	510	89	2,355	1.00
Total	2,355			

of patients who were 49 years old or less is simply the sum of 385, a value appearing in cell D6, and 270, the entry listed in cell B7. As should be verified, the other values appearing in the distribution are then computed by (1) placing the cursor on cell D6 and (2) using the "Copy" function to calculate the values appearing in the other cells of the cumulative frequency distribution.

The cumulative distribution of relative frequencies is also easily calculated. Specifically, the total number of observations was obtained by applying the "AutoSum" function in cell B12. Similar to the previous example, the distribution of relative frequencies is obtained by

1. Locating the cursor on cell E5.
2. Entering = B5/$B$12.
3. Using the "Copy" function to calculate the remaining relative frequencies that appear in the final column of the exhibit.

The results, which are easily verified, indicate that 150 or 0.06 of the 2,355 patients were 29 years old or less and that 385 individuals or 0.16 of the sample were 39 years old or less.

The data depicting the distribution of patients regarding age also form the basis for the construction of a "more than" cumulative distribution. Suppose the administrator is interested in the number and proportion of patients who were 20 years of age or older, 30 years old or more, and so on. The process of preparing the cumulative distribution is shown in Exhibit 2.3.

In this case, the original frequency distribution was reproduced in cells A7 to B13. The values appearing in cells C7 to C13 define the terms of the cumulative distribution (i.e., 20 years or more and 30 years or more). In cell B13, observe that 510 of the patients were 80 years old or older, and as a result, either 510 or = B13 is entered in cell D13. An inspection of the original frequency distribution reveals that 510 + 450 (or 960) of the patients were 70 years old or older. Hence, the corresponding value in the cumulative distribution is obtained by entering = D13 + B12 in cell D12. The remaining values in the cumulative distribution were acquired by placing the cursor on cell D12 and copying the expression to the other cells of the cumulative "more than" frequency distribution.

The relative frequencies appearing in the final column of the exhibit were calculated as follows: First, the "AutoSum" function was used to determine the total number of observations that appear in cell B14. Next, the expression = D7/$B$14 was entered in cell E7. The cursor was located on cell E7, and the expression to the remaining cells of the relative distribution was copied. The results indicate that 1,970 (or 0.84) of the 2,355 patients were 40 years old or older and that 1,360 (or 0.58) of the patients were 60 years old or older. The cumulative distributions and relative cumulative distributions are merely an extension of the original data and provide a mechanism for developing an alternate expression of the idea that is of interest to management.

Exhibit 2.3 **Cumulative More Than Distribution of Inpatients, Grouped by Age, Presenting Diseases of the Respiratory System**

Age	Number of Patients	Years or More	Cumulative Frequency	Relative Frequency
20–29	150	20	2,355	1.00
30–39	235	30	2,205	0.94
40–49	270	40	1,970	0.84
50–59	340	50	1,700	0.72
60–69	400	60	1,360	0.58
70–79	450	70	960	0.41
80–89	510	80	510	0.22
Total	2,355			

The Use of Excel to Prepare Graphic Presentations

As indicated in the previous section, frequency distributions summarize data in a more understandable form. Although frequency distributions are valuable when presenting information, data that are interesting to the health administrator might be presented in a more appealing form by using a graph or a chart. This section focuses on the use of health information to make a histogram or bar chart, a pie chart, a radial chart, and a line chart.

The Bar Chart

The data used to construct a frequency distribution or a distribution of relative frequencies can be used to develop a bar chart. The bar chart is a common graphical presentation of data and consists of a series of rectangles with the area of each given by the product of its base and height. The height of each rectangle is measured by class frequencies or relative frequencies that appear on the vertical scale. The base of each is measured by the class interval that appears on the horizontal scale. If the class intervals are of equal length, the area of a given rectangle indicates the relative importance of the class in the set of categories that defines the distribution.

Exhibit 2.4 shows the frequency and relative frequency distributions that depict the number of patients, grouped by secondary diagnoses, have been reproduced. The upper and lower limits of the classes are presented in cells A6 to A9, whereas the corresponding class frequencies are listed in cells B6 to B9. The bar chart is constructed by

1. Selecting the "Chart Wizard" function from the tool bar
2. Selecting "Column" as the chart type from the menu
3. Selecting "next"
4. Identifying the range in which data appear (i.e., cells A6 to B9)
5. Entering the chart title
6. Entering variable names that appear on the vertical and horizontal axes
7. Entering finish

Because the class intervals are equal in length, the areas of the rectangles that make the bar chart indicate the relative importance of each category. A graph that depicts the relative frequency distribution conveys this feature.

Exhibit 2.5 shows a bar chart that is based on the distribution of relative frequencies. The upper and lower class limits appear in cells A5 to A8, whereas the relative frequencies are listed in cells B5 to B8. The process of constructing the distribution of relative frequencies in Exhibit 2.5 is identical to the development of the frequency distribution presented in Exhibit 2.4. Both images show the distribution of the patients regarding the number of secondary diagnoses and indicate case complexity, a factor that might influence the use of service and related costs.

Bar charts frequently present the rectangles parallel to the horizontal axis. As mentioned previously, the rectangles that form the bar chart should have bases of

Exhibit 2.4 **A Histogram Depicting the Number of Secondary Diagnoses**

Number of Secondary Diagnoses	Number of Patients
1 to 4	7
5 to 8	7
9 to 12	4
13 to 16	2

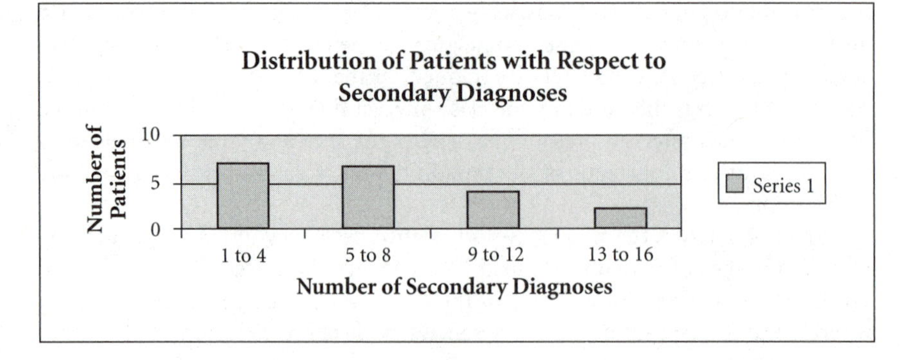

Exhibit 2.5 **A Histogram Depicting the Relative Frequency of Secondary Diagnoses**

Number of Secondary Diagnoses	Relative Frequency
1 to 4	0.35
5 to 8	0.35
9 to 12	0.20
13 to 16	0.10

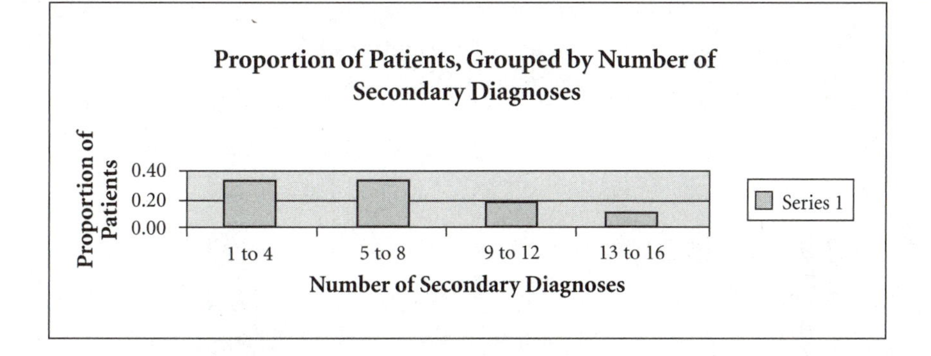

equal width, suggesting that the areas of individual rectangles indicate the relative importance of the class. Relying on the distribution of patients with respect to secondary diagnosis, a horizontal bar chart is presented in Exhibit 2.6. In this case, the class limits are listed in cells A7 to A10, whereas the class frequencies appear in cells B7 to B10. The bar chart was constructed by

1. Selecting the "Chart Wizard" function from the tool bar
2. Selecting "bar" as the chart type from the menu
3. Entering "next"
4. Entering the data range (i.e., A7 to B10)
5. Selecting "finish"

The horizontal bar chart is commonly used to present health information and an alternate view of the same distribution.

Pie Charts

Information that is interesting to the health administrator might also be presented as a pie chart. In this case, the area of the chart represents the total of the phe-

Exhibit 2.6 **A Bar Chart Depicting the Frequency Distribution of Secondary Diagnoses**

Number of Secondary Diagnoses	Number of Patients	Relative Frequency
1 to 4	7	0.35
5 to 8	7	0.35
9 to 12	4	0.20
13 to 16	2	0.10

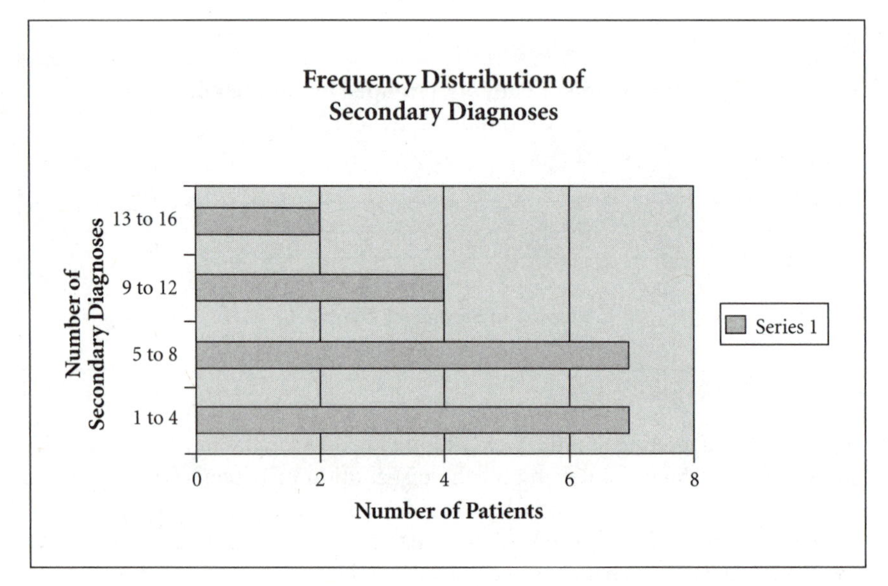

nomenon of interest, and each slice represents the relative importance of each category or class. Exhibit 2.7 shows that the limits of the categories are presented in cells A7 to A10, whereas the class frequencies appear in cells B7 to B10. The pie chart that is based on these data is developed by

1. Selecting the "Chart Wizard" function from the tool bar
2. Selecting "pie" from the menu and entering next
3. Entering the range in which the data appear (i.e., A7 to B10)
4. Entering the "finish" command

As shown in Exhibit 2.7, the area of the pie chart corresponds to all patients, and each slice represents the number of patients in each category. An inspection of the chart indicates that the classes with limits of 1 to 4 and 5 to 8 secondary di-

Exhibit 2.7 **A Pie Chart Depicting the Frequency Distribution of Secondary Diagnoses**

Number of Secondary Diagnoses	Number of Patients
1 to 4	7
5 to 8	7
9 to 12	4
13 to 16	2

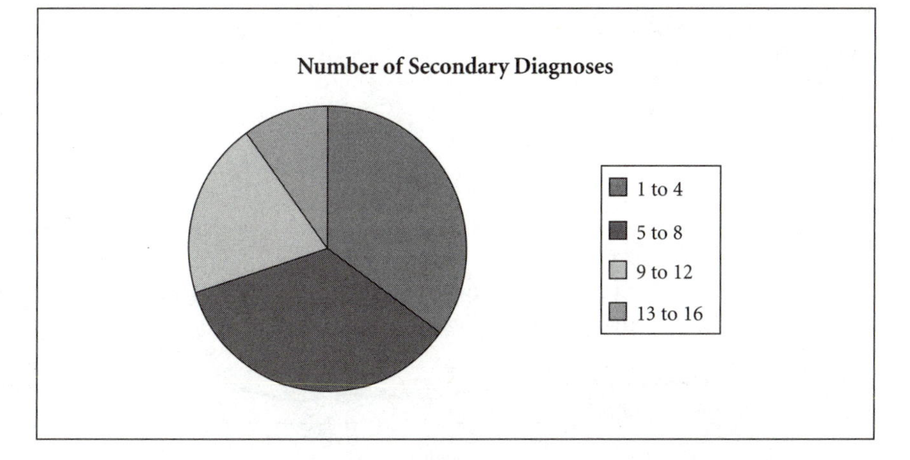

agnoses contain the same number of patients and more individuals than the other groups.

Line Charts

Line charts are frequently used to condense information about two or more variables and to portray the interrelation among the variables of interest. In addition, line charts show changes in the value of one or more variables during a study period. For example, suppose that a multi-institutional arrangement is interested in reviewing the average length of stay that Medicare beneficiaries and Medicaid recipients experience.

After assembling the data and calculating the average length of stay for the two groups during the past 10 years, a line chart is constructed using the data listed in Exhibit 2.8. An inspection of the two series of data reveals that the average length of stay for both groups declined during the period and that, on average, Medicare beneficiaries appeared to experience a longer hospital episode than their Medicaid counterparts. A line chart showing these observations is constructed by

Exhibit 2.8 **Line Chart Depicting the Average Number of Days of Care Consumed by the Typical Medicare Beneficiary and Medicaid Recipient**

Year	Medicare Beneficiary	Medicaid Recipient
1	7.6	5.4
2	7.5	5.3
3	7.4	5.2
4	7.5	5.1
5	7.3	4.9
6	7.2	4.8
7	6.9	4.8
8	7.1	4.7
9	6.8	4.5
10	7.3	4.3

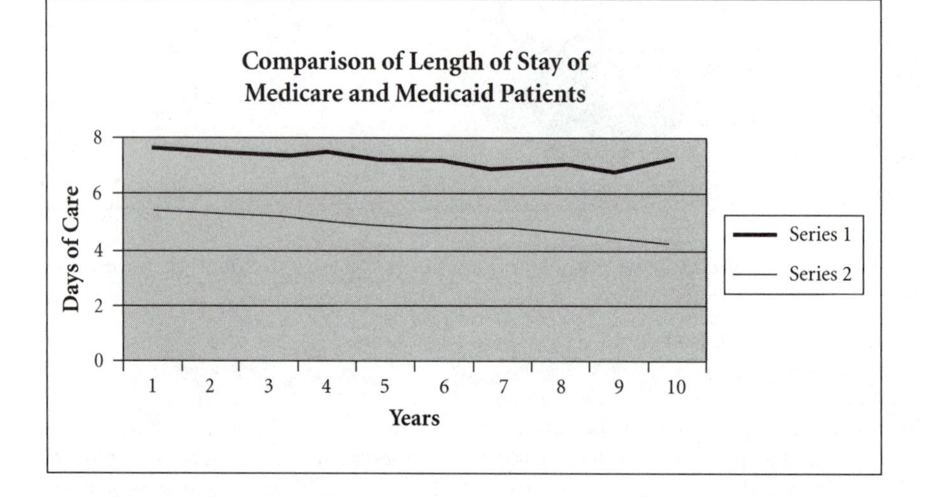

1. Selecting the "Chart Wizard" function from the tool bar
2. Selecting the "line" function from the menu and "next"
3. Entering the data range (i.e., cells A5 to C14)
4. Entering the "finish" command

An inspection of the line chart suggests two tentative conclusions. First, the vertical distance between the two series indicates that Medicare beneficiaries, on average, used more days of care per hospital episode than Medicaid recipients.

Second, both series decline from left to right, suggesting that the length of stay for both groups decreased during the study period.

Radar Charts

Finally, information that is interesting to the health administrator can be presented as a radar chart. A radar chart is a visual image that enables the administrator to assess remedial policies or compare the performance of entities that comprise the health service organization. Values that refer to multiple dimensions are recorded on one of several axes that form the radar chart. Straight lines then connect the coordinate points, forming a figure that portrays the information about the variable of interest.

For example, suppose that the performance of each department is evaluated in terms of multiple dimensions. Assume that a common scale is used in the evaluation, with the following numeric values assigned for excellent, good, average, fair, and poor:

1. Excellent = 5
2. Good = 4
3. Average = 3
4. Fair = 2
5. Poor = 1

Furthermore, suppose that the administrator evaluated the laboratory for timeliness, which refers to the lapse of time required to respond to a request for diagnostic procedures; accuracy, which refers to the defective rate; efficiency, which refers to the costliness of operations; and synergy, which measures the department's interrelation with other units comprising the organization. Based on the results of an initial evaluation, suppose that the administrator decided that the ratings appearing in Exhibit 2.9 represented an organizational weakness and that remedial policies were required. After implementing remedial action, a second evaluation was conducted, resulting in the second set of ratings that appear in Exhibit 2.9.

The radar chart, based on the two sets of data, was developed by

1. Selecting the "Chart Wizard" function from the tool bar
2. Selecting "Radar" chart from the menu
3. Highlighting the range in which the data appear (i.e., B7 to C10)
4. Entering the command to "finish"

As the chart indicates, the outer figure represents "excellent" in all four dimensions. However, because the difference between actual performance in each dimension and an excellent rating is unfavorable, it is clear that the unit represents

Exhibit 2.9 **A Radar Chart Depicting the Performance of the Laboratory**

Dimension	Initial Evaluation	After Remedial Policy
Timeliness	3	5
Accuracy	2	4
Efficiency	2	5
Synergy	2	4

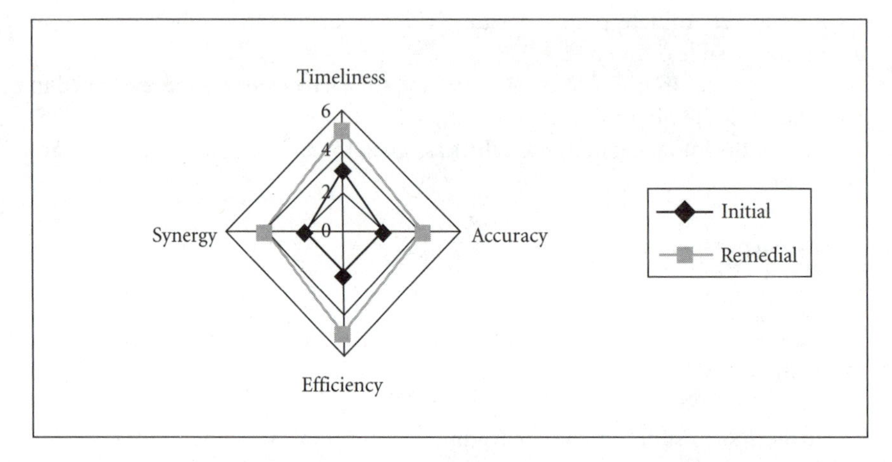

an area of weakness and requires the implementation of remedial policies or actions. Finally, a comparison of the ratings of the department after the implementation of remedial actions with those derived from the initial assessment allows management to evaluate the improvement in departmental performance and the potential need to implement additional policies that might reduce remaining deficiencies in the performance of the unit.

The radar chart also is useful when comparing the overall performance of multiple units, such as the laboratory, radiologic services, and various nursing units. Similarly, the chart might be used to summarize data depicting the overall performance of components that comprise a multi-institutional arrangement. A visual comparison of multiple units or components obviously enhances the ability of the administrator to identify areas of organizational weakness but also to improve the performance of the entire institution.

Applications to Health Administration

The methods described here enable the health administrator to summarize, condense, and present information in a more understandable and usable form. The application of the techniques described here is limited only to the needs of the health service organization. For example, line charts might be used to depict periodic changes in the organization's fiscal performance, occupancy rate, payer mix, or the intensity of using resources. Similarly, the radar chart might be used to develop an image of changes in the strengths or weaknesses of the organization that result from the implementation of remedial policies or actions. The bar or pie chart is valuable for describing the characteristics of patients, the distribution of inpatients, grouped by diagnostic or risk category, and the use of service, grouped by public or private insurer. Indeed, the list is virtually endless, and the techniques described in this chapter should be used when it is necessary to rearrange a large set of information into a more usable and understandable form.

Exercises

1. Suppose the health service organization is interested in the number of visits per person per year. After selecting 25 individuals from the insured population, the following data were obtained:

   1, 2, 5, 3, 7, 8, 0, 4, 3, 7, 10, 2, 2, 4, 2, 6, 7, 8, 3, 2, 1, 1, 6, 5, 0

   Use Excel to construct a frequency distribution, a relative frequency distribution, a cumulative less than distribution, and a cumulative more than distribution.
2. Using the results obtained from Exercise 1, use Excel to construct a bar chart and a pie chart from the frequency and relative frequency distributions derived for the distribution of patients, grouped by number of visits per person per year.
3. Assume the administrator wishes to assess the efficiency of two technicians: A and B. Measured in minutes, the amount of time required to provide a given procedure on 20 different occasions by each was as follows:

   Technician A: 10, 15, 12, 16, 13, 16, 20, 21, 13, 22, 24, 17, 18, 19, 22, 12, 21, 22, 14, 15

   Technician B: 21, 22, 23, 26, 19, 18, 25, 23, 25, 15, 18, 27, 14, 23, 29, 16, 15, 23, 28, 16

   Use Excel to construct a frequency, a relative frequency, and cumulative more than frequency distribution for each technician.
4. Referring to Exercise 3, use Excel to construct a bar chart and a pie chart that depict the frequency distribution and relative frequency distribution that were derived from the amount of time required to perform the procedure. Compare the results obtained for the two technicians. Does there appear to be a difference in their performance?
5. The following data depict the occupancy rate, expressed as a percentage, during the past 12 months:

   97, 98, 95, 94, 93, 91, 89, 90, 87, 88, 86, 85

Use Excel to construct a line chart depicting monthly changes in the occupancy rate. Describe the implications of the chart.

6. Assume the health service organization is concerned about the amount of bad debt that has been incurred. Expressed as a percentage of gross income, the following represents the bad debt experience of the organization during the past 10 years:

   7, 8, 7, 10, 11, 10, 12, 11, 13, 14

   Use Excel to construct a line chart that depicts the annual change in the bad debt rate. What conclusions does the chart suggest?

7. Suppose that the health administrator evaluated the performance of the dietary department in terms of efficiency, quality, synergy, and adherence to the patient's selections from the menu. At the end of the first period, the results of the evaluation were as follows:

   Efficiency, 2
   Quality, 3
   Synergy, 2
   Selection, 4

   In this case, the values correspond to the following evaluation:

   Excellent = 5
   Good = 4
   Average = 3
   Below average = 2
   Poor = 1

   At the end of the second period, the unit was evaluated as follows:

   Efficiency, 4
   Quality, 4
   Synergy, 3
   Selection, 5

   Construct a radar chart that depicts the performance of the unit at the end of the two periods. What conclusion does the chart suggest?

8. Suppose that a multi-institutional arrangement assessed the quality of care provided by two of its clinics: the Eastern Clinic and the Northern Clinic. Based on the responses of 100 patients seen at each, the following results, expressed as percentages, were obtained:

Rating	Eastern	Northern
Superior	40	20
Good	30	10
Average	15	25
Below Average	10	35
Poor	5	10

   Based on these results, use Excel to assess the performance of the two clinics.
   What conclusions do the results suggest regarding the strengths and weaknesses of the organization?

CHAPTER 3 The Distribution and Its Properties[R,O]

OBJECTIVES

1. Describe measures of central tendency, the weighted mean, the geometric mean, and the set of fractiles, defined as the percentile, the decile, and the quartile.
2. Describe the range, the variance, and the standard deviation as measures of scatter or dispersion.
3. Describe symmetrical and asymmetrical distributions.
4. Define skewness and kurtosis.
5. Use Excel to calculate a Paasche Index and a Laspeyres Index.
6. Use Excel to calculate measures of central tendency, dispersion, the weighted mean, and the geometric mean.
7. Use Excel to identify percentiles, deciles, and quartiles.

The Properties of a Distribution[R]

In this chapter, we conclude our discussion of descriptive statistics and develop measures of location, dispersion or scatter, symmetry or skewness, and kurtosis. The indicators described in the following discussion pertain to either a population or a sample. As defined in Chapter 1, the term *population* or *universe* refers to a set of data that consists of all conceivable or theoretically possible observations concerning a phenomenon or variable that is of administrative interest. A sample is a subset or a portion of the data that are associated with a given population or universe.

Depending on the purpose of the analysis, a set of data might be regarded as a sample or as a finite population. For example, consider a daily census consisting of 400 inpatients, and suppose that the administrator of the hospital is interested in the use of ancillary services per case. After selecting 100 patients and measuring the amount of service that each consumed, the administrator is in a position to derive an indicator of the amount of care per case. In this situation, the 100 patients represent a sample that was selected from a population of 400 inpatients. It also is possible to regard the daily census of 400 patients as a subset or a sample of all previous inpatients and all those who will be admitted in the future.

The notation used in this chapter differentiates a sample from a population. Specifically, when describing measures of central location, $\overline{X}$ (pronounced x-bar) is used when referring to the arithmetic mean. When assessing the total observations associated with a finite population, μ (the Greek letter mu) is used to identify the mean. When measuring the scatter or dispersion exhibited by sample data, S and S^2 are used to identify the standard deviation and variance, respectively. The standard deviation and variance of a finite population are identified by σ and σ^2, respectively. In this case, σ is the Greek letter sigma.

Selecting the Sample[R]

As indicated, a sample is a subset of a population or universe that is of interest to the administrator. The sample, in turn, is selected so that we may derive inferences from the sample data about the universe. As indicated in Chapter 1, a sample is frequently less costly and timelier than a census. In addition, a sample enables the analyst to assemble data that are as accurate as or more accurate than those obtained from a census. Furthermore, information concerning an infinite population may be obtained only from a sample. Because a distribution and its properties frequently depend on a sample, this section considers methods of selecting a sample from a finite and an infinite population.

A probability sample is one in which elements of the population are selected according to known or specified probabilities. The selection of elements from the population in accordance with known or specified probabilities prevents the analyst from exercising discretion about which elements are included in the sample. Two main advantages of a probability sample should be mentioned. First, the bias that might accompany the exercise of judgment or discretion in the selection of a sample from the universe is avoided. Second, and perhaps more important, the data derived from a probability sample may be used to determine the error in the results that are obtained when sample data are used.

Sampling from a Finite Population

Although numerous types of probability samples exist, our focus is on a simple random sample. A simple random sample selected from a finite population is one in which each observation and each sample combination has an equal probability of being chosen. For example, consider a finite population consisting of the set {2, 4, 6, 8, 10}. If we select a sample of n equal to 2, the possible sample combinations are {2, 4}, {2, 6}, {2, 8}, {2, 10}, {4, 6}, {4, 8}, {4, 10}, {6, 8}, {6, 10}, and {8, 10}. Ten combinations are possible when we select a sample consisting of two values from the finite population defined by the five values. A simple random sample requires that each of the 10 sample combinations has a probability of 1/10 or 0.10 of being selected.

A random sample requires that each element and each of the sample combinations must have an equal chance of being selected. For example, using an example of interest to a health administrator, suppose we wished to select 25 physicians from a finite population of 100 physicians and that the physicians are distributed equally, with 25 physicians assigned to each of four groups: A, B, C, and D. If we selected one of the groups as our sample and if each group has a 25% chance of selection, then each of the physicians has an equal chance of selection. However, such an approach fails to satisfy the requirements of a simple random sample. Specifically, the sampling scheme prevents us from selecting a physician from group A and a physician from group B (i.e., if we selected group A as our sample, none of the physicians in group B would be chosen). Thus, in random sampling, every element and each of the possible sample combinations must have an equal chance of selection.

We generally rely on random numbers to select the elements that are included in the sample. Tables of random numbers are constructed by listing the digits 0, 1, . . . , 9 in such a manner that each has a probability of 1 in 10 of appearing at a given location. In the problem of selecting 25 physicians from a finite population of 100 physicians, we simply assign a unique value represented by 001, 002, and so forth to each of the 100 physicians. We then select 25 random numbers that are included in the interval 001 to 100. Once the 25 random numbers have been chosen, we simply select as our sample the physicians whose identification numbers correspond to the set of random digits.

Sampling from an Infinite Population

When the population is infinite, a sample is the only available method of obtaining information that describes the universe. Unfortunately, it is not possible to rely on a probability mechanism for selecting the sample. The process associated with the infinite population furnishes sample observations. However, two conditions must be satisfied if the selection process results in a simple random sample. First, all observations must be selected from the same population. Second, the sample observations must be statistically independent. There is no way of proving that a sample selected from a finite population is random. The assumption of random sampling must be verified by reliability and usefulness of the data.

Measures of Location[R,O]

In this section, we rely on sample data to calculate measures of location. The most familiar indicator of location is the arithmetic mean. However, other indicators of central tendency are also valuable to the health administrator. The weighted mean, the geometric mean, and the mode might be used to describe a set of data. This section also considers other techniques that might be used to locate data in a distribution. Among these indicators of location, the median, the quartile, the decile, and the percentile are the most commonly used.

The Arithmetic Mean[R]

The arithmetic mean is routinely used to summarize or represent a set of data by means of a single value. The average length of stay, the average daily census, the average number of admissions, or the average number of outpatient visits are of interest to the health administrator and may be described by calculating the arithmetic mean. For example, suppose we selected 10 patients who required outpatient care during the past year and recorded the number of visits to the clinic that our health service organization operates. Suppose further that the data were arranged as follows:

$$x = [2, 3, 1, 4, 3, 5, 2, 2, 3, 6]$$

In this case, the values contained in the brackets are the number of patient visits included in the sample. The arithmetic mean of these data is obtained by

$$(2 + 3 + 1 + 4 + 3 + 5 + 2 + 2 + 3 + 6)/10$$

or 3.1 visits per person.

Because of its importance in statistical analyses, the arithmetic mean adopts a special notation when being calculated. Specifically, when analyzing sample data represented by the set $[x_1, \ldots, x_i, \ldots x_n]$, the arithmetic mean, represented by $\bar{X}$, is given by

$$\bar{X} = \Sigma x_i/n \qquad \text{(Equation 3.1)}$$

In Equation 3.1, simple addition is indicated by the symbol Σ, whereas x_i corresponds to the values included in the summation that appears in the numerator. The lowercase n represents the sample size or the number of observations that is included in the calculation. In contrast, the arithmetic mean of a finite population is given by

$$\mu = \Sigma x_i/N \qquad \text{(Equation 3.2)}$$

In this case, μ is the arithmetic mean of the finite population. The x_i represents the values assigned to the item of interest, and N denotes the size or number of observations that define the finite population.

Given the importance of the arithmetic mean, several observations about its properties are notable. First, the arithmetic mean is familiar and easy to calculate. Second, the mean is unique and always exists for a given set of data. The mean also is subject to further manipulation that simplifies the calculation of other statistics, such as those that measure the dispersion or scatter exhibited by data. Finally, unlike other statistical descriptors, the mean is relatively stable and exhibits little variation from sample to sample.

The calculation of the arithmetic mean, which has several advantages, is based on all observations, a feature that increases the sensitivity of the statistic to extreme values. An extreme value is an observation that is either much larger or smaller than the main body of data. Because the arithmetic mean is sensitive to extreme values, it may not represent the entire set of data. For example, suppose that we measured the length of stay for five patients and obtained this information:

$$x_1 = 3$$
$$x_2 = 2$$
$$x_3 = 2$$
$$x_4 = 4$$
$$x_5 = 34$$

In this case, the value of the arithmetic mean is given by

$$\overline{X} = (3 + 2 + 2 + 4 + 34)/5$$

or 9 days. Although mathematically correct, the mean value of 9 days fails to show accurately any of the data contained in the original set of information. The sensitivity of the arithmetic mean to extreme values may reduce its ability to describe a set of data accurately.

The Mode[R]

In addition to the arithmetic mean, the mode is also frequently used as an indicator of central location. When describing ungrouped information, the *mode* is the value that occurs with the greatest frequency in a set of data. The mode may be used as an indicator of location for grouped data that are portrayed by a bar chart or a continuous distribution and for ungrouped information. Furthermore, the mode frequently is used to describe data that are presented in qualitative terms.

Consider first the use of the mode when describing a set of ungrouped data. Assume that we gathered information about the age of 10 patients admitted to the pediatric unit. The ages of the patients (in years) were

10, 11, 12, 12, 12, 13, 14, 15, 9, 8

Twelve years is the modal age because it appears three times, whereas the other values appear only once. Unlike the mean, the mode may not exist and may not be unique. For example, consider the following observations:

1, 2, 3, 4, 5, 6, 7, 8, 9

In this case, no mode exists because all of the values occur with the same frequency. On the other hand, this set of data

10, 12, 13, 14, 14, 15, 15, 16, 17

is characterized by two modal values (i.e., 14 and 15). We refer to such a distribution as bimodal, implying that the mode may not be unique.

The mode of a distribution that is presented as a bar chart is defined as the class mark or midpoint of the category with the most observations. Furthermore, the category for which class frequencies are greatest is the modal class, and as a result, the midpoint of the modal class is used to measure the mode. On the other hand, suppose that the distribution is approximated by a smooth, continuous function. Figure 3.1 shows that the mode is the value that corresponds to the maximum point of the distribution.

The mode might be used as an indicator of central tendency when the item of interest is expressed quantitatively. In addition, the mode might also be applied to qualitative information. For example, a set of data might suggest that more people die from cardiovascular disease than from any other illness. Cardiovascular disease is referred to as the modal cause of death caused by illness. The discussion also indicates that the identification of the mode requires little if any calculation. Instead, the mode is determined by simply selecting the value that occurs with the greatest frequency.

Fractiles[R]

A *fractile* is a value below which lies a given proportion or percentage of the data. The specific fractiles that are discussed in this chapter are the median, the decile, the quartile, and the percentile.

The *median*, the value below which lies 50% of the data, is perhaps the most familiar fractile. As described previously, the arithmetic mean is sensitive to ex-

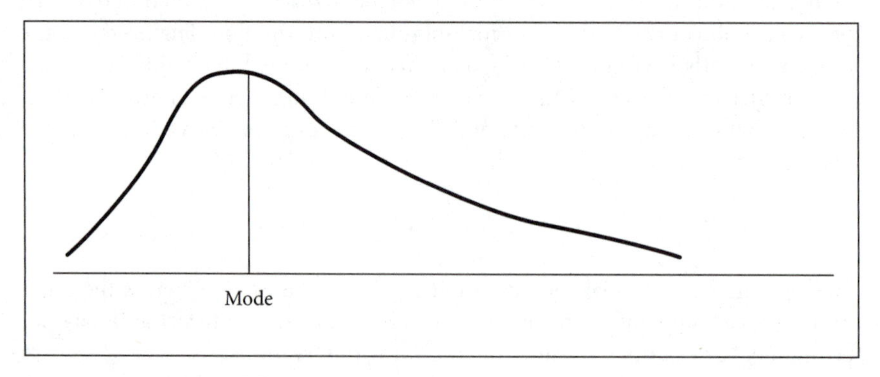

Figure 3.1 **The Modal Value**

treme values, a feature that may reduce its ability to describe a set of data with precision. To avoid the difficulties associated with the sensitivity of the mean to extreme values, central location may be described in terms of the median. The median is simply the value of the middle item or the average of the two middle items in a set of data that are arranged in ascending or descending order.

If the data consist of an odd number of observations, the median always exists, and the value of the middle item is the median. Assume that the daily cash balance (in thousands) during each day of the past 5 days was as follows:

$80, $85, $90, $97, $175

In this case, the value of the middle item, $90,000, is the median cash balance. If the number of observations is odd, the value of the middle item is the median. Then, if the set of data consist of n observations, where n is odd, the median is the value of the $(n + 1)/2$ largest item. For example, if n is 23, the value of the 12th largest item is the median.

Consider next a situation in which the number of observations is even. In this case, no middle item exists, and as a result, the median is defined as the arithmetic mean of the two middle observations in a set of data that have been arranged in ascending or descending order. For example, suppose that the administrator is interested in the delayed discharges, and the following observations represent the lapse of time, measured in days, between the date of discharge and the day when each of six patients was prepared clinically for release.

2, 3, 6, 8, 10, 30

In this case, the location of the median item is given by $(6 + 1)/2$ (or 3.5), implying that the middle item is midway between the third and fourth observations. The median length of delay is given by the arithmetic mean of 6 and 8 days or 7 days. It is important to emphasize that the ratio $(n + 1)/2$ identifies the location or position of the observation, the value of which is the median.

Several important features of the median should be noted. First, unlike the mode, the median always exists and is unique for a given set of information. Unlike the mean, the median is not influenced by extreme values. For example, consider the following set of data that depicts the ages (in years) of five patients.

10, 12, 15, 18, 62

The median is 15 years, irrespective of the age of the fifth patient.

As described previously, a fractile is a value below which lies a given proportion, percentage, or fraction of the data. *Quartiles* divide the distribution into four equal parts. Specifically, the first quartile, represented by Q_1, is a value below which lies 25% of the data, whereas the second quartile, Q_2, is a value below which lies 50% of the data. Accordingly, the second quartile is equivalent to the median. The third quartile, represented by Q_3, is a value below which lies 75% of the data.

After grouping the data in ascending order, the process of locating each of the quartiles is virtually identical to the method of locating the position of the median. In the following, let n correspond to the number of observations in the set of data. Adopting this notation and proceeding from the smallest value, the observation below which lies 25% of the data is identified by counting n/4 items. Similarly, beginning with the smallest value, the item whose value defines the second quartile or the median is identified by counting n/2 items, whereas the third quartile is obtained by counting 3n/4 items.

The *decile* divides the distribution into 10 equal parts. The first decile is the value below which lies 10% of the data; the second decile is the value below which lies 20% of the data, and the fifth decile is the value below which lies 50% of the data. Thus, the fifth decile is equivalent to the second quartile and the median. The other deciles are interpreted in a similar fashion. In the following, let Di correspond to the ith decile, suggesting that $i = 1, \ldots, 9$. After arranging the data in ascending order and proceeding from the smallest value, each of the deciles is determined by counting $(i/10) \times n$ of the observations.

Finally, *percentiles* divide the distribution into 100 equal parts. For example, the 5th percentile, represented by P_5, is the value below which lies 5% of the observations, whereas the 50th percentile, P_{50}, is the value below which lies 50% of the data. Therefore, the median, the 2nd quartile, the 5th decile, and the 50th percentile are equivalent.

The method of identifying the location of each percentile is similar to the process of determining the value of the median, quartiles, and percentiles. Similar to the previous discussion, let n correspond to the number of observations and P_k for $k = 1, \ldots, 99$, represent the kth percentile. After arranging the data in ascending order and beginning with the smallest value, the location of the kth percentile is identified by counting $(k/100) \times n$ items or observations. For example, suppose $n = 200$ and $k = 30$. The location or position of the 30th percentile is identified by counting $(30/100) \times 200$ or 60 observations.

Fractiles and their interpretation not only simplify understanding of large amounts of data, but they are also valuable to the health administrator. For example, suppose that in a comparison of 200 similar institutions, our organization ranks in the 76th percentile in the distribution of costs that were incurred during the previous period and in the 40th percentile in a distribution that depicts the volume of care provided during the same time. Compared with similar institutions, the two measures of location clearly indicate that the cost per unit of service in our organization is relatively high, thus possibly identifying an internal weakness.

The Weighted Mean[R]

The weighted mean is a variant on the arithmetic mean and is used when it is necessary to account for differences in the relative importance of the various observations.

Suppose, for example, that the administrator is interested in determining the cost per unit of inventory used to provide ambulatory care. Assume further that the data summarized in Exhibit 3.1 were assembled for analysis. We suppose that the unit consumes six items of supply, that the price or cost per unit varied, and that the volume of each item used during the period differed. In this case, we might be tempted to calculate the cost per unit of item by employing the arithmetic mean to obtain

$$\bar{X} = (1 + 10 + 3 + 7 + 9 + 18)/6$$

or $8.00. Unfortunately, an unmodified arithmetic mean fails to reflect the relative importance of the cost per unit for each item.

In order to determine the cost per unit, it is necessary to divide total spending by the amount of inventory consumed during the period. The total spending on the items is given by the sum of products

$$1(50) = 10(850) + 3(160) + 7(400) + 9(30) + 18(310)$$

or $17,680. Because 1,800 units were used to provide ambulatory care during the period, the average cost per unit of supply is given by this ratio:

$$17{,}680/1{,}800$$

or approximately $9.82. The average is referred to as the *weighted mean* because the relative importance of the different prices is adjusted for the amount of each supply item consumed.

The weighted mean for a set of data represented by $x_1, \ldots x_i, \ldots x_n$ and for which the corresponding weights are $w_1, \ldots w_i, \ldots, w_n$ is given by

$$\bar{X}_w = \Sigma w_i x_i / \Sigma w_i \qquad \text{(Equation 3.3)}$$

Exhibit 3.1 **The Weighted Average Supply Cost of Providing Ambulatory Care**

Supply Item	Price Per Unit	Quantity Used	Cost
A	1	50	50
B	10	850	8,500
C	3	160	480
D	7	400	2,800
E	9	30	270
F	18	310	5,580
Total	48	1,800	17,680
Weighted Mean	9.82		

In this case, $\Sigma w_i x_i$ is the sum of products among the observations x_i and the corresponding weights; Σw_i merely represents the sum of the weights.

Although the weighted mean appears complicated, Excel allows the analyst to perform the calculations easily. Exhibit 3.1 shows that the supply items are identified in the cells A6 to A11, whereas the corresponding price per unit appears in cells B6 to B11. The amount of each supply item consumed during the period is listed in cells C6 to C11. After placing the cursor on cell D6, enter the expression = B6*C6, and use the "Copy" function to transfer the product from cell D6 to cells D7 to D11. Next, place the cursor in cell C12, and use the "AutoSum" function to find the total number of units consumed. Similarly, place the cursor on cell D12, and use the "AutoSum" function to determine the total spending. Finally, calculate the weighted average cost per unit by entering the expression = D11/C11. As shown in cell B16, the weighted average cost per unit of inventory used during the period is $9.82, an amount equal to the average calculated earlier in this section.

Ratios and Indices[O]

Ratios and indices are valuable when it is necessary measure changes in a variable over time. For example, the preparation of the budget or an evaluation of the purchasing function frequently requires a measure of the average rate of change in the price of consumable supplies. The administrator may be interested in the growth in the number of individuals in the market area or the variation in the use of service during the past 10 years. In each situation, it is necessary to compare a current value with one from the past.

For example, suppose the administrator was interested in the number of outpatient visits to one of several clinics that are operated by the health service organization and assembled the data that appear in Table 3.1. The annual number of visits, measured in thousands, is presented in the second column. The ratio appearing in the third column expresses the number of visits in a given year relative to those that occurred in the previous period. The first ratio, defined as 125/120, indicates that the number of visits in the second year was 4% higher than the vol-

Table 3.1 **Annual Rate of Change in Visits**

Year	Visits (in Thousands)	Rate of Change
1	120	
2	125	1.04
3	129	1.03
4	131	1.02
5	132	1.01

ume in the first. Similarly, the ratio, given by 129/125, indicates that the number of visits in third year was only 3% higher than in the second year. The other values listed in the column are interpreted similarly. The ratios indicate that the number of visits to the clinic increased each year but at a slower pace than in the preceding period. The information derived from the construction of the time series index summarizes the data in a form that enables the analyst to assess periodic changes and, as in the case of the number of visits provided during the past 5 years, to identify an emerging or potential weakness that should be addressed or an organizational strength that might be exploited.

Indices[O]

Indices are valuable when measuring the rates of change in the prices or quantities of the resources that the health service organization uses. For example, suppose that the administrator is interested in the periodic rate of change in the prices of disposable syringes and penicillin. When considered alone, the index for disposable syringes was 120% and that of penicillin was 180%. In an attempt to construct a single value that represents changes in the prices of the two items, the analyst might adopt the arithmetic mean to obtain (120 + 180)/2 or 150. Based on the mean value, the administrator might conclude that the prices of the two items increased by 50%. Although the result is mathematically correct, it has little value. As in the case of the weighted mean, the values included in the average are of different importance, and it is necessary to apply weights in the calculation of an index that accurately measures the phenomenon of interest.

The selection of weights is rarely a simple matter and depends, in part, on the phenomenon or variable that we wish to measure. However, when measuring periodic changes in prices, quantities are usually used as weights. In the following, let P_{io} and Q_{io} represent the base year price and quantity of item i, respectively. The base year is the period that is compared with others. P_{in} and Q_{in} are used to identify the given year price and quantity, respectively.

Although several approaches are possible, the Laspeyres Index (LI) and the Paasche Index (PI) are considered next. The LI is defined by

$$LI = (\Sigma P_{in}\, Q_{io} / \Sigma P_{io}\, Q_{io})100 \qquad \text{(Equation 3.4)}$$

where the sum includes all items for which we wish to measure variation in price. The base year quantities for each item, Q_{io}, appear in both the numerator and denominator. In contrast, the set of given year prices, P_{in}, appears in the numerator, whereas the set of base year prices, P_{io}, appears in the denominator. Thus, the denominator measures total spending on the set of items in the base year, whereas the numerator represents spending on the same mix, assuming that the prices in the given year prevailed. When multiplied by 100, the LI indicates the average percentage change in prices, after adjusting for the relative importance of the items.

To illustrate the use of the LI, refer to the data recorded in Exhibit 3.2, where it is assumed that a department of the health organization routinely consumes six supply items. Appearing in the second column from cell B5 to B10 are the set of base year prices, whereas the given year prices appear in the third column from cell C5 to C10. The numerator of the LI is calculated in the third column of the exhibit. Specifically, each value in the column is a product of the price in the given year and the base year quantity. These values were calculated by (1) entering in cell E5 the expression = C5*D5; (2) locating the cursor on cell E5, where the equation resides; and (3) using the "Copy" function to transfer the expression to the remaining cells. As before, the "AutoSum" function was used to determine the column total, which appears in cell E11.

The values appearing in the last column represent the product of the base year price and the base year quantity for each item. These values were calculated by (1) entering the expression = B5*D5 in cell F5, (2) locating the cursor on F5 where the equation resides, and (3) using the "Copy" function to transfer the expression to the remaining cells. The total appearing in cell F11 was obtained by the "AutoSum" function. Finally, the LI appears in cell B14 and is obtained by entering = (E11/F11)*100. These results indicate that on average the prices of the six items increased by approximately 11% during the lapse of time between the base and the given period.

Unlike the LI, the PI adopts the given year quantities as the weights that are applied to the different prices. By using the previously mentioned notation, the PI may be expressed as

$$PI = (\Sigma P_{in}\, Q_{in}/\Sigma P_{io}\, Q_{in})100 \qquad \text{(Equation 3.5)}$$

The numerator of the PI is the sum of products among the given year prices and quantities, a result that measures spending on the items during the period. In con-

Exhibit 3.2 **The Laspeyres Price Index**

Inventory Item	Base Year Price	Given Year Price	Base Year Quantity	Numerator LI	Denominator LI
A	2.50	3.00	800	2,400.00	2,000.00
B	4.75	5.25	1,250	6,562.50	5,937.50
C	1.25	1.75	478	836.50	597.50
D	2.30	3.10	350	1,085.00	805.00
E	5.60	6.10	900	5,490.00	5,040.00
F	7.60	8.15	1,260	10,269.00	9,576.00
Total				26,643.00	23,956.00
LI	**1.112164**				

trast, the sum of products appearing in the denominator is based on the given year quantities and the base year prices.

Exhibit 3.3 shows Excel simplifying the process of calculating the PI. The base year prices, appearing in cells B5 to B10, are listed in the second column. The given year prices appear in cells C5 to C10, whereas the quantity of each item used during the given year is shown in cells D5 to D10. The numerator of the PI index is shown in cells E5 to E10. These values were calculated by (1) entering the expression = C5*D5 in cell E5, (2) locating the cursor on cell E5, and (3) using the "Copy" function to record the expression to the remaining cells. The denominator of the PI was calculated by (1) entering the expression = B5*D5 in cell F5, (2) locating the cursor on cell F5, and (3) using the "Copy" function to transfer the expression to the remaining cells. The totals that appear in cells E11 and F11 were obtained by using the "AutoSum" function. Finally, the PI appearing in cell B15 was obtained by the expression = (E11/F11) × 100. These calculations indicate that the prices of the inventory items rose, on average, by approximately 13% during the study period.

The LI is perhaps more convenient to apply than the PI. As indicated, the LI relies on base year quantities as weights that are applied to prices, whereas the PI requires the use of given year quantities. The weights required when applying the LI remain constant, whereas those associated with the PI vary, thereby making it necessary to assemble new information for each period considered. Unfortunately, these data are frequently expensive and perhaps difficult to obtain.

Unless dramatic changes occur during the lapse of time between the given and base periods, the difference between PI and LI will be small. However, if prices increase or decrease dramatically, the difference between the LI and PI may be large. In such a situation, it may be necessary to average the two indices. One approach is to use the Fisher Ideal, FI, index which is defined by

$$FI = (PI \times LI)^{1/2}$$

Exhibit 3.3 **The Paasche Index**

Inventory Item	**Base Year Price**	**Given Year Price**	**Given Year Quantity**	**Numerator PI**	**Denominator PI**
A	2.50	3.00	1,200	3,600.00	3,000.00
B	4.75	5.25	1,400	7,350.00	6,650.00
C	1.25	1.75	750	1,312.50	937.50
D	2.30	3.10	530	1,643.00	1,219.00
E	5.60	6.10	1,200	7,320.00	6,720.00
F	7.60	8.15	850	6,927.50	6,460.00
Total				28,153.00	24,986.50
PI	**112.67**				

For example, suppose that the value of the PI was 209.6% and that the value of the LI was 267.5%. The FI index is given by

$$FI = (209.6 \cdot 267.5)^{1/2}$$

or 236.8%. As described in the next section, the FI is simply the geometric mean of the two indices and results in an average of the LI and the PI.

With a slight modification, the LI and PI might be used to measure changes in quantities rather than prices. By substituting p for q and q for p, the LI and the PI represent a quantity index in which the prices are used as weights. The construction of such an index indicates the relative change in the average use of resources because the prices appearing in the numerator and denominator are the same.

The Geometric Mean[O]

Time series indices, to include those that are derived from the PI or the LI, form the basis for developing an estimate of the average rate of periodic change. As indicated in this section, the time series indices are represented by a set of ratios, for which the geometric mean is an appropriate indicator of location. Suppose the set of data defined by

$$\{x1, \ldots xi, \ldots, x_n\}$$

is comprised of ratios or indices. The geometric mean of the set of ratios or indices is given by

$$G = \{(x_1)(x_2) \ldots (x_n)\}^{1/n} \qquad \text{(Equation 3.6)}$$

In this case, the *geometric mean*, represented by G, is obtained by finding the nth root of the product among the n ratios or indices. For example, suppose that after assembling data depicting the prices of inventory items the administrator constructed the following PI for each of 4 years. Each x_i represents the price index for the corresponding year.

$$x_1 = 1.04$$
$$x_2 = 1.06$$
$$x_3 = 1.02$$
$$x_4 = 1.05$$

Using these data, the geometric mean is calculated by

$$G = \{1.04 \times 1.06 \times 1.02 \times 1.05\}^{1/4}$$

or approximately 1.04. Thus, these results indicate that, on average, the prices of the items increased by approximately 4% per year during the study period. Although valuable to the administrator, the geometric mean is undefined for a set of data that contains a zero or a negative value.

Measures of Dispersion^R

The measures of location described previously in this chapter are single values that might be used to represent or portray a given distribution or set of data. Although useful, these indicators need to be supplemented with measures of dispersion or scatter. Measures of variation indicate the extent of scatter in a set of data, a feature that is important to the health administrator. Suppose, for example, that the administrator of a health maintenance organization is interested in the amount of time required to complete an initial visit by physicians assigned to one of two clinics. The results (measured in minutes) from a sample of 10 initial visits completed at Nevada Street Clinic were as follows:

21, 22, 25, 23, 25, 27, 24, 27, 22, 24

Similarly, the results (measured in minutes) from a sample of 10 initial visits provided at the Boulder Street Clinic were

10, 36, 21, 31, 19, 25, 26, 34, 20, 18

The mean time required to complete an initial evaluation was 24 minutes at each of the clinics, and if the analysis was based on the mean values only, the administrator might conclude that the amount of time required to complete each initial visit is the same at the Boulder and Nevada Street Clinics.

However, a more careful inspection reveals that the difference between the mean and the amount of time required to complete each of the visits at the Nevada Street Clinic was relatively small. In contrast, the difference between the mean and the amount of time required to complete the each of the visits at the Boulder Street Clinic was relatively large. Thus, the distribution of times derived for the Boulder Street Clinic exhibited greater variability, and it may not be possible to conclude that amount of time devoted to the initial visit is the same at both clinics.

As is indicated in our discussion of inferential statistics, the variability in the population from which a sample was selected might influence an administrative decision or the development and implementation of institutional policy. For example, suppose that the administrator of a multi-institutional arrangement is interested in the age of inpatient population of a short-term hospital and residents of the organization's long-term care facility. Furthermore, assume that the ages of the inpatients range from newborns to 95 years of age. In contrast, the ages of residents in the long-term care facility vary from 65 to 98 years. After selecting a sample of 100 patients from each setting, the data selected from the long-term care facility probably will exhibit less variability than those obtained from the short-term hospital. It also is likely that the difference between the sample mean and the population mean will be less for the long-term care facility than for the short-term hospital. Furthermore, in order to evaluate the accuracy of the sample mean as an estimate of the corresponding parameter, a measure of the variation exhibited by the population from which the sample was selected needs to be calculated. As the variation present in the population grows, the dispersion exhibited by data derived from a sample also is likely to increase. The focus of the following discussion is on measures of variability.

The Range

The *range* is perhaps the simplest measure of variation and is defined as the difference between the largest and smallest values in a given set of data. For example, this information depicts the length of stay for each of five patients.

2, 4, 6, 7, 10

In this case, the range is 8 days, given by the difference between the longest hospital stay of 10 days and the shortest of 2 days.

Although the range is easy to calculate and understand, it conveys inadequate information about the dispersion that is present in a set of data. Consider, for example, the three sets of data depicting the use of laboratory services, measured in units of service.

1, 4, 5, 6, 7, 10
1, 1, 1, 1, 1, 10
1, 10, 10, 10, 10, 10

In each case, the range is nine procedures, even though the sets of data do not exhibit the same degree of variability. Given the deficiency in the range as an indicator of dispersion, other measures of scatter are required.

Variance and the Standard Deviation

An understanding of the variance and the standard deviation might be enhanced by referring to the continuous distributions shown in Figures 3.2 and 3.3. Assuming that the scale of measurement is the same in the figures, a visual inspection reveals that the dispersion or scatter of data in Figure 3.2 is less than the variation exhibited by the distribution shown in Figure 3.3.

The purpose of the analysis is to develop a single measure of the dispersion exhibited by a given distribution. A deviation is the difference between an observa-

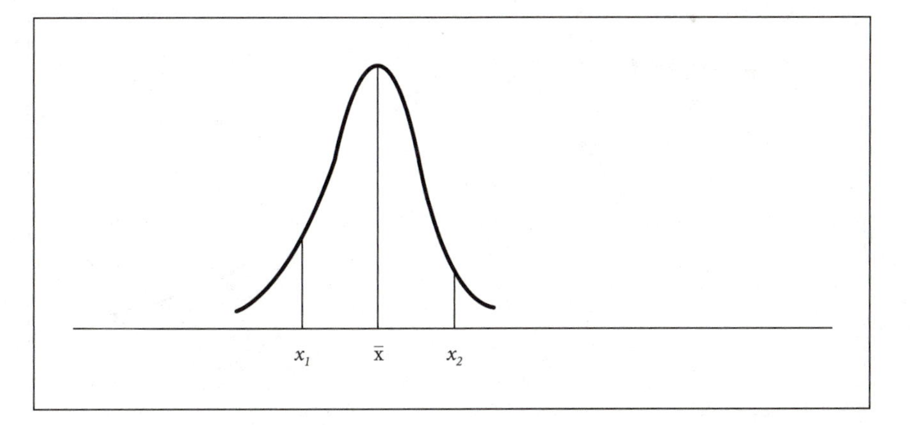

Figure 3.2 **Small Dispersion**

tion, say x_i and $\bar{X}$. The distance between x_i and $\bar{X}$ measures the difference between the observation and the mean (Figure 3.2). Figure 3.2 indicates that x_1 lies below $\bar{X}$, implying that the deviation $x_1 - \bar{X}$ is negative. In contrast, the observation x_2 lies above the mean, implying that the deviation $x_2 - \bar{X}$ is positive. Also, $\Sigma(x_i - \bar{X})$ must equal zero, a feature that is shown by the set {1, 2, 3, 4, 5}. The mean of these data is 3, and the deviations relative to the mean are summarized here:

x_i	$x_i - \bar{X}$
1	−2
2	−1
3	0
4	1
5	2
	0

Importantly, the sum of the deviations is zero.

The difficulty associated with using signed deviations relative to the mean to measure dispersion is avoided by first squaring each deviation and summing the results. Here, we define variation as

$$Variation = SS(X) = \Sigma(x_i - \bar{X})^2$$

for a sample and as

$$Variation = SS(X) = \Sigma(x_i - \mu)^2$$

for a finite population. As implied previously here, variation and SS(X) refer to the sum of squared deviations of the observations from the mean.

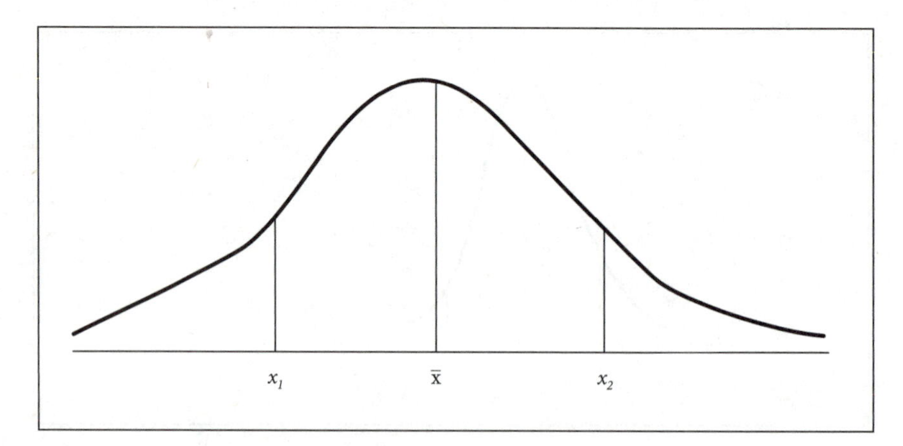

Figure 3.3 **Large Dispersion**

To express indicators of dispersion symbolically, we let σ^2 correspond to the variance of a finite population defined by $x_1, \ldots x_i, \ldots, x_n$. The variance of the population is given by

$$\sigma^2 = \Sigma(x_i - \mu)^2/N \qquad \text{(Equation 3.7)}$$

Hence, the variance of a finite population of size N is simply the average of the sum of squared deviations. To compensate for the fact that the deviations were squared, we compute the square root of the average of the sum of squared deviations to obtain the standard deviation of a finite population. Letting σ represent the standard deviation, we find that

$$\sigma = [\Sigma(x_i - \mu)^2/N]^{1/2}$$

In this case, the exponent $^1/_2$ is equivalent to and is frequently used as an alternate for the square root symbol; σ is nothing more than the square root of the mean of squared deviations and is often referred to as the *root-mean square deviation.*

Consider next the variance and standard deviation derived from sample data. Letting n represent the sample size, we might be mistakenly tempted to simply substitute $\overline{X}$ for μ and obtain $\Sigma(x_i - \overline{X})^2/n$. However, our objective is to derive an unbiased estimate of the population variance, and because $(\overline{X} - \mu)^2$ is routinely positive

$$\Sigma(x_i - \mu)^2/n = [\Sigma(x_i - \overline{X})^2 + (\overline{X} - \mu)^2]/n$$

After a slight rearrangement, the right-hand side of the equation reduces to

$$\Sigma(x_i - \overline{X})^2/n + (\overline{X} - \mu)^2$$

Because $(\bar{X} - \mu)^2$ is usually positive, the ratio $\Sigma(x_i - \bar{X})^2/n$ underestimates the population variance. To avoid the problem of underestimation, the unbiased estimate of the population variance, S^2, is defined by

$$S^2 = \Sigma(x_i - \bar{X})^2/n - 1 \qquad \text{(Equation 3.8.1)}$$

where n − 1 rather than n appears in the denominator. Using the notation introduced earlier, the variance might be expressed as

$$S^2 = SS(X)/n - 1 \qquad \text{(Equation 3.8.2)}$$

In this instance, n − 1 is referred to as the number of degrees of freedom, which requires a brief explanation. As demonstrated earlier, $\Sigma(x_i - \bar{X})$ must equal zero. The values of the first n − 1 deviations determine the value of the difference between the mean and the last observation, represented by x_n. Because the variance is based on squared deviations from the mean, the calculation of S^2 is based on n − 1 independent values, implying that the number of degrees of freedom is given by n − 1. In general, a degree of freedom is sacrificed on each occasion that a statistic is used as an estimate of a parameter. As indicated previously, we defined variation as the sum of squared deviations, represented by $\Sigma(x_i - \bar{X})^2$, and as a result, the sample variance also might be expressed as

$$S^2 = \textit{Variation/degrees of freedom} \qquad \text{(Equation 3.9.1)}$$

or by

$$S^2 = \textit{SS(X)/degrees of freedom} \qquad \text{(Equation 3.9.2)}$$

As described in Chapter 8, the concept of variance defined as the ratio of variation or SS(X) to degrees of freedom will enhance our understanding of analysis of variance and the evaluation of multiple means.

We define the standard deviation of a sample, represented by S, as the square root of the sample variance, a practice that compensates for the fact that the deviations were squared initially. As a consequence, the standard deviation of a sample is given by

$$S = [\Sigma(x_i - \bar{X})^2/n - 1]^{1/2} \qquad \text{(Equation 3.10)}$$

The standard deviation, S, is a point estimate of σ and is measured in units that express the variable on which it is based.

The process of calculating the standard deviation, S, is illustrated in the Excel spreadsheet shown in Exhibit 3.4. We suppose that the administrator of the health facility is interested in the use of laboratory services by inpatients. After selecting

Exhibit 3.4 **The Calculation of the Variance and Standard Deviation**

Patient	**Laboratory Use (in Units)**	**Squared Deviations SS(X)**
1	3	64
2	5	36
3	8	9
4	10	1
5	19	64
6	4	49
7	5	36
8	18	49
9	23	144
10	3	64
11	8	9
12	9	4
13	11	0
14	13	4
15	15	16
16	16	25
17	17	36
18	14	9
19	12	1
20	7	16
Total	220	636
Mean	11	
Variance	33.47	
Standard Deviation	5.79	

a sample of 20 patients, the volume of laboratory care used by each appears in cells B8 to B27. The third column shows the squared deviations of each observation relative to the mean of 10 procedures, a value that was calculated in cell B30. The squared deviations were calculated by entering the expression = (B38 − $B$30)^2 in cell C8 and copying the expression to cells C9 to C27. The "Auto Sum" function was used to determine the sum of squared deviations that appears in cell C28. The variance for the sample was calculated by entering the expression = C28/19 in cell B32, indicating that S^2 is equal to 33.47 procedures. Finally, the standard deviation was calculated by entering the expression = B32^.5 in cell

B34. The spreadsheet indicates that the standard deviation for the sample is approximately 5.79 laboratory procedures.

Skewness and Kurtosis[R,O]

As indicated previously, measures of location and dispersion are routinely used to describe a distribution. In addition, a distribution might assume multiple shapes and sizes. For example, consider a distribution that depicts the annual number of admissions by individuals enrolled in a managed-care organization. It is likely that most of the enrolled members experience no hospital episodes and a fewer number were admitted once during the year. Similarly, it is probable that an even fewer number of members were admitted twice, and a lesser number were admitted three times. In such a situation, the distribution would decline from left to right.

The health administrator also might encounter a distribution that is "U" shaped. For example, consider a distribution of use by groups characterized by differing ages. The young and the old tend to consume large quantities of health care, whereas individuals of intermediate ages consume relatively fewer units of service. Thus, the distribution of use, grouped by age, usually forms a "U" shape.

Although the health administrator might encounter distributions of different sizes and shapes, the focus of this section is on skewness and kurtosis. Skewness is applied to asymmetrical distributions, whereas kurtosis is an indicator of the distribution's peakedness.

Skewness[R]

A distribution is *symmetrical* if it is possible to make a perpendicular line that divides it into two identical halves. If a tail appears at either end, as shown in Figure 3.4, the distribution is asymmetrical and is said to be skewed. Even though two distributions have the same mean and standard deviation, one might be symmetrical, whereas the other exhibits skewness.

The symmetry or asymmetry that a distribution exhibits might be expressed as similarities or differences between the mode, the mean, and the median. Figure 3.5 shows that the mode, the mean, and the median assume the same value if the distribution is symmetrical and unimodal. Hence,

$$Mean = Median = Mode$$

for symmetrical and unimodal distributions.

However, in the case of asymmetry, recall that the median is a value below which lies 50% of the data, whereas the mean is influenced by extreme values. Figure 3.6 shows that the mean exceeds the median and that the median exceeds the

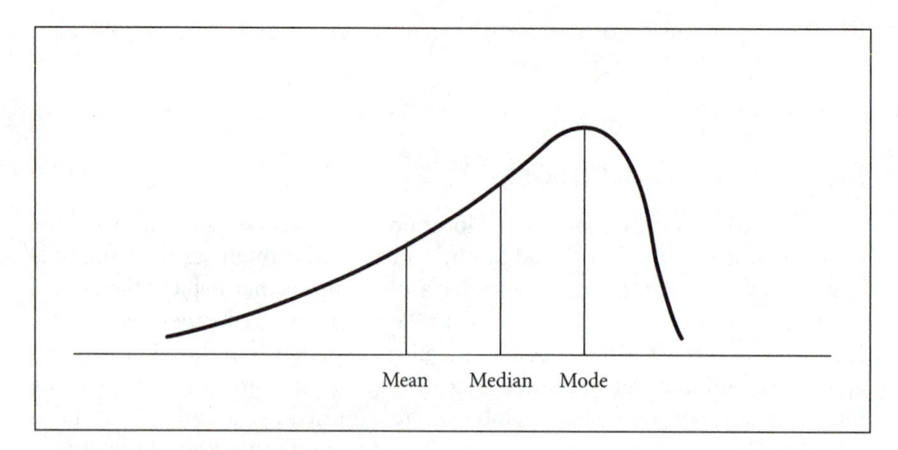

Figure 3.4 **Negatively Skewed Distribution**

mode in a distribution that is skewed to the right. Hence, for distributions similar to the one in Figure 3.6,

$$Mean > Median > Mode$$

However, Figure 3.4 shows that the median exceeds the mean in a distribution characterized by a tail that appears on the left. For distributions that are skewed to the left, the inequalities are reversed, so that

$$Mean < Median < Mode$$

As indicated later here, differences between the median and the mean enable us to measure and identify skewed distributions.

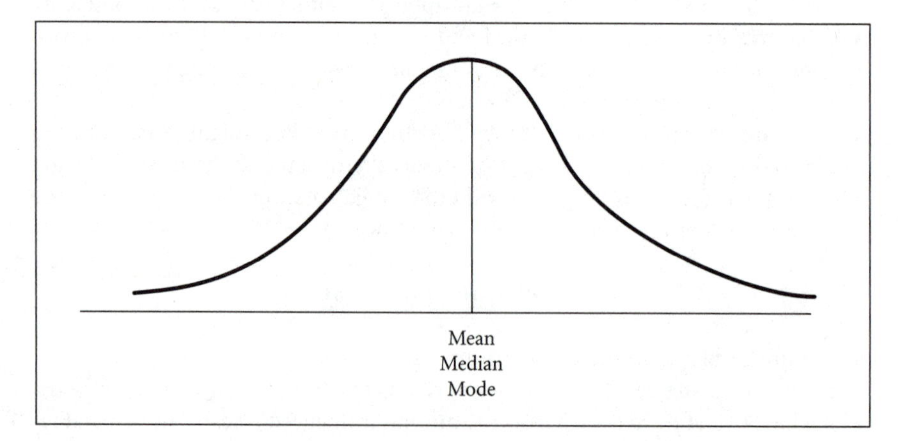

Figure 3.5 **Symmetrical Distribution**

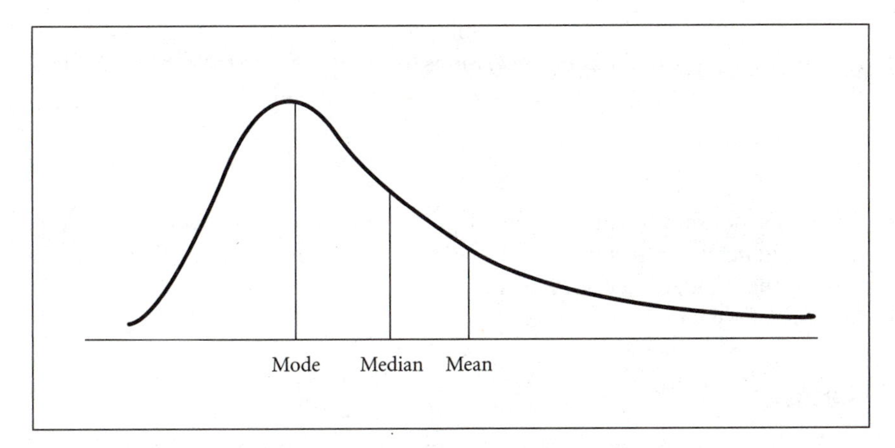

Figure 3.6 **Positively Skewed Distribution**

For moderately skewed distributions, the Pearsonian coefficient of skewness, represented by S_k, is frequently used to measure the shape of the distribution. It can be shown that S_k might be expressed as

$$S_k = 3(Mean - Median)/Standard\ Deviation \quad \text{(Equation 3.11)}$$

The standard deviation appears in the denominator of the Pearsonian coefficient of skewness, an aspect of S_k that reduces or eliminates the influence of differences in scale on the measure of asymmetry.

For example, consider a distribution that is similar to Figure 3.6, and suppose that the mean is 15 units, the median is 11 units, and the standard deviation is 10 units. After substituting appropriately, the value of the coefficient of skewness is given by

$$S_k = 3(15 - 11)/10$$

or 1.2. In this case, the coefficient is positive, and as a result, distributions that are skewed to the right are positively skewed. In contrast, consider a distribution similar to the one presented in Figure 3.4. Suppose that the mean is equal to 12, that the value of the median is 17, and that the standard deviation is 10. After substituting, the value of the Pearsonian coefficient of skewness is given by

$$S_k = 3(12 - 17)/10$$

or −1.5. Because the coefficient is negative, distributions that are skewed to the left are negatively skewed. The value of the coefficient of skewness for a symmetrical distribution is zero.

In addition to the Pearsonian coefficient, skewness also is measured by the ratio of the average of the cubed deviations from the mean to the cube of the standard deviation. Symbolically, we define α_3 (alpha-three) by

$$\alpha_3 = 1/n\ \Sigma(x_i - \mu)^3/\sigma^3 \qquad \text{(Equation 3.12)}$$

By cubing deviations, the directional property of each deviation is preserved, thereby indicating a positively or negatively skewed distribution. As before, the cube of the standard deviation is used to eliminate the influence of scale on the measure of skewness.

Kurtosis[O]

Although not used frequently in analyses, measures of kurtosis might be used to describe the shape of the distribution. Represented by α_4, the measure of kurtosis is

$$\alpha_4 = 1/n\ \Sigma(x_i - \mu)^4/\sigma^4 \qquad \text{(Equation 3.13)}$$

If α_4 exceeds 3, the distribution is leptokurtic or peaked. In contrast, if α_4 is less than 3, the distribution is broad humped or platykurtic.

An Application of Excel[R]

The statistics that are used to describe a distribution are calculated easily when Excel is used to perform the analysis. For example, suppose the administrator of a managed-care organization is interested in the number of visits per person per year for those that are insured. After selecting a sample of 20 individuals, the number of visits for each individual was recorded in cells B5 to B24 (Exhibit 3.5). The set of descriptive statistics are obtained by

1. Selecting "Tools" and then "Data Analysis" from the menu
2. Selecting "Descriptive Statistics" from the menu
3. Entering the range in which the data are recorded (i.e., B5 to B24)
4. Identifying the output range, beginning in cell A27
5. Selecting "Summary Statistics"
6. Entering "OK"

The results are reported immediately and are interpreted as follows: First, the arithmetic mean is 2.95 visits per person per year; the median is 2.5 visits, and the mode, the most frequently occurring value in the set of data, is one visit. The mean exceeds the median, implying that the coefficient of skewness (0.54) is positive and that the distribution is positively skewed. The variance S^2 is given by the ratio of variation to degrees of freedom and amounts to 4.05 visits, whereas the

Exhibit 3.5 **An Application of Excel**

Identification Number	Annual Number of Visits
1	2
2	3
3	1
4	1
5	3
6	5
7	2
8	4
9	0
10	3
11	4
12	6
13	1
14	1
15	5
16	2
17	6
18	7
19	2
20	1

Column1	
Mean	2.95
Standard Error	0.45
Median	2.5
Mode	1
Standard Deviation	2.01246118
Sample Variance	4.05
Kurtosis	−0.759502511
Skewness	0.549209679
Range	7
Minimum	0
Maximum	7
Sum	59
Count	20

standard deviation is 2.01 visits. Exhibit 3.5 shows that the range is simply the difference between the largest value, 7 visits, and the smallest value in the set of data. Finally, the standard error of the mean (0.45) is a measure that is discussed in Chapter 6.

The set of fractiles is also easily calculated when Excel is used to perform the analysis. Exhibit 3.6 shows the data that pertain to the use of visits; these data were initially examined in Exhibit 3.5. The first quartile is a value below which lies 25% of the data. Hence, the first quartile is equivalent to the 25th percentile. The first quartile was calculated by

1. Locating the cursor on cell B27
2. Selecting the "f_x" function that is adjacent to the cell identifier

Exhibit 3.6 **An Application of Excel to Calculate Fractiles**

Identification Number	Annual Number of Visits
1	2
2	3
3	1
4	1
5	3
6	5
7	2
8	4
9	0
10	3
11	4
12	6
13	1
14	1
15	5
16	2
17	6
18	7
19	2
20	1
First Quartile	1
Second Quartile	2.5
Third Quartile	4.25
Second Decile	1
Third Decile	1.7
Sixth Decile	3

3. Selecting "PERCENTILE" from the menu
4. Identifying, as an "ARRAY" the range in which the data appear (i.e., B6 to B25)
5. Entering 0.25 as the value for K
6. Selecting OK

The second and third quartiles were calculated by replicating these steps and assigning 0.5 and 0.75 as the value for K, respectively.

The exhibit also illustrates the method of finding several of the deciles. Specifically, the second decile corresponds to the 20th percentile. The third decile is equivalent to the 30th percentile, and the sixth decile is equivalent to the 60th percentile. Hence, beginning in cell B32, the second, third, and sixth deciles were calculated by repeating the steps described previously here and by sequentially assigning values of 0.2, 0.3, and 0.6 to K, respectively.

EXERCISES

1. The lengths of stay of 20 patients hospitalized with a digestive disorder are as follows:

   10, 4, 5, 8, 5, 7, 9, 11, 4, 3, 6, 9, 8, 5, 13, 4, 6, 8, 9, 3

   Similarly, the lengths of stay of 15 patients hospitalized with coronary heart disease are as follows:

   11, 13, 16, 12, 5, 8, 9, 5, 6, 7, 4, 8, 9, 7, 8

   Use Excel to find the mean, the mode, the median, the standard deviation, the range, and the coefficient of skewness for both sets of data. In addition, use Excel to find the 1st quartile, the 3rd decile, and the 40th percentile.
2. The following data depict the length of delay in discharging 18 older patients to a long-term care facility:

   5, 3, 4, 1, 2, 6, 7, 4, 8, 10, 3, 5, 3, 5, 4, 6, 7, 9

   Use Excel to find the mean, the mode, the median, the standard deviation, the range, the coefficient of skewness, the 3rd quartile, the 6th decile, and the 25th percentile.
3. Suppose the following represents compensation per hour and the number of hours worked by six employees of our organization during the past week. Use these data to calculate the average wage rate of the employees.

Employee	Hours	Wage
1	20	$15.00
2	40	$18.00
3	35	$12.00
4	30	$20.00
5	37	$14.00
6	25	$23.00

4. Suppose that we measured the amount of time (measured in minutes) required to perform an appendectomy on 20 different occasions and obtained the following data:

   109, 180, 150, 114, 160, 92, 142, 135, 126, 154 201, 149, 165, 185, 178, 159, 149, 148, 89, 175

   Use Excel to determine the mean, the mode, the median, the standard deviation, the range, the coefficient of skewness, the 1st quartile, the 8th decile, and the 45th percentile.

5. Suppose the following represents the base and given year prices and quantities of six supply items that are used in our laboratory. Use these data to construct a Laspeyres and a Paasche price index.

Supply Item	Base Year Price	Base Year Quantity	Given Year Price	Given Year Quantity
A	$50.00	100	$30.00	75
B	35.00	200	25.00	125
C	40.00	150	32.00	110
D	80.00	300	76.00	250
E	10.00	650	8.50	420
F	65.00	450	49.00	380

6. Use the data presented in Exercise 5 to construct a Laspeyres and a Paasche quantity index.
7. The following results were derived by constructing a price index for each of 5 years. Use these data to find the geometric mean.

Year	Price Index
1	1.03
2	1.05
3	1.02
4	1.03
5	1.04

8. Suppose our institution invests $10,000 in a security that earns 4%, $15,000 in another that earns 8%, and $40,000 in another that earns 9%. What is the average rate of return on these investments?
9. Suppose we selected a sample of 15 accounts receivable and determined the number of days that each was past due. The results derived from our sample are as follows:

   120, 90, 67, 34, 56, 78, 134, 145, 156, 80, 96, 67, 89, 23, 89

   Use Excel to find the mean, mode, median, standard deviation, range, coefficient of skewness, the 3rd decile, and the 15th percentile.

10. The following represents the number of procedures and the cost per procedure for each of five laboratory tests provided by our organization. Use these data to determine the average cost per procedure provided by the laboratory.

Procedure	Number	Cost/ Procedure
A	500	$25.00
B	1,000	$50.00
C	2,000	$15.00
D	900	$85.00
E	5,000	$45.00

11. The price index for food items used by the dietary department for each of the past 6 years is as follows: Use these data to calculate the geometric mean of the price indices.

Year	Index
1	1.08
2	1.09
3	1.02
4	1.10
5	1.03
6	1.07

12. Measured in 1,000 staff hours, suppose the use of personnel, grouped by occupational category, and the related payment per hour during the base and given year are as follows:

Occupation	Wage Rate		Hours	
	Base Year	Given Year	Base Year	Given Year
A	$12.00	$15.00	10.8	11.2
B	32.00	38.00	6.2	7.1
C	19.00	21.00	9.7	10.2

Use these data to construct a Paasche and a Laspeyres price index.

13. Use the data presented in Exercise 12 to construct a Paasche and a Laspeyres quantity index.
14. The following data depict the hourly wages paid to technicians by 15 institutions located in the same market area:

    $25.00, $28.00, $30.00, $29.00, $24.50, $28.00, $27.50, $31.50, $26.00

    $23.40, $27.50, $28.50, $32.30, $29.80, $28.70

    Use Excel to determine the mean, the mode, the median, the standard deviation, the range, the coefficient of skewness, the 1st quartile, the 3rd decile, and the 15th percentile.
15. The total number of visits to each of 10 physicians practicing in a given area was as follows:

    1,250, 1,750, 24,300, 1,570, 960, 1,854, 3,420, 2,114, 895, 672

    Use Excel to determine the mean, the mode, the median, the standard deviation, the range, the coefficient of skewness, the 1st quartile, the 2nd decile, and the 18th percentile.
16. Measured in $1,000, the supply expenses of our laboratory during each month of the past year were as follows:

    $21.1, $46.2, $36.8, $28.5, $19.2, $20.0, $21.7, $27.4, $29.3, $30.4, $33.1, and $34.7

    Use Excel to determine the mean, the mode, the median, the standard deviation, the range, the coefficient of skewness, the 1st quartile, the 4th decile, and the 34th percentile.

CHAPTER 4 The Fundamentals of Probability[R]

OBJECTIVES

1. Define probability in objective and subjective terms.
2. Define random experiment, outcomes, sample space, and events.
3. Portray the sample space, outcomes, and events in both tabular and graphic forms.
4. Define unions, intersections, and complements.
5. Describe the basic postulates of probability.
6. Use the general and special rules of addition to address issues or problems that occur in the health facility.
7. Define and calculate conditional probability.
8. Use the general and special rules of multiplication to address problems or issues that occur in the health service organization.
9. Use Excel and the rules of addition to address problems or issues that occur in the health service organization.
10. Use Excel and the rules of multiplication to address problems or issues that occur in the health service organization.

This chapter shifts the discussion from descriptive statistics to inferential statistics. A basic objective of inferential statistics is to increase the administrator's ability to make decisions or to develop institutional policy under conditions of uncertainty. Probability and the concepts of probability play a central role in inferential statistics. Hence, if applied appropriately, probability and the techniques associated with inferential statistics are immensely valuable to the successful administrator.

Basic Approaches to Probability

As described in the next section, probability is measured by a relative frequency, a proportion, or percentage. On the other hand, subjective probability is used to depict the occurrence or nonoccurrence of a unique event or an outcome that can occur only once. The fundamentals of both approaches are considered in this section.

Relative Frequency

The relative frequency interpretation defines probability as the percentage or proportion of time that similar events or outcomes occur in a set of repeated trials or in the long run. For example, suppose that we selected 100 laboratory tests and determined that 10 yielded false-positive or false-negative results. The findings are consistent with the suggestion that

1. The test yielded faulty results with a relative frequency of 10/100.
2. The proportion of tests that yielded faulty results is 0.10.
3. Ten percent of the tests yielded faulty results.

In this case, the proportion or percentage of the time that an event or outcome occurs is measured by a relative frequency, and the relative frequency that an event or outcome occurs is called its probability.

When defined in terms of relative frequency, probability is understood easily by referring to a finite population. A finite population is bounded and is limited in size such that it is possible to list all of the observations. For example, suppose that the director of human resources is interested in projecting the number of future retirees, suggesting that a distribution of employees, grouped by age, is required. The health service organization employs 100 individuals who are distributed with respect to age, as shown in Part A of Exhibit 4.1. The frequency distribution and the distribution of relative frequencies can be derived using the methods described in Chapter 2. In this case, the class frequencies are defined by the number of employees assigned to each of the age categories. The relative frequencies were derived by the ratios in which the class frequency appears in the numerator; the total number of employees is the denominator.

Consistent with our introductory comments, let n correspond to the number of elements or members assigned to a finite population and x represent the number of times that a well-defined result, outcome, or event occurs. The ratio x/n defines a relative frequency. The relative frequency calculated for the age category of 60 to 69 years is 18/100 (0.18). Eighteen percent of the employees are between 60 to 69 years old, and as a consequence, the distribution of relative frequencies might be interpreted as a probability distribution.

If an employee is randomly selected (the probability of selection is the same for each member of the population), the distribution of relative frequencies indicates the probability that the individual will be chosen from each of the age groups. The probability of selecting an individual who is between 20 and 29 years old is 0.12 or 12%, whereas the probability of choosing an employee who is between 50 and 59 years old is 0.25 or 25%.

The display in Part B of Exhibit 4.1 shows probability. Similar to the discussion in Chapter 2, suppose that the bases of the rectangles are identical and that the width of each is equal to one. The height of each rectangle is the relative frequency

Exhibit 4.1 **Age Distribution of Employees**

Part A

Age Group	Number of Employees	Relative Frequency
20–29	12	0.12
30–39	15	0.15
40–49	30	0.30
50–59	25	0.25
60–69	18	0.18
Total	100	1.00

Part B

of the corresponding age group and indicates the probability of selecting an employee assigned to the category. Because the base of each rectangle is one, the area of each rectangle, defined as the product of height and width, also represents the probability of selecting an employee from the corresponding age group. The area of each rectangle ranges from zero to one, and the sum of the areas is one.

Although health administrators frequently focus on finite populations, a number of situations require the analysis of an infinite universe. An infinite population is unbounded and has no upper constraint, eliminating the potential for listing or enumerating all elements of the universe. An infinite population usually is defined as the results or outcomes that are derived when a process is operated indefinitely under constant conditions.

For example, suppose that we are interested in measuring the amount of time required to provide a given laboratory procedure. After calibrating the equipment and selecting 1,000 units of the service, we recorded, in minutes, the amount of time required to complete the production cycle that results in the service. Figure 4.1 shows that the time required to provide the service formed a unimodal, continuous, and symmetric distribution. An inspection of Figure 4.1 reveals that the arithmetic mean was 10 minutes. Because the median and the arithmetic average are identical, on 50% of the occasions, 10 minutes or more were required to provide the procedure. As a consequence, the probability is 0.5 that the provision of the procedure will require 10 minutes or more, implying that the area under a continuous distribution corresponds to probability.

Consider next the interpretation attached to the probability of 0.5 that the service will require 10 minutes or more to provide. The probability statement means that in a large number of trials, the proportion of procedures requiring 10 minutes or more will approach 0.5 as more and more of the service is provided under constant conditions. As before, then, we define probability in terms of the relative frequency x/n as the number of trials, represented by n, increases indefinitely under constant conditions.

However, the probability statement does not enable us to identify which occasion will require 10 minutes or more to provide the procedure. Similarly, suppose we are told that the probability is 0.16 that a 45- to 50-year-old male will die from a cardiovascular disease. The probability does not allow us to identify which male will die with the disease; the probability simply indicates that 16% of a large number of 45- to 50-year-old males diagnosed with cardiovascular disease will die.

In general, if an event or outcome rarely occurs, the probability of the event or outcome is close to zero. In contrast, if an event or outcome is almost certain to occur, the probability of its occurrence is close to one. If an event or outcome is certain to occur, the probability of its occurrence is one. On the other hand, if an event or out-

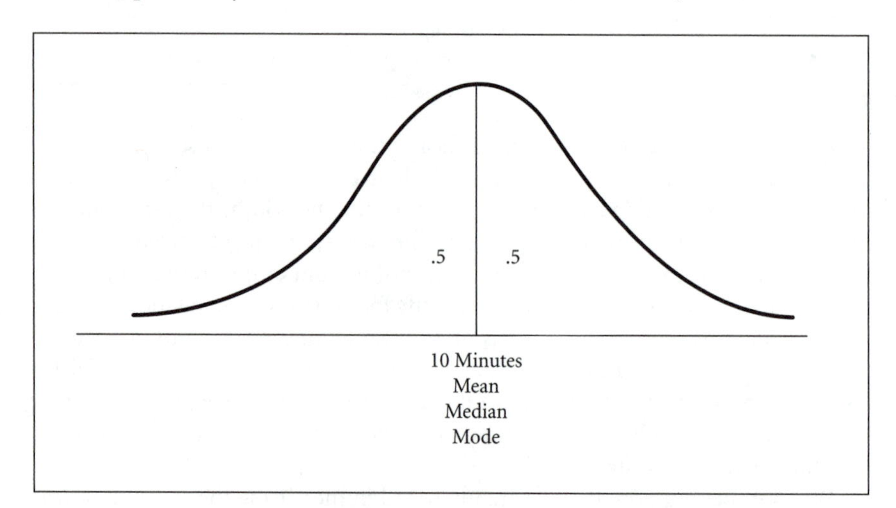

Figure 4.1 **Time Required to Provide a Service**

come never occurs, the probability of its occurrence is zero. In these situations, the occurrence or nonoccurrence of the events or outcomes is known with certainty.

Subjective Probability

As described in the previous section, a relative frequency, percentage, or proportion refers to the occurrence or nonoccurrence of an event or outcome in a large number of trials or replications. However, these measures may not be applied to an event or outcome that is unique or occurs only once. In many situations, there is little or no direct evidence concerning the occurrence or nonoccurrence of the item of interest.

For example, the administrator is unable to rely on direct evidence when assessing (1) the success of a new managed-care organization that might be introduced in the market area, (2) the relative success of new clinics located at multiple sites, (3) patients' acceptance of a new program or service, or (4) the need to dispose of marketable securities before the end of the current period. In each of these examples, the analyst must rely on subjective probability to evaluate the occurrence or nonoccurrence of the subject of interest. Subjective probability is directly related to the strength of the analyst's belief in the occurrence or nonoccurrence of an event. The relationship between subjective and objective probability is as follows: If an individual is prepared to offer odds of H:J that an event or outcome will occur, the corresponding objective probability is given by $H/(H + J)$.

For example, suppose that a multi-institutional group is evaluating a proposal to construct a new clinic at one of three sites. After assessing expected patterns of use in each of the clinics, the administrator assigned the following odds of success, represented by a predetermined level or rate of profitability.

Site	Odds
Tejon Street	2:1
Institute Street	4:1
Meade Avenue	3:1

Adopting the approach introduced earlier, the calculation and related objective probability of success at each site is as follows:

Site	Calculation	Probability
Tejon Street	$2/(2 + 1)$	0.67
Institute Street	$4/(4 + 1)$	0.80
Meade Avenue	$3/(3 + 1)$	0.75

Based on these results, the Institute Street location is most likely to be successful, followed by the Meade Avenue and Tejon Street sites.

Basic Concepts

Based on our discussion of the interpretation of probability, we look at the basic concepts that form the foundation for determining or calculating probabilities of more complex events from known or assumed probabilities of simpler events. This section focuses on random experiments, outcomes, events, and sample spaces.

Random Experiment

A *random experiment* is any process that randomly leads to one of several results for which the concepts and rules of probability are applicable. In a given random experiment, the administrator might be interested in several results. For example, we might wish to assess the quality of care that one of our clinics provides. In this situation, we might describe the experiment as the development and administration of a questionnaire to patients who visited the clinic. Similar to an earlier example, the administrator might be interested in the amount of time required to provide a given procedure or in the insurance status of individuals who were admitted as inpatients through the emergency department. The subject of interest usually dictates the nature or parameters of the experiment.

Outcomes

Basic outcomes are the results that are obtained from an experiment. For example, suppose the experiment consisted of selecting a patient from the daily census and recording the individual's gender. In this case, two outcomes are possible: male and female.

Sample Space

A *sample space* consists of all basic outcomes or results associated with a given random experiment. The basic outcomes derived from a random experiment are frequently characterized as mutually exclusive and collectively exhaustive. *Mutual exclusion* implies that only one of the outcomes will result from the random experiment. Because the sample space consists of all outcomes, it is *collectively exhaustive*, and as a consequence, a random experiment must result in only one of the basic outcomes.

Sample spaces might be defined in terms of the number of dimensions that are of interest to the administrator. A univariate sample space consists of basic outcomes that refer to a single dimension or characteristic such as age, sex, or diagnosis. Similarly, a bivariate sample space consists of outcomes or results that refer to two characteristics, such as age and sex. In general, we let O_i represent a basic outcome in a given sample space. Consider a sample space that is defined by age and sex. Suppose that the focus of the analysis is on those who are less than 65 years old and those who are 65 years old or more. In this case, the outcomes might correspond to

O_1: Males who are less than 65 years old
O_2: Males who are 65 years old or more
O_3: Females who are less than 65 years old
O_4: Females who are 65 years old or more

Finally, sample spaces might be defined in three or more characteristics or dimensions. In these situations, the focus of the analysis is on a multivariate sample space.

Events

It is often necessary to focus on results that are broader than the basic outcome of an experiment. An *event* consists of one or more outcomes or results derived from a random experiment. Thus, an event is a subset of the basic outcomes of a given sample space and an event occurs if one of the outcomes contained in the event occurs. Furthermore, as described later in this chapter, different events might share outcomes or a subset of the sample space in common. On the other hand, two or more events that share no basic outcomes in common are mutually exclusive.

An Illustration

A simple example might illustrate random experiment, basic outcomes, the sample space, and events. Suppose that the administrator of a managed-care organization is interested in evaluating the health status of the insured population. The evaluation, in part, consists of responses to this question: "During the past year, how would you rate your health?"

Suppose the responses to the question, with the numeric equivalent in parentheses, were good (3), average (2), and poor (1). In this case, we might regard the question as random experiment, whereas the outcomes or results of the experiment are represented by the responses of good, average, and poor.

To simplify the discussion of the related sample space, suppose that we are interested in the responses of the first two members. The sample space that represents the potential responses of the two individuals might be portrayed as shown in Figure 4.2. A coordinate of the form (x,y) has been listed beneath each of the outcomes that comprise the sample space. The first value indicates a response of the first insured member, and the second identifies a response of the second individual. For example, the coordinate (1,2) indicates that the first person reported a poor health status, whereas the second reported an average health status. Similarly, (3,3) indicates that both individuals rated their health status as good.

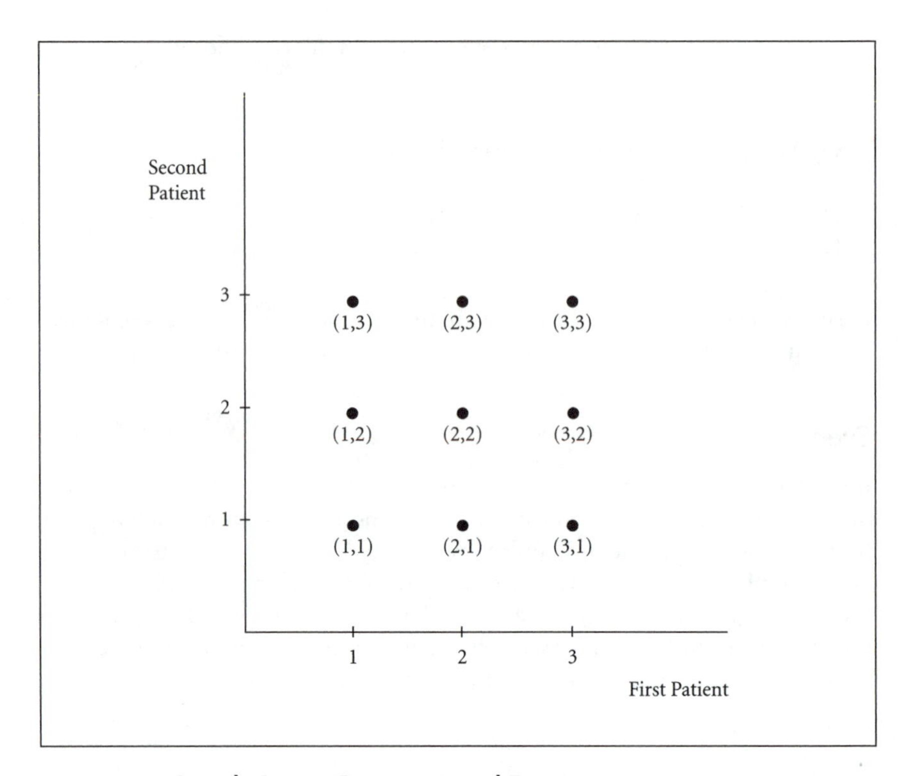

Figure 4.2 **Sample Space, Outcomes, and Events**

Thus far, the focus has been on the potential responses of two individuals. However, if the number of individuals increased from two to three insured members, the sample space would grow from 3^2 (or 9) to 3^3 (or 27) outcomes. One of the basic outcomes in the sample space defined by three members is (3,3,2), implying that the first two individuals rated their health status as good, and the third reported an average health status. In general, a sample space derived for n individuals would consist of 3^n basic outcomes represented by the set $\{r_1, \ldots r_n\}$. In this case, each value represents a response or an evaluation by one of the n respondents.

Next consider events that are defined by one or more of the outcomes portrayed in the sample space. Let A_1 correspond to the event that the two members reported the same health status, A_2 represent the event that at least one of the two members rated his or her health status as average, and A_3 represent the event that one member reported poor health and the other reported good health (Figure 4.2).

Consider the outcomes that comprise event A_1. An inspection of Figure 4.2 indicates that the event consists of outcomes (1,1), (2,2), and (3,3) because in all other instances the responses of the two individuals differ. Similarly, the event A_2, defined as outcomes in which at least one reported an average health status, consists of outcomes (1,2), (2,2), (3,2), (2,1), and (2,3). Finally, event A_3 consists of outcomes in which one respondent reported a poor health status and the other reported a good health status. An inspection of Figure 4.2 reveals the basic outcomes (1,3) and (3,1).

After the outcomes that comprise each of the events have been identified, it is possible to establish the relationships among A_1, A_2, and A_3. Figure 4.3 describes the previously mentioned events and shows that event A_3 shares no points in common with either event A_1 or event A_2. When events share no basic outcomes in common, they are mutually exclusive, implying that both cannot occur simultaneously in the same random experiment.

We also might be interested in forming more complex events from their simpler counterparts. For example, we might be interested in the event that both members rated their health the same *and* that at least one of the individuals reported an average health status. In this case, we are interested in the event that A_1 and A_2 both occur, which is indicated by the basic outcome (2,2). Alternatively, we might be interested in the event in which the individuals responded in the same way *or* one of the patients reported a poor health status and the other reported a good health status. Our interest is in the event that *either* A_1 *or* A_3 occurs.

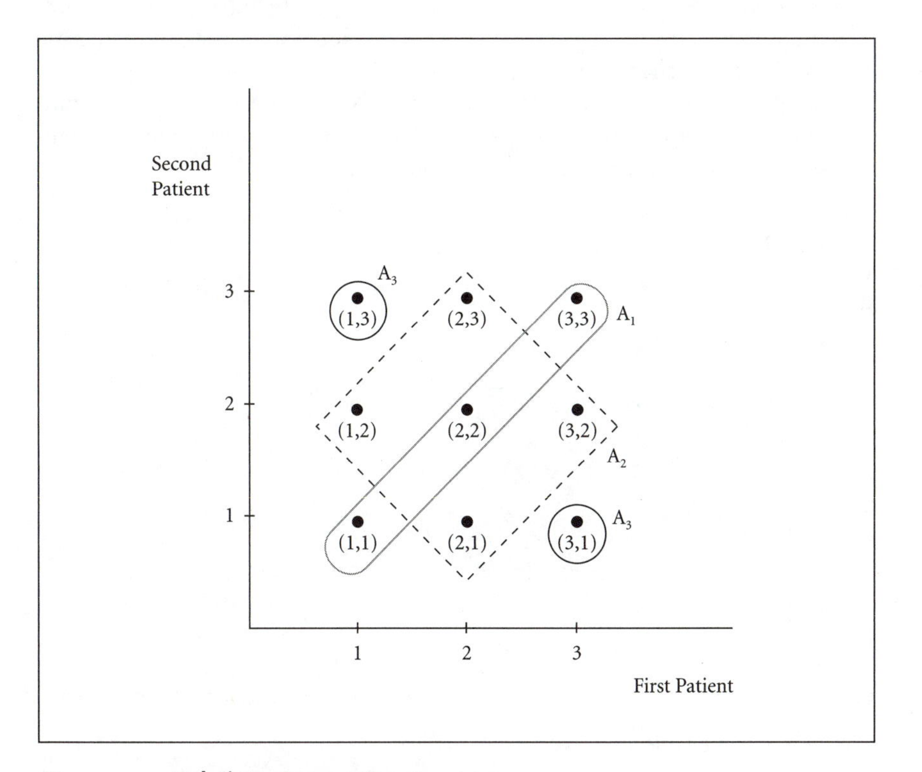

Figure 4.3 **Relations Among Events**

Referring to the figure, the outcomes comprising the event that either A_1 *or* A_3 occurs are (1,1), (2,2) (3,3), (3,1), and (1,3).

Unions, Intersections, and Complements

Let A and B represent two events. We define their *union*, represented by $A \cup B$, as the event consisting of all basic outcomes contained either in A, in B, or in both A and B. The example from the previous section showed that the union of A_1 and A_2 is the set {(1,1), (2,2), (3,3), (1,2), (3,2), (2,1), (2,3)}.

The sample space, events, and relations among events might also be presented by relying on a Venn diagram. A rectangle customarily represents the sample space and the events or subsets of the basic outcomes by regions or areas of the rectangle. Figure 4.4 shows that circles and parts of circles are used to depict events or subsets of outcomes in the sample space. An inspection of the figure also reveals that the union of two events A and B is depicted by the lined area.

If A and B are two events, we define their *intersection*, represented by $A \cap B$, as the outcome or outcomes that are common to both. The intersection of A_1 and A_2 that is shown in Figure 4.3 is the basic outcome (2,2). The intersection of events A and B is defined by the region that is shared in common by the two events and is identified by the shaded area (Figure 4.5).

The *complement* of event A is represented by A′ and consists of all basic outcomes that are not contained in A. Figure 4.6 depicts the event A and the complement of A, which is represented by the lined area.

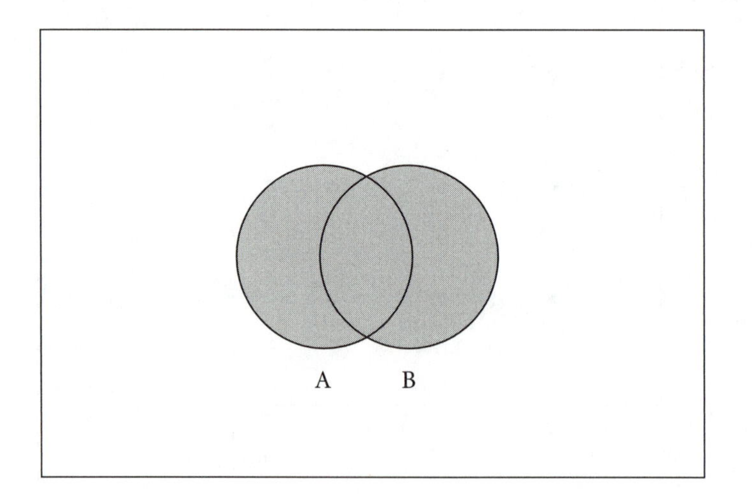

Figure 4.4 **The Union of Two Events**

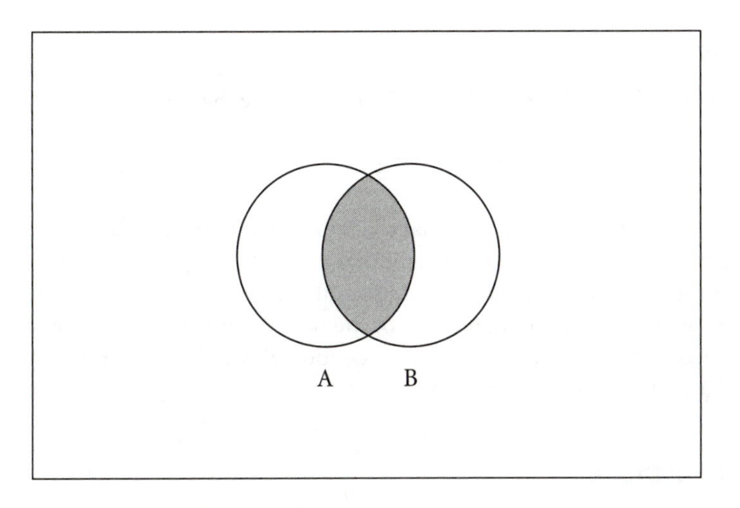

Figure 4.5 **The Intersection of Two Events**

THE POSTULATES OF PROBABILITY

In the following, we let $O_1, \ldots O_i, \ldots O_n$ represent the basic outcomes of a random experiment. Also, we let $P(O_i)$ represent the probability that outcome O_i will be the result of the random experiment. Based on this, the following discussion is devoted to the basic postulates of probability.

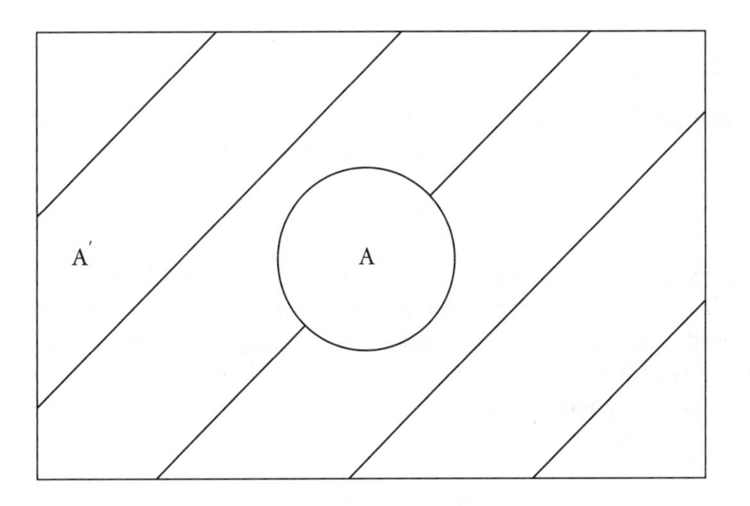

Figure 4.6 **The Complement of an Event**

The First Postulate

The first postulate is that each probability $P(O_i)$ must satisfy the expression

$$0 \leq P(O_i) \leq 1 \qquad \text{(Equation 4.1)}$$

In this formula, $\leq$ means "less than or equal to," implying that the probability of outcome O_i cannot be less than zero or greater than one. Thus, the probability of any outcome must range from zero to one. As a result, an outcome cannot occur less than 0% of the time or more than 100% of the time. Similarly, when viewed from the perspective of subjective probability, the ratio defined by $H/(H + J)$ can never be less than zero or more than one.

The Second Postulate

Basic outcomes are mutually exclusive, and the sample space is collectively exhaustive. As a consequence, the probability of a given sample space is one, as expressed by

$$\Sigma P(O_i) = 1 \qquad \text{(Equation 4.2)}$$

This asserts that one of the basic outcomes in the sample space will result from the random experiment and that the sum of related probabilities is one. When expressed in terms of relative frequencies, Equation 4.2 indicates that one of the basic outcomes contained in the sample space will occur 100% of the time.

The Third Postulate

Assume that an event A is defined by basic outcomes O_1, O_2, and O_3. If the basic outcomes are mutually exclusive, the probability of the event, $P(A)$, is given by

$$P(A) = P(O_1) + P(O_2) + P(O_3)$$

In general, the probability of an event A is simply the sum of the probabilities of the outcomes that comprise that event. For example, suppose that insured members of a managed-care organization reported identical ratings of their health and that the probability of the outcome (1,1) is 0.05, the probability of the outcome (2,2) is 0.1, and the probability of the result (3,3) is 0.02. In this case, the probability of event A_1 is given by

$$P(A_1) = 0.05 + 0.1 + 0.02$$

or 0.17.

Rules of Addition

Consider first the *special rule of addition*. Assume that two events A and B are mutually exclusive, implying that one and only one of the events will result from the random experiment. In this case, we employ the special rule of addition to find the probability that A or B will occur. The special rule of addition is given by

$$P(A \cup B) = P(A) + P(B) \qquad \text{(Equation 4.3)}$$

For example, suppose event A consists of outcomes O_1, O_2, and O_3, whereas event B consists of O_4 and O_5. Consider event A and assume that

$$P(O_1) = 0.05$$
$$P(O_2) = 0.01$$
$$P(O_3) = 0.15$$

Similarly, suppose that the probabilities of the outcomes comprising event B are

$$P(O_4) = 0.02$$

whereas

$$P(O_5) = 0.03$$

The probability of event A is 0.05 + 0.01 + 0.15 (or 0.21), whereas the probability of event B is 0.02 + 0.03 (or 0.05). Thus, the probability that either event A or B will occur is 0.21 + 0.05 (or 0.26). An identical result is obtained by the sum of the outcomes that comprise A and B (i.e., [0.05 + 0.01 + 0.15] + [0.02 + 0.03]).

A Venn diagram can used to illustrate the union of two mutually exclusive events. Figure 4.7 shows that events A and B share no basic outcomes in common. The probability of event A occurring is 0.4, whereas the probability of event B occurring is 0.15. Thus, using Equation 4.3, we find that the probability that either A or B will occur is simply 0.4 + 0.15 (0.55).

Thus far our discussion has assumed that the events were mutually exclusive. However, if two events share one or more outcomes in common, a slightly different approach must be used when calculating the probability that an outcome either in A, in B, or in both A and B will occur. Using the previous example, suppose that event A consists of outcomes O_1, O_2, and O_3. However, event B now consists of outcomes O_3, O_4, and O_5, and as a result, outcome O_3 is common to both. The probability of event A is, as before, the sum of the probabilities 0.05, 0.01, and 0.15 (0.21). Similarly, the revised probability of event B is the sum of 0.02, 0.03, and 0.15 (0.20). If we mistakenly applied the special rule of addition, we would conclude that the probability of A union B is 0.41, a value that includes the probability of outcome O_3 twice. To accommodate the inclusion of the outcome in the

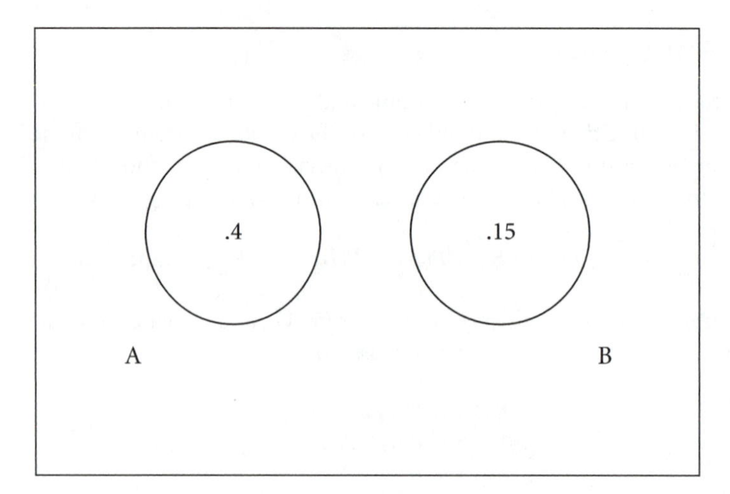

Figure 4.7 **The Union of Two Mutually Exclusive Events**

calculation of P(A) and P(B), probability of outcome O_3 must be subtracted from the sum 0.41 to obtain 0.26.

Based on these observations, we may express the *general rule of addition* in the form

$$P(A \cup B) = P(A) + P(B) - P(A \cap B) \qquad \text{(Equation 4.4)}$$

For example, an application of Equation 4.4 yields

$$P(A \cup B) = (0.21 + 0.20) - 0.15$$

or 0.26. Equation 4.4 also might be applied to the problem of calculating the probability of the union between two mutually exclusive events because the $P(A \cap B)$ is zero.

The general rule of addition also might be shown by the Venn diagram that is in Figure 4.8. In this case, the probability of A occurring is given by the sum 0.3 + 0.1 (0.4), whereas the probability of event B occurring is 0.2 + 0.1 (0.3). Thus, the probability of A intersect B is 0.1, suggesting that an application of Equation 4.4 yields

$$P\,(A \cup B) = (0.4 + 0.3) - 0.1$$

or 0.6. An identical result is obtained by adding mutually exclusive areas identified in Figure 4.8. As before, we find that

$$P\,(A \cup B) = 0.3 + 0.1 + 0.2$$

or 0.6.

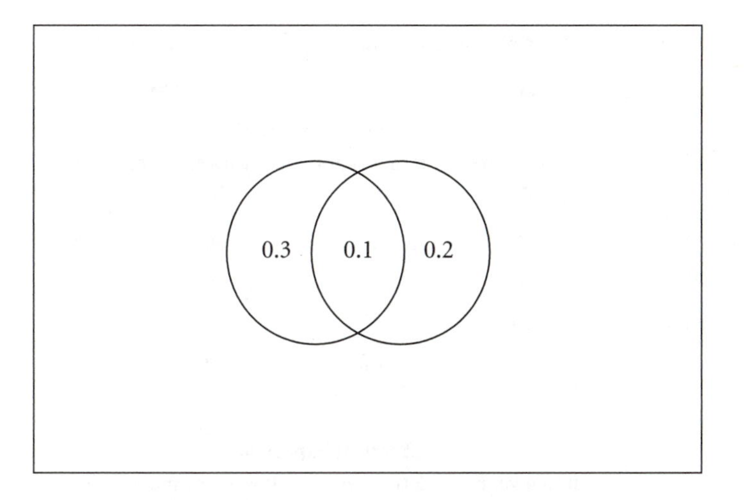

Figure 4.8 **The Union of Two Events: The General Rule of Addition**

Finally, the general and special rules of addition might be illustrated using data that are presented as a table. For example, suppose the director of human resources is interested in inequities that might result from a failure to adjust the salaries of registered nurses employed by a multi-institutional organization. After adjusting for shift differentials, the information presented in Part A of Exhibit 4.2 depicts the annual income of 200 registered nurses, grouped by years of experience. In this case, the categories 0 to 4 years, 5 to 9 years, and 10 years or more are used to measure the experience of the nursing staff. Similarly, the categories defined as $30,000 to $49,999, $50,000 to $69,999, and $70,000 or more reflect the annual salaries of the 200 registered nurses who are employed by the health service organization. In this case, a total of 20 nurses earned a salary of $70,000 or more and reported between 0 and 4 years of experience. The exhibit indicates that 32 of the nurses with 5 to 9 years of experience earned between $50,000 and $69,999 per year.

Using the previously described procedures, the frequency distribution may be transformed into a distribution of relative frequencies, as shown in Part B of Exhibit 4.2. In this case, the number of nurses who had 0 to 4 years experience and who earned an annual income between $30,000 and $49,999 appears in cell B6, whereas the total number of observations appears in cell E9. The distribution of relative frequencies appearing in Part B of Exhibit 4.2 was calculated by

1. Locating the cursor on cell B17
2. Entering the expression = B6/$E$9
3. Using the "copy" function to transfer the expression to the other cells of the exhibit

The resulting data are interpreted as follows. Suppose that we choose a nurse at random, implying that each has the same probability of selection. Referring to

Exhibit 4.2 **The Distribution of Nurses, Grouped by Salary and Experience**

Part A

	Years of Experience			
Salary	**0 to 4 years (B_1)**	**5 to 9 years (B_2)**	**10 years or more (B_3)**	**Total**
\$30,000 to \$49,999 (A_1)	8	20	40	68
\$50,000 to \$69,999 (A_2)	10	32	30	72
\$70,000 or more (A_3)	20	30	10	60
Total	38	82	80	200

Part B

	Years of Experience			
Salary	**0 to 4 years (B_1)**	**5 to 9 years (B_2)**	**10 years or more (B_3)**	**Total**
\$30,000 to \$49,999 (A_1)	0.04	0.10	0.20	0.34
\$50,000 to \$69,999 (A_2)	0.05	0.16	0.15	0.36
\$70,000 or more (A_3)	0.10	0.15	0.05	0.30
Total	0.19	0.41	0.40	1.00

the row totals, the probability of selecting a nurse with 0 to 4 years experience, represented by $P(B_1)$, is 0.19. Similarly, the probability of selecting a nurse with an income between \$50,000 and \$69,999 per year, represented by $P(A_2)$, is 0.36.

Suppose that the director of human resources is (using the distribution of relative frequencies) interested in the probability that either event B_1 or B_3 will occur. In this case, we are interested in the probability that the nurse selected has either 0 to 4 years or 10 years or more of experience. Recognizing that the two events are mutually exclusive, an application of the special rule of addition (given by Equation 4.3) yields

$$P(B_1 \cup B_3) = 0.19 + 0.40$$

or 0.59. Similarly, suppose the director is interested in the union of events A_1 or A_2, implying that the individual selected earns an annual income of \$30,000 to \$49,999 or \$50,999 to \$69,999. Again, the two events are mutually exclusive, suggesting that

$$P(A_1 \cup A_2) = 0.34 + 0.36$$

or 0.70.

Next consider the likelihood that event A_1 or B_1 will occur. In this case, we are interested in the likelihood that the nurse has 0 to 4 years of experience or earns an income of $30,000 to $49,999 per year. The probability of event A is 0.34, whereas the probability of event B is 0.19. Furthermore, the calculation of P(A) and P(B) includes the probability of selecting a nurse who has 0 to 4 years experience *and* earns an income of $30,000 to $49,999 per year (i.e., $P[A_1 \cap B_1] = 0.04$). Accordingly, an application of the general rule of addition yields

$$P(A_1 \cup B_1) = (0.19 + 0.34) - 0.04$$

or 0.59. In this case, failure to adjust for the intersection of the two events results in a 0.04 overstatement of the probability.

Conditional Probability

Health administrators are frequently required to assess conditional probabilities. For example, the probability that an individual will appear in the emergency department, given that he or she is 65 years old or more, may need to be calculated. We might be interested in the probability that an individual is admitted as an inpatient, given that he or she visited the emergency department. Similarly, the financial officer is frequently interested in the probability that an account will be recognized as uncollectible if the patient earns an annual income of $10,000 or less. In each example, the probability of interest is contingent on the occurrence of a well-defined event or outcome; the corresponding probability is called a *conditional probability*.

Suppose that we are interested in two events, A and B, that pertain to a given sample space. The conditional probability of A, given B, is noted by $P(A \mid B)$. To illustrate the nature of conditional probability, refer to the distribution of 200 nurses, grouped by experience and income. Suppose that the administrator is interested in the probability that a nurse earns an income of $30,000 to $49,999 per year, if the individual has 10 years or more experience. Referring to the frequency distribution presented in Part A of Exhibit 4.2, the analysis is limited to the 80 nurses who have experience of 10 years or more. Because 40 of the 80 also earn an income of $30,000 to $49,999 per year, the corresponding conditional probability might be calculated by

$$P(A_1 \mid B_3) = 40/80$$

or 0.5. Letting N correspond to the number of observations, the numerator is defined by $N(A_1 \cap B_3)$, whereas the denominator corresponds to $N(B_3)$. We might also calculate the probability that a nurse earns a salary of $70,000 or more if the individual has 10 years or more of experience. Once again, the analysis is limited to the 80 nurses that have 10 years or more of experience. In this case, however, only 10 of them earn $70,000 or more per year. Using the notation introduced earlier, the conditional probability required by the director might be expressed in this form:

$$P(A_3 \mid B_3) = N(A_3 \cap B_3)/N(B_3)$$

After substituting appropriately, we get

$$P(A_3 \mid B_3) = 10/80$$

or 0.125.

Conditional probability might be expressed more conveniently by relying on the concept of relative frequency. Let N correspond to the number of observations associated with a given event and T the total number of observations on which the distribution is based.

$$P(A \cap B) = N(A \cap B)/T$$

while

$$P(B) = N(B)/T$$

Referring to Part B of Exhibit 4.2, recall that the probabilities appearing on the bottom row correspond to $P(B_j)$ where the index j represents one of the three categories of professional experience and that $P(A_i \cap B_j)$ represents the probability defined by the intersection of row i and column j. For example, $P(A_2 \cap B_1)$ represents the probability of selecting a nurse who earns an income of $50,000 to $69,999 per year *and* has 0 to 4 years of experience. We conclude, in general, that

$$P(A_i \mid B_j) = P(A_i \cap B_j)/P(B_j) \qquad \text{(Equation 4.5)}$$

For example, suppose that we wished to derive a conditional probability distribution of income if the individual has 10 years or more of experience. In this case, the conditional probability distribution is represented by $P(A_i \mid B_3)$. The calculations of the distribution are as follows:

Conditional Probability	Calculation	Result
$P(A_1 \mid B_3)$	0.20/0.40	0.50
$P(A_2 \mid B_3)$	0.15/0.40	0.375
$P(A_3 \mid B_3)$	0.05/0.40	0.125
Total		1.00

Two observations concerning the conditional probability distribution listed in the last column are important. First, consistent with postulate 1, each probability ranges from zero to one. Second, consistent with postulate 2, the sum of the probabilities is equal to one.

The Venn diagram that is presented in Figure 4.9 shows the conditional probability. In this case, the intersection of A and B is identified by the lined area that represents a probability of 0.2. Also, the probability of event B is the sum of 0.3 and 0.2 (0.5). Hence, the probability of A, given B, is obtained by

$$P(A \mid B) = 0.2/0.5$$

or 0.4.

The Interpretation of Conditional Probability

As described in the previous section, conditional probability is valuable to the administrator when assessing operating activity or in situations in which we wish to assess the association of one event with another. Consider first a situation in which one event is independent of another. The Venn diagram in Figure 4.10 shows that the $P(A \cap B)$ is 0.2, whereas P(B) is 0.4. We find that

$$P(A \mid B) = 0.2/0.4$$

or 0.5. The Venn diagram also shows that the P(A) also is 0.5, indicating that

$$P(A \mid B) = P(A) = 0.5$$

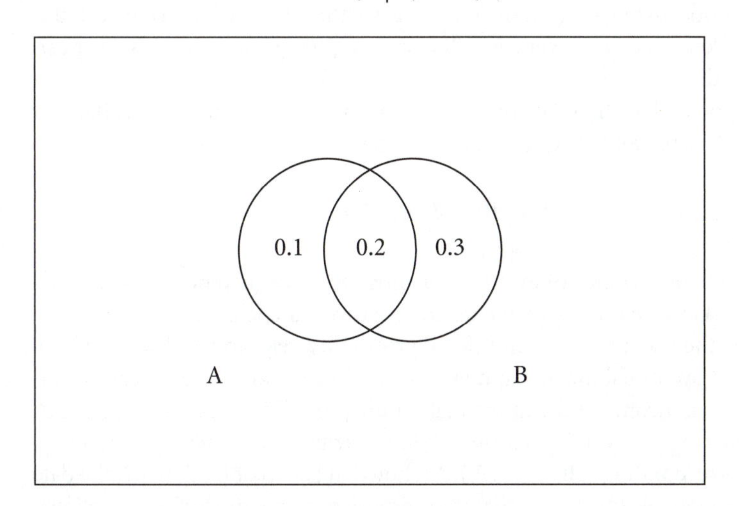

Figure 4.9 **Conditional Probability**

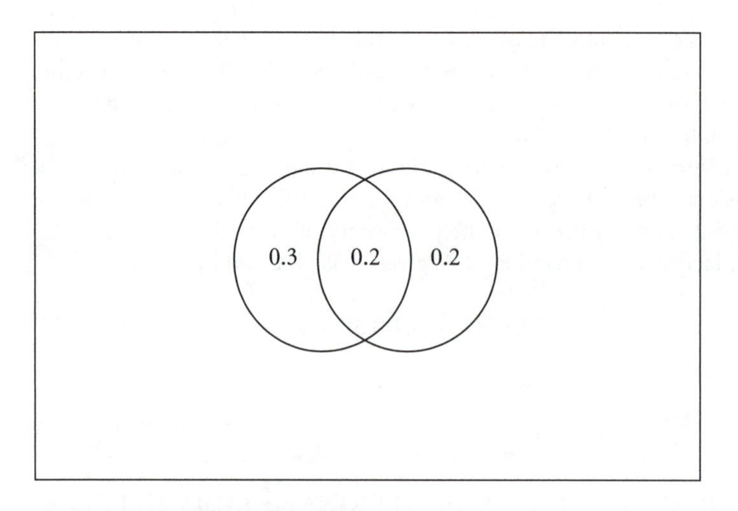

Figure 4.10 **Independent Events**

These results indicate that the occurrence of event A does not depend on the occurrence or nonoccurrence of event B. In these circumstances, event A is said to be *independent* of event B.

Consider next a situation in which the probability of A, given B, differs from the probability of A. For example, suppose that P(A | B) = 0.8 and that P(A) = 0.2, implying that

$$P(A \mid B) - P(A) > 0$$

The inequality indicates that the occurrence of event A is dependent on the occurrence or nonoccurrence of event B. It suggests that the occurrence of event B increases the likelihood that event A will occur, implying that A and B are positively associated.

Finally, suppose that the probability of A, given B, is less than the probability of A. If P(A | B) is 0.4 and P(A) is 0.6, the inequality

$$P(A \mid B) - P(A) < 0$$

indicates that the occurrence of event A depends on the occurrence or nonoccurrence of event B and that the two events are negatively associated.

To illustrate the usefulness of conditional probability, refer to the distribution of nurses, grouped by annual income and experience. In general, as the experience increases, the annual income of the individual should grow. This idea might be examined by considering the conditional probability distribution, represented by $P(A_i \mid B_3)$ with the corresponding value of $P(A_i)$. As shown in Part B of Exhibit 4.2, the data that relate to personnel with 10 or more years experience are summarized as follows:

Income	$P(A_i \mid B_3)$	$P(A_i)$	Association
$30 to $49,999	0.50	0.34	Positive
$50 to $69,999	0.375	0.36	Positive
$70,000 or more	0.125	0.30	Negative

These results suggest that those with experience of 10 years or more are relatively more likely to earn an income of $30,000 to $49,999 per year and less likely to earn an income of $70,000 or more.

The data derived for nurses with 0 to 4 years of experience support the idea that the salary policy of the organization requires evaluation and quite possibly modification. After calculating the conditional probability distribution represented by $P(A_i \mid B_1)$, we obtain the following comparisons:

Income	$P(A_i \mid B_1)$	$P(A_i)$	Association
$30 to $49,999	0.21	0.34	Negative
$50 to $69,999	0.26	0.36	Negative
$70,000 or more	0.53	0.30	Positive

These results indicate that nurses with 0 to 4 years of experience are relatively less likely to earn an annual income of either $30,000 to $49,999 or $50,000 to $69,000. The data also suggest that those with 0 to 4 years experience are relatively more likely to earn an income of $70,000 or more. Because the set of nurses with greater experience seems to earn a lower annual income than their less experienced counterparts, the analysis of the conditional probability distributions alerts management to a potential deficiency in the salary policy of the institution and a need to adjust the salaries of existing staff so as to reflect changes in the market rate of compensating registered nurses.

Rules of Multiplication

As described previously here, the general and special rules of addition might be applied to problems requiring the calculation of $P(A \cup B)$. Thus far, however, we have not considered methods that might be applied to the calculation of probabilities that reflect the intersection of two events, A and B. Here the general and special rules of multiplication that govern the calculation of $P(A \cap B)$ are introduced.

The previous discussion of conditional probability indicated that the conditional probability of A given B is given by

$$P(A \mid B) = P(A \cap B)/P(B)$$

After multiplying both sides of the equation by P(B) and rearranging them slightly, we obtain the *general rule of multiplication* that is expressed by

$$P(A \cap B) = P(A \mid B) \times P(B) \qquad \text{(Equation 4.6)}$$

Suppose that A represents the event that an individual will be admitted as an inpatient and that B corresponds to the event that a resident of the organization's service area will visit the emergency department. Suppose also that P(A | B) is 0.4 and that P(B) is 0.005. An application of the general rule of multiplication yields

$$P(A \cap B) = (0.4)(0.005)$$

or 0.002. These calculations indicate that the probability of an individual visiting the emergency department and requiring an inpatient stay is 0.002. Suppose that a population of 50,000 resides in the service area, implying that the health service organization might expect (50,000)(0.002) or 100 inpatient admissions after a visit to the emergency department. If each stay is expected to last an average of 5 days, an application of the general rule of multiplication suggests that the administrator should reserve (0.002)(50,000)(5) or 500 bed days of care to treat patients admitted after a visit to the emergency department.

Consider next the *special rule of multiplication*, an approach that is applied to independent events. As described in the previous section, event A is independent of B if

$$P(A \mid B) = P(A)$$

After substituting P(A) for P(A | B) in Equation 4.6, we obtain the *special rule of multiplication*, which is defined by

$$P(A \cap B) = P(A) \times P(B) \qquad \text{(Equation 4.7)}$$

It should be emphasized that the special rule of multiplication may be applied only when A is independent of B. As described in Chapter 7, the special rule of multiplication also plays a pivotal role when it is necessary to assess the association of one variable with another.

The special rule of multiplication might be extended to more than two events. Suppose that $A_1, \ldots A_i, \ldots A_n$ represents a set of events for which the probabilities are $P(A_1), \ldots P(A_i), \ldots P(A_n)$, respectively. The probability of the intersection among the n events is given by

$$P(A_1 \cap A_2 \ldots \cap A_i \cap \ldots \cap A_n) = P(A_1) \times \ldots \times P(A_i) \times \ldots \times P(A_n)$$

Hence, the intersection among n independent events is simply the product of the probabilities that each will occur.

Exercises

1. As indicated in this Venn diagram, the probability that a patient will visit our emergency room, represented by event A, is 0.40. The probability that an individual will be admitted as an inpatient, represented by event B, is 0.25. Find P(A ∪ B), P(A ∩ B), and P(A | B). Is event A independent of B, or is event A related to B? If A is related to B, is the association positive or negative?

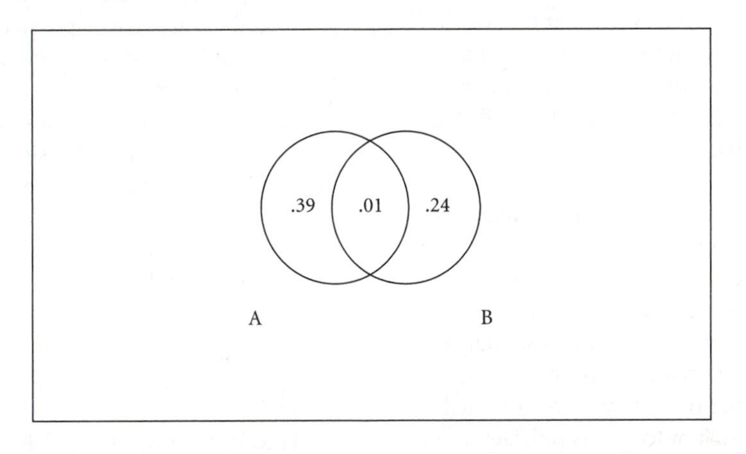

2. Suppose that we are considering a proposal to include productivity as a factor when adjusting the rates of compensating employees of our health service organization. We are interested in whether employees favor the proposal, oppose the proposal, or are undecided. Limited to two employees, we might portray the sample space concerning their responses as follows.

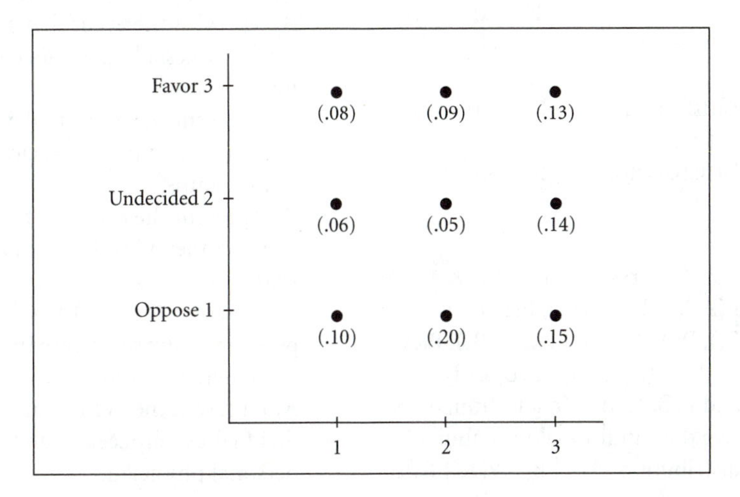

The values appearing in parentheses correspond to the probabilities of each of the basic outcomes. We now let A correspond to the event that the two employees responded in the same way, B represent the event that at least one of the employees was undecided, and C represent the event that one of the employees opposed the plan and the other favored the proposal. Find P(A), P(B), P(C), $P(A \cup B)$, $P(A \cup C)$, $P(B \cup C)$, and $P(B \mid A)$.

3. Suppose that our organization employs three laboratory technicians who perform a given procedure. When evaluating their performance, suppose that we selected a sample of procedures performed by each and rated each outcome as satisfactory or unsatisfactory. The following data were assembled as a part of the assessment.

Rating	Technician		
	I (B_1)	II (B_2)	III (B_3)
Satisfactory (A_1)	40	50	40
Unsatisfactory (A_2)	20	40	10

Use these results to find $P(A_1)$, $P(A_2)$, $P(B_1)$, $P(B_2)$, $P(B_3)$, $P(A_1 \cap B_3)$, $P(A_1 \cap B_2)$, $P(A_2 \cap B_1)$, $P(A_2 \cap B_3)$, $P(A_1 \cup B_1)$, $P(B_1 \cup B_2)$, and $P(B_2 \cup B_3)$. In addition, derive the conditional probability distribution $P(A_i \mid B_1)$, $P(A_i \mid B_2)$, $P(A_i \mid B_3)$ for i = 1 and 2. Use these results to evaluate the performance of each technician.

4. In the following let
   1. B_1 represent the event that an individual is insured.
   2. B_2 correspond to the event that an individual is unisured.
   3. A_1 represent the event that an individual visits a physician on at least one occasion during the year.
   4. A_2 represent the event that an individual will not visit a physician during the year.

   Based on data derived from a survey of our market area, suppose we found that

   $P(B_1) = 0.75$.
   $P(A_1 \mid B_1) = 0.8$.
   $P(A_2) = 0.30$.

   Find $P(A_1 \cap B_1)$, $P(A_2 \cap B_2)$, $P(A_1 \cup B_2)$ and the conditional probabilities $P(A_1 \mid B_1)$ and $P(A_1 \mid B_2)$. Are use of service and insurance status independent in this area?

5. In the following let
   B_1 represent the event that a person occupies a high socioeconomic status.
   B_2 represent the event that a person occupies a middle socioeconomic status.
   B_3 represent the event that a person occupies a low economic status.
   A_1 represent the event that a person usually seeks care in our emergency room.
   A_2 represent the event that an individual usually seeks care from a personal physician.

Suppose that a survey of our market area revealed the following results:

	Socioeconomic Status			
Source	High (B_1)	Middle (B_2)	Low (B_3)	Total
ED (A_1)		80	400	500
Physician (A_2)	320	600		
Total	380	680		1,500

Complete the table and use the results to find $P(B_3)$, $P(A_2)$, $P(A_1 \cap B_1)$, $P(A_2 \cap B_3)$, $P(A_1 \mid B_1)$, $P(A_1 \mid B_2)$, and $P(A_1 \mid B_3)$. Based on the conditional probabilities, is the source of care independent of socioeconomic status?

6. Let

   B_1 represent the event that a person has less than a high school education.
   B_2 represent the event that a person has a high school education.
   B_3 represent the event that a person has more than a high school education.
   A_1 represent the event that a person will visit one of our dental clinics during the year.
   A_2 represent the event that an individual will not visit one of our dental clinics during the year.

   Based on a survey of our market area, suppose that we know that

   $P(A_1) = 0.7$
   $P(B_1) = 0.45$
   $P(B_3) = 0.08$
   $P(A_1 \mid B_2) = 0.85$
   $P(A_1 \mid B_3) = 0.90$

   Use these results to find $P(A_1 \cap B_3)$, $P(A_1 \cup B_3)$, and $P(A_1 \mid B_1)$. Are these two variables independent in the study population? If not, describe the conclusions that these results suggest.

7. Let

   B_1 represent the event that an initial visit to one of our physicians lasts less than 20 minutes.
   B_2 represent the event that an initial visit to one of our physicians lasts 20 to 25 minutes.
   B_3 represent the event that an initial visit to one of our physicians lasts more than 25 minutes.
   A_1 represent the event that a visit was provided at the Royer Street Clinic.
   A_2 represent the event that a visit was provided at the Peak Street Clinic.
   A_3 represent the event that a visit was provided at the Unita Street Clinic.

   Suppose further that we obtained the following information:

		Site		
Length of Visit	Royer (A_1)	Peak (A_2)	Unita (A_3)	Total
0–19 (B_1)	30		55	165
20–25 (B_2)		500	55	
25+ (B_3)	80	100		270
Total	120		200	1,000

Use these data to calculate $P(A_2)$, $P(B_2)$, $P(B_3 \cap A_3)$, $P(B_1 \cap A_2)$, and $P(B_2 \cap A_3)$. Construct a conditional probability distribution of the length of visit given that a visit occurred at the (1) Royer Street Clinic, (2) the Peak Street Clinic, and (3) the Unita Street Clinic.

8. In the following, let A represent the event that a bill was prepared properly and B correspond to the event that the insurer delayed payment.
   Find $P(A)$, $P(B)$, $P(A \cap B)$, $P(A \cup B)$ and $P(B \mid A)$. Does the accuracy of submitted bills influence delays in receiving payment?

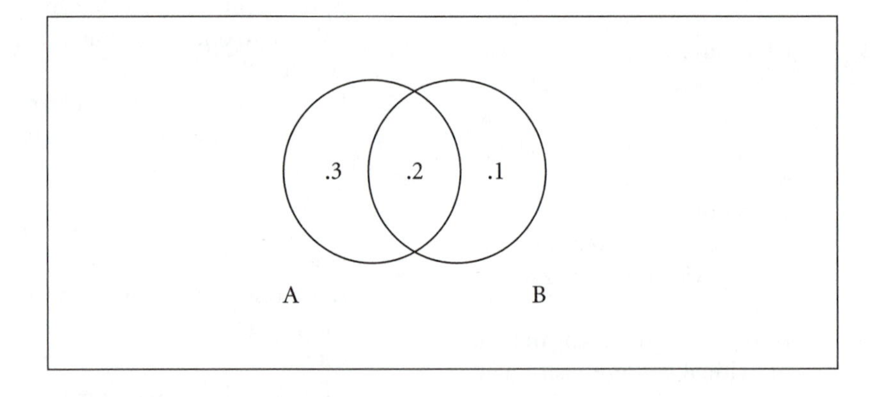

9. In the following let
   B_1 represent the event that the delay in transferring a patient from the hospital to a long-term care facility was 1 to 10 days, identified as "Short."
   B_2 represent the event that the delay in transferring a patient from the hospital to a long-term care facility was 11 to 20 days, identified as "Medium."
   B_3 represent the event that the delay in transferring a patient from the hospital to a long-term

care facility was more than 20 days, identified as "Long."
A_1 represents the event that post hospital care was financed by the Medicaid Program.
A_2 represent the event that post hospital care was financed by the private insurance.

Based on a review of medical records, suppose that we obtained the following distribution:

	Length of Delay			
Source of Payment	Short B_1	Medium B_2	Long B_3	Total
Medicaid (A_1)	0.1		0.4	0.6
Private (A_2)	0.2	0.15		
Total	0.3	0.2		1.0

Use these data to calculate $P(A_1 \cap B_2)$, $P(A_2 \cap B_3)$, $P(B_3 \mid A_1)$, and $(B_3 \mid A_2)$, $(B_2 \mid A_1)$, and $P(B_2 \mid A_2)$.

Based on these results, is the length of delay in transferring the patient independent of the source of financing post hospital care?

CHAPTER 5 PROBABILITY DISTRIBUTIONS[R]

OBJECTIVES

1. Define the term probability function.
2. Distinguish between a continuous and a discrete random variable.
3. Use Excel, the binomial, and the Poisson distributions to calculate probability.
4. Apply the results derived from the binomial and Poisson distributions to problems or issues that occur in health service organizations.
5. Describe the standard normal distribution.
6. Use the standard normal distribution to calculate desired probabilities and apply the results to problems or issues that occur in the health service organization.
7. Distinguish between an experimental and theoretical sampling distribution of the mean.
8. Describe the properties of the theoretical sampling distribution.
9. Describe the central limit theorem.
10. Use the central limit theorem to calculate desired probabilities, and apply the results to address problems or issues that are of interest to the health administrator.

We have thus far examined the fundamentals of probability, the interpretation of probability, conditional probability, the rules of addition, and the rules of multiplication. In this chapter, we continue our discussion of probability and examine the probability functions and distributions that form the foundation for many of the techniques that comprise inferential statistics.

In general, the number of probability distributions is indefinite, each differing from others in one or more aspects, such as central tendency, variation or scatter, symmetry, and kurtosis. However, a limited number of probability distributions can be applied in a wide range of situations. This chapter focuses on the binomial probability distribution, the Poisson probability distribution, and the normal distribution. However, before considering these distributions, we must introduce the concept of a probability function.

The Probability Function

Health administrators are frequently interested in the probability that a random variable will assume a given value in a set of attainable or possible values. On the other hand, the value of a random variable is determined by chance or the outcome of a random experiment. Thus, when the focus is on a probability function, we are interested in the likelihood that a random variable will assume a given value.

For example, if we are interested in evaluating the quality of care that one of several clinics renders, the random experiment asks, "In general, how would you rate the care you received at the clinic?"

We also assume that the outcomes consist of the responses good (3), average (2), and poor (1), where the values in parentheses correspond to the ratings of the three responses. Limited to the possible responses of only two patients, the sample space is presented in Figure 5.1. The values 0, 1, and 2 appear above the outcomes appearing in the sample space and indicate the number of patients who rated the care as average. The designation of the number of patients who rated the care as average enables us to define a probability function based on the sample space, suggesting that random variables are functions.

A probability function lists the likelihood that the random variable will assume each value in the set of possible values. Figure 5.1 shows the probability of each

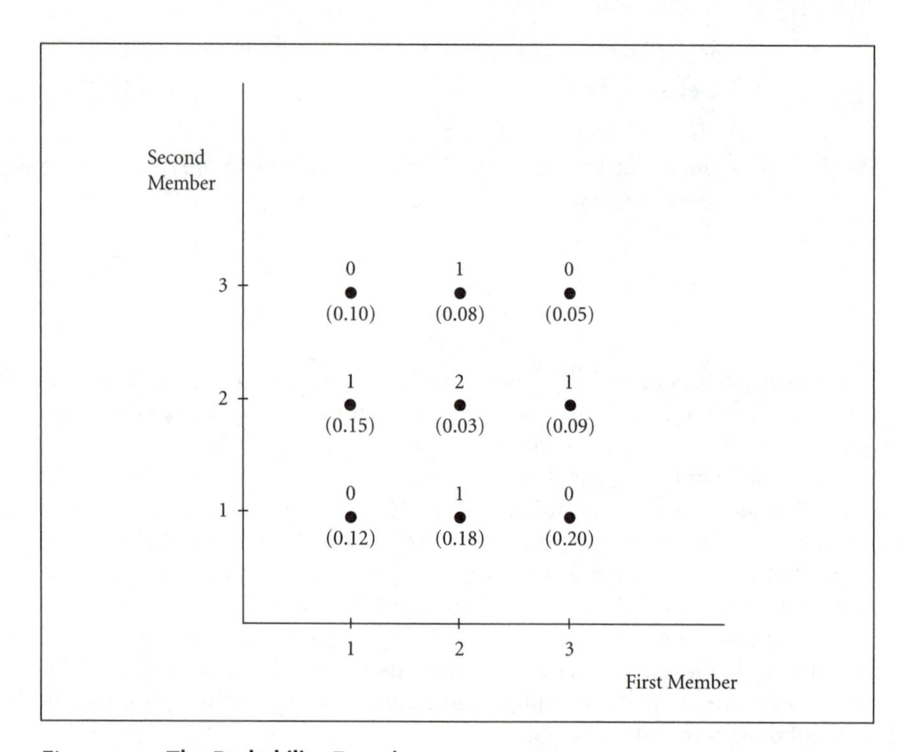

Figure 5.1 **The Probability Function**

outcome in parentheses. For example, the probability of outcome (2, 2) is 0.03, whereas the probability of the outcome represented by (1, 3) is 0.10. Given these probabilities, the probability that none of the patients rated the care as average is given by the sum of 0.10, 0.05, 0.12, and 0.20 or 0.47, whereas the probability that one of the patients rated the care as average is given by the sum of 0.15, 0.09, 0.08, and 0.18 or 0.50. Figure 5.1 also reveals that the probability of two patients rating the care as average is 0.03. These results are summarized as follows:

Number of Patients Rating Care as Average (x)	Probability f(x)
0	0.47
1	0.50
2	0.03
Total	1.00

The probabilities range from zero to one, and their sum is one. In this example, f(x) denotes a probability function and indicates the likelihood that the random variable x will assume the values 0, 1, and 2. In general, the probability function, represented by f(x), indicates the probability that the random variable will assume each value in the set of possible values. We let f(x) represent the probability that 0, 1, or 2 patients rate the care as average. Using this notation, we find that

$$f(0) = 0.47$$
$$f(1) = 0.50$$
$$f(2) = 0.03$$

These results indicate that the probability that 0, 1, or 2 of the patients rate the care as average is 0.47, 0.50, and 0.03, respectively.

Discrete Probability Distributions

Random variables are customarily described as discrete or continuous. A continuous random variable assumes any value on the real number line. Examples of continuous random variables include age, time, and distance. In contrast, a discrete random variable assumes positive integer values such as 0, 1, 2, 3, or 4. A discrete random variable can assume an indefinite number of integer values. In this section, we consider discrete random variables and the theoretical probability distributions that are valuable to the health administrator. The binomial and the Poisson probability distributions are next examined.

The Binomial Probability Distribution

The binomial probability distribution enables the administrator to calculate the probability that an event will occur on x occasions in n trials. The binomial probability distribution is based on three conditions. First, an application of the binomial probability distribution requires that the probability of an event occurring remains constant from trial to trial. The first condition implies that the analyst wishes to examine an infinite population or a process that operates indefinitely under constant conditions. Alternatively, the first condition implies that data are derived from a finite population and that we sample with replacement. Second, an application of the binomial probability distribution requires that trials are independent, implying that the outcome of a given trial is influenced in no way by the result of any other trial. Finally, the binomial probability distribution may be applied to only a binary or dichotomous outcome. For example, the results of a laboratory procedure might be either correct or defective, represented by a false-negative or a false-positive outcome.

For example, consider an application of the binomial probability distribution to the problem of quality assessment. Assume that the health service organization monitors and evaluates the performance of the laboratory department by characterizing procedures as either correct or defective as indicated by false-positive or false-negative results. To simplify this example, suppose that the focus is on a sample of three procedures that are rated as correct, represented by *C*, or defective, identified by *D*. There is only one way that all of the procedures yield correct results, suggesting that none are defective. The outcome in which no procedures are defective might be represented by the set {C,C,C}.

Suppose that an expert indicates that, after calibration, we might expect 20% of the procedures to yield defective results. We believe that the normal defective rate is 0.20, implying that the probability of a correct result is 0.8. If the trials are independent, we employ the special rule of multiplication and find that the probability of identifying no defective procedures in a sample of three is given by

$$0.8 \times 0.8 \times 0.8$$

or 0.512. This result also might be expressed in the form $(1)(0.2^0)(0.8^3)$ where 0.2^0 is equal to one.

Consider next the probability of identifying one defective result in a sample of three. For example, the first procedure included in the sample might yield defective results, whereas the results of the other two are correct. Alternatively, the results of the first and third procedure might be correct, whereas the results of the second were defective. The number of ways in which only one procedure was defective in a sample of three might be summarized as

1. {D,C,C}
2. {C,D,C}
3. {C,C,D}

The probability of a defective result is 0.2, whereas the probability of a correct result is 0.8. Because we assume that the trials are independent, an application of the special rule of multiplication yields the probability of each of the ways in which one result is defective. These calculations are summarized as follows:

Result	Calculation	Probability
1. {D,C,C}	$0.2 \times 0.8 \times 0.8$	0.128
2. {C,D,C}	$0.8 \times 0.2 \times 0.8$	0.128
3. {C,C,D}	$0.8 \times 0.8 \times 0.2$	0.128
Total		0.384

The probability of 0.384 also might be calculated by

$$f(1) = 3 \cdot 0.2^1 \cdot 0.8^2$$

where 3 is the number of ways in which one defective procedure might be selected from the sample of three services.

Adopting a similar approach, the number of occasions and probabilities associated with observing two defective results in a sample of three procedures is as follows:

Outcome	Calculation	Probability
1. {D,D,C}	$0.2 \times 0.2 \times 0.8$	0.032
2. {D,C,D}	$0.2 \times 0.8 \times 0.2$	0.032
3. {C,D,D}	$0.8 \times 0.2 \times 0.2$	0.032
Total		0.096

The probability of .096 is equivalent to

$$f(2) = 3 \cdot 2^2 \cdot 0.8$$

Finally, the number of occasions and probabilities associated with identifying three defective results in our sample is given by

Outcome	Calculation	Probability
{D,D,D}	$0.2 \times 0.2 \times 0.2$	0.008

These results might be expressed in the form

$$f(3) = 1 \times 0.2^3 \times 0.8^0$$

The calculation of the number of ways in which a given result might occur in n trials requires the introduction of a binomial coefficient. In this text, the binomial coefficient is represented by ${}_nB_x$ and is defined as the number of distinct permutations that might be formed from n objects of which x items are of one type and $n - x$ are of another. Thus, {D,C,D} and {C,D,D} are two distinct permutations obtained when two defective items are selected from three procedures. The binomial coefficient is defined by

$$ {}_nB_x = n!/x!\,(n - x)! \qquad \text{(Equation 5.1)}$$

The notation introduced in Equation 5.1 requires a brief explanation. The numerator of ${}_nB_x$ requires the calculation of n factorial, represented by n!. By definition, 0! is equal to one, whereas n! is defined by $n \times (n - 1) \times (n - 2) \times \ldots \times (n - n + 1)$. For example, if $n = 4$, we find that

$$4! = 4 \times 3 \times 2 \times 1$$

or 24. Similarly, $(5 - 2)!$ is equivalent to 3! or $3 \times 2 \times 1$.

Consider the sample of three laboratory procedures and the situation in which two results are identified as defective. In this case, the use of Equation 5.1 yields

$$\begin{aligned} {}_3B_2 &= 3!/2! \times (3 - 2)! \\ &= (3 \times 2 \times 1)/2 \times 1 \times 1 \end{aligned}$$

or 3, a result that agrees with the previous discussion. Similarly, consider a situation in which only one of the results was identified as defective. In this case, we find that

$$\begin{aligned} {}_3B_1 &= 3!/1!\,(3 - 1)! \\ &= (3 \times 2 \times 1)/1 \times 2 \times 1 \end{aligned}$$

or 3. Again, these results are identical to those derived when each possibility was listed in detail.

Based on our understanding of the binomial coefficient, we now develop the definitional formula for the binomial probability distribution. In the following, let P correspond to the probability that the event of interest will occur and its complement, defined by $(1 - P)$, represent the probability that another event will occur in any one of the n trials. The probability that the event of interest will occur exactly x times in n trials is given by

$$f(x) = {}_nB_xP^x(1 - P)^{n-x} \qquad \text{(Equation 5.2)}$$

for $x = 0, 1, 2, \ldots, n$ and a given value of P. For example, return to the assessment of the laboratory procedure, and use Equation 5.2 to determine the probability that two of the three results are defective.

$$f(2) = (3!/2!\,1!)\,0.2^2\,0.8^1$$

or 0.096.

The task of calculating probabilities is greatly reduced when the analyst uses Excel. In Exhibit 5.1, the information in column A identifies the number of defective results in three procedures. The probability function appearing in column B was obtained by

1. Selecting the function f_x from the tool bar
2. Selecting the "statistical" function
3. Selecting BINOMDIST
4. Highlighting the values in cells A8 to A11
5. Indicating that the analysis is based on three trials
6. Indicating that the probability is 0.2
7. Entering false, a logical command to calculate the probabilities f(x)
8. Entering OK
9. Copying the results in cell B5 to B11

The cumulative distribution, identified by F(x), was obtained by repeating these steps. However, in step 7, the cumulative distribution is obtained by entering true rather than the logical false. The results obtained with Excel are identical to those that were derived by the detailed calculations.

The mean and standard deviation of the binomial probability distribution are particularly important to our discussion of inferences concerning the proportion that appears in Chapter 7. In general, if we are given the probability function f(x), the mean of the probability distribution is given by

$$\mu = \Sigma f(x_i)\, x_i \qquad \text{(Equation 5.3)}$$

For example, suppose that we are interested in the number of emergent cases that requires an MRI. Let n = 10 and P = 0.3 (Exhibit 5.2). Cells A7 to A17 show the values $x_i = 0, 1, \ldots, 10$, whereas the corresponding probabilities $f(x_i)$ that are listed in cells B7 to B17 were calculated using the BINOMDIST function. Cells C7 to C17 show the products of $f(x_i)$ and x_i, whereas the "AutoSum" function in cell C18 calculated the sum of the products. These results indicate that, on average, we would expect 3 of the 10 patients to require an MRI.

Exhibit 5.1 **The Binomial Probability Distribution and Excel**

Number of Defective Results x	**Probability f(x)**	**Cumulative Probability F(x)**
0	0.512	0.512
1	0.384	0.896
2	0.096	0.992
3	0.008	1

Exhibit 5.2 **The Mean of the Binomial Probability Distribution**

Number Requiring a Scan x	Probability f(x)	Expected Number
0	0.028248	0
1	0.121061	0.121061
2	0.233474	0.466949
3	0.266828	0.800484
4	0.200121	0.800484
5	0.102919	0.514597
6	0.036757	0.220541
7	0.009002	0.063012
8	0.001447	0.011574
9	0.000138	0.00124
10	5.9E-06	5.9E-05
Total	1	3

The process shown in Exhibit 5.2 is greatly simplified by noting that identical results are obtained by the product of P and n (i.e., 0.3×10 or 3). Thus, we define more simply the mean of the binomial distribution by

$$\mu = nP \qquad \text{(Equation 5.4)}$$

Without formal derivation, we simply assert that the variance of the binomial distribution is given by

$$\sigma^2 = nP(1 - P) \qquad \text{(Equation 5.5)}$$

which implies that the equation

$$\sigma = (nP[1 - P])^{1/2} \qquad \text{(Equation 5.6)}$$

is the standard deviation of the binomial distribution. The standard deviation for the number of patients requiring an MRI is given by

$$\sigma = (10 \times 0.3 \times 0.7)^{0.5}$$

or approximately 1.45 patients.

The Poisson Distribution

The Poisson distribution is another important probability function. The Poisson distribution may be applied to processes that involve the demand or need for service. For example, the function might be applied to emergency arrivals during a well-defined period, the number of times a given individual might be admitted during the year, or the frequency of cardiovascular accidents requiring treatment during a day or a week.

The Poisson distribution, like the binomial, applies to random variables that assume integer values. For example, there might be 0, 1, 2, 3, or 4 emergency visits during a given hour. The Poisson and the binomial probability distributions also are based on similar assumptions. For example, suppose that we are interested in the arrival of emergent cases, which may be approximated by the Poisson distribution if

1. The number of occurrences in mutually exclusive time intervals is statistically independent
2. The number of occurrences in a given time interval has the same probability for all time intervals
3. The probability of two or more occurrences is small relative to the probability of one occurrence, implying that the probability of two or more emergent cases during an interval of 1 minute is very small
4. The probability of occurrences is approximately proportional to the length of the interval (e.g., the probability of admitting an emergent case during an interval of 1 minute must be approximately twice the likelihood of an emergent admission during an interval of 0.5 minute or 30 seconds).

The four conditions define a Poisson process to which the Poisson probability distribution might be applied.

For example, suppose that the four conditions are satisfied and that the administrator is interested in the number of emergent admissions. The outcomes are either that an emergent admission will occur or that an emergent arrival will not occur during a given time interval. Because only a few emergent conditions are admitted during a short time, the corresponding probability P is small, whereas for a large n, the corresponding mean, given by nP, frequently is small. In this case, the product of n and P represents the average number of occurrences during the time interval. It is necessary for calculation to estimate the product of n and P rather than derive values for n and P separately. However, if we are able to estimate the value of P from available data, it is necessary to determine the appropriate n, thereby enabling the analyst to estimate the average number of occurrences during a given interval.

Using the previous notation, the Poisson probability distribution is defined by

$$f(x) = [(nP)^x e^{-nP}]/x! \qquad \text{(Equation 5.7)}$$

In Equation 5.7, e represents the base for natural logarithms and is equal to approximately 2.71828. After calculating the product nP, the Poisson probability distribution enables us to determine the likelihood that exactly x occurrences will occur during the period; e^{-np} is calculated only once, whereas x is the number of occurrences during the time interval for which the probability is calculated.

To illustrate the applicability of the Poisson distribution, suppose that the administrator is assessing the staffing pattern in the emergency department and wishes to be 90% certain that personnel are available to diagnose and treat emergent cases. Assume that the market area consists of 150,000 residents and that the probability of one of the individuals requiring emergent care between 2 and 3 a.m. is 0.00001. The average number of emergent arrivals during the time interval is 1.5. Recalling that 0! = 1, an application of Equation 5.7 yields

$$f(0) = (1.5^0 e^{-1.5})/0! = 0.22$$
$$f(1) = (1.5^1 e^{-1.5})/1! = 0.34$$
$$f(2) = (1.5^2 e^{-1.5})/2! = 0.25$$
$$f(3) = (1.5^3 e^{-1.5})/3! = 0.12$$
$$f(4) = (1.5^4 e^{-1.5})/4! = 0.05$$
$$f(5) = (1.5^5 e^{-1.5})/5! = 0.01$$

These calculations show that the value of x! becomes large quickly and that as a consequence f(x) declines rapidly. These observations indicate that the number of required calculations is usually limited by the rapid decline in f(x).

Returning to the example, the probability distribution is transformed into a cumulative distribution:

Number of Emergent Cases	Probability Distribution f(x)	Cumulative Distribution F(x)
0	0.22	0.22
1	0.34	0.56
2	0.25	0.81
3	0.12	0.93
4	0.05	0.98
5	0.01	0.99

These calculations indicate that the organization is 90% certain that three or fewer emergent cases will arrive during the time interval. If, after adjusting for the mix of skills, 2 hours are required for each emergent case, the organization should plan to employ 6 staff hours during the period from 2 to 3 a.m.

The use of Excel reduces or eliminate the need to perform the complex calculations that are associated with the Poisson distribution. Exhibit 5.3 shows that x = 0 is in cell A8. The probabilities in cells B8 to B15 are calculated as follows:

1. Select the function "f_x."
2. Select the "statistical" function from the menu.

3. Select "Poisson" from the next menu.
4. Highlight the cells in which the values of x appear (i.e., cells A8 to A15).
5. Enter the mean number of arrivals (1.5).
6. Enter the logical "false" for the cumulative distribution.
7. Locate the cursor on cell B5. and copy the results to the remaining cells (i.e., cells B6 to B15).

The cumulative distribution listed in cells C8 to C15 is calculated in a similar fashion. However, in this case, enter the logical "true" in order to obtain the cumulative distribution.

Continuous Random Variables: The Normal Distribution

A second set of probability distributions should be applied when analyzing continuous random variables (i.e., variables that assume any value on the real number line). The statistical methods described in this text require an understanding of the normal distribution, the t distribution, the χ^2 (pronounced chi square) distribution, and the F distribution. The normal distribution is considered here. The t distribution and the F distribution are introduced in Chapter 6, and the χ^2 distribution is examined in Chapter 7.

The normal distribution is perhaps the most important of the theoretical distributions that are applied to continuous random variables. The following discussion focuses on the properties of the normal distribution, the use of the distribution in deriving probability, and the application of derived probabilities to problems or issues that occur in an administrative setting.

Exhibit 5.3 **An Application of the Poisson Probability Distribution**

Number of Emergent Cases x	Probability Distribution f(x)	Cumulative Probability Distribution F(x)
0	0.223	0.223
1	0.335	0.558
2	0.251	0.809
3	0.126	0.934
4	0.047	0.981
5	0.014	0.996
6	0.004	0.999
7	0.001	1.000

Rectangles that were constructed with equal width were used to form a bar chart (see Chapter 2). When a distribution depicts a relative frequency distribution and the width of the rectangles is equal to one, the area of each is interpreted as probability. For example, Exhibit 2.5 portrays the relative frequency distribution of patients, grouped by the number of secondary diagnoses. The area of the first rectangle indicates that if we select a patient at random the probability is 0.35 that the individual presents between one and four secondary conditions. Similarly, the probability of selecting a patient at random who presents 9 to 12 secondary conditions is 0.20. Consistent with the postulates of probability, the area of a given rectangle is interpreted as a probability; the probability ranges from zero to one, and the sum of the areas of the rectangles that comprise the bar chart is equal to one.

Figure 5.2 shows that the histogram constructed from the relative frequency distribution might be approximated by a smooth or continuous function. That the area *aegfd* of the continuous function is equivalent to area *abcd*, one of the rectangles forming the histogram, is demonstrated as follows. The area *aegcd* is common to both areas. Area *ebg* is equivalent to area *gcf*. Hence, area *aegfd* is equivalent to area *abcd*, and by extending this process, it can be demonstrated that the area formed by the continuous function is equivalent to the area that the histogram defined. Because the area formed by the histogram corresponds to probability, we conclude that the area under the continuous function also represents probability.

Similar to the smooth curve shown in Figure 5.2, the normal distribution is a continuous function and is perhaps the most important probability distribution that is used in inferential statistics. Figure 5.3 shows that the normal distribution is symmetrical, unimodal, and characterized by tails that are asymptotic with respect to the x axis. The property of symmetry implies that it is possible to con-

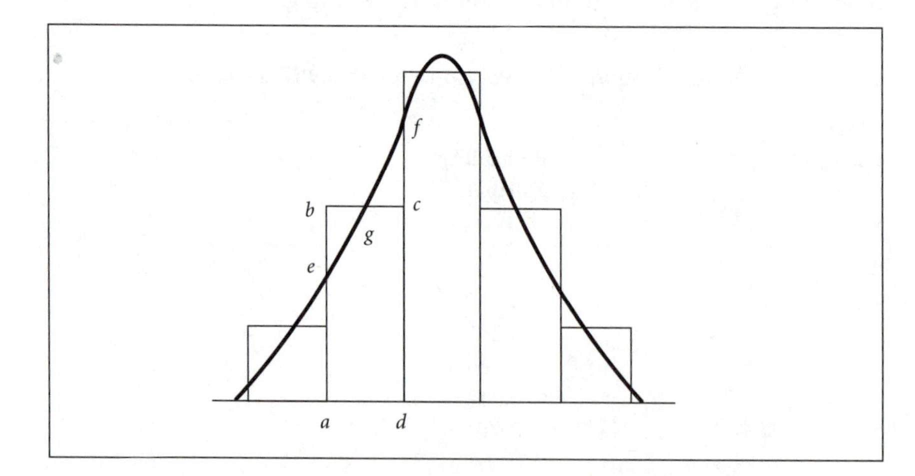

Figure 5.2 **Approximation of a Histogram by a Smooth Curve**

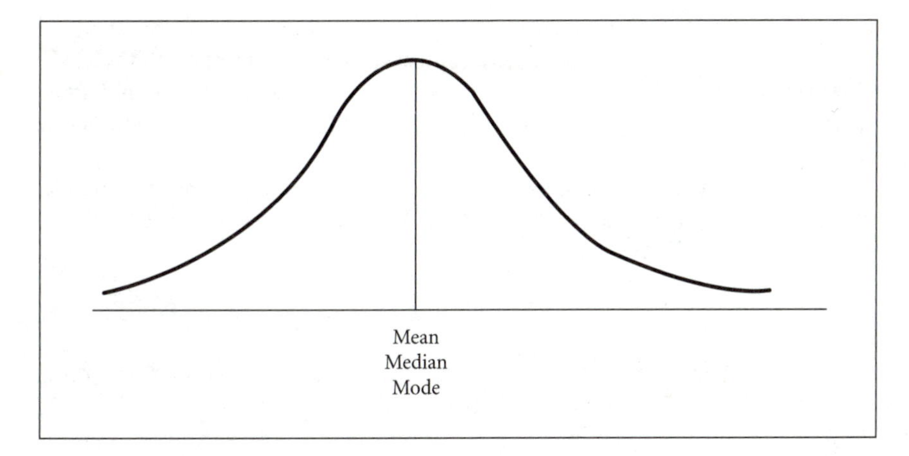

Figure 5.3 **The Normal Distribution**

struct a perpendicular line that divides the distribution into two identical halves (see Chapter 3). In addition, a symmetrical distribution is characterized by a mean, mode, and median that assume the same value.

Numerous distributions might be characterized as normal but differ in terms of scatter or variation and the value assumed by the arithmetic mean. For example, the distributions presented in Figure 5.4 are unimodal, symmetrical, and asymptotic with respect to the x axis. However, the two distributions differ in terms of the values assumed by the mean and the standard deviation. The probability density function for the normal distribution is determined by two parameters: the mean (μ) and the standard deviation (σ). In this case, the *probability density function* determines the height of the normal distribution relative to the x axis.

It is not possible to calculate the area under the probability density function for all possible values of μ and σ. Instead, after performing a scale transformation, we rely on the values that are presented in Table D.1 of Appendix D to determine the

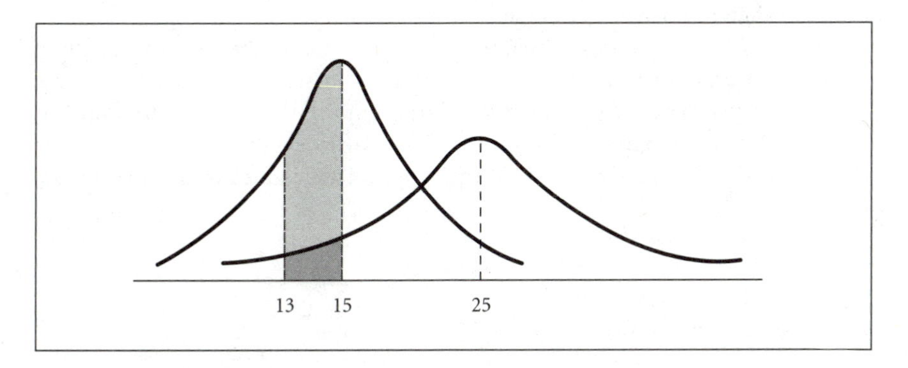

Figure 5.4 **Two Different Normal Curves**

area under a standard normal curve and, hence, probability. As before, a standard normal curve is unimodal, symmetrical, and asymptotic with respect to the x axis. However, the probability density function of the standard normal curve is defined specifically by a mean value of zero (i.e., $\mu = 0$) and a standard deviation of one (i.e., $\sigma = 1$).

The scale transformation to which we referred enables us to express a variable, measured in natural units, in terms of a standard normal deviate. Specifically, we define the standard normal deviate, represented by Z, by

$$Z = (x_i - \mu)/\sigma \qquad \text{(Equation 5.8)}$$

In this case, x_i represents the value of a continuous variable, measured in natural units. For example, suppose the administrator is assessing the staffing patterns in the operating theater and is interested in the time required to perform a given surgical procedure. Based on previous data, we assume that time required to perform the procedure is normally distributed with a mean time of 180 minutes and a standard deviation of 20 minutes. Suppose that the administrator is interested in an operative procedure with a duration of 220 minutes (Equation 5.8). In this case, we find that

$$Z = (220 - 180)/20$$

yields a standard normal deviate of 2.0. This suggests that an operative procedure lasting 220 minutes exceeds the mean time of 180 minutes by 2.0 standard deviations. Consider next a procedure that requires 150 minutes to complete. In this case, we find that

$$\begin{aligned} Z &= (150 - 180)/20 \\ &= -1.5 \end{aligned}$$

These calculations indicate that duration of the procedure is 1.5 standard deviations less than or below the average.

Equation 5.8 also might be used to transform a standard normal deviate into the original units of measure. Referring to the illustration involving the time required to perform the surgical procedure, suppose that the administrator is interested in the length of time that is 3 standard deviations in excess of the mean. In this case, we simply substitute appropriate values into Equation 5.8 and obtain

$$3.0 = (x_i - 180)/20$$

After rearranging slightly, we obtain

$$x_i = 3.0 \times 20 + 180$$

or 240 minutes. If we were interested in a procedure lasting 1 standard deviation less than the average, we would obtain

$$-1.0 = (x_i - 180)/20$$

After a slight rearrangement, we find that

$$x_i = -1.0 \times 20 + 180$$

or 160 minutes.

The results when Equation 5.8 is used allow us to determine probabilities from Table D.1. As indicated in Table D.1, values are presented for values of Z that range from Z = 0 to Z = 3.09. Suppose, for example, that we wished to determine and interpret the value for a standard normal deviate equal to 1.96. In this case, the desired value appears in the cell that corresponds to the intersection of the row identified by the value 1.9 and the column identified by the value 0.06 (i.e., the sum of 1.9 and 0.06 is the desired standard normal deviate). After locating the cell identified by the intersection, we observe that the value is 0.4750, implying that 47.5% of the area under the probability density function ranges from Z = 0 to Z = 1.96. Thus, we conclude that the probability of obtaining a standard normal deviate that is greater than or equal to zero or less than or equal to 1.96 is 0.4750. This result might be expressed as

$$P(0 \leq Z \leq 1.96) = 0.4750$$

The probability of obtaining a standard normal deviate in excess of 1.96 is 0.025 or less (i.e., the difference between 0.5000 and 0.4750).

For example, if the administrator is interested in the probability that an operative procedure will last more than 210 minutes, the corresponding standard normal deviate is given by

$$Z = (210 - 180)/20$$

or 1.5. Table D.1 shows that a standard normal deviate of 1.5 is 0.4332, implying that the probability of a given operative procedure lasting more than 210 minutes is 0.5000 − 0.4332. These calculations indicate that the likelihood of the operative procedure requiring more than 210 minutes is 0.0668 or less.

It might be interesting to determine the probability that an operative procedure will last between 190 and 220 minutes. In this case, the standard normal deviate corresponding to 190 minutes is given by

$$Z_{190} = (190 - 180)/20$$

or 0.5, whereas the standard normal deviate corresponding to 220 minutes is given by

$$Z_{200} = (220 - 180)/20$$

or 2.0. The value of Z_{190} or 0.5 is 0.1915. On the other hand, the tabular value of Z_{200} or 2.0 is 0.4772. Thus, consistent with Figure 5.5, we assert that

$$\begin{aligned} P(0 \leq Z \leq 2.0)&: \quad 0.4772 \\ P(0 \leq Z \leq 0.5)&: \quad -\underline{0.1915} \\ P(0.5 < Z < 2.0) &= 0.2875 \end{aligned}$$

Thus, the probability of the procedure lasting between 190 and 220 minutes is approximately 0.29.

As a final example, if the administrator wishes to determine the probability that a given procedure will last between 140 and 250 minutes, we transform 140 and 210 minutes into standard normal deviates as follows:

$$\begin{aligned} Z_{140} &= (140 - 180)/20 \\ &= -2.0 \\ Z_{210} &= (210 - 180)/20 \\ &= 1.5 \end{aligned}$$

Regarding the finding that $Z_{140} = -2.0$, the standard normal curve is symmetrical, implying that the probability $P(0 \leq Z \leq 2.0)$ is identical to $P(-2.0 \leq Z \leq 0)$, and as a consequence, no negative values for the standard normal deviate appear in the

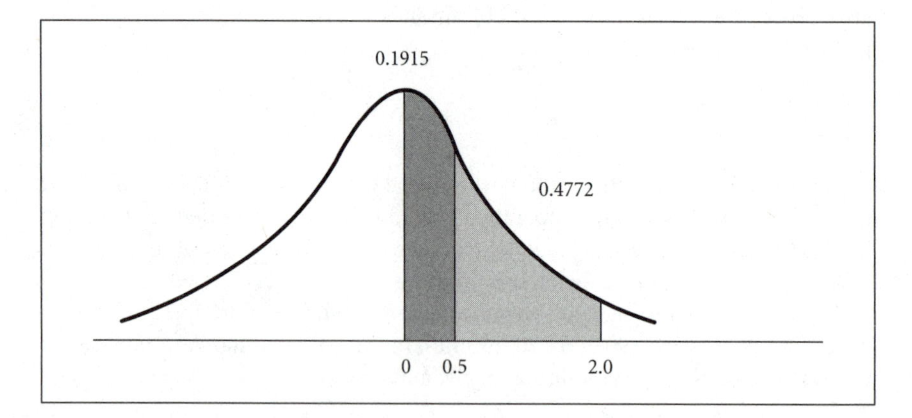

Figure 5.5 **The P (0.5 < Z < 2.0)**

table. Because $P(0 \leq Z \leq 2.0)$ and $P(-2.0 \leq Z \leq 0)$ are the same, we simply substitute the value that corresponds to $Z = 2$ for the value of $Z = -2$ and obtain

$$P(-2.0 \leq Z \leq 0) = 0.4772$$

The table value for a standard normal deviate of 1.5 is 0.4332, and Figure 5.6 shows that the desired probability is given by the sum

$P(-2.0 \leq Z \leq 0)$:	0.4772
$P(0 \leq Z \leq 1.5)$:	<u>0.4332</u>
$P(-2.0 \leq Z \leq 1.5)$:	0.9104

These results indicate that the probability of an operative procedure lasting between 140 and 210 minutes is approximately 0.91.

Sampling Distributions

We now turn attention to perhaps the most important of the concepts in inferential statistics: the sampling distribution of a statistic, a concept that emphasizes chance variation and the role of dispersion in inferential statistics. It is possible to identify essentially two approaches to the study of sampling distributions. The first results in an experimental or an observed sampling distribution that is based on the data obtained by selecting a series of repeated samples from a given population. The second approach relies on mathematical theory and results in a theoretical sampling distribution of the statistic. Each of the two approaches is discussed here.

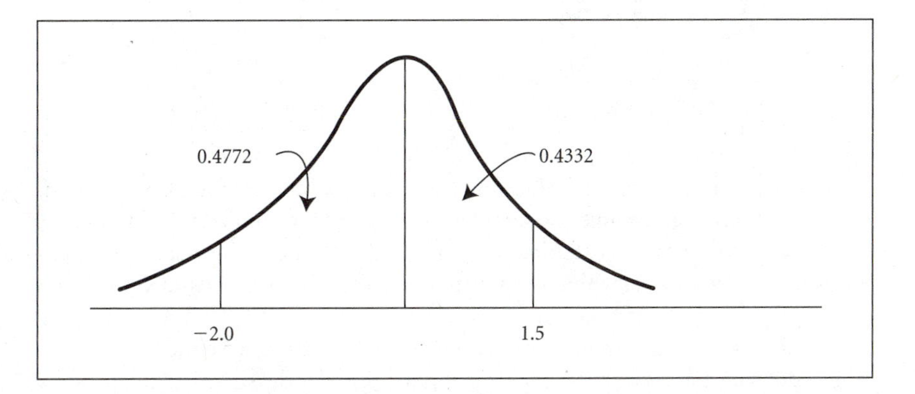

Figure 5.6 **Finding the Probability P $(-2.0 \leq Z \leq 1.5)$**

Experimental Sampling Distribution of the Mean

An experimental sampling distribution is obtained by calculating the mean for each sample in a series of samples that are selected from a given population. For example, suppose that management's focus is on the length of stay that patients with a respiratory system disease experienced. Suppose also that the analysis is limited to 200 patients who were hospitalized with a respiratory system disease and that the administrator selected 10 random samples of size n = 5. After reviewing each medical record and recording the length of stay for each patient, suppose that the results of the multiple samples yielded the following results that are expressed in days of care:

Sample 1: 3, 4, 8, 5, 10
Sample 2: 10, 7, 4, 2, 9
Sample 3: 7, 2, 6, 8, 3
Sample 4: 5, 7, 11, 3, 9
Sample 5: 7, 9, 5, 9, 8
Sample 6: 13, 5, 7, 8, 4
Sample 7: 6, 4, 8, 5, 2
Sample 8: 5, 9, 7, 10, 11
Sample 9: 6, 8, 4, 10, 13
Sample 10: 13, 10, 8, 9, 3

An examination of the variation exhibited by the sample means requires us to calculate the average length of stay for each of the 10 samples. The results of these calculations are as follows:

Sample	Mean
1	6.0
2	6.4
3	5.2
4	7.0
5	7.6
6	7.4
7	5.0
8	8.4
9	8.2
10	8.6

The mean of the sampling distribution is 6.98 days, and the standard deviation is 1.29 days. Thus, even though the samples were selected from the same population, the corresponding means exhibited variation, an outcome that is related to differences in the length of stay that each of the patients who were included in the set of repeated samples experienced.

The distribution of sample means might be presented as a frequency distribution. Adopting classes defined by 5 to 5.9 days, 6 to 6.9 days, 7 to 7.9 days, and 8 to 8.9 days, the frequency distribution of sample means is as follows:

Mean	Frequency
5 to 5.9	2
6 to 6.9	2
7 to 7.9	3
8 to 8.9	3

The frequency distribution is particularly important when determining the probability of obtaining a sample mean that is between 5 and 5.9 days and so forth. A distribution that indicates the probability of obtaining different sample means is called an experimental sampling distribution of the mean.

Theoretical Sampling Distribution

Unlike their experimental counterparts, theoretical sampling distributions are derived from an appropriate mathematical theory. The discussion is now simplified by focusing on a finite population that consists of the values 2, 4, 6, 8, and 10. The mean of the population (μ) is given by

$$\mu = (2 + 4 + 6 + 8 + 10)/5$$

or 6, whereas the variance of the population (σ^2) is

$$\sigma^2 = [(2 - 6)^2 + (4 - 6)^2 + (6 - 6)^2 + (8 - 6)^2 + (10 - 6)^2]/5$$

or 8. Accordingly, the standard deviation of the population (σ) is

$$\sigma = (8)^{1/2}$$

We now select repeated samples of size $n = 2$ from the population and obtain all possible combinations that consist of the values (2,4), (2,6), (2,8), (2,10), (4,6), (4,8), (4,10), (6,8), (6,10), and (8,10). Based on the samples of size $n = 2$, the corresponding sample means are as follows:

Sample	Mean
(2,4)	3
(2,6)	4
(2,8)	5
(2,10)	6
(4,6)	5
(4,8)	6
(4,10)	7
(6,8)	7
(6,10)	8
(8,10)	9

These calculations result in a distribution of sample means when samples of size n = 2 are selected from the finite population. The selection of a sample consisting of the values 2 and 4 has a sample mean of (2 + 4)/2 or 3, whereas a sample consisting of 4 and 8 has a mean of (4 + 8)/2 or 6.

Our attention is now turned to the mean and standard deviation of the theoretical sampling distribution. In the following, we let $\mu_{\bar{x}}$ represent the mean of the theoretical sampling distribution:

$$\mu_{\bar{x}} = (3 + 4 + 5 + 6 + 5 + 6 + 7 + 7 + 8 + 9)/10$$

or 6. Thus, it can be shown that the mean of the theoretical sampling distribution, $\mu_{\bar{x},}$ is equal to the mean, μ, of the population from which the samples were selected. Thus, we conclude that

$$\mu_{\bar{x}} = \mu \qquad \text{(Equation 5.9)}$$

We now turn attention to the standard deviation of the theoretical sampling distribution. In this case, we modify the approach in Equation 3.7 and define the variance of the theoretical sampling distribution by

$$\sigma_{\bar{x}}^{2} = \Sigma(\bar{X} - \mu)^2/n \qquad \text{(Equation 5.10)}$$

We find that the variance is

$$\sigma_{\bar{x}}^{2} = ([3 - 6]^2 + [4 - 6]^2 + \ldots + [9 - 6]^2)/10$$

or 3. Thus, the standard error of the mean, which is the standard deviation of the theoretical sampling distribution, is

$$\sigma_{\bar{x}} = (3)^{1/2}$$

The finding that the standard deviation of the population from which the samples were selected differs from the standard error of the mean or the standard deviation of the theoretical sampling distribution is particularly important. In particular, the calculations indicated that the standard deviation of the population σ, assumed a value of $\sqrt{8}$, whereas the standard error of the estimate amounted to $\sqrt{3}$. However, when the focus is on a finite population, the standard error of the mean might be calculated from the standard deviation of the universe by

$$\sigma_{\bar{x}} = \sigma/(n)^{1/2} \times (N - n/N - 1)^{1/2} \qquad \text{(Equation 5.11)}$$

Recall that the finite population consisted of five observations, that we selected samples that were n = 2, and that the standard deviation of the population is

$(8)^{1/2}$. After substituting appropriately, we find that the standard error of the mean that Equation 5.11 defined is

$$\sigma_{\bar{x}} = ((8)^{1/2}/(2)^{1/2}) \times (5 - 2/5 - 1)^{0.5}$$

which reduces to $(3)^{1/2}$. The results from Equation 6.11 are identical to those that were derived when we applied Equation 5.10 to the problem of determining the standard error.

The previously presented calculations required the use of the finite correction factor that is represented by $(N - n / N - 1)^{1/2}$. In general, the finite correction factor is used when two conditions are satisfied. In particular, the adjustment is required when calculating the standard error of the mean for a sample selected from a finite population and when the sample represents a relatively large portion of the universe. If the sample size is small relative to the size of the population, the finite correction factor approaches one and thus exerts little or no influence on the standard error of the mean. For example, suppose that a finite population consists of 100,000 observations and that we select a sample of 100 items. In this case, the finite correction factor is given by the square root of the quotient $(100{,}000 - 100)/(100{,}000 - 1)$ or approximately 0.999. However, as the sample size grows, the finite correction factor decreases, indicating that the value of the standard error declines as more information about the universe is included in the sample. As a general rule, the finite correction factor is not used if the sample size is 5% or less of the corresponding population.

The finite correction factor is ignored when the sample size is small relative to the population or when the analysis pertains to an infinite population. In this case, the standard error of the mean is given by

$$\sigma_{\bar{x}} = \sigma/(n)^{1/2} \qquad \text{(Equation 5.12)}$$

Equation 5.12 indicates that as the standard deviation of the population grows the standard error of the mean increases. Thus, if considerable variation exists in the population from which the sample is selected, the distribution of the means will also exhibit considerable scatter. Second, if other factors remaining constant, an increase in the sample size reduces the standard error of the mean. In such a situation, more information is conveyed by a larger sample, and the difference between the sample mean and the mean of the population, μ, declines with additional observations.

In summary, *if samples of size n are selected from a population having a mean μ and a standard deviation σ, the theoretical sampling distribution has a mean μ and a standard deviation $\sigma_{\bar{x}}$ that is defined by either Equation 5.11 or Equation 5.12.* The standard error of the mean plays a pivotal role in inferential statistics because it measures the chance variation that is present in the distribution of the mean.

The Central Limit Theorem

The previous section focused on measures of the central tendency and scatter exhibited by the sampling distribution of the mean. When combined with the central limit theorem, these features form the foundation of inferential statistics and the assessment of an alternate courses of action under conditions of uncertainty. As indicated here, the central limit theorem links the attributes of the theoretical sampling distribution of the mean to the standard normal curve and enables the administrator to calculate probabilities of obtaining various values of the sample mean.

The central limit theorem states that if the sample size n and degrees of freedom are large, the theoretical sampling distribution may be approximated by the standard normal curve. Thus, if n is large, the sampling distribution of the statistic

$$Z = (\bar{X} - \mu)/\sigma_{\bar{x}} \qquad \text{(Equation 5.13)}$$

is a standard normal deviate or a normally distributed random variable.

Generally, we assert that the approximation is appropriate if n is greater than 30. Given that the sample size is large, our reliance on the central limit theorem is not contingent on the configuration of the distribution from which the sample was selected. Furthermore, it can be shown that the central limit theorem is valid if n is small and the population from which the sample is selected is approximately normal.

To illustrate the usefulness of the central limit theorem, suppose that we are interested in the length of stay that patients hospitalized with a given diagnosis experienced. Based on previous experience, suppose that patients who were admitted with the diagnosis and did not require posthospital care experienced an average stay of 5 days with a standard deviation of 4 days. Limited to those for whom postdischarge care was required, suppose that we selected a sample of 100 patients who were transferred to a long-term care facility and found the sample mean was 6 days. In this case, the administrator might be interested in the probability that the number of days of care consumed by the typical patient requiring postdischarge services is 5 days or less. Based on these data, the standard error of the mean is given by

$$\sigma_{\bar{x}} = 4/(100)^{1/2}$$

or 0.4. Thus, the corresponding standard normal deviate is

$$Z = (6 - 5)/0.4$$

or 2.5. The tabular value for a standard normal deviate of 2.5 is 0.4938 (Table D.1). Consistent with Figure 5.7, the desired probability is obtained by 0.5000 less

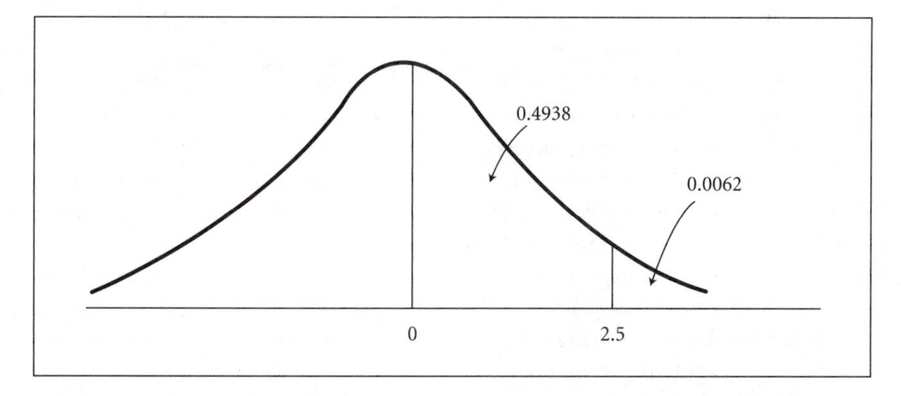

Figure 5.7 **The Probability of Obtaining a Standard Normal Deviate Greater than 2.5**

0.4938 or 0.0062 or less. Thus, with other factors remaining constant, these results are consistent with the proposition that it is highly unlikely that patients admitted with the diagnosis and required postdischarge care experienced a length of stay that was 5 days or less. The findings also indicate that the need for postdischarge care contributes to a longer hospital stay. When viewed from a fiscal perspective, the results also suggest a need to evaluate the process of discharge planning and to ensure a smooth transition from the hospital to a source of postdischarge care, particularly when services are financed by a fixed payment per patient, grouped by diagnostic nomenclature.

Exercises

1. Find the probability that exactly four of six patients will experience an injury resulting from a fall. Assume that the probability of any patient experiencing an injury from a fall is 0.4.
2. Find the probability that 7 of 12 scheduled appointments at one of our outpatient clinics will be canceled. Assume that the probability of canceling an appointment is 0.3.
3. Assume that the probability of an error appearing on a patient's bill is 0.6. Find the probability that on 10 bills we will identify
   a. No errors
   b. Five errors
   c. Seven errors
4. If 2% of all children in an area have not been vaccinated against polio, what is the probability in a sample of 200 that exactly 6 will not have been vaccinated (Poisson distribution)?
5. Suppose that, on average, 2.8 emergent cases arrive in the emergency room of a large metropolitan hospital between 1 and 2 a.m. Use the Poisson

distribution to find the probability that (1) there will be no emergent cases, (2) there will be four emergent cases, and (3) there will be two emergent cases.

6. If on average 0.2 ambulances arrive per hour, use the Poisson distribution to find the probability that (1) no ambulances will arrive during the hour, (2) one ambulance will arrive during the hour, and (3) two ambulances will arrive during the hour. Suppose further that we wish to staff the emergency department to ensure that we are able to treat 95% of the ambulance arrivals. How many arrivals should we plan to diagnose and treat?
7. Find the mean and standard deviation of the binomial distribution presented in Exercise 1.
8. Find the mean and standard deviation of the binomial distribution presented in Exercise 2.
9. Find the area under the normal curve that resides
   a. $Z = 0$ and $Z = 2.51$
   b. $Z = -1.69$ and $Z = 0$
   c. $Z = 1.69$ and $Z = 1.84$
   d. To the right of $Z = 0.87$
   e. To the left of $Z = 0.87$
   f. To the left of $Z = -1.23$
   g. Between $Z = -0.69$ and $Z = -1.72$
   h. To the right of $Z = -0.69$
   i. Between $Z = -0.75$ and $Z = 1.83$
   j. Between $Z = 0.23$ and $Z = 2.58$
10. Suppose that the length of an office visit at one of our clinics is a random variable that is distributed normally with a mean of 25 minutes and a standard deviation of 5 minutes. What is the probability that an office visit will require
    a. Less than 23 minutes
    b. More than 31 minutes
    c. Between 26 and 29 minutes
    d. Between 22 and 24 minutes
    e. Between 23 and 27 minutes
11. If the duration of a given operative procedure has a normal distribution with a mean of 240 minutes and a standard deviation of 40 minutes, what is the probability of a procedure of this type lasting
    a. Less than 200 minutes
    b. More than 190 minutes
    c. Between 220 and 260 minutes
    d. Between 230 and 270 minutes
12. Suppose that, on average, 90 minutes are required to perform a given procedure. If the standard deviation is 25 minutes and the random variable is normally distributed, what is the probability that the procedure will require
    a. More than 120 minutes
    b. Less than 110 minutes
    c. Between 80 and 98 minutes
    d. More than 70 minutes

CHAPTER 6

Inferences Concerning the Mean[R,O]

OBJECTIVES

1. Distinguish between a point and an interval estimate.
2. Use Excel to construct a confidence interval for the mean based on large and small samples.
3. Develop null and alternate hypotheses.
4. Distinguish between directional and nondirectional alternate hypotheses.
5. Distinguish between Type I and Type II errors.
6. Examine presumed values of the mean based on data derived from large and small samples.
7. Examine the difference between two means if the corresponding variances are equal.
8. Examine the difference between two means if the corresponding variances are unequal.
9. Use Excel to examine the difference between two means.
10. Determine the sample size required to achieve a desired precision when estimating the population mean from data derived from a sample.
11. Calculate the sample size that is required to control Type I and Type II errors.

This chapter focuses on problems requiring an estimate or an inference concerning the mean. We examine (1) the difference between a point and an interval estimate; (2) methods of developing an interval estimate for the population mean, μ, based on the results of both large and small samples; (3) the construction of hypotheses concerning the mean to include an understanding of the errors that might occur when examining expectations; (4) based on large and small samples, the tests that are used to evaluate hypotheses or expectations concerning the mean; (5) methods of examining the difference between two means; and (6) the process of determining the sample size that is required to achieve a given degree of precision. As in previous chapters, we rely on Excel to perform calculations and derive statistical summaries of the analyses.

Decisions that the administrator implements might be based on statistical analyses and objective evidence. However, subjective considerations are always present and, by necessity, must be regarded as factors that influence the analysis of the administrator. For example, subjective factors influence the standards by which a decision is evaluated. Similarly, subjective considerations influence the degree of precision or certainty required in a given situation. Although the emphasis is on the objective aspects of the statistical methods that are applied to the mean, an element of subjectivity or administrative judgment is present in formulating the nature of the problem requiring statistical analysis, the risks the health service organization is prepared to assume, and the relative certainty of results that management requires.

Point and Interval Estimates of the Mean[R]

The health service organization requires an estimation when data are incomplete, particularly in the case of an infinite population or a finite population for which a census is either impossible or impractical. In these situations, the administrator is forced to derive an estimate of the population parameter, based on a statistic derived from a sample.

Estimates are fundamentally important to the health administrator, who is responsible for ensuring efficient operations and the continued viability of the health organization. The administrator may wish to estimate the average amount of labor, grouped by occupational category, that is required to provide a unit of a given service, the average amount of time required to perform a given surgical procedure, the average length of stay provided to older patients, grouped by diagnosis, or the average delay in discharging patients to an alternate source of care. The administrator might be interested in estimating the proportion of laboratory results that are either false positive or false negative, the proportion of laboratory results that are reported to the physician within 1 hour of the request, the proportion of patients with a given diagnosis that are admitted after an initial assessment in the emergency department, or the diagnostic mix, represented by the proportion of patients admitted or discharged with one of several conditions. In each of these situations, estimates of a mean or a proportion (discussed here and in Chapter 7, respectively) may be necessary.

The difference between a point and an interval estimate is important to the problem of estimation. For example, we might find that 25% of the patient population is admitted with a given diagnosis or that the discharge of 15% of the patients assigned to the medical/surgical department is delayed. We might assert that on average 0.23 staff hours are required to provide a given service or that the typical appendectomy requires an average of 140 minutes to complete. In these examples, we used a *point estimate* to convey information that is useful, as each consists of a single value. However, a point estimate fails to reveal information concerning (1) the reliability or precision of the methods used to derive the mean or proportion, (2) the size of the sample, or (3) the variability in the data.

These observations suggest a need to supplement a point estimate with additional information. This section discusses the development of interval estimates that are based on the sample size and the variability of the data. As illustrated later here, interval estimates also reflect the administrator's subjective preference for the relative certitude that characterizes the estimate. However, before discussing the methods that are used to develop interval estimates, basic notation needs to be reviewed.

Basic Notation

Chapter 5 discussed that the arithmetic mean is expected to vary from sample to sample, an outcome that results from differences in the observations selected in each of the samples. It also indicated that the mean of the sampling distribution of the mean is μ, the mean of the population from which the sample was selected. The discussion also indicated that when the focus is on an infinite population the standard error of the mean is given by $\sigma/\sqrt{n}$, where σ is the standard deviation of the population from which the sample was selected. The discussion of the central limit theorem also indicated that if n is large and greater than 30 observations, the quotient

$$Z = (\bar{X} - \mu)/(\sigma/\sqrt{n})$$

is a standard normal deviate.

We now combine the review of the central limit with new notation to form an interval estimate for the mean. In the following, we let Z_α correspond to the standard normal deviate for which the area under the standard normal curve to its right is α. In Figure 6.1, the value of α is indicated by the shaded area. We also define $-Z_\alpha$ as the standard normal deviate for which the area residing under the curve to its left is α. If Z equals $-Z_\alpha$, the corresponding value of α is indicated by the shaded area in Figure 6.2. For future reference, commonly used values of α, the corresponding standard normal deviates, and related tabular values are summarized in Table 6.1.

The tabular value for a standard normal deviate of $\pm Z_{0.10}$ (i.e., ± 1.282) is 0.4000, implying that the area to the right of $Z_{0.10}$ or 1.282 is 0.5000 − 0.4000 or 0.10. Because the standard normal curve is symmetrical, the area residing under the density function to the left of $-Z_{0.10}$ (i.e., -1.282) also is 0.5000 − 0.4000 or 0.10.

In the next situation, we let α equal .025. The tabular value of $Z_{0.025}$ or 1.96 and $-Z_{0.025}$ (i.e., -1.96) is 0.4750. We conclude that the area under the normal curve to the right of $Z_{0.025}$ or 1.96 is 0.5000 − 0.4750 or 0.025, whereas the area to the left of $-Z_{0.025}$ or -1.96 also is 0.025. The other standard normal deviates and related tabular values are interpreted similarly. To simplify future calculations, we employ standard normal deviates of ± 1.64, ± 1.96, ± 2.33, and ± 2.58 as approximations of those summarized in Table 6.1.

The standard normal deviate represented by $Z_{\alpha/2}$ is pivotal in constructing an interval estimate. In Figure 6.3, the area under the normal curve to the right of

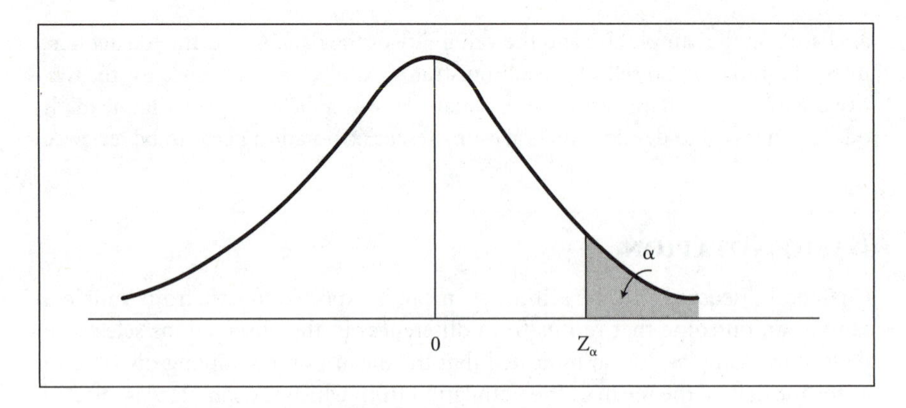

Figure 6.1 **The Area to the Right of Z_α**

$Z_{\alpha/2}$ is $\alpha/2$, whereas the area under the curve to the left of $-Z_{\alpha/2}$ also is $\alpha/2$. As before, each area is interpreted as probability and indicates the likelihood of obtaining a standard normal deviate that is less than $-Z_{\alpha/2}$ or greater than $Z_{\alpha/2}$. The combined area to the right of $Z_{\alpha/2}$ and to the left of $-Z_{\alpha/2}$ is $\alpha/2$ plus $\alpha/2$ or α. In Figure 6.3, with a probability of $1 - \alpha$, the standard normal deviate Z will range from $-Z_{\alpha/2}$ to $Z_{\alpha/2}$.

Commonly used values for $\pm Z_{\alpha/2}$, the corresponding tabular value, and the related values of α, $\alpha/2$, and $1 - \alpha$, are summarized in Table 6.2. The value of α is simply the sum of $\alpha/2$ and $\alpha/2$. The standard normal deviates summarized in Table 6.2 are frequently used when constructing an interval estimate for the population mean. Similar to Table 6.1, the tabular value for $\pm$ 1.96 is 0.4750, implying that the value of $\alpha/2$ is 0.025, the value of α is 0.05, and the value of $1 - \alpha$ is 0.95. The tabular value for standard normal deviates $\pm$ 2.33 is approximately

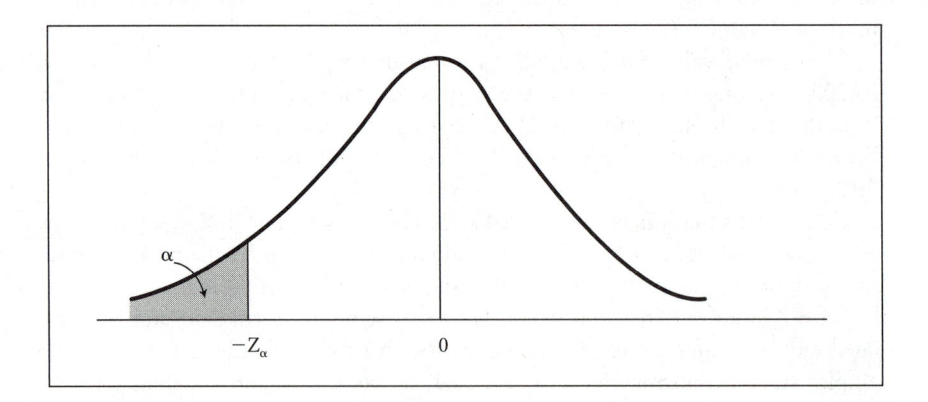

Figure 6.2 **The Area to the Left of $-Z_\alpha$**

Table 6.1 **Standard Normal Deviates and Tabular Values of α**

Standard Normal Deviate	Tabular Value	Value of α
1.282–1.282	0.4000	0.10
1.645–1.645	0.4500	0.05
1.96–1.96	0.4750	0.025
2.326–2.326	0.4900	0.01
2.576–2.576	0.4950	0.005

0.4900. Thus, the value of $\alpha/2$ is approximately 0.01, and the value of α is 0.02. The value of $1 - \alpha$ is 0.98.

Interval Estimates of the Mean[R]

We now consider the methods that are used to develop an interval estimate for the mean of the population from which a sample is selected. We rely on the central limit theorem and the standard normal curve to develop an interval estimate when the sample size is large. However, when the sample size is small, we must rely on an alternate theoretical probability distribution. Both situations are considered in this section.

Interval Estimates of μ Based on Large Samples

Limited to situations in which n is greater than 30, methods of deriving an interval estimate of the mean μ based on the results derived from a sample are now

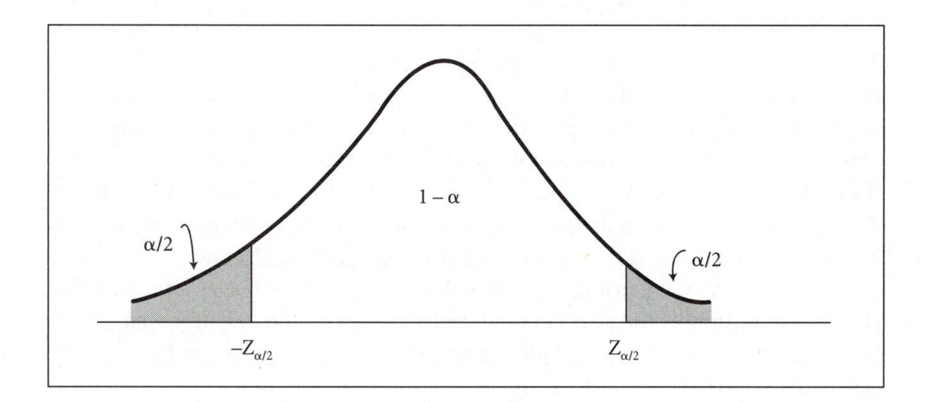

Figure 6.3 **The Area to the Right of $-Z_{\alpha/2}$ and to the Left of $-Z_{\alpha/2}$**

Table 6.2 **Standard Normal Deviates, Tabular Values, and Values of α, $\alpha/2$, and $1 - \alpha$**

Normal Deviate	Tabular Value	Value of $\alpha/2$	Value of α	Value of $1 - \alpha$
−1.64, 1.64	0.4500	0.05	0.10	0.90
−1.96, 1.96	0.4750	0.025	0.05	0.95
−2.33, 2.33	0.4900	0.01	0.02	0.98
−2.58, 2.58	0.4950	0.005	0.01	0.99

considered. If the sample size is large, we rely on the central limit theorem to assert that

$$Z = (\bar{X} - \mu)/(\sigma/\sqrt{n})$$

is a standard normal deviate. The discussion in the previous section also indicated that the expression

$$-Z_{\alpha/2} \leq Z \leq Z_{\alpha/2}$$

is satisfied with a probability of $1 - \alpha$. Thus, after substituting $(\bar{X} - \mu)/(\sigma/\sqrt{n})$ for Z, the expression

$$-Z_{\alpha/2} \leq (\bar{X} - \mu)/(\sigma/\sqrt{n}) \leq Z_{\alpha/2} \qquad \text{(Equation 6.1)}$$

is also satisfied with a probability of $1 - \alpha$. After a slight rearrangement, it can be shown that

$$\bar{X} - Z_{\alpha/2}\,(\sigma/\sqrt{n}) \leq \mu \leq \bar{X} + Z_{\alpha/2}\,(\sigma/\sqrt{n}) \qquad \text{(Equation 6.2)}$$

The result obtained from this expression is called a confidence interval, and the probability of $1 - \alpha$ is referred to as degree of confidence. The parameter that we wish to estimate, namely μ, appears in the middle of this expression. As a result, with a confidence of $1 - \alpha$, the mean of the population from which we selected the sample ranges from $\bar{X} - Z_{\alpha/2}\,(\sigma/\sqrt{n})$ to $\bar{X} + Z_{\alpha/2}\,(\sigma/\sqrt{n})$. The expression $\bar{X} - Z_{\alpha/2}\,(\sigma/\sqrt{n})$ is referred to as the lower limit of the confidence interval, whereas $\bar{X} + Z_{\alpha/2}\,(\sigma/\sqrt{n})$ is called the upper limit of the confidence interval.

A final comment regarding the confidence interval should be emphasized. The standard deviation of the population appears in Equation 6.2. Unfortunately, the standard deviation of the population is seldom known, and as a result, we substitute S, the standard deviation of the sample, for σ and obtain

$$\bar{X} - Z_{\alpha/2}\,(S/\sqrt{n}) \leq \mu \leq \bar{X} + Z_{\alpha/2}\,(S/\sqrt{n}) \qquad \text{(Equation 6.3)}$$

Equation 6.3 is routinely used when calculating the $1 - \alpha$ confidence interval for the mean of the population.

For example, consider the general problem of a delay in transferring patients to another source of care after a hospital stay. Suppose that we selected a sample of 36 patients who were transferred from our hospital to a nursing home and measured the delay in discharge by the number of days that lapsed between the time the patient was ready for transfer and the date of discharge. The results of the sample are presented in Exhibit 6.1. After using the "descriptive statistics" function that is available in Excel, Exhibit 6.1 also indicates that the average length of delay was approximately 17.14 days. Without additional information, the mean of the sample represents a point estimate and might be used to approximate the mean of the population, μ. Exhibit 6.1 also reveals that the standard deviation, S, was approximately 4.73 days and that the standard error of the mean was approximately 0.788. Now suppose that the administrator wishes to construct a 95% confidence interval for the mean delay in transferring patients. Table 6.2 shows that the corresponding standard normal deviate is 1.96, implying that the confidence interval is

$$17.14 \pm 1.96\ (0.788)$$

Thus, the 95% confidence interval is

$$17.14 \pm 1.54$$

which implies that

$$15.60 \leq \mu \leq 18.68$$

With a probability of 0.95, the average delay in transferring patients to a source of postdischarge care ranges from 15.60 to 18.68 days.

Suppose that the administrator wants to construct a 98% confidence interval. We find that the confidence interval is

$$17.14 \pm 2.33\ (0.788)$$

or

$$17.14 \pm 1.84$$

After performing the calculations, we find that the 98% confidence interval may be expressed as

$$15.30 \leq \mu \leq 18.98$$

Exhibit 6.1 **The Delay in Transferring Patients to an Alternate Source**

Patient	Delay (Days)
1	10
2	14
3	13
4	21
5	15
6	18
7	19
8	21
9	16
10	18
11	13
12	15
13	25
14	22
15	17
16	13
17	12
18	19
19	20
20	25
21	12
22	26
23	8
24	23
25	24
26	12
27	10
28	16
29	18
30	14
31	17
32	18
33	11
34	19
35	21
36	22

Descriptive Summary

Column1	
Mean	17.13888889
Standard Error	0.787957756
Median	17.5
Mode	18
Standard Deviation	4.727746535
Sample Variance	22.3515873
Kurtosis	−0.838702882
Skewness	0.060961571
Range	18
Minimum	8
Maximum	26
Sum	617
Count	36

Based on these calculations, we are 98% confident that the mean time required to provide the service ranges from 14.92 to 17.52 minutes.

Finally, suppose that we wish to construct a 99% confidence interval. Table 6.2 indicates that the value of the corresponding standard normal deviate is 2.58, suggesting that

$$17.14 \pm 2.58\ (0.788)$$

The corresponding confidence interval is given by

$$17.14 \pm 2.03$$

Thus, the 99% confidence interval is defined as

$$15.11 \leq \mu \leq 19.17$$

After comparing the upper and lower limits of the 95%, 98%, and 99% confidence intervals, we note that as the degree of confidence increases the range of values that define the confidence interval also grows. As the degree of confidence increases, we can be less precise about the value that we want to estimate.

Excel performs the previously summarized calculations with ease. The value of the product $Z_{\alpha/2}\ (S/\sqrt{n})$ is calculated as follows:

1. Select the "f_{ix}" function.
2. Select the "CONFIDENCE" function.
3. Enter the value of α (0.05, 0.02, or 0.01).
4. Enter the value of the standard deviation.
5. Enter the sample size.

Excel automatically calculates the value that is added to or subtracted from the mean $\bar{X}$ to construct the corresponding confidence interval for μ.

Interval Estimates for μ Based on Small Samples

Thus far, we have used a large sample and the central limit theorem to develop the confidence interval for the mean of the population. However, if the sample size is small, $n \leq 30$, the standard normal curve cannot approximate the sampling distribution of the mean. Fortunately, the distribution of the ratio

$$(\bar{X} - \mu)/s/\sqrt{n}$$

has been determined when the sample size is small.

Without benefit of formal derivation, we simply assert that our methods are based on the t distribution and particularly on

$$t = (\bar{X} - \mu)/s/\sqrt{n} \qquad \text{(Equation 6.4)}$$

The t distribution is similar to the standard normal curve because it is unimodal, symmetrical, and characterized by a mean of zero. However, Figure 6.4 shows that the probability of getting a value that resides in the two tails is greater in the t than the standard normal curve. Also, the precise configuration of the t distribution depends on the number of degrees of freedom, which is given by n − 1.

In the previous section, $Z_{\alpha/2}$ was defined so that the area to its right represents a probability of $\alpha/2$ and $-Z_{\alpha/2}$ as the standard normal deviate for which the area to its left also represents a probability of $\alpha/2$. Based on these definitions, $P(-Z_{\alpha/2} \leq Z \leq Z_{\alpha/2})$ is $1 - \alpha$. In Figure 6.4, a similar approach to the definition of $\pm t_{\alpha/2,n-1}$ is adopted. The values in the t distribution that correspond to $-Z_{\alpha/2}$ and $Z_{\alpha/2}$ are $-t_{\alpha/2,n-1}$ and $t_{\alpha/2,n-1}$, respectively. The main difference is that the corresponding tabular value for t is dependent on the number of degrees of freedom.

In Table D.2, the rows are defined by the number of degrees of freedom from 1 to an infinite number. On the other hand, the columns are defined by $t_{0.05}$, $t_{0.025}$, $t_{0.01}$, and $t_{0.005}$. Also, as the number of degrees of freedom increases indefinitely, the tabular value of $t_{0.025}$ approaches 1.96, which is the value of $Z_{\alpha/2}$ when α is 0.05. The tabular values for $t_{\alpha/2}$ approach 2.33 and 2.58 as the number of degrees of freedom increase indefinitely. The tabular values of 2.33 and 2.58 correspond to $Z_{\alpha/2}$ for $\alpha = 0.02$ and 0.01, respectively. Thus, as the number of degrees of freedom increases, the t distribution approaches the standard normal curve.

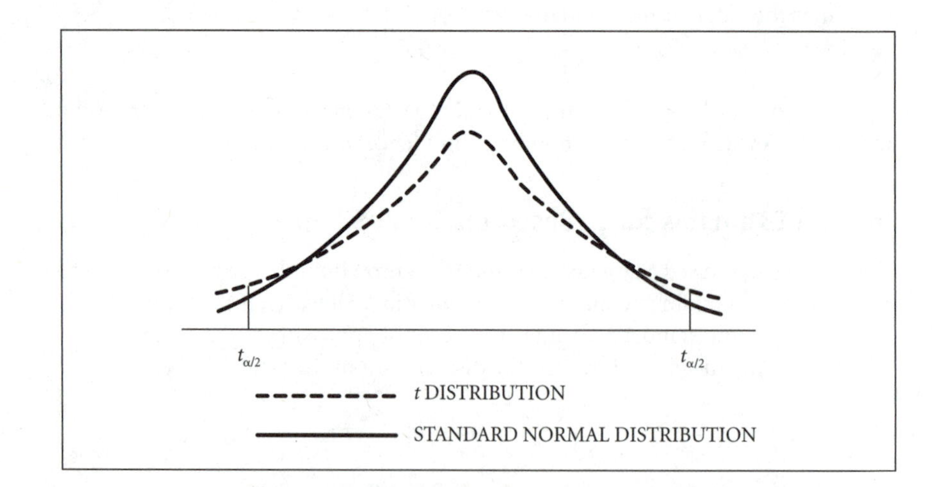

Figure 6.4 **Comparison of the *t* and Standard Normal Distributions**

The approach used here is similar to the development of a $1 - \alpha$ confidence interval based on a large sample. When n is small, the confidence interval with a degree of confidence equal to $1 - \alpha$ is given by

$$\bar{X} - t_{\alpha/2,n-1}\,(S/\sqrt{n}) \le \mu \le \bar{X} + t_{\alpha/2,\,n-1}\,(S/\sqrt{n}) \qquad \text{(Equation 6.5)}$$

The only difference in the method of constructing a confidence interval based on a large and small sample is the substitution of $t_{\alpha/2,\,n-1}$ for $Z_{\alpha/2}$ and $-\,t_{\alpha/2,\,n-1}$ for $-\,Z_{\alpha/2}$.

For example, suppose that after selecting a sample of 25 medical records we find that the mean length of stay is 7.2 days and the standard deviation is 1.5 days. If the degree of confidence equals 0.95, the degrees of freedom are $25 - 1$ or 24. Table D.2 reveals that the tabular value for $t_{0.025,24}$ is 2.064 and that, after substituting appropriately, the confidence interval is

$$7.2 \pm 2.064\ (1.5/5)$$

Based on these calculations, we are able to assert with a probability of 0.95 that

$$6.58 \le \mu \le 7.82$$

Similar to the interpretation of a confidence interval based on a large sample, the calculations indicate that we are 95% confident that the mean length of stay ranges from 6.58 to 7.82 days.

Introduction to Hypotheses and Related Risks[R]

Inferential statistics and the examination of hypotheses or assertions concerning the mean play a pivotal role in assessing other courses of action and identifying strengths or weaknesses in the health service organization. In each of these situations, the administrator is frequently required to form and implement decisions under conditions of uncertainty or in the absence of complete information.

For example, suppose that the health service organization is considering a strategic plan that requires the construction of a clinic in a given market area. When considering the planned size of the clinic, we might need to examine the claim that the typical resident of the market area experienced five visits during the past year. In this situation, a hypothesis concerning the average number of visits per person per year needs to be examined. If the average number of visits is less than five per person per year, the planned capacity might be excessive. In contrast, if the average number of visits is greater than five per person per year, the planned size might be too small. Thus, an examination of an assumption or claim of the mean is valuable when evaluating plans to construct a clinic of given size.

The assertion might be evaluated by selecting a sample of patients or individuals in the insured population who reside in the market area. Based on the experience of a comparable population and market area, the standard deviation is four visits per person per year. Suppose that we select a sample of 100 individuals and calculate the mean number of visits per person per year. Figure 6.5 shows that the situation might be assessed by accepting the claim as valid if the mean of the sample is between four and six visits per person per year. In this case, we have adopted clear criteria that enable us to assess the assertion that μ is equal to five visits per person per year.

The criteria on which the decision is based are not infallible. It is possible for the mean derived from the sample to be greater than six visits per person per year or less than four visits per person per year even though the true mean is five visits per person per year. If the sample mean is greater than six visits per person per year and the true mean is five visits per year, the administrator might mistakenly decide to build a clinic that is too large. In contrast, if the sample mean is less than four visits per person per year and the true mean is five visits per year, the administrator might decide to build a clinic that is too small or to abandon the project.

Using the initial decision criteria, consider next the probability of getting a sample mean that is less than four visits per person per year or greater than six visits per person per year when the true mean is five visits per person per year. Because the sample is large (n = 100), the central limit theorem suggests that the sampling distribution of the mean may be approximated by a normal distribution. Figure 6.5 reveals that when calculating the desired probability it is necessary to express the original decision limits in terms of standard normal deviates. If the standard deviation is four visits, the standard error of the mean is

$$S_x = 4/(100)^{1/2}$$

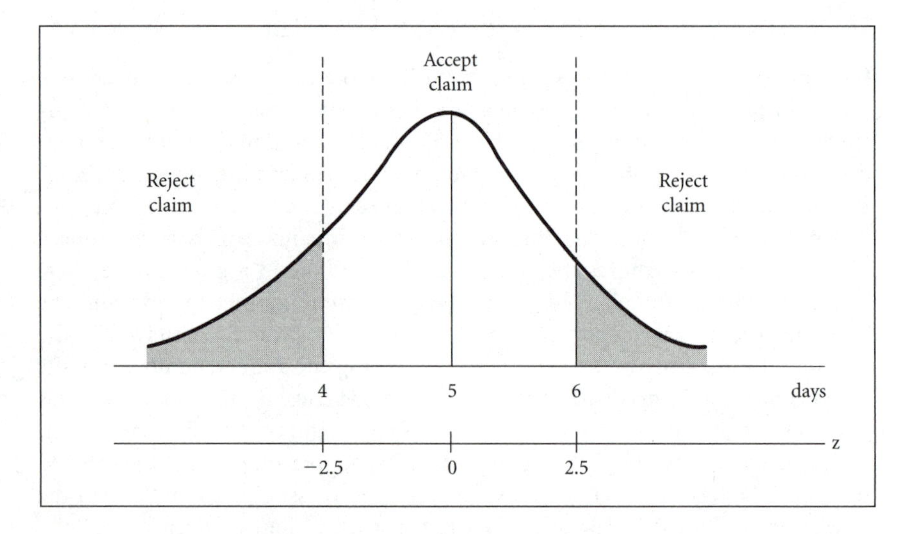

Figure 6.5 **The Decision Criteria, Expressed in Days**

or 0.4. The standard normal deviates that correspond to the lower and upper limit of the decision criteria are given by

$$Z_4 = (4 - 5)/0.4$$

and

$$Z_6 = (6 - 5)/0.4$$

respectively. These calculations indicate that the upper limit of the decision criteria is equal to a standard normal deviate of 2.5, whereas the lower limit of the decision criteria is equal to a standard normal deviate of −2.5.

Table D.1 reveals that the tabular value for a standard normal deviate of 2.5 is 0.4938. Thus, the probability of obtaining a standard normal deviate that is greater than 2.5 (i.e., a sample mean that exceeds six visits per person per year) is 0.0062 or less (i.e., 0.5000 − 0.4938). The probability of obtaining a standard normal deviate of −2.5 or less is 0.0062 or less. The likelihood of obtaining a sample mean that forces us to reject a true assertion is given by the sum of 0.0062 and 0.0062 or 0.0124.

The potential for getting a sample mean that forces us to reject a true assertion might be reduced by selecting other values for the decision criteria. For example, suppose that the administrator decides to accept the claim that the true mean is five visits per person per year if the sample mean is greater than three visits or less than seven visits per person per year. Unfortunately, an extension of the decision criteria exposes the administrator to a second risk. An increase in the range of the decision limits also increases the risk of having a sample mean ranging from three to seven visits per person per year even though the true mean is *not* five visits per person per year. The results of the sample might result in a decision to accept a false assertion or claim.

Consider next the probability that the results of the sample and the original decision criteria fail to detect that the true mean is not five visits per person per year. Assume that the true mean is 6.5 visits person per year rather than 5 visits per person per year as originally claimed. In Figure 6.6, the desired probability is given by the sum of the areas residing under the normal distribution to the left of four visits per person per year and to the right of six visits per person per year. The standard normal deviate that corresponds to four visits is given by

$$Z_4 = (4 - 6.5)/0.4$$

or −6.5. The probability $P(Z \leq -6.5)$ is zero or nearly so, suggesting that we may ignore the area to the right of four visits per person per year in our calculations. On the other hand, the standard normal deviate that corresponds to the upper limit of the decision criteria is

$$Z_6 = (6 - 6.5)/0.4$$

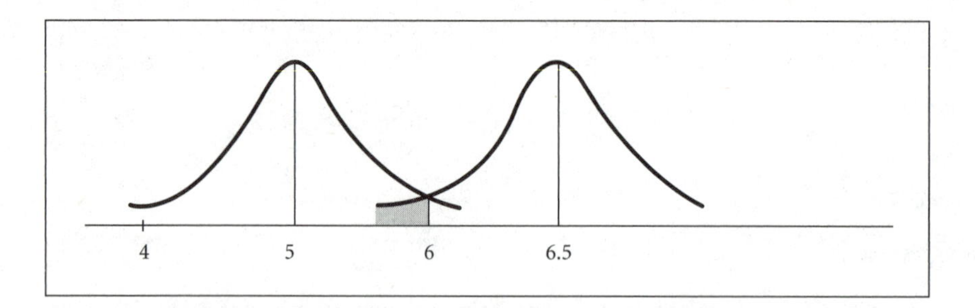

Figure 6.6 **The Probability of Accepting a False Hypothesis**

or −1.25. Since the tabular value for a standard normal deviate of −1.25 is 0.3944, the probability of obtaining a sample mean that is less than 6 visits per person per year is given by 0.5000 less 0.3944 or 0.1056. If μ is in fact 6.5 visits per person per year, these calculations suggest that the probability of obtaining a sample mean that results in the acceptance of a false assertion is approximately 11%.

This discussion indicates that when we evaluate an assertion, a claim, or hypothesis, we encounter two types of risk. Table 6.3 shows that a decision to reject a true hypothesis results in a Type I error. In contrast, if a false hypothesis or claim is accepted, we commit a Type II error.

When assessing claims or assertions, we wish to control the magnitude of both types of risk. As suggested later here, it is possible to control the likelihood of committing both types of errors when the size of the sample is not predetermined. However, as is commonly the case, we may control or specify only the probability of committing a Type I error when the sample size is predetermined.

Specification of Hypotheses[R]

The health administrator is frequently required to examine the association of one variable with another. For example, if primary diagnosis remains the same, it is possible that the presence of comorbidity increases the use of care, resource consumption, and costs. In this case, we might expect the average length of stay re-

Table 6.3 **Type I and Type II Errors**

	Assertion Is True	**Assertion Is False**
Accept	Correct	Type II error
Reject	Type I error	Correct

quired by patients with two or more diagnoses to exceed the average number of days of care used by those with only one diagnosis. We might express the expectation by claiming that on average the length of stay required by those with a single diagnosis is less than or equal to the average number of days of care required by those with two or more diagnoses.

When examining assertions or claims, the administrator is frequently required to decide whether a difference is statistically significant or attributable to chance variation. In turn, the difference of interest is defined as a contrast or comparison that is governed by a null hypothesis, represented by H_o, and an alternate hypothesis, represented by H_a. When comparing of the length of stay by comorbid patients with those with only one diagnosis, let LOS_c represent the average length of stay associated with a group of patients who are diagnosed with multiple diagnoses. Let LOS_{nc} represent the average length of stay for a group of patients who are not comorbid or who have only one diagnosis. In this case, we might express the null hypothesis as

$$H_o: LOS_c \leq LOS_{nc} \qquad \text{(Equation 6.6.1)}$$

The null hypothesis that Equation 6.6.1 defines is equivalent to

$$H_o: LOS_c - LOS_{nc} \leq 0 \qquad \text{(Equation 6.6.2)}$$

The alternate hypothesis defines the contrast or comparison of interest and might be expressed as

$$H_a: LOS_c > LOS_{nc} \qquad \text{(Equation 6.7.1)}$$

The alternate hypothesis in Equation 6.7.1 might be expressed as

$$H_a: LOS_c - LOS_{nc} > 0 \qquad \text{(Equation 6.7.2)}$$

When forming the null hypothesis, we employed $\leq$, which means "less than or equal to," whereas the alternate hypothesis used $>$, which means "greater than."

Three aspects of the null and alternate hypotheses should be noted. First, the null and alternate hypotheses are mutually exclusive because either the null hypothesis, $LOS_c - LOS_{nc} \leq 0$, or the alternate hypothesis, $LOS_c - LOS_{nc} > 0$, is true. Second, the expected value derived from a contrast or comparison is specified by the null and alternate hypotheses. For example, if the null hypothesis is true, a contrast or comparison represented by $LOS_c - LOS_{nc}$ will be approximately zero or a negative value. In contrast, if the alternate hypothesis is true, we expect the comparison or contrast to result in a positive value. Third, the null and alternate hypotheses were derived from a conceptual framework that indicates the administrative importance of the contrast or comparison.

The process of developing hypotheses and related decision criteria consists of three phases. The null and alternate hypotheses are formulated during the first phase. In general, the null hypothesis represents the opposite of what we wish to examine or prove. The alternate hypothesis is frequently derived from a conceptual framework and, as the following discussion demonstrates, may be directional or nondirectional.

To illustrate the formulation of a directional or one-sided alternative, suppose that the chief financial officer believes that if the average length of stay required by a Medicare beneficiary who is admitted with a given diagnosis is equal to or greater than 5 days, the organization will sustain a loss. If the length of stay is less than 5 days, the organization will have a net surplus and an improvement in the net cash flow derived from operations. The null hypothesis might be expressed as

$$H_o: \mu \leq 5$$

In this case, the null hypothesis indicates that if the average length of stay is 5 days or less no losses are sustained. On the other hand, the alternative hypothesis might be expressed as

$$H_a: \mu > 5$$

implying that, on average, the organization sustains a net loss if the length of stay is more than 5 days.

To illustrate the second form of the directional or one-sided alternate hypothesis, suppose that the administrator of an outpatient clinic is concerned that the quality of care is compromised by a relatively short initial visit. Based on previous experience, physicians who practice at the clinic claim that the initial examination and the completion of the patient's medical history require at least 45 minutes. If the initial visit is less than 45 minutes, it is possible that the examination, the medical history, or both may be incomplete. In this instance, the null hypothesis might be

$$H_o: \mu \geq 45$$

To accommodate the administrator's concern, the directional alternate hypothesis might be expressed as

$$H_a: \mu < 45$$

Suppose that the evaluation of the average time required to complete an initial visit is significantly less than 45 minutes. These results require us to reject the null hypothesis in favor of the alternative. The statistical analysis and related interpretation suggest the existence of a potential problem and the need to investigate the adequacy of initial visits provided by the organization.

The alternate hypothesis may also be expressed in nondirectional terms. For example, suppose that, on average, 15 minutes are required to complete a given procedure. In this case, we might form a null hypothesis represented by

$$H_o\colon \mu = 15$$

The nondirectional or two-sided alternative assumes

$$H_a\colon \mu \neq 15$$

which implies that the true mean is not equal to 15 minutes. After appropriate evaluation, the null hypothesis might be rejected if the true mean is found to be either significantly greater or less than 15 minutes.

In the following, we let μ_o correspond to a presumed value for the mean μ. Similar to our assessment of the length of stay and related potential losses, consider a statement of the null and alternate hypotheses in situations in which we are concerned that the true mean is greater than a prescribed value. In this case, the null and alternate hypothesis might be expressed as

$$H_o\colon \mu - \mu_o \leq 0$$
$$H_a\colon \mu - \mu_o > 0$$

respectively. Similar to the situation in which we wished to evaluate the length of the initial visit, the assertion that the true mean is less than a prescribed or assumed value might be expressed by

$$H_o\colon \mu - \mu_o \geq 0$$
$$H_a\colon \mu - \mu_o < 0$$

The null and alternate hypotheses are equal statements of our concern about the average length of the initial visit.

Finally, similar to the problem about the length of time to complete a given procedure, the null and alternate hypotheses might be expressed as

$$H_o\colon \mu - \mu_o = 0$$
$$H_a\colon \mu - \mu_o \neq 0$$

The alternate hypothesis corresponds to a nondirectional or two-sided alternative.

The second phase of formulating hypotheses requires the analyst to specify the probability of committing a type I error and, if possible, to comment on the likelihood of committing a Type II error. In testing hypotheses, claims, or assertions, we are interested in the statistical significance of the difference measured by a comparison or contrast. If the difference is relatively small, we are tempted to accept the null hypothesis, a decision that exposes us to the risk of committing a Type II error. If the administrative situation permits, we might reserve judgment and thereby entirely avoid the risk of accepting a false claim, assertion, or hypothesis. The last section of this chapter is committed to the relationship of sample size to Type II errors, and as a consequence, the following discussion focuses on the probability of committing a Type I error.

For example, suppose the comparison or contrast results in a difference that is relatively large and consistent with expectations that the alternate hypothesis expressed. For example, in the situation in which we wished to assess the average length of stay in relationship to a specified value of 5 days, suppose that the mean length of stay of a sample of 144 patients was 9.2 days. In this case, the mean obtained from the sample is much more than the postulated value, and we are tempted to reject the null hypothesis in favor of the alternate, which indicates the true mean stay exceeds 5 days.

When the null hypothesis is rejected, risks associated with committing a Type I error are encountered. The probability or risk of committing a Type I error is represented by the Greek letter α, which enabled us to specify the degree of confidence when constructing a confidence interval. Similar to our discussion of constructing a confidence interval, suppose that we wish to be 95% confident that the results of the test will allow us to avoid a Type I error. In this case, we implicitly assign a value of 0.05 to α, indicating that the probability of committing a Type I error is 0.05 or less. Although the choice is somewhat arbitrary, analysts routinely let α equal 0.05, 0.02, or 0.01 when evaluating the results derived from a test of significance.

The third phase of formulating hypotheses is to employ the specified value of α to construct the decision criteria that enable us to evaluate the results of the statistical test. It is possible to identify three approaches to the specification of the decision criteria, each yielding equivalent results.

When the first is adopted, the decision criteria are expressed in units that measure the item of interest. For example, consider the problem of evaluating the average length of stay in which the alternate hypothesis might be expressed by

$$H_a\text{: } \mu - 5 > 0$$

Suppose that we selected 100 inpatients and calculated a standard deviation of 3 days. If the sample size is large, the central limit theorem is used in our evaluation. If we wished to be 95% certain of avoiding a Type I error, an inspection of Table 6.1 indicates that the corresponding standard normal deviate is 1.64. Thus, we find that

$$1.64 = (\bar{X} - 5)/3/\sqrt{100}$$

After solving for $\bar{X}$, we find that decision criteria require us to reject the null hypothesis if the sample mean is greater than or equal to 5.492 days. In contrast, if the sample mean is less than 5.492 days, we should either accept the null hypothesis or reserve judgment.

When the second approach is adopted, the decision criteria are specified by first selecting the desired value for α and then identifying the corresponding critical standard normal deviate. For example, Table 6.1 reveals that if $\alpha = 0.05$, the corresponding critical values of the standard normal deviate are 1.64, -1.64, or ± 1.96, depending on the nature of the alternate hypothesis. As described in the next section, the calculated value of Z is compared with the critical value when deciding to accept or reject the null hypothesis.

The third approach, described in our discussion of Excel, requires a comparison of the exact probability of obtaining a calculated value of Z if the null hypothesis is correct with the value of α. The exact probability indicates the likelihood of obtaining the value of the calculated standard normal deviate based on the proposition that the null hypothesis is correct. If the exact probability is less than α, the chance that the null hypothesis is true is correspondingly small. If the exact probability is less than α, the null hypothesis must be rejected in favor of the alternate.

Tests of Significance: Presumed Values of the True Mean[R]

Here we consider claims that the true mean is equal to a presumed or specified value. The tests of significance are contingent on the size of the sample. We consider first comparisons or contrasts that are based on large samples for which the degrees of freedom are 30 or more. We also consider tests of specified or presumed values of the mean that are based on small samples.

Tests of Significance: Large Samples

As before, μ_o represents the specified value of the true mean. The focus of the assessment is on an alternate hypothesis about the true value of the mean. As indicated in the previous section, alternate hypotheses might be expressed as one of the following directional or nondirectional forms:

1. $\mu - \mu_o > 0$
2. $\mu - \mu_o < 0$
3. $\mu - \mu_0 \neq 0$

Thus, the alternate hypothesis states that the true mean μ is greater than, less than, or not equal to a presumed or prescribed value represented by μ_0.

After the null and alternate hypotheses have been formulated, the desired probability or risk of committing a Type I error (i.e., the possibility of rejecting a true assertion as expressed by the null hypothesis) must be specified. In this case, the most commonly used values of α are 0.05, 0.02, or 0.01. The critical values that correspond to each of the probabilities of committing a Type I error are summarized for the directional and nondirectional hypotheses in Table 6.4.

If n, the sample size, is large, we next rely on the central limit theorem to assert that

$$Z = (\bar{X} - \mu_o)/\sigma/\sqrt{n} \qquad \text{(Equation 6.8)}$$

is a normally distributed variable or a standard normal deviate. In this case, $\bar{X}$ is a point estimate of μ, and σ is the standard deviation of the population from which the sample was selected; μ_o is the value of the true mean posited by the null hypothesis, and the ratio translates units used to measure the variable of interest into standard normal deviates. In the future, we refer to the ratio as the calculated value of Z or the calculated value of the standard normal deviate.

To illustrate the decision criteria, consider the first of the alternate hypotheses that were summarized previously here. Assume that our focus is on the alternate hypothesis represented by $\mu - \mu_o > 0$, implying that the mean of the population exceeds the specified value μ_o. Recalling that $\bar{X}$ is a point estimate of the population mean, we see that the alternate hypothesis is supported if the contrast $\bar{X} - \mu_o$ results in a positive value. Thus, if $\bar{X} - \mu_o > 0$ the corresponding standard normal deviate must also be positive. If the alternate hypothesis represented by $\mu - \mu_o > 0$ is true, we would expect the calculated value of Z to be large and positive, an outcome that results in the rejection of the null hypothesis in favor of the alternative.

A decision criterion must be developed that defines with precision the standard that must be exceeded before rejecting the null hypothesis and accepting the alternate. Figure 6.7 shows that the decision criterion is expressed in terms of a critical value for the standard normal deviate, represented by Z_α. We define Z_α as the standard normal deviate for which the proportion of the area under the probability distribution to its right is α. The decision criterion also has been identified graphically by constructing a perpendicular line from the point $Z = Z_\alpha$. The perpendicular line divides the distribution into two regions. The first of these regions, known as the rejection or critical region, requires us to reject the null hypothesis and accept the alternate. The second region, known as the acceptance

Table 6.4 **Critical Values for Commonly Used Values of α**

Alternate	Probability of Type I Error		
Hypothesis	**0.05**	**0.02**	**0.01**
$\mu - \mu_o > 0$	1.64	2.06	2.33
$\mu - \mu_o < 0$	−1.64	−2.06	−2.33
$\mu - \mu_0 \neq 0$	±1.96	±2.33	±2.58

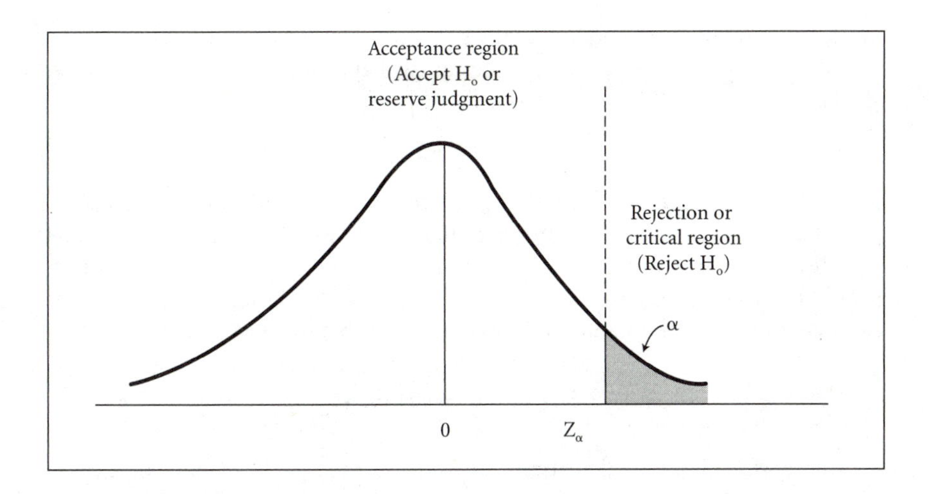

Figure 6.7 **The Decision Criteria: H_a: $\mu - \mu_o > 0$**

region, requires us to either accept the null hypothesis or reserve judgment. In summary, if the calculated value of the test statistic exceeds the critical value (i.e., resides to the right of the perpendicular line), we reject the null hypothesis in favor of the alternate, recognizing that the probability of committing a Type I error is α or less. In contrast, if the calculated value is equal to or less than the critical value, the null hypothesis is accepted or judgment is reserved, thereby avoiding the risks of committing a Type II error.

For example, consider a problem that requires an assessment of the average length of time required to complete one cycle of providing a given procedure. After adjusting for fatigue, breaks, and other routine interruptions, a technical expert informs us that on average no more than 15 minutes should be required to complete a particular procedure. If the mean time is 15 minutes or less, resources were used efficiently. In contrast, if on average more than 15 minutes are required, resources were used less efficiently than planned, and a potential problem exists. We form the following null and alternate hypotheses to examine the situation:

$$H_o: \mu - 15 \leq 0$$
$$H_a: \mu - 15 > 0$$

After selecting a sample of 36 occasions in which a given technician performed the procedure, suppose that we obtained the data in Exhibit 6.2.

Excel obtained the summary statistics that accompany the exhibit. These results are derived by

1. Selecting data analysis
2. Selecting the "DESCRIPTIVE" Function

3. Identifying the field containing the time required in minutes
4. Identifying the field in which the results will appear
5. Selecting the "SUMMARY STATISTICS" function
6. Selecting "OK"

Excel's results may then be used to assess the situation. The sample mean is approximately 16.22 minutes, and the standard deviation is approximately 3.34 minutes, resulting in a standard error of the mean of approximately 0.56. If $\alpha = 0.05$, Table 6.4 indicates that the critical value of Z is 1.64. Using Equation 6.8, the calculated value for the standard normal deviate is obtained as follows:

$$Z = (16.22 - 15)/0.56$$

After performing the calculations, we find that the calculated value of Z is approximately 2.18. Because the calculated value of Z (2.18) exceeds the critical value (1.64), the statistical test indicates that we should reject the null hypothesis in favor of the alternate, recognizing that the probability of committing a Type I error is 0.05 or less. In this case, the analysis suggests the existence of a potential problem in the operational performance of the health service organization. Thus, the results suggest a need for additional administrative examination and perhaps the implementation of corrective policies.

If we had specified a nondirectional alternative, the rejection of the null hypothesis would require a calculated value of Z that is either greater than the critical value of 1.96 or is less than -1.96. Thus, relative to a critical value of 1.64, the nondirectional or two-sided alternative imposes a more stringent standard that must be satisfied before rejecting the null hypothesis. These observations indicate that a nondirectional or two-sided alternative is a more conservative test of significance.

Consider next the second of the two alternate hypotheses. As before, suppose that our focus is on the time required to complete an initial visit and that if on average less than 45 minutes are needed, the patient's history and examination may be incomplete. In this situation, we are interested in examining the following null and alternate hypotheses that are specified by

$$H_o: \mu - 45 \geq 0$$
$$H_a: \mu - 45 < 0$$

Assume that we wish to be 95% certain of avoiding aType I error, implying that the value of α is 0.05. After assembling data derived from 81 visits, suppose that we found that the mean time was 40 minutes and that the standard deviation was 18 minutes. The calculated value of Z is obtained by

$$Z = (40 - 45)/18/\sqrt{81}$$

Exhibit 6.2 **The Time Required to Provide a Service**

Observation	Time (in Minutes)
1	12
2	15
3	10
4	11
5	13
6	18
7	17
8	10
9	19
10	21
11	22
12	13
13	14
14	18
15	13
16	15
17	17
18	19
19	21
20	22
21	17
22	18
23	17
24	15
25	14
26	18
27	15
28	13
29	17
30	18
31	19
32	22
33	12
34	18
35	16
36	15

Descriptive Summary

	Column1
Mean	16.22222222
Standard Error	0.556507122
Median	17
Mode	18
Standard Deviation	3.339042729
Sample Variance	11.14920635
Kurtosis	−0.684746326
Skewness	−0.034571631
Range	12
Minimum	10
Maximum	22
Sum	584
Count	36

We find that the calculated value of the standard normal deviate is equal to −2.50. In Figure 6.8, if the calculated value of Z is less than the critical value, represented by $-Z_{\alpha}$, we should reject the null hypothesis and accept the alternate. Returning to the problem involving the average length of the initial visit, we note that the calculated

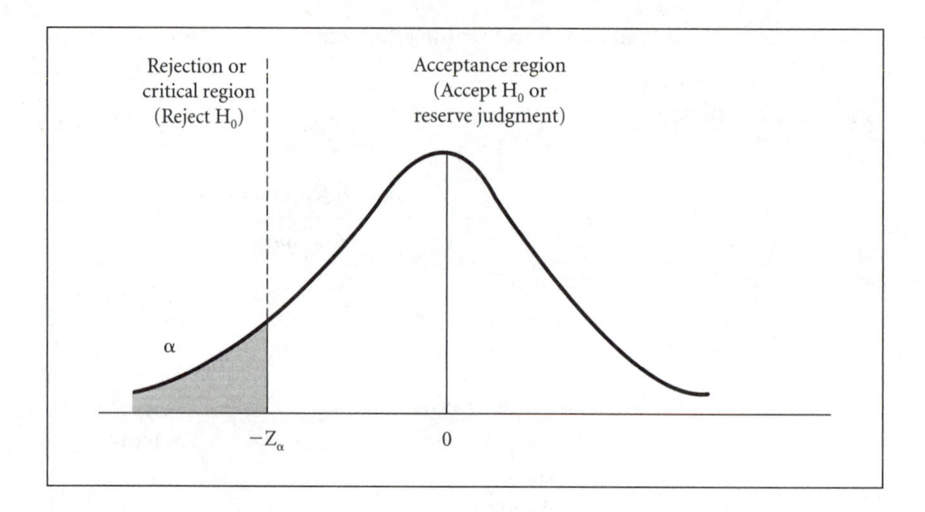

Figure 6.8 **The Decision Criteria: H_a: $\mu - \mu_o < o$**

value of Z (−2.50) is less than the critical value (−1.64). Thus, the results of the statistical test indicate that we must reject the null hypothesis in favor of the alternative, concluding that the average length of the initial visit is less than 45 minutes.

Finally, consider the nondirectional or two-sided hypothesis. As indicated previously, the critical values are represented by $Z_{\alpha/2}$ and $-Z_{\alpha/2}$. In Figure 6.9, as before, the critical values divide the distribution into two regions. Specifically, if the condition $-Z_{\alpha/2} \leq Z \leq Z_{\alpha/2}$ is satisfied, the statistical analysis indicates that we should accept the null hypothesis or, if possible, reserve judgment, thereby avoiding a Type II error. In contrast, if the calculated value of Z exceeds $Z_{\alpha/2}$ or is less than $-Z_{\alpha/2}$, the null hypothesis should be rejected and the alternate accepted, recognizing that the probability of committing a Type I error is $\alpha/2$ or less. The calculated value of Z is obtained using the procedures outlined in this section.

Tests of Significance: Small Samples

The analysis has thus far focused on a situation in which the size of the sample is large. However, when the sample size is small, the examination of a presumed value of the mean requires a slightly different approach. In general, the sample size is regarded as small when less than 30 degrees of freedom (i.e., n − 1) are available for analysis. In this case, we posit a null and an alternate hypothesis as described in the previous sections. Similar to our discussion of constructing a confidence interval, the analysis is based on a t-ratio rather than a standard normal deviate. Specifically, when the sample size is small, our decisions are based on

$$t = (\bar{X} - \mu)/s/\sqrt{n}$$

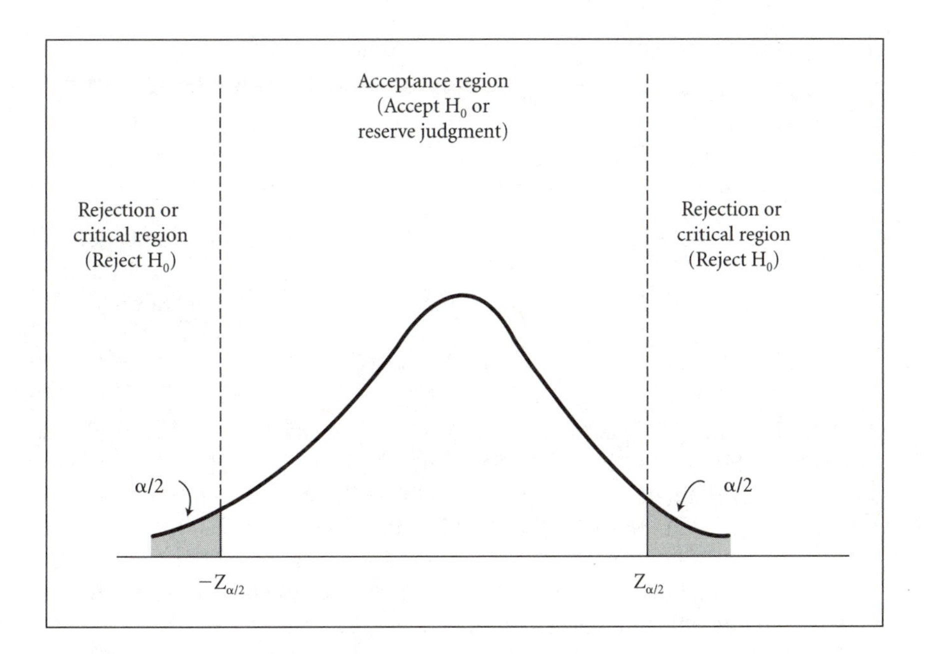

Figure 6.9 **The Decision Criteria: H_a: $\mu - \mu_o \neq 0$**

If the calculated value of t exceeds $t_{\alpha, n-1,}$ the null hypothesis is rejected in favor of the directional alternate represented by

$$H_a\text{: } \mu - \mu_o > 0$$

If the calculated value of t is less than $-t_{\alpha, n-1}$, the analysis indicates that we should reject the null in favor of the alternate hypothesis specified by

$$H_a\text{: } \mu - \mu_o < 0$$

Finally, if the calculated value of t is less than $-t_{\alpha/2, n-1}$ or greater than $t_{\alpha/2, n-1}$, we are forced to reject the null hypothesis in favor of the nondirectional alternate defined by

$$H_a\text{: } \mu - \mu_o \neq 0$$

The subscript $n - 1$ represents the degrees of freedom that are available. For example, suppose that the administrator of several clinics is concerned that patient satisfaction declines as the amount of time between a scheduled appointment and the patient's contact with the physician time increases. The administrator is also worried that the average lapse of time between the scheduled time for the patient's appointment and the initial contact with the physician is more than 20 minutes. In this situation, we are interested in the following hypotheses:

$$H_o: \mu - 20 \leq 0$$
$$H_a: \mu - 20 > 0$$

Suppose that we wish to be 99% certain of avoiding a Type I error and after selecting a sample of 25 visits found that the mean waiting time was 23.9 minutes and that the standard deviation was 6 minutes. The calculated value of t is

$$t = (23.9 - 20)/6/\sqrt{25}$$

or 3.25. The critical value of t, represented by $t_{0.01,24}$, is 2.49. Because the calculated value of t (3.25) exceeds the critical value of t (2.49), we reject the null hypothesis in favor of the alternate, recognizing that the probability of committing a Type I error is .01 or less. In this case, the statistical analysis suggests that the process of scheduling physician visits should be investigated and perhaps improved to reduce the time between the scheduled appointment and the first contact with the provider, an outcome that may enhance patient satisfaction.

Contrasts Involving Two Means[R]

In addition to examining a presumed value of the mean, the health administrator is frequently required to assess the difference between two means. For example, we might be interested in determining whether

1. African Americans experience a longer delay in seeking care than their white counterparts.
2. The delay in transferring inpatients to a nursing home is greater for males than females.
3. A given diagnosis results in higher treatment costs than another.
4. Older persons use fewer days of hospital care than their younger counterparts.
5. The poor travel a greater distance for outpatient care than wealthier members of society.

In each case, our interest is in comparing one mean with another. Similar to our earlier discussion, the focus is on the following null and alternate hypotheses:

1. $H_o: \mu_1 - \mu_2 \leq 0$
   $H_a: \mu_1 - \mu_2 > 0$
2. $H_o: \mu_1 - \mu_2 > 0$
   $H_a: \mu_1 - \mu_2 < 0$

3. $H_a: \mu_1 - \mu_2 = 0$
   $H_a: \mu_1 - \mu_2 \neq 0$

The alternate hypotheses are directional or one sided and nondirectional or two sided. The first of the directional or one-sided alternate hypotheses asserts that μ_1 exceeds μ_2, whereas the second assumes that μ_1 is less than μ_2. The nondirectional or two-sided alternate hypothesis asserts that μ_1 is not equal to μ_2.

When comparing two means, the object is to determine whether the difference between two means is statistically significant or attributable to chance variation. In general, we select a sample from the first population of interest and calculate the mean $\bar{X}_1$, which is an estimate of the true mean μ_1 and S_1^2, which serves as an estimate of σ_1^2. We select a sample from the second population of interest and calculate the mean $\bar{X}_2$, which serves as an estimate of the true mean μ_2, and S_2^2, which serves as a point estimate of σ_2^2. We rely on $\bar{X}_1 - \bar{X}_2$ as an estimate of $\mu_1 - \mu_2$. As indicated, the data derived from the two samples also form the basis for the calculation of S_1^2 and S_2^2, which serve as estimates of the variances exhibited with the two populations.

The criteria for evaluating the null and the alternate hypothesis are identical to those specified previously. Specifically, suppose that the alternate hypotheses is

$$H_a: \mu_1 - \mu_2 > 0$$

The corresponding null hypothesis is rejected in favor of the alternate if the calculated value of t exceeds the critical value represented by t_α that corresponds to $n_1 + n_2 - 2$ degrees of freedom. Otherwise, we accept the null hypotheses or reserve judgment.

Suppose that the alternate hypothesis is expressed as

$$H_a: \mu_1 - \mu_2 < 0$$

If the calculated value of t is less than $-t_\alpha$ for $n_1 + n_2 - 2$ degrees of freedom, the null hypothesis is rejected in favor of the alternate; otherwise, we accept the null hypothesis or reserve judgment. As indicated, the degrees of freedom usually are determined by adjusting the combined sample size (i.e., $n_1 + n_2$) for degrees of freedom sacrificed when a statistic is used as an estimate of a parameter. In this case, we sacrifice one degree of freedom when $\bar{X}_1$ is used to estimate μ_1 and another because $\bar{X}_2$ is used to estimate μ_2.

Equal Variances

The test statistic is expressed as

$$t = (\bar{X}_1 - \bar{X}_2)/SE_{(\bar{X}1-\bar{X}2)}$$

The denominator, represented by $SE_{(\bar{X}1-\bar{X}2)}$, is referred to as the standard error of the difference between two means. The calculation of the standard error of the difference between two means is in turn contingent on the assumption that σ_1^2 is equal to σ_2^2. If the two populations are characterized by the same variance, the property of homoscedasticity is satisfied. *Homoscedasticity* refers to a situation in which two or more variances are equal. If the assumption is satisfied, the standard error of the difference between two means is based on a pooled variance, represented by S_p^2. The pooled variance is usually defined by

$$S_p^2 = ([n_1 - 1]S_1^2 + [n_2 - 1]S_2^2)/(n_1 + n_2 - 2)$$

When calculating S_p^2, it is important to note that n_1 is the size of the sample selected from the first population; n_2 is the size of the sample from the second population, and S_1^2 and S_2^2 are the variances derived from each of the two samples. If we conclude that the variances of the two populations are equal, the test statistic is given by

$$t = (\bar{X}_1 - \bar{X}_2)/(S_p^2\,[1/n_1 + 1/n_2])^{1/2} \qquad \text{(Equation 6.9)}$$

The denominator of the t ratio measures chance variation in the difference between means.

Before using Equation 6.9, the assumption of equal variances must be examined. Perhaps the simplest approach is to rely on the F distribution. The F distribution is based on the ratio S_1^2/S_2^2, given that S_1^2 exceeds S_2^2, or S_2^2 / S_1^2, assuming that S_2^2 is greater than S_1^2. The probability distribution for F assumes that

1. Two random samples are selected from normally distributed populations
2. The variances of the two populations are equal (i.e., homoscedastic)
3. The sample variances S_1^2 and S_2^2 are unbiased or accurate estimates of $\sigma_1{}^2$ and σ_2^2, respectively
4. F is defined by S_1^2/S_2^2 or S_2^2/S_1^2, where the larger of the two variances appears in the numerator

F is a family of probability distributions, each defined by the number of degrees of freedom in the numerator and the number of degrees of freedom in the denominator. If n_1 corresponds to the size of sample 1 and n_2 corresponds to the size of sample 2, the corresponding degrees of freedom are $n_1 - 1$ and $n_2 - 1$, respectively.

When examining the assumption that the variances are equal, we form a null hypothesis as follows:

$$H_o\!: \sigma_1^2 - \sigma_2^2 = 0$$

If the null hypothesis is true, the ratio σ_1^2/σ_2^2 is one, and as a result, the ratio S_1^2/S_2^2 will be relatively small. In contrast, the alternate hypothesis, represented by

$$H_a: \sigma_1^2 - \sigma_2^2 \neq 0$$

implies that the variances are unequal. Thus, the ratio S_1^2/S_2^2 or S_2^2/S_1^2 will be greater than one and large. In this case, the test statistic is given by

$$F = S_1^2/S_2^2 \qquad \text{(Equation 6.10.1)}$$

or

$$F = S_2^2/S_1^2 \qquad \text{(Equation 6.10.2)}$$

where the larger of the two sample variances appears in the numerator.

We require a criterion that enables us to decide whether the variances are equal or unequal. Specifically, we rely on the F distribution and related critical values. In Figure 6.10, the critical value of F_α divides the distribution into two regions. Specifically, if the null hypothesis is correct, the probability of obtaining a calculated value F that exceeds the critical value F_α is α or less. Thus, if the calculated value of F exceeds the critical value, we are forced to reject the null hypothesis and the presumption that the variances are equal. In contrast, if the calculated value of F is less than or equal to the critical value, we are unable to reject the null hypothesis and conclude that the variances are equal or homoscedastic.

For example, suppose that we selected 21 observations from the first population and obtained a variance of 10. After selecting 20 observations from the second population, we obtained a sample variance of 4. The calculated value of F is given by the ratio 10/4 or 2.5. The critical values of F when we let α equal 0.05 and 0.01, respectively, are listed in Tables D.3 and D.4. In the example, 20 degrees of freedom are assigned to the numerator and 19 degrees of freedom to the denominator. If we wish to be 95% certain of avoiding a Type I error, the critical value of F is 2.16. Comparing the calculated value of F (2.5) with the critical value (2.16), we are forced to reject the null hypothesis and conclude that the variances are unequal.

An examination of the difference between two means might be illustrated as follows. Suppose that the administrator believes that the use of urine analyses is greater among mothers who experience a caesarean delivery than among their counterparts who deliver vaginally. The following information was assembled to assess the situation:

Caesarean Delivery (Sample 1)	Vaginal Delivery (Sample 2)
n = 10	n = 10
$S_1^2 = 4.9$	$S_2^2 = 2.04$
$\bar{X}_1 = 5.3$	$\bar{X}_2 = 3.6$

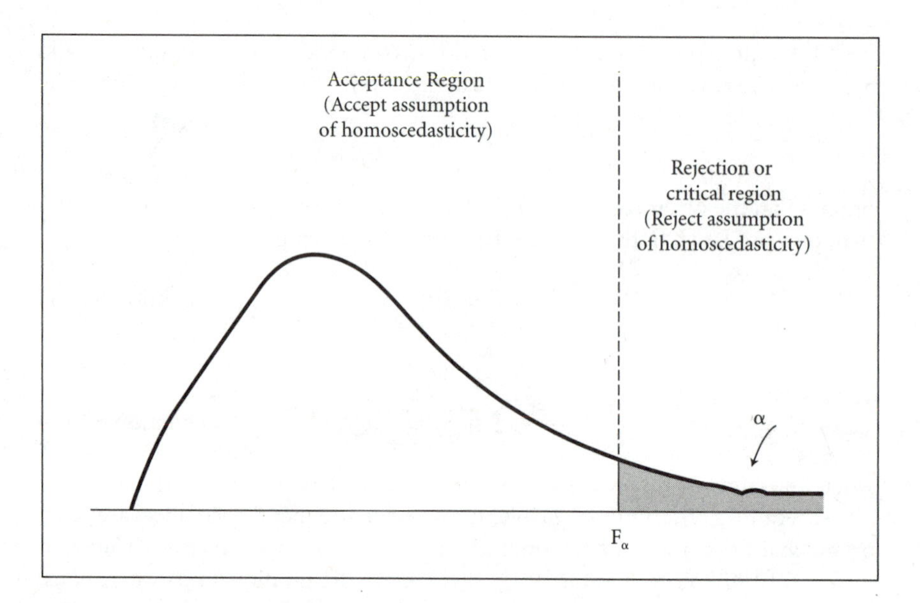

Figure 6.10 **The F Distribution and the Critical Value**

The first step is to examine the assumption that the two variances are equal in contrast with the possibility that they are unequal. The calculated value of F is given by

$$F = 4.9/2.04$$

or approximately 2.40. If α equals 0.05, the critical value of F for 9 degrees of freedom in the numerator and 9 degrees of freedom in the denominator is 3.18. Recognizing that the calculated value of F (2.4) is less than the critical value, we are unable to reject the presumption of homoscedasticity and conclude that the variances are equal.

As mentioned previously, the null and alternate hypotheses about the mean use of urine analyses must be established. Specifically, we establish the null hypothesis as follows:

$$H_0: \mu_1 - \mu_2 = 0$$

If the administrator believes that the use of urine analyses is greater among mothers experiencing a caesarean delivery, the alternate hypothesis is expressed as

$$H_a: \mu_1 - \mu_2 > 0$$

If the variances are equal, we next calculate the pooled variance as follows:

$$S_p^2 = (9 * 4.9 + 9 * 2.04)/18$$

After performing the calculations, we find that the pooled variance is approximately 3.47, suggesting that the standard error of the difference between two means is

$$SE_{(X1-X2)} = [3.47(1/10 + 1/10)]^{0.5}$$

or approximately 0.83. These results allow us to form the test statistic

$$t = (5.3 - 3.6)/0.83$$

or approximately 2.04. The critical value of $t_{0.05,\,8}$ is 1.73, a value that is less than the value of the test statistic. In this case, we are forced to reject the null hypothesis, recognizing that the probability of committing a Type I error is 0.05 or less, and conclude that mothers who experience a caesarean delivery use significantly more urine analyses than those who deliver vaginally.

Unequal Variances

If sample variances are unequal or heteroscedastic, the standard error of the difference between two means may be approximated by

$$SE_{(\bar{X}1-\bar{X}2)} = (S_1^2/n_1 + S_2^2/n_2)^{1/2}$$

The test statistic is a t ratio of the general form

$$t = (\bar{X}_1 - \bar{X}_2)/(S_1^2/n_1 + S_2^2/n_2)^{1/2} \qquad \text{(Equation 6.11)}$$

The contrast $\bar{X}_1 - \bar{X}_2$ is an estimate of $\mu_1 - \mu_2$, and the test statistic is interpreted as described previously.

Using Equation 6.11, suppose that our organization purchases supplies from two vendors, A and B, and that we are interested in the lapse of time between placing and receiving an order. Focusing on supplier A, assume that on 11 occasions, the average lapse of time between placing and receiving an order was 15 days and that the standard deviation was 5 days. With supplier B, suppose that on 16 occasions the average lapse of time between placing and receiving an order was 12 days and that the standard deviation was 2 days.

Similar to the discussion presented in the previous section, the first task of the administrator is to examine the null hypothesis that is specified as follows:

$$H_o: \sigma_1^2 - \sigma_2^2 = 0$$

The alternate hypothesis is that the two variances are unequal as indicated by

$$H_a: \sigma_1^2 - \sigma_2^2 \neq 0$$

We examine the assumption of homoscedasticity by constructing the F ratio

$$F = 5^2/2^2$$

If $\alpha = 0.05$, we find that the calculated value of F (i.e., 6.25) is greater than the critical value of F (i.e., 2.54). Thus, we must reject the null hypothesis and conclude that the variances are unequal.

The second task is to examine the null hypothesis concerning the difference between the two means. In this case, the null hypothesis might be expressed as

$$H_o: \mu_1 - \mu_2 = 0$$

whereas the alternate hypothesis is given by

$$H_a: \mu_1 - \mu_2 \neq 0$$

Based on the results of our sample, the test statistic is

$$t = (15 - 12)/[5^2/11 + 2^2/16]^{0.5}$$

or approximately 1.89. Because the value of the test statistic, 1.89, is less than the critical value of $t_{0.05,\,25}$ (i.e., 2.06), we are unable to reject the null hypothesis and conclude that the difference in the lapse of time between placing and receiving an order from the two suppliers is not significant.

The Use of Excel to Perform the Calculations[R]

As indicated previously here, the calculations required to examine assumptions concerning the difference between two means are somewhat excessive. However, after entering the basic data, Excel performs the analysis with ease and precision.

Limited to caesarean deliveries, suppose that we are interested in the potential difference in the length of stay associated with commercially insured patients and Medicaid beneficiaries. In this case, the null and alternate hypotheses might be expressed as

$$H_o: \mu_1 - \mu_2 = 0$$
$$H_a: \mu_1 - \mu_2 \neq 0$$

Suppose also that we selected 20 recent mothers whose care was financed by the Medicaid program and 21 mothers who were commercially insured. In Exhibit 6.3, the data depict the lengths of stays by members of these two groups. The DESCRIPTIVE Function indicated that the variances in the length of stay by the

Exhibit 6.3 The Difference Between Two Means: Equal Variances

Part A: The Data

Observation	Length of Stay Commercial	Length of Stay Medicaid
1	7	6
2	5	4
3	3	7
4	9	8
5	11	9
6	7	4
7	8	3
8	4	6
9	6	8
10	9	7
11	10	8
12	10	9
13	5	3
14	5	4
15	4	5
16	7	6
17	9	8
18	8	9
19	11	10
20	12	11
21	9	

Part B: The F-Test

F-Test Two-Sample for Variances

	Variable 1	Variable 2
Mean	7.571428571	6.75
Variance	6.657142857	5.565789474
Observations	21	20
df	20	19
F	1.196082405	
P(F ≤ f) one-tail	0.349852424	
F Critical one-tail	2.155495338	

Part C: The Analysis

t-Test: Two-Sample Assuming Equal Variances

	Variable 1	Variable 2
Mean	7.571428571	6.75
Variance	6.657142857	5.565789474
Observations	21	20
Pooled Variance	6.125457875	
Hypothesized Mean Difference	0	
df	39	
t Stat	1.062265906	
P(T ≤ t) one-tail	0.1473244	
t Critical one-tail	1.684875315	
P(T ≤ t) two-tail	0.2946488	
t Critical two-tail	2.022688932	

commercially insured and Medicaid recipients were approximately 6.66 and 5.57 days, respectively. The F ratio is

$$F = 6.66/5.57$$

or approximately 1.20. In Table D.3, the critical value of F for 20 degrees of freedom in the numerator and 19 degrees in the denominator is 2.16. Because the calculated value of F is less than the critical value, we are unable to reject the assumption of homoscedasticity and conclude that the variances are equal.

Excel can be used to examine the assumption that the two variances are equal or homoscedastic. In Part B of Exhibit 6.3, the previously described analysis might be performed by

1. Selecting the "DATA ANALYSIS" function
2. Selecting the "F-Test Two Sample Variances" function
3. Identifying the field in which the data about the lengths of stay experienced by commercially insured patients is located (i.e., cell B9 to B29)
4. Identifying the field in which the lengths of stay experienced by Medicaid patients is located (i.e., cells C9 to C28)
5. Identifying the field in which the results appear (i.e., cell A33)
6. Selecting "OK"

Part B of Exhibit 6.3 shows the results of the F test. As before, the calculated value of F is approximately 1.20, a value that is less than the critical value of F of approximately 2.16. If the assumption of homoscedasticity is satisfied, the probability of obtaining a calculated value of F equal to 1.20 is approximately 0.35, a value that is greater than 0.05. Excel's results force us to accept the assumption that the two variances are equal.

Based on these findings, we employ Excel to assess the difference in use. If $\alpha = 0.05$, the statistical results in Part C of Exhibit 6.3 were obtained by

1. Selecting the "DATA ANALYSIS" function
2. Selecting the "t-TEST: TWO SAMPLE ASSUMING EQUAL VARIANCES" function
3. Identifying the field in which the data are located
4. Identifying the field in which the results will appear
5. Selecting "OK"

A blank appearing as the expected difference between the two means automatically results in a value of zero.

The results indicate that the difference between the average lengths of stay is not statistically significant. In particular, the calculated value of t (approximately

1.06) is clearly less than the critical value of 2.02 for a nondirectional or two-sided alternative. If the two variances are equal, the probability of obtaining a calculated value of t equal to 1.06 is approximately 0.29, a value that is clearly greater than the probability of committing a Type I error (i.e., 0.05). Both sets of findings indicate that we are unable to reject the null hypothesis, and as a consequence, we conclude that the two groups experienced a similar length of stay.

Consider next a situation in which the variances are unequal or heteroscedastic. For example, suppose that we are interested in the difference in the length of delay in transferring African American and white patients to a postdischarge source of care, such as a nursing home. Based on the date that the individual was prepared for discharge, the data listed in columns 2 and 3 of Part A of Exhibit 6.4 measure the days of delay in discharge for each patient.

The first task is to examine the proposition that the two variances are equal. As described previously, the "F-Test Two Sample or, for Variances" function was used to examine the assumption that the two variances are equal. In Part B of Exhibit 6.4, the calculated value of F was equal to approximately 14.25 and exceeded the critical value of F of approximately 2.69. If the variances are equal, the chance of obtaining a calculated value of F equal to 14.25 is 0.00003, a probability that is much less than 0.05. Thus, the findings in Part B of Exhibit 6.4 force us to reject the assumption of homoscedasticity and conclude that the variances are unequal or heteroscedastic.

Based on these results, we analyze the difference between the two means by

1. Selecting "t-TEST: TWO SAMPLE ASSUMING UNEQUAL VARIANCES" function
2. Identifying the fields in which the two sets of data appear
3. Identifying the area in which the results will appear
4. Selecting "OK"

Unlike the situation in which the two variances are equal, the results in Part C of Exhibit 6.4 suggest that no pooled variance is reported.

Excel's results are interpreted as described throughout this section. In particular, the results indicate that the calculated value for the t ratio was approximately 9.39 and greatly exceeded the critical value of either 1.76 or 2.03. As before, the null hypothesis specifies that there is no difference between the mean delays experienced by the two groups. If the null hypothesis is correct, the probability of obtaining a calculated value of t equal to 9.39 is approximately 0.0000001, a value that is much less than the probability of committing a Type I error. As a consequence, we are forced to reject the null hypothesis in favor of the alternate that asserts the two means differ significantly. Because of the calculated value of t, we are forced to conclude that the delay in discharging African Americans is greater than that experienced by their white counterparts. In turn, these results may identify a potential weakness and a need to improve discharge planning in the health service organization.

Exhibit 6.4 **The Difference Between Two Means: The Case of Unequal Variances**

Part A: The Data

Patient	African Americans	Whites
1	18	12
2	19	12
3	20	13
4	21	14
5	23	15
6	24	13
7	26	14
8	23	13
9	27	13
10	27	14
11	28	15
12	29	14
13	30	15

Part B: The F-Test

F-Test Two-Sample for Variances

	Variable 1	Variable 2
Mean	24.23076923	13.61538462
Variance	15.52564103	1.08974359
Observations	13	13
df	12	12
F	14.24705882	
P(F ≤ f) one-tail	2.75557E-05	
F Critical one-tail	2.686633138	

Part C: The Analysis

t-Test: Two-Sample Assuming Unequal Variances

	Variable 1	Variable 2
Mean	24.23076923	13.61538462
Variance	15.52564103	1.08974359
Observations	13	13
Hypothesized Mean Difference	0	
df	14	
t Stat	9.389710681	
P(T ≤ t) one-tail	1.013E-07	
t Critical one-tail	1.76130925	
P(T ≤ t) two-tail	2.02601E-07	
t Critical two-tail	2.144788596	

Sample Size: Precision of the Estimate[O]

In this section, we use the central limit theorem and the sampling distribution of the mean to determine the sample size that is required to achieve a preferred or desired degree of precision when estimating the mean of the population with the mean derived from a sample. Suppose that we wish to assert with a probability of $1 - \alpha$ that the error will be less than $\bar{X} - \mu$. Let E correspond to the maximum error, represented by $\bar{X} - \mu$ that we are prepared to tolerate. After substituting $Z_{\alpha/2}$ for Z and E for $\bar{X} - \mu$, we rely on the standard normal deviate

$$Z = (\bar{X} - \mu)/S/\sqrt{n}$$

to form

$$Z_{\alpha/2} = E/S/\sqrt{n}$$

A slight algebraic rearrangement yields

$$n = (Z_{\alpha/2} \times S/E)^2 \qquad \text{(Equation 6.12)}$$

Suppose that we wish to be 98% certain that the maximum error in the average length of stay is 0.5 days and that based on previous experience we believe that the standard deviation is 3 days. As indicated previously, the standard normal deviate corresponding to the probability of 0.98 is 2.33. These data indicate that the required sample size is

$$n = (2.33 \times 3/0.5)^2$$

or approximately 195 hospital episodes. Thus, we may be 98% certain that with a sample size of $n = 195$, the mean derived from sample data will differ from the population mean by no more than 0.5 days.

Sample Size: Type I and Type II Errors[O]

Thus far, the discussion has focused on Type I errors and the likelihood of rejecting a true null hypothesis. However, Type II errors and the related potential for accepting a false null hypothesis have received little or no attention. This section focuses on the selection of an appropriate sample size, n, that allows the analyst to control the probability of committing a Type I error, represented as before by α, and the likelihood of committing a Type II error, which we represent by the Greek letter β (beta).

For example, suppose that we are interested in evaluating the length of time required to perform a given operative procedure. Suppose also that we believe the mean time, represented by μ_o, is 45 minutes and that we let $\alpha = 0.01$. In Figure 6.11, the area to the right of 2.33 corresponds to the probability of committing a Type I error. The sample mean that corresponds to a standard normal deviate of 2.33 is represented by $\overline{X}_d$ in Figure 6.11. If the sample yields a mean greater than $\overline{X}_d$ or a test statistic that is greater than 2.33, we are forced to reject the null hypothesis in favor of the alternate, recognizing that the probability of committing a Type I error is 0.01 or less.

The second distribution shown in the figure resides to the right of the first. In this case, the second of the two distributions represents a situation in which we wish to avoid failing to detect the fact that the true mean, represented by μ_a, is, for example, 52 minutes. If the sample yields a mean that is less than $\overline{X}_d$, we are unable to reject the null hypothesis and are at risk of accepting a false hypothesis. A failure to recognize that the true mean is μ_a, or 52 minutes, constitutes a Type II error. In the example, we assume that we wish to be 90% certain of avoiding a Type II error. As a consequence, we assign a value of 0.10 to β, implying that the corresponding value of the standard normal deviate is -1.28.

Based on Figure 6.11, the sample size that limits the risks of committing a Type I error (0.01) and the probability of committing a Type II error (0.10) can be de-

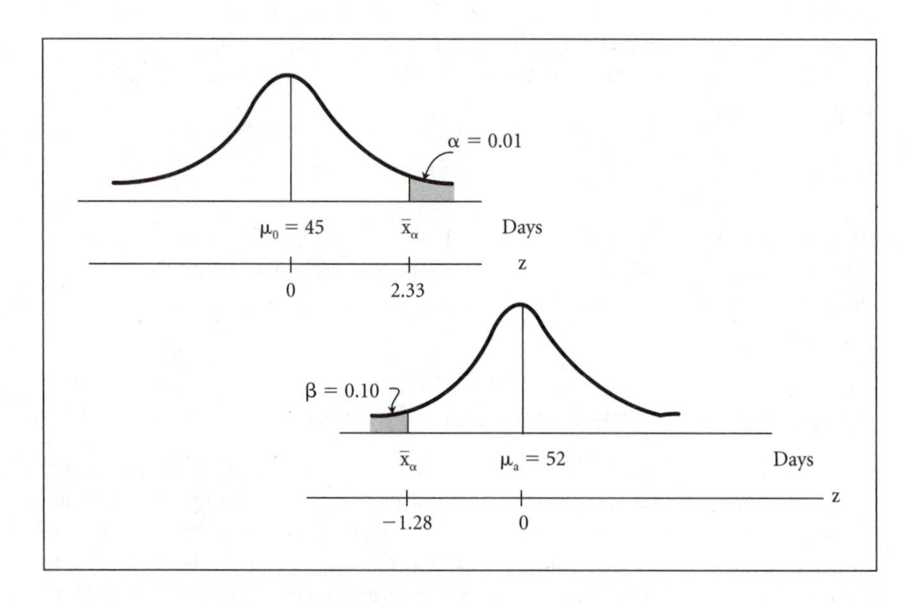

Figure 6.11 **Sample Size Required to Control Probabilities of a Type I and Type II Error**

rived. The length of the interval from μ_a to μ_o corresponds to the distance that represents the potential to commit both types of errors and may be expressed by

$$\mu_a - \mu_o = 52 - 45$$

or 7 minutes. We now express the distance, expressed in minutes, as standard normal deviates. Relying on the central limit theorem, we can easily show that

$$\bar{X}_d - \mu_a = -1.28(\sigma/\sqrt{n}) \qquad \text{(Equation 6.13.1)}$$

Also

$$\bar{X}_d - \mu_o = 2.33(\sigma/\sqrt{n}) \qquad \text{(Equation 6.13.2)}$$

Because we are interested in the distance $\mu_a - \mu_o$, we employ absolute values and, after a slight rearrangement, Equations 6.13.1 and 6.13.2 may be used to obtain

$$|\mu_a - \mu_o| = (|1.28| + |2.33|)\,(\sigma/\sqrt{n}) \qquad \text{(Equation 6.13.3)}$$

These results indicate that the distance represented by $|\mu_a - \mu_o|$ is equal to $3.61(\sigma/\sqrt{n})$ minutes. Equation 6.13.3 might be expressed as follows:

$$|\mu_a - \mu_o| = (|Z_a| + |Z_o|)\,(\sigma/\sqrt{n}) \qquad \text{(Equation 6.14)}$$

In Equation 6.14, $|Z_a|$ is the absolute value of the standard normal deviate that corresponds to the probability of committing a Type II error, whereas $|Z_o|$ is the standard normal deviate that corresponds to the likelihood of committing a Type I error. After squaring all terms and rearranging slightly, we obtain

$$n = [\sigma^2(|Z_a| + |Z_o|)^2/(|\mu_a - \mu_o|)^2 \qquad \text{(Equation 6.15)}$$

For example, suppose that the standard deviation is 12 minutes and that we wish to limit the values of α and β to 0.01 and 0.10, respectively. The corresponding sample size that is required in this case is obtained by

$$n = [(12)^2\,(1.28 + 2.33)^2]/(7)^2$$

After performing the calculations, the results indicate that a sample of 38 procedures is required to control the probabilities of committing Type I and Type II errors.

Exercises

1. To estimate the time required to provide a given laboratory procedure, suppose that we measured the amount of time required when the service was provided on 60 occasions. Based on this sample, we obtained a mean of 20.32 minutes and a standard deviation of 3.82 minutes. What can we say with a probability of 0.95 about the size of the error when we use 20.32 minutes as an estimate of the true average time required to provide the procedure? (Hint: $\bar{X} - \mu = Z_{\alpha/2} [S/\sqrt{n}]$)
2. Use the data in Exercise 1 to construct a 98% confidence interval.
3. Based on a sample of 90 patients, suppose that we found that the average cost of diagnosing and treating an upper respiratory infection is $490 with a standard deviation of $50. Use these data to construct a 95% confidence interval. What can be said with a probability of 0.99 about the possible size of the error that results if we use $490 as an estimate of the true average cost of treating an upper respiratory infection? (Hint: $\bar{X} - \mu = Z_{\alpha/2} [S/\sqrt{n}]$)
4. Our health organization is interested in estimating the average value of outstanding accounts receivable. After selecting a sample of 100 accounts, suppose that the mean was $120 and the standard deviation was $40. Use these data to construct a 98% confidence interval.
5. Suppose that we know that the average length of stay for 100 patients was 3.5 days and that the standard deviation was 2.5 days. Construct a 95% confidence interval for the true mean length of stay.
6. In a study of 10 patients treated for a kidney infection, the following data refer to the use of urinary analysis.

   1, 2, 5, 7, 3, 1, 4, 3, 6, 4

   Use these data to construct a 99% confidence interval for the true mean use of the procedure.
7. In a study of the cost per case of treating patients admitted with a disease of the digestive system, the following data were obtained:

   $5,000, $5,500, $9,000, $8,000, $10,500, $11,000, $490

   Use these data to construct a 98% confidence interval for the true mean cost per case.
8. Suppose that we selected 12 outstanding accounts and measured the time that was required to convert each into cash after the first billing. The results in days are as follows:

   120, 50, 40, 180, 230, 250, 30, 60, 70, 180, 270, 190

   Use these data to construct a 98% confidence interval for the true mean time required to transform accounts into cash after the first billing.

9. Suppose that the data in Exercise 8 were collected after the introduction of a new collection method. Before the use of the new method, the average time required to transform an account into cash was 230 days. If $\alpha = 0.05$, determine whether the new procedure was successful in reducing the collection period.
10. Suppose that a labor union claims that a given procedure requires 20 minutes to perform. To evaluate this, suppose that we measured the amount of time required to complete the procedure on each of 36 occasions.

    12, 15, 18, 14, 19, 21, 16, 17, 18, 13, 19, 21, 22, 15, 16, 17, 18, 22

    23, 14, 16, 18, 23, 13, 16, 18, 19, 15, 13, 21, 23, 14, 15, 16, 17, 21

    Assuming we wish to be 95% certain of avoiding a Type I error, use these data to evaluate the union's claim.
11. Suppose that a health plan asserts that a patient hospitalized with coronary heart disease requires no more than 6.5 days of hospital care. However, we believe that a stay of 6.5 days is too low. To examine the claim of the health plan, assume further that we collected data depicting the lengths of stay of 40 patients who were hospitalized recently with coronary heart disease. The results of the sample are as follows:

    5, 8, 9, 12, 7, 9, 10, 11, 4, 7, 8, 5, 8, 13, 11, 10, 6, 5, 8, 9,

    5, 12, 7, 9, 4, 8, 7, 7, 11, 5, 8, 10, 5, 8, 2, 11, 3, 6, 8, 7

    If $\alpha = 0.05$, use these data to evaluate the claim by the health plan.
12. Suppose that our multi-institutional arrangement serves a well-defined population and operates two clinics that serve two separate market or service areas. We believe that distance keeps people from seeking care and are concerned that, on average, the distance traveled from the patient's residence to Clinic A exceeds that of Clinic B. To assess the existence of a potential problem, suppose that we surveyed 25 individuals in each market and obtained information describing the miles to the clinic

    A: 4, 7, 10, 13, 21, 14, 1, 2, 6, 7, 1, 4, 2, 14, 18, 2, 3, 10, 2, 7, 11, 4, 6, 6, 3

    B: 2, 4, 1, 6, 7, 10, 3, 2, 5, 9, 11, 13, 2, 1, 4, 6, 8, 8, 9, 3, 2, 5, 1, 6, 7

    If we wish to be 95% certain of avoiding a Type I error, use these data to examine differences in the average distance traveled to the two clinics.
13. Suppose that we wish to evaluate the performance of two technicians and measure the amount of time each required to perform a given procedure on 20 different occasions. The results of the two samples are as follows:

    Technician 1: 30, 31, 29, 32, 30, 29, 28, 27, 29, 30, 31, 29, 28, 30, 31, 30, 29, 29, 32, 31

    Technician 2: 28, 29, 29, 32, 33, 28, 27, 28, 29, 30, 27, 30, 28, 29, 27, 27, 29, 30, 27, 28

If we wish to be 99% confident of avoiding a Type I error, use these data to evaluate the performance of the two technicians.

14. Suppose that our institution is concerned about the delay in transferring older patients to long-term care after hospitalization. In particular, we are concerned that the delay in transfer from Memorial Hospital is longer than the delay in discharge from Hill Street Hospital. To evaluate our concerns, we randomly selected 15 recent discharges from each hospital and measured, in days, the length of delay in transferring each to a source of long-term care. The results of the two samples are as follows:

    Memorial: 15, 13, 16, 19, 10, 22, 23, 19, 18, 17, 15, 19, 16, 12, 8

    Hill Street: 10, 13, 16, 18, 12, 9, 18, 15, 19, 11, 13, 9, 15, 18, 20

    If $\alpha = 0.05$, use these data to evaluate the difference in the delay in transfer from the two hospitals.
15. Suppose that we wish to be 95% sure that the maximum error in the average number of laboratory procedures per case is no more than 0.5. If the standard deviation is 12 procedures per patient, what is the required sample size?
16. Assume that we are interested in estimating the true length of stay required by patients with an endocrine system disease. Based on previous experience, we believe the mean length of stay is 5.2 days and fear that we will fail to detect the true mean of 6.1 days. If the standard deviation is 1.2 days, what sample size is required to avoid a Type I error with a probability of 0.95 and a Type II error with a probability of 0.90?

CHAPTER 7

Inferences Concerning the Proportion[R]

OBJECTIVES

1. Distinguish between a proportion that is derived from a sample and the proportion of the corresponding universe.
2. Construct a confidence interval for the population proportion.
3. Examine a postulated value of the population proportion.
4. Examine the difference between two proportions.
5. Use Excel and χ^2 to examine differences among three or more proportions.
6. Use Excel and χ^2 to examine the relationship of one variable to another.

This chapter focuses on the techniques that are used to develop estimates and inferences about the proportion. We previously defined probability as a relative frequency, a proportion, or a percentage. On the other hand, a percentage is a proportion or a relative frequency that has been multiplied by 100. Probability is also the percentage of occasions that an event will occur in the long run.

A proportion or relative frequency is similar to the arithmetic mean. For example, assume that we selected 10 results from a given laboratory procedure and evaluated each for precision. Zero was assigned to each result that was correct, and one was assigned if the test yielded a false-positive or false-negative result. Suppose also that six of the procedures yielded defective results and that the remaining four were correct. These findings are shown as

$$x = \{1, 1, 1, 1, 1, 1, 0, 0, 0, 0\}$$

The mean of six ones and four zeros is 6/10 or 0.6, and after multiplying it by 100, it is 60%. Thus, the proportion is simply a variant of the arithmetic mean in which the value of a random variable is either zero or one. These observations suggest that with a slight modification the methods described in the previous chapter might be applied to proportions. The methods of deriving estimates and inferences concerning the arithmetic mean are basically the same as those that are applied to the proportion.

Our discussion of the sampling distribution of the mean also applies to the proportion. If all possible random samples were selected from a population, the mean of the sample proportions would equal the proportion of the population from which the samples were chosen. In the following, p represents the proportion of items from a sample that exhibits a characteristic of interest. The proportion of the population that exhibits the attribute of interest is designated by the Greek letter π (Pi). We also represent the proportion of observations in the sample and the population that fails to exhibit the characteristic of interest by $1-p$ and $1-\pi$, respectively.

Estimation of the Population Proportion, π

In Chapter 6, we use $\bar{X}$ as a point estimate of μ. We also employ p as a point estimate of π and assume that

1. The variable of interest is binary or dichotomous.
2. Trials are independent.
3. The probability that the event will occur remains constant from trial to trial.

These conditions must be satisfied when applying the binomial probability distribution. After adopting the previously introduced notation, we see that the sampling distribution of the frequencies on which the methods are based is the binomial probability distribution with a mean of

$$\mu = n\pi \qquad \text{(Equation 7.1)}$$

and a standard deviation of

$$\sigma = [n\pi(1-\pi)]^{1/2} \qquad \text{(Equation 7.2)}$$

In the following, x represents the number of items that exhibit the characteristic of interest in a sample of size n. If n is large and π is close to neither zero nor one, the binomial probability distribution may be approximated by the standard normal curve. Previously, we defined the standard normal deviate Z by

$$Z = x - \mu/\sigma$$

After substituting $n\pi$ for μ and $[n\pi(1-\pi)]^{1/2}$ for σ, we obtain

$$Z = (x - n\pi)/[n\pi(1-\pi)]^{1/2} \qquad \text{(Equation 7.3)}$$

which is a normally distributed random variable. In Figure 7.1, with a probability of $1-\alpha$, the standard normal deviate ranges from $-Z_{\alpha/2}$ to $Z_{\alpha/2}$. The expression

$$-Z_{\alpha/2} \leq Z \leq Z_{\alpha/2}$$

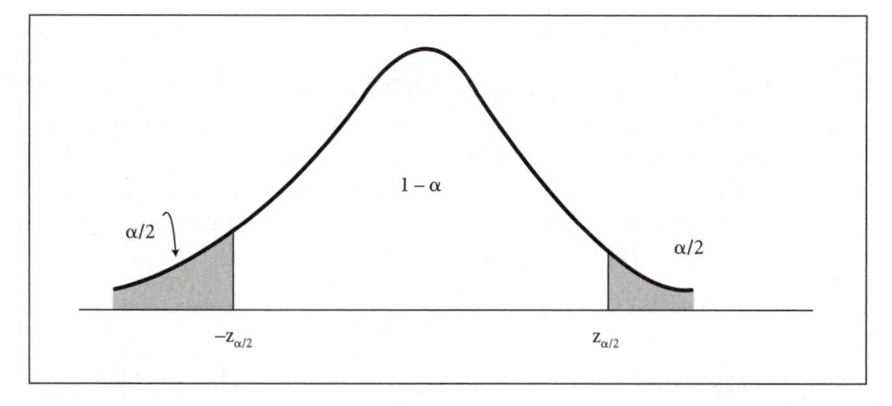

Figure 7.1 **The 1 – α Confidence Interval**

is satisfied with a probability of 1 − α. After substituting the right-hand side of Equation 7.3 for Z, we obtain

$$-Z_{\alpha/2} \leq (x - n\pi)/[n\pi(1 - \pi)]^{1/2} \leq Z_{\alpha/2} \qquad \text{(Equation 7.4)}$$

In general, the value of the population proportion is unknown, and we base our estimate of the population proportion, π, on sample data. Our objective is to construct an interval estimate for the true value of the population proportion. A slight algebraic manipulation of Equation 7.4 yields

$$x/n - Z_{\alpha/2}[\pi(1 - \pi)/n]^{1/2} \leq \pi \leq x/n + Z_{\alpha/2}[\pi(1 - \pi)/n]^{1/2} \qquad \text{(Equation 7.5.1)}$$

where $[\pi(1-\pi)/n]^{1/2}$ is the standard error of the proportion, represented by SE (π). *Similar to the standard error of the mean, the standard error of the proportion is the standard deviation of the sampling distribution of sample proportions.* Although π appears in the middle of Equation 7.4, the upper and lower limits of the interval also contain the parameter that we wish to estimate; p or x/n is an unbiased estimate of π, and we may thus substitute the relative frequency x/n or the sample proportion for π. After substituting p for π in the standard error of the proportion, we obtain

$$SE(\pi) = [p(1 - p)/n]^{1/2} \qquad \text{(Equation 7.5.2)}$$

The 1 − α confidence interval for π may be expressed as

$$p - Z_{\alpha/2}\,[SE(\pi)] < \pi < p + Z_{\alpha/2}\,[SE(\pi)] \qquad \text{(Equation 7.6)}$$

The expression $p - Z_{\alpha/2}\,[SE(\pi)]$ is the lower limit of the 1 − α confidence interval, whereas $p + Z_{\alpha/2}\,[SE(\pi)]$ is the upper limit of the confidence interval.

To show the construction of a $1 - \alpha$ confidence interval for π, suppose that the administrator is interested in the proportion of older patients whose hospital stay is more than 5 days. Limited to a given diagnosis, suppose also that the administrator wished to construct a 98% confidence interval, implying that the corresponding standard normal deviate is approximately 2.33. After selecting a sample of 100 discharges, 60 patients experienced a length of stay greater than 5 days. We must first calculate the standard error of the proportion in accordance with Equation 7.5 and obtain

$$SE(\pi) = [(0.6)(0.4)/100]^{1/2}$$

or approximately 0.05. Thus, the 98% confidence interval is obtained by

$$0.6 \pm 2.33\ (0.05)$$

After completing the required calculations, with a probability of 0.98,

$$0.48 < \pi < 0.72$$

The resulting confidence interval indicates that between 48% and 72% of the older patients assigned to the diagnosis had a stay that was more than 5 days.

Relative frequencies or probabilities must range from 0 to 1. The lower limit of the confidence interval can never be less than zero, and the upper limit may not exceed one. Thus, the maximum allowable value for the upper limit is one, and the minimum allowable value for the lower limit is zero.

Tests of Significance: Presumed Values of the True Proportion

The administrator may be interested in examining claims, assertions, or hypotheses about a presumed value of π (as discussed in Chapter 6). For example, suppose that an expert tells us that the number of false negatives and false positives associated with a given procedure should not exceed 10%. In this case, a defective rate of greater than 0.10 might indicate an organizational weakness or an operational problem requiring the development and implementation of a remedial plan. Also, the administrator might want to examine the suggestion that no less than 80% of outstanding accounts receivable should result in a cash receipt or no more than 15% of all fatalities should result from nosocomial infections or other patient errors. In each of these cases, an assumed value of the true or population proportion needs to be evaluated.

As in our discussion of inferences concerning the mean, the probability of committing a Type I error, the null hypothesis and the alternate hypothesis must be specified. We let π_o represent the assumed or presumed value that is associated with the null hypothesis, and as mentioned before, the population proportion is represented by π. The three sets of null and alternate hypotheses might be summarized as follows:

1. $H_o: \pi - \pi_o \geq 0$
   $H_a: \pi - \pi_o < 0$
2. $H_o: \pi - \pi_o \leq 0$
   $H_a: \pi - \pi_o > 0$
3. $H_o: \pi - \pi_o = 0$
   $H_a: \pi - \pi_o \neq 0$

In each case, the structures of the null and alternate hypotheses are identical to those presented in Chapter 6. As before, the first two sets consist of directional or one-sided alternate hypotheses, whereas the third is a nondirectional or two-sided alternate hypothesis.

When examining the null and alternate hypothesis, we assume that the sample size is large, implying that more than 30 degrees of freedom, represented by $n - 1$, are available for analysis. When examining a null and alternate hypothesis, we approximate the binomial probability distribution by the standard normal distribution, implying that

$$Z = (x - n\pi_o)/[n\pi_o(1 - \pi_o)]^{1/2} \qquad \text{(Equation 7.7)}$$

is normally distributed. In Equation 7.7, we assume that the null hypothesis is correct and let π equal π_o when calculating the mean shown in the numerator and the standard error shown in the denominator. After dividing the numerator and denominator of Equation 7.7 by n, we obtain

$$Z = (x/n - \pi_o)/[\pi_o(1 - \pi_o)/n]^{1/2} \qquad \text{(Equation 7.8)}$$

The ratio x/n in the numerator is the proportion of observations in our sample that exhibits the attribute of interest and represents a point estimate of π, the true proportion. Thus, the contrast represented by $x/n - \pi_o$ forms the basis for evaluating each of the alternate hypotheses summarized previously here.

To illustrate the use of Equation 7.8, suppose that after evaluating the cash received in payment of outstanding accounts receivable the financial officer determines that, if the collection rate is less than 0.75, the ability of the health service organization to honor its obligations is impaired. In this case, let π_o equal 0.75 and form the following null and alternate hypotheses:

$$H_o: \pi - 0.75 \geq 0$$
$$H_a: \pi - 0.75 < 0$$

After selecting a sample of 100 outstanding accounts, we found that 65 resulted in a full payment and that 45 were uncollectible. The point estimate of π is 0.65, and as a result, the test statistic is given by

$$Z = (0.65 - 0.75)/[(0.75)(0.25)/100]^{1/2}$$

After performing the calculations, we find that the calculated value of Z is approximately -2.31. If we want to be 95% certain of avoiding a Type I error, the corresponding value of α is 0.05, and the critical value of Z is -1.64. The evaluation of the null and alternate hypotheses requires a comparison of the calculated and critical values of Z. In particular, the calculated value (approximately -2.31) is less than the critical value (-1.64), and as a result, we are forced to reject the null hypothesis and accept the alternate, recognizing that the probability of committing a Type I error is 0.05 or less. These results alert the administrator to the existence of a financial problem or weakness that requires an investigation of credit or collection practices and perhaps the implementation of a remedial policy.

Contrasts Involving Two Proportions

As in Chapter 6, we now consider methods of examining the difference between two proportions. Health administrators are frequently required to determine whether two populations differ with respect to an attribute of interest. For example, suppose that the focus is on a multi-institutional arrangement that consists of several hospitals, outpatient clinics, and long-term care facilities. In such a situation, we might be interested in the difference in

1. The proportion of inpatients admitted to one hospital and the proportion of their counterparts who were admitted to another that require long-term care
2. The proportion of patients with a scheduled appointment at one clinic and the proportion of patients scheduled for a visit at another who fail to appear for their appointments
3. The proportion of patients assigned to one diagnosis and the proportion of patients assigned to another who require 15 or more urine analyses
4. The proportion of men and women whose care is financed by the Medicaid program
5. The proportion of African Americans and Native Americans whose hospital discharge is delayed

In each of these examples, we are interested in the difference in the proportion of observations associated with two populations that exhibit an attribute of interest.

In the following, let π_1 and π_2 correspond to the proportion of two populations that exhibit the characteristic of interest. Furthermore, let p_1 and p_2 represent sample proportions and point estimates of π_1 and π_2, respectively. We employ $p_1 - p_2$ as a point estimate of $\pi_1 - \pi_2$, which allows us to evaluate the statistical significance of the difference between the two proportions. In this case, the use of $p_1 - p_2$ is similar to our previous reliance on $\bar{X}_1 - \bar{X}_2$ to evaluate the difference between the means of two populations. As before, our object is to determine whether an observed difference is statistically significant or attributable to chance variation.

When examining the difference between two proportions, the first step is to specify the null and alternate hypotheses. Adopting the format developed previously, the directional and nondirectional hypotheses are as follows:

1. $H_o: \pi_1 - \pi_2 \leq 0$
   $H_a: \pi_1 - \pi_2 > 0$
2. $H_o: \pi_1 - \pi_2 \geq 0$
   $H_a: \pi_1 - \pi_2 < 0$
3. $H_o: \pi_1 - \pi_2 = 0$
   $H_a: \pi_1 - \pi_2 \neq 0$

The structures of the null and alternate hypotheses listed here are identical to those in Chapter 6.

When examining the null hypothesis regarding the difference between two proportions, we must select two large independent samples from the two populations. In the following, let n_1 represent the size of the sample selected from the first population and n_2 correspond to the sample size selected from the second. In addition, let x_1 represent the number of observations in the first sample that exhibits the characteristic of interest such that x_1/n_1 is the proportion of the observations in first sample that exhibits the characteristic. Similarly, let x_2 correspond to the number of observations in the second sample that exhibits the attribute of interest, and as a consequence, the relative frequency x_2/n_2 is the proportion of items or observations in the second sample that exhibits the characteristic of interest.

Statistical theory allows us to assert that the sampling distribution of the difference between two proportions, represented by $p_1 - p_2$ or $(x_1/n_1) - (x_2/n_2)$, can be approximated by a normal distribution that has a mean of $\pi_1 - \pi_2$ and a standard deviation that is given by

$$SE(\pi_1 - \pi_2) = [\pi_1(1 - \pi_1)/n_1 + \pi_2(1 - \pi_2)/n_2]^{1/2} \quad \text{(Equation 7.9)}$$

In this case, the quantity given by $[\pi_1(1 - \pi_1)/n_1 + \pi_2(1 - \pi_2)/n_2]^{1/2}$ is the *standard error of the difference between two proportions.* Similar to our earlier discussion, the standard error of the difference between two proportions measures the chance variation in differences among proportions.

To illustrate the meaning of the sampling distribution of the distribution of two proportions, suppose that we are interested in the proportion of males in a given population and the proportion of females who visited our outpatient facility in the last year. Suppose also that we selected repeated samples from each group and obtained the difference

$$(x_1/n_1) - (x_2/n_2)$$

for each sample. The difference will likely differ from sample to sample, resulting in an experimental sampling distribution. Without formal derivation, we simply assert that the theoretical sampling distribution of the difference between two proportions is a normal distribution with mean $\pi_1 - \pi_2$ and standard deviation given by $[\pi_1(1 - \pi_1)/n_1 + \pi_2(1 - \pi_2)/n_2]^{1/2}$.

If two large independent samples are selected, we employ the difference represented by $(x_1/n_1) - (x_2/n_2)$ as a point estimate of $\pi_1 - \pi_2$ and define the standard error of the difference between two proportions by

$$\mathrm{SE}(p_1 - p_2) = \{[(x_1 + x_2)/(n_1 + n_2)][1 - (x_1 + x_2)/(n_1 + n_2)(1/n_1 + 1/n_2)]\}^{1/2} \quad \text{(Equation 7.10)}$$

When evaluating the null and alternate hypotheses, we employ a pooled estimate of the common value of π_1 and π_2. We define P^* by

$$P^* = (x_1 + x_2)/(n_1 + n_2)$$

The numerator of P^* is defined by the sum $x_1 + x_2$, which is the combined number of observations in the two samples that exhibit the attribute of interest. The denominator is defined by $(n_1 + n_2)$, which is the size of the combined samples. Thus, $(x_1 + x_2)/(n_1 + n_2)$ is the proportion of observations in both samples that exhibits the attribute of interest. The complement, defined by

$$1 - P^* = 1 - (x_1 + x_2)/(n_1 + n_2)$$

indicates the proportion of observations in both samples that fails to exhibit the attribute of interest. After appropriate substitution, the standard error of the difference between two proportions may be expressed as

$$\mathrm{SE}(p_1 - p_2) = [P^*(1 - P^*)(1/n_1 + 1/n_2)]^{1/2} \quad \text{(Equation 7.11)}$$

The test statistic is given by

$$Z = (x_1/n_1) - (x_2/n_2)/\mathrm{SE}(p_1 - p_2) \quad \text{(Equation 7.12)}$$

which is a random variable that may be approximated by the standard normal distribution.

For example, we return to the problem requiring an evaluation of the difference in the proportion of males and females who visited an outpatient facility during the previous year. Suppose that we wished to be 95% confident of avoiding a Type I error, implying that $\alpha = 0.05$. We also wish to examine the null and alternate hypotheses that are summarized by

$$H_o\colon \pi_1 - \pi_2 = 0$$
$$H_a\colon \pi_1 - \pi_2 \neq 0$$

If the alternate hypothesis is nondirectional or two tailed, the critical value of the standard normal deviate is ± 1.96. After selecting a sample of 100 males and 100 females, assume the following results were obtained:

Males	Females
$x_1 = 27$	$x_2 = 43$
$n_1 = 100$	$n_2 = 100$
$x_1/n_1 = 0.27$	$x_2/n_2 = 0.43$

Based on these data, we find that the common proportion, P*, is given by

$$P^* = (27 + 43)/(100 + 100)$$

or 0.35. Using these results, the standard error of the difference between the two proportions is given by

$$\text{SE}(p_1 - p_2) = [(0.35)(0.65)(1/100 + 1/100)]^{1/2}$$

or approximately 0.07. Thus, the calculated value of the test statistic is obtained by

$$Z = (0.27 - 0.43)/0.07$$

After performing the calculations, we find that the value of the calculated value of Z is approximately -2.29. Because the calculated value of Z is less than -1.96, the critical value, we reject the null hypothesis, accept the alternate, and conclude that a greater proportion of women visited the outpatient facility than men.

In general, the decision rules that accompany directional or one-tailed and nondirectional or two-tailed alternate hypotheses are as follows:

Alternate Hypothesis	Reject H_o
$\pi_1 - \pi_2 > 0$	$Z > Z_\alpha$
$\pi_1 - \pi_2 < 0$	$-Z < -Z_\alpha$
$\pi_1 - \pi_2 \neq 0$	$-Z < -Z_{\alpha/2}$ or $Z > Z_{\alpha/2}$

These rules are identical to those developed previously and may be applied to a statistical assessment of the difference between two proportions.

Test Concerning Multiple Proportions

Although it is useful to examine the difference between two proportions, the health administrator is frequently required to evaluate differences among multiple proportions. In the previous section, we identified two subgroups, males and females, as the focus of analysis. However, it is possible to partition a population into three or more groups. For example, we might be interested in employee satisfaction, grouped by occupational categories such as physicians, nurses, technicians, and support staff. Similarly, we might be interested in the evaluation of care by individuals of different socioeconomic groups or variation in the use of care by individuals whose service is financed by different types of payment. In each of these cases, three or more subgroups are of interest to the analyst.

In general, we presume that the population of interest consists of k subgroups and classify the number of observations in each in terms of the presence or absence of the attribute of interest. For example, we might be interested in patients whose discharge from the hospital to a long-term care facility was delayed versus those individuals who experienced a timely transfer. Thus, the focus is on the presence or absence of a delay in transferring the patient to a source of care after the hospital episode. We also might group patients into k categories that depict the racial status of the patient or the individual's source of insurance coverage.

After the k categories are defined, the analyst can construct a table consisting of two rows, defined by the presence or absence of a delay in discharge, and k columns, each of which corresponds to one of several ethnic backgrounds or one of several sources of insurance coverage. After determining the number of patients or observations in each cell of the table, the analyst is in a position to determine whether the observed distribution of observations is compatible or consistent with a postulated theory or a presumption that is specified by the null hypothesis.

For example, suppose that the administrator is interested in employees' satisfaction with their conditions of employment. Assume that a survey was administered to employees and that in addition to a set of questions that addressed specific areas of their employment nurses, technicians, and support staff were asked to respond to the following question:

In general, are you satisfied with the conditions of your employment?

Yes ____ No ____

Table 7.1 summarizes the actual responses of 70 nurses, 50 technicians, and 80 support personnel who were included in the survey.

Table 7.1 **Satisfaction or Dissatisfaction with Conditions of Employment**

	Nurses	Technicians	Support Staff
Satisfied	35 (**24.5**)	20 (**17.5**)	15 (**28**)
Dissatisfied	35 (**45.5**)	30 (**32.5**)	65 (**52.0**)
Total	70	50	80

Fifty percent (i.e., 35/70 × 100) of the nurses and 40% (i.e. 20/50 × 100) of the technicians were satisfied with the general conditions of their employment. However, only 18.75% (i.e., 15/80 × 100) of the support staff expressed satisfaction with working conditions. In this case, the object is to determine whether the observed differences in the proportions or percentages of employees reporting a general satisfaction are significant or attributable to chance variation.

The first step is to specify the null and alternate hypotheses. In the following, let π_1 correspond to the proportion of nurses who expressed satisfaction with working conditions and π_2 represent the proportion of technicians who were similarly satisfied. Finally, let π_3 correspond to the proportion of the support staff that reported general satisfaction with their conditions of employment. The null hypothesis, which assumes that the three proportions are identical, might be specified as follows:

$$H_o: \pi_1 = \pi_2 = \pi_3$$

In contrast, the alternate hypothesis assumes that the three proportions are not equal. We specify the alternate hypothesis as

$$H_a: \pi_1 \neq \pi_2 \neq \pi_3$$

As in the examination of the difference between two proportions, we assume that the null hypothesis is true and that π_1, π_2, and π_3 are equal to a common proportion represented by P*. As discussed in the previous section, P* is defined by

$$P^* = (x_1 + x_2 + x_3)/(n_1 + n_2 + n_3)$$

We let x_1 represent the number of nurses who expressed satisfaction with the working environment whereas the number of technicians and support staff reporting satisfaction with their conditions of employment is represented by x_2 and x_3, respectively. Finally, the number of nurses, technicians and staff members responding to the survey is indicated by n_1, n_2 and n_3, respectively. Thus, the common proportion, P*, is obtained by

$$P^* = (35 + 20 + 15)/(70 + 50 + 80)$$

or 0.35. The complement of P*, 1 − P*, is 0.65.

We now presume that the null hypothesis is correct and that the proportions π_1, π_2, and π_3 are estimated by the numeric value of the common proportion P* or 0.35. If the null hypothesis were true, we would expect 35% of each group to express satisfaction with their working conditions and 65% to report dissatisfaction with the work environment. Based on these data, the expected cell frequencies depicting members of each group who are satisfied with the terms of their employment are calculated as follows:

Group	Calculations	Number Satisfied
Nurses	0.35 (70)	24.5
Technicians	0.35 (50)	17.5
Support staff	0.35 (80)	28.0

These calculations suggest that if the null hypothesis is correct 35% of the 70 nurses ought to report that they are satisfied with the terms of their employment and 35% of the 50 technicians ought to report that they also are satisfied with working conditions. The expected number of employees reporting dissatisfaction, grouped by occupational category, is calculated as follows:

Group	Calculations	Number Dissatisfied
Nurses	0.65 (70)	45.5
Technicians	0.65 (50)	32.5
Support staff	0.65 (80)	52.0

The calculations refer to expected cell frequencies that are based on the presumption that the null hypothesis is correct. The expected cell frequencies are summarized in Table 7.1 and appear in parentheses as bold-faced entries.

Differences between the observed frequencies derived from responses to the survey and the expected cell frequencies that are based on the presumption that the null hypothesis is true might be interpreted as follows:

1. If the null hypothesis is true, the absolute value of the differences between the observed and expected cell frequencies will, on balance, be small.
2. If the null hypothesis is false and the alternate hypothesis is true, the absolute value of the differences between the observed and expected cell frequencies will, on balance, be large.

In this case, we require a test statistic and a critical value that enable us to determine whether the differences are large or small.

In the following, let *O* correspond to the observed frequency appearing in a given cell and *e* represent the corresponding expected frequency. Using this notation, we evaluate the differences between the distribution of observed and expected frequencies by relying on the χ^2 distribution, where χ is the Greek letter chi. The test statistic is given by

$$\chi^2 = \Sigma(O - e)^2/e \qquad \text{(Equation 7.13)}$$

The calculated value of χ^2 is obtained by first squaring the difference between the observed and expected frequency and dividing by the expected value for each cell. We then simply sum the results obtained for each cell in the table. The calculated value of χ^2 is interpreted as follows:

1. If the null hypothesis is true, the absolute value of $(O - e)$ will, on balance, be small, suggesting that the ratio $(O - e)^2/e$ will, on balance, be small and that the calculated value of χ^2 will be small.
2. If the null hypothesis is false and the alternate hypothesis is true, the absolute value of $(O - e)$ will be large, suggesting that the ratio $(O - e)^2/e$ will, on balance, be large and that the calculated value of χ^2 will be large.

In Table 7.1, the calculated value of χ^2 is given by

$$\chi^2 = (35 - 24.5)^2/24.5 + (20 - 17.5)^2/17.5 + (15 - 28)^2/28 + (35 - 45.5)^2/45.5 + (30 - 32.5)^2/32.5 + (65 - 52)^2/52$$

or approximately 16.76.

In Exhibit 7.1, an Excel spreadsheet can be used to calculate the value of χ^2. The original or observed frequencies that were derived from the survey are listed in Part A of Exhibit 7.1. The common proportion, P*, is shown in cell B13, whereas its complement is listed in cell B14. Based on the presumption that the null hypothesis is correct, the expected frequencies are shown in Part B of the exhibit and were calculated as follows:

1. Enter = $B$13*B$10 in cell B23.
2. Use the "COPY" function to record the equation in the other two cells of the first row.
3. Enter = $B$14*B$10 in cell B24.
4. Use the "COPY" function to record the equation in the other two cells of the second row.

In this case, $B$14 is a fixed cell address, whereas B$10 limits the calculations to the 10th row of the spreadsheet. The distribution of expected frequencies calculated in Part B of Exhibit 7.1 is identical to the set of results appearing in the set of parentheses shown in Table 7.1.

The process of calculating the value of χ^2 is illustrated in Part C of Exhibit 7.1. The calculated value of χ^2 is obtained by

1. Entering the equation = (B8 − B23)^2/B23 in cell B33
2. Using the "Copy" function to record the remaining cells of Part C
3. Using the "AutoSum" function to calculate row, column, and grand totals

Referring to the equation (B8 − B23)^2/B23, the symbol "^" indicates the operation of exponentiation and results in the square of the difference between the value appearing in cells B8 and B23. The value of χ^2 (16.76) computed in Exhibit 7.1 is identical to the corresponding value listed in Table 7.1.

If the calculated value of χ^2 is large, the differences between the observed and expected frequencies are large. Thus, we are tempted to reject the null hypothesis in favor of the alternate. In contrast, if the calculated value of χ^2 is small, the differences between observed and expected frequencies are also small and probably attributable to chance variation. In such a situation, we are tempted to accept the null hypothesis or reserve judgment.

When evaluating the calculated value of χ^2, we rely on the χ^2 probability distribution. As indicated in Figure 7.2, the χ^2 distribution is unimodal, continuous, and limited to positive values; χ^2 is a family of probability distributions, each determined by a single parameter defined as degrees of freedom. For a relatively

Exhibit 7.1 **Satisfaction or Dissatisfaction with Conditions of Employment**

Part A: The Original Data

Response	Nurses	Technicians	Support Staff	Total
Satisfied	35	20	15	70
Dissatisfied	35	30	65	130
Total	70	50	80	200
P*	0.35			
1–P*	0.65			

Part B: Expected Values: Assuming the Null Hypothesis Is Correct

Response	Nurses	Technicians	Support Staff
Satisfied	24.5	17.5	28
Dissatisfied	45.5	32.5	52

Part C: The Calculation of Chi Square

Response	Nurses	Technicians	Support Staff	Total
Satisfied	4.50	0.36	6.04	10.89
Dissatisfied	2.42	0.19	3.25	5.87
Total	6.92	0.55	9.29	**16.76**

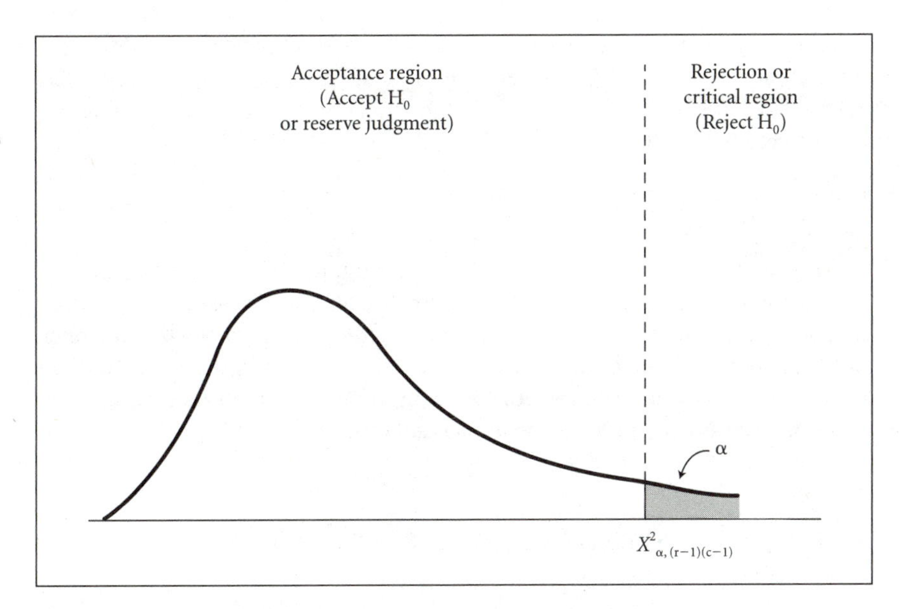

Figure 7.2 **The χ^2 Distribution and the Decision Criteria**

small number of degrees of freedom, the χ^2 distribution is asymmetrical and skewed to the right. However, as the number of degrees of freedom increases, the χ^2 distribution becomes more symmetrical and approaches the normal distribution. When examining the difference between the observed and expected frequencies that appear in a table consisting of r rows and c columns, we see that the number of degrees of freedom is given by the product $(r - 1)(c - 1)$. The data have been organized into a table consisting of two rows and three columns. Thus, we find that $(2 - 1)(3 - 1)$ or 2 degrees of freedom are available for analysis.

The χ^2 probability distribution is in Table D.5. As indicated, the number of degrees of freedom defines the rows of the table, whereas the values of χ^2_α define the columns of the table. Thus, each row of the table corresponds to one of the distributions known as χ^2. The columns of the table are defined for different values of α or $1 - \alpha$. Similar to our discussion of Z_α and t_α, we define $\chi^2_{\alpha, (r-1)(c-1)}$ as the value of chi-square for which the area to its right is α. Figure 7.1 indicates that $\chi^2_{\alpha, (r-1)(c-1)}$ is a critical value that divides the distribution into two regions. Specifically, if the calculated value of χ^2 exceeds the critical value $\chi^2_{\alpha, (r-1)(c-1)}$, we conclude that the differences among the observed and expected frequencies are significant. In this situation, we reject the null hypothesis and accept the alternate, recognizing that the probability of committing a Type I error is α or less. In contrast, if the calculated value of χ^2 is less than the critical value, we conclude that the differences among the expected and observed frequencies are small and not significant. As a consequence, we are forced to accept the null hypothesis or if possible reserve judgment.

Returning to the example, suppose that $\alpha = 0.05$. Given that two degrees of freedom are available, the corresponding value of chi-square, $\chi^2_{0.05,2}$ is 5.991, implying that if the null hypothesis is true the probability of obtaining a value of χ^2 that exceeds 5.991 is 0.05 or less. In Table 7.1 or Exhibit 7.1, the calculated value of χ^2 was 16.76. Because the calculated value of χ^2 exceeds the critical value, we reject the null hypothesis and accept the alternate, recognizing that the probability of committing a Type I error is 0.05 or less.

Viewed from an administrative perspective, the results also indicate that the proportion of employees, grouped by occupational category, expressing satisfaction with their conditions of employment differed significantly and that members of the support staff appear to be the most dissatisfied. Thus, the results indicate the presence of a potential problem or organizational weakness that requires further investigation and perhaps the implementation of a remedial policy.

Tests of Independence or Relationship

The χ^2 distribution is also valuable when the data are arranged in a contingency table and the independence or the association of one variable with another needs to be examined. In general, a contingency table is constructed to assess the relationship of one variable with another or to determine whether the two variables are unrelated or independent. The health administrator might examine two kinds of problems.

The first is a situation in which three or more outcomes are possible while the size of the corresponding samples is known and held constant. For example, suppose that the health service organization is evaluating a proposal to extend the hours of operation in the outpatient clinic and that the opinions of employees will be considered when assessing the suggestion. Assume also that 50 physicians, 70 nurses, and 25 technicians were surveyed and asked to respond to the following question:

In general, do you favor increasing the hours of operation in the clinic by 1 hour?

Favor ____ Oppose ____ Undecided _____

In this case, the size of each sample is fixed and equal to 50 physicians, 70 nurses, and 24 technicians. The outcomes consist of responses that indicate employees who favor the proposal, oppose the proposal, or are undecided. Even though the sample sizes are fixed, responses are allowed to vary and represent the values assumed by the random variable that depicts the opinions of employees included in the survey. In this case, we are interested in examining the null hypothesis that the reaction of employees to the proposal is independent of occupational category. The alternate hypothesis specifies that the reaction of employees is dependent on the type of occupation.

The second kind of problem involves a situation in which sample sizes and outcomes are allowed to vary. For example, suppose that we are interested in any association between the socioeconomic status of patients and their evaluation of the care provided by our organization. Suppose also that we asked 1,000 patients to rate the care that they received as excellent, fair, or poor. After assigning each individual to a social category as low, middle, or high, suppose that we obtained the distribution as shown in Table 7.2.

As before, we are interested in a null hypothesis that assumes that the evaluation of the care provided by our organization is independent of social class. The alternate hypothesis indicates that the evaluation of care is dependent on or related to social class.

To illustrate the approach that is used to assess this situation, we assume initially that the null hypothesis is correct and that the evaluation of care is independent of social class. If the null hypothesis of independence is correct, recall that we may apply the special rule of multiplication, which specifies that

$$P(A \cap B) = P(A)P(B)$$

We now consider the probability of randomly selecting a patient who is of high social class *and* rated the care provided by the organization as excellent. In Table 7.1, A_1, A_2, and A_3 represent an individual of low, middle, and high social class, respectively. Similarly, B_1, B_2, and B_3 identify a response of excellent, fair, or poor to the question. Thus, the desired probability might be expressed as

$$P(A_1 \cap B_1) = P(A_1)P(B_1)$$

After appropriate substitution we find that

$$P(A_1 \cap B_1) = (300/1{,}000)(290/1{,}000)$$

Table 7.2 **Evaluation of Patient Care by Social Class**

	Social Class			
Evaluation	**Low**	**Middle**	**High**	**Total**
	(A_1)	**(A_2)**	**(A_3)**	
Excellent	30	150	110	290
(B_1)	**(87)**	**(145)**	**(58)**	
Fair	120	190	60	370
(B_2)	**(111)**	**(185)**	**(74)**	
Poor	150	160	30	340
(B_3)	**(102)**	**(170)**	**(68)**	
Total	300	500	200	1,000

or 0.087. Furthermore, if the null hypothesis is correct, we would expect (0.087)(1,000) or 87 patients to occupy a high social class *and* rate the care as excellent. If e_{11} corresponds to the expected frequency assigned to the cell defined by the intersection of row one and column one, this result is equivalent to

$$e_{11} = (300/1{,}000)(290/1{,}000)1{,}000$$

or (300)(290)/1,000. These calculations suggest that the expected cell frequency is the product of an appropriate row and column total divided by the total number of observations.

Similarly, we may calculate the probability of selecting a patient who was assigned to the high social class *and* rated the care as poor by

$$P(A_3 \cap B_3) = (200/1{,}000)(340/1{,}000)$$

or 0.068. Hence, if the null hypothesis were correct, we would expect

$$[(200/1{,}000)(340/1{,}000)](1{,}000)$$

or 68 members of the high social class to evaluate the care as poor. Using this approach, the frequency expected in the cell defined by the intersection of the third row and third column is given by

$$e_{33} = (200)(340)/1{,}000$$

or 68 patients.

The calculations summarized here suggest that the expected cell frequency is given by the product of the appropriate row and column totals divided by the total number of observations. In general, let the subscript i correspond to a row in the table and the subscript j represent one of the columns. In addition, let R_i correspond to the total of row i and C_j represent the total of column j. The expected frequency in the cell defined by the intersection of row i and column j is given by

$$e_{ij} = (R_i)(C_j)/\, T \qquad \text{(Equation 7.14)}$$

where T is the total number of observations. After applying Equation 7.14 to each cell of Table 7.2, we obtain the distribution of expected frequencies that appears in bold face and parentheses.

As discussed in the previous section, if differences among the observed and expected frequencies are, on balance, small, we might believe that the null hypothesis is correct (i.e., the social class is independent of the evaluation of care). On the other hand, if the differences among the observed and expected frequencies are large, we tend to believe that the null hypothesis should be rejected in favor of the alternate. Equation 7.13 is used to calculate the value of χ^2 as follows:

$$\chi^2 = (30 - 87)^2/87 + (150 - 145)^2/145 + (110 - 58)^2/58 + (120 - 111)^2/111 + (190 - 185)^2/185 + (60 - 74)^2/74 + (150 - 102)^2/102 + (160 - 170)^2/170 + (30 - 68)^2/68$$

After performing the calculations, we find that the value of χ^2 is approximately 132.06.

The calculations required to determine the value of χ^2 are tedious and may result in errors. However, with Excel, the calculated value of χ^2 is determined with relative ease. In Exhibit 7.2, the original information from the survey was summarized in Part A. The expected cell frequencies were then calculated as follows:

1. Enter the equation = (B$10*$E7)/$E$10 in cell B18.
2. Use the "COPY" function to record the equation in the remaining cells of Part B.
3. Use the "AutoSum" function to calculate row totals, column totals, and the total number of observations.

The address B$10 restricts calculations to the 10th row of the spreadsheet, whereas $E7 restricts calculations to column E of Exhibit 7.2. Finally, $E$10 is a fixed cell address in which the total number of observations is recorded.

The method of calculating the value of χ^2 is shown in Part C of Exhibit 7.2. Similar to Exhibit 7.1, the calculated value of χ^2 is obtained by

1. Entering =(B7 – B18)^2/B18 in cell B29
2. Using the "Copy" function to record the equation in other cells forming the body of the exhibit
3. Using the "AutoSum" function to determine row totals, column totals, and the grand total

These calculations indicate that the calculated value of χ^2 is approximately 132.06.

As before, if the calculated value of χ^2 is large, we conclude that the differences among the observed and expected frequencies are large, an outcome that forces us to reject the assumption of independence and conclude that social class is associated with the evaluation of care. On the other hand, if the calculated value of χ^2 is small, the differences among the observed and expected frequencies are small, and we are forced to accept the null hypothesis (i.e., social class and the evaluation of care are independent) or reserve judgment.

From our earlier discussion, it is clear that a comparison of the calculated and critical value of χ^2 forms the basis for evaluating the null and alternate hypothe-

Exhibit 7.2 **The Evaluation of Social Class and the Evaluation of Care**

Part A: The Original Data

	Social Class			
	Low	Middle	High	Total
EVALUATION				
Excellent	30	150	110	290
Fair	120	190	60	370
Poor	150	160	30	340
Total	300	500	200	1,000

Part B: Expected Cell Frequencies

	Social Class			
	Low	Middle	High	Total
EVALUATION				
Excellent	87	145	58	290
Fair	111	185	74	370
Poor	102	170	68	340
Total	300	500	200	1,000

Part C: The Calculation of Chi-Square

	Social Class			
	Low	Middle	High	Total
EVALUATION				
Excellent	37.34482759	0.172413793	46.62068966	84.13793103
Fair	0.72972973	0.135135135	2.648648649	3.513513514
Poor	22.58823529	0.588235294	21.23529412	44.41176471
Total	60.6627261	0.895784222	70.50463242	132.0632093

sis. If $\alpha = 0.05$, Table D.5 reveals that the critical value of χ^2 for four degrees of freedom is 9.488. Because the calculated value (132.06) greatly exceeds the critical value, we are forced to reject the null hypothesis in favor of the alternate, recognizing that the probability of committing a Type I error is 0.05 or less. Because of magnitude of the calculated value, one might conclude that there is virtually no chance of committing a Type I error.

The analysis clearly indicates that social class and the evaluation of care are associated. An inspection of the observed frequency distribution clearly indicates that those patients assigned to the high socioeconomic group were more likely to rate their care as excellent, whereas those in the low socioeconomic class were more likely to rate their care as poor. As a consequence, the analysis suggests that the treatment of patients of different social groups varies and that further examination or administrative investigation into potential inequities in the services provided by the organization may be required.

Exercises

1. In a sample survey, 200 of 800 individuals enrolled in our managed-care organization indicated that they favored a proposal to extend office hours from 5:00 to 8:00 p.m. Construct a 95% confidence interval for the corresponding true proportion.
2. Suppose that we conducted a survey in which we asked 800 people the following question: "In the event of an emergency, would you seek medical assistance at the emergency room of our hospital?" If 180 of the respondents indicated that they would seek care at the emergency room, construct a 95% confidence interval for the true proportion.
3. In a random sample of 800 older members of our managed-care organization, 260 indicated that they intended to visit one of our clinics for a flu vaccination. Construct a 99% confidence interval for the corresponding true proportion.
4. In a random sample of 1,200 bills submitted to a given insurer, 250 contained an error. Construct a 98% confidence interval for the true proportion of bills that contain an error.
5. Suppose that we believe that no fewer than 60% of members of a prepaid group practice received a physical examination last year. In a sample survey of 800 members, suppose that we found that 352 individuals received an exam during the previous year. If $\alpha = 0.01$, use these results to examine the null hypothesis that the proportion of the membership receiving a physical examination is 0.60.
6. In a random sample of 640 recent discharges, it was found that a hospital-acquired infection was reported in the medical records of 262. We believe that no less than 20% of inpatients should acquire a hospital-related infection. If $\alpha = 0.05$, use these data to evaluate the performance of the hospital.
7. Suppose that an expert tells us that the defective rate (i.e., false positive or false negative) associated with a given laboratory procedure should be no more than 10%. In a random sample of 400 results, suppose that we found that 100 were either a false positive or a false negative. If $\alpha = 0.05$, use these data to examine the null hypothesis that the probability of a defective result is 0.10.
8. Suppose that we operate two long-term care facilities and are concerned that the quality of care provided by the two facilities differs. In an initial assessment, suppose that we randomly selected 100 patient records from facility A and found that bed sores were

reported in 40 cases. Similarly, we randomly selected 150 records from facility B and found that bed sores were reported in 70 cases. Let $\alpha = 0.05$, and use these data to find the difference, if any, in the performance of the two facilities.

9. Suppose that we operate a multi-institutional organization and that we are concerned that the rate of birth by caesarean sections at the Tejon Hospital exceeds that of Memorial Hospital. Using only those with a similar clinical condition, we selected 200 records of patients discharged from Tejon Hospital and found that a caesarean section was performed on 98 of the cases. A random sample of 150 recent discharges from Memorial Hospital revealed that 60 of the cases received a caesarean section. If $\alpha = 0.01$, evaluate the difference in the rates of performing caesarean sections by the two hospitals.
10. In examining the appointment procedures in four outpatient clinics, suppose that we interviewed 90 patients from each of the clinics and asked them whether they experienced excessive waiting times during the past year. Using only the responses of "Yes" or "No," suppose that 60 of the patients at clinic A, 20 of the patients at clinic B, 30 of the patients at clinic C, and 45 of the patients at clinic D indicated that they experienced excessive waiting times during the previous year. Use $\alpha = 0.05$ to examine the proposition that the differences among population proportions are attributable to chance.
11. Suppose that the medical staff indicates that the results of a given laboratory procedure must be available 30 minutes after the physician submits a request for the service. In this situation, if the results arrived 30 minutes or less after the request, we regard the performance of the laboratory as timely. If results arrived more than 30 minutes after the request, we regard the performance as tardy. Focusing on the day, evening, and night shifts, suppose that we selected a random sample and obtained the following results:

	Shift		
Performance	Day	Evening	Night
Timely	100	80	40
Tardy	20	30	40

If $\alpha = 0.05$, use these results to test the proposition that the performance of the laboratory is independent of shift.

12. Suppose that we are interested in examining the relation between the use of physician care and the age of the patient. After surveying 173 individuals enrolled in our managed-care organization, suppose that we obtained the following results:

Age	Use	Nonuse
10–24	49	14
25–39	23	65
40–54	4	18

Let $\alpha = 0.01$ and determine whether the use or nonuse of physician service is the same for the three age groups.

13. Suppose that we are interested in the relationship between socio-economic status and the type of prenatal care received. A sample survey yielded the following results:

Socioeconomic status	Midwife	Generalist	Specialist
High	15	30	96
Middle	20	15	14
Low	60	10	7

Let $\alpha = 0.05$ to determine whether the source of prenatal care is independent of socioeconomic status.

14. Examining the medical records of 400 patients admitted to the medical, the surgical, and the pediatric unit, suppose that we calculated the average daily costs for each. Using the categories, low, middle, and high to characterize the resulting cost data, suppose that the distribution of patients was as follows:

Unit	Low	Middle	High
Medical	46	62	70
Surgical	45	22	85
Pediatric	10	50	10

Use $\alpha = 0.05$ to determine whether costs are independent of the unit in which patients are hospitalized.

CHAPTER 8 ANALYSIS OF VARIANCE[R,O]

OBJECTIVES

1. Define the structural model for one-way analysis of variance, two-way analysis of variance without interaction, and two-way analysis of variance with interaction.
2. Describe the process of partitioning total variation when using a one-way analysis of variance, a two-way analysis of variance without interaction, and a two-way analysis of variance with interaction.
3. Describe the role of the F distribution when evaluating the results produced by an analysis of variance.
4. Use Excel to perform an analysis of variance.
5. Interpret the statistical results when an analysis of variance is applied to issues or problems that occur in the health service organization.
6. Apply the statistical analysis to the functions or roles of the administrator.

As described in Chapter 7, χ^2 is a generalization of the approach that is used to examine the difference between two proportions. We found that χ^2 enabled us to assess differences among multiple proportions and to evaluate the proposition that k proportions, where k exceeds 2, might be treated as having been selected from a given population with a proportion of π. Similarly, analysis of variance (ANOVA) is a generalization of the methods used to evaluate the difference between two means. Similar to χ^2, ANOVA allows us to examine differences among k means where k exceeds 2. The primary purpose of ANOVA is to determine whether the differences among the means of multiple samples are a product of chance variation or whether variation among sample means is significant and attributable to differences among the means of the populations from which the data were selected. Thus, ANOVA allows us to evaluate the assumption that the k means were selected from the same population with a mean of μ.

ANOVA is very valuable to the administrator of a health service organization. For example, the administrator of a multi-institutional arrangement might want to determine whether the average lengths of stay of four of the organization's hospitals differ significantly or if the costs per visit in several of the clinics differ significantly. We might be interested in evaluating variation in the average use of ancillary care by patients with one of several diagnoses or in determining whether variation in the average length of delay in transferring patients of different backgrounds to long-term care is significant or attributable to chance.

This chapter is developed in essentially three phases. The first focuses on the fundamentals of ANOVA and introduces the simplest form of ANOVA, namely one-way ANOVA. The purpose of one-way ANOVA is to determine whether the variation exhibited by multiple means is attributable to chance or to the systemic effects of a single factor. The second section discusses two-way ANOVA. Two-way ANOVA is simply an extension of one-way ANOVA and enables us to assess whether differences by multiple means are attributable to chance or to the effects of two factors. Finally, the chapter concludes with an examination of two-way ANOVA with interaction or replication.

One-Way or One-Factor ANOVA[R]

For example, suppose that the administrator of a multi-institutional arrangement is interested in the average lengths of stay associated with four of the organization's hospitals, represented by A_1, A_2, A_3, and A_4. The compensation of all four hospitals is derived from a prospective payment system. The payer mix of hospitals A_1 and A_2 uses a prospective pricing system in which a fixed per diem represents the unit of payment. Thus, we might speculate that a relatively long length of stay might improve the fiscal performance of these two institutions. In contrast, hospitals A_3 and A_4 use a prospective payment system in which the patient or discharge represents the unit of payment; thus, in order to increase the organization's net surplus, the length of stay should be shortened. If these hospitals are taking advantage of the financial incentives created by the unit of payment, the length of stay will be relatively short.

Assume that we selected a sample of six patients from each of the four hospitals and recorded the corresponding lengths of stay, as shown in Table 8.1. The average length of stay for each of the hospitals is as follows:

Hospital	Average Length of Stay
A_1:	3.0
A_2:	5.0
A_3:	7.0
A_4:	10.0

These results indicate that the average lengths of stay showed variation, and our objective is to determine whether differences in the lengths of stay are attributable to chance variation or to characteristics of the hospital.

Similar to previously described approaches, the null hypothesis needs to be specified. We assume that

$$H_o: \mu_1 = \mu_2 = \mu_3 = \mu_4 = \mu$$

Table 8.1 **Length of Stay and One-Way ANOVA**

Patient	Hospital			
	A_1	A_2	A_3	A_4
1	2	3	5	10
2	3	6	8	11
3	4	7	9	13
4	3	5	10	8
5	4	4	4	9
6	2	5	6	9
Total	18	30	42	60
Mean	3.0	5.0	7.0	10.0

In this case, μ_1, μ_2, μ_3, and μ_4 represent the true mean length of stay in hospital A_1, A_2, A_3, and A_4, respectively. The null hypothesis assumes that the average length of stay is the same in each of the hospitals and that, in turn, the means μ_1, μ_2, μ_3, and μ_4 also are equal to the mean μ. The null hypothesis assumes that means were selected from the same population and that each is equal to the common mean μ where μ is given by

$$\mu = (\mu_1 + \mu_2 + \mu_3 + \mu_4)/4$$

The alternate hypothesis states that two or more of the means are unequal or differ significantly.

It is useful to express the four means as

$$\begin{aligned} \mu_1 &= \mu + \lambda_1 \\ \mu_2 &= \mu + \lambda_2 \\ \mu_3 &= \mu + \lambda_3 \\ \mu_4 &= \mu + \lambda_4 \end{aligned}$$

In the following, we refer to λ_1, λ_2, λ_3, and λ_4 as *treatment effects* and μ as the *grand mean*. Using this notation, the null hypothesis also might be expressed as

$$H_o\colon \lambda_1 = \lambda_2 = \lambda_3 = \lambda_4 = 0$$

Thus, the null hypothesis indicates that the treatment effects are equal to zero.

To verify, we now let μ_j correspond to the true mean length of stay for one of the four hospitals and λ_j represent the related treatment effect.

$$\mu_j = \mu + \lambda_j$$

If λ_j is zero, then $\mu_j = \mu$ for all j, and we conclude that the treatment effects or, as is the case in the example, that characteristics of the hospitals exert no influence on the average length of stay. Furthermore, because the sum of the treatment effects $\Sigma\lambda_j$ must equal zero, the alternate hypothesis states that not all of the λ_j are equal to zero, suggesting that two or more of the treatment effects are nonzero.

The logic of the null and alternate hypotheses is as follows. If the variation among the means is small, we are tempted to believe that the differences might be due to chance. Thus, we might conclude that the null hypothesis is true and that the treatment effects, represented by attributes of the hospitals, are not significant. In contrast, if the variation among the sample means is large, we might be tempted to reject the null hypothesis in favor of the alternate, concluding that the treatment effects or observed differences among sample means are significant. Thus, to evaluate the null and the alternate hypothesis, we require a precise indicator of the variation shown by the means and a decision criterion that allows us to judge the size of observed differences.

When one-way ANOVA is used, the total variation in the data is partitioned into two components. The first represents the variation that is related to the treatment effects, and the second measures the variation that is attributable to chance. Specifically, one-way ANOVA is based on the mathematical identity

$$SS(TOT) = SS(TR) + SS(ERROR) \qquad \text{(Equation 8.1)}$$

In Equation 8.1, SS(TOT) refers to the total variation of the data and is measured by the sum of squared deviations of observations relative to the grand mean. The components that combine to determine total variation are represented by SS(TR), a measure of the variation exhibited by treatment means relative to the grand mean and by SS(ERROR), an indicator of the chance variation existing within the samples.

The relationship of the null and alternate hypotheses to the components that determine the total variation shown by the data is as follows. SS(ERROR) measures the variation within the samples and is therefore attributable to chance. On the other hand, SS(TR) measures the variation among column means (i.e., the average lengths of stay for the four hospitals) and, therefore, represents the effects of chance and the systemic effects, if any, of the treatment (i.e., attributes of the hospital). If the null hypothesis is correct, both SS(ERROR) and SS(TR) are influenced by only chance variation. After adjusting for degrees of freedom (represented by "d.f."), a true null hypothesis leads to the expectation that

$$SS(TR)/d.f. \sim SS(ERROR)/d.f.$$

Thus, if the null hypothesis is correct, we would expect that the ratio [SS(TR)/d.f.]/[SS(ERROR)/d.f.] will not differ significantly from one.

Consider next expectations derived from the presumption that the null hypothesis is false. The term SS(ERROR) measures the effects of chance or the way in which samples were selected. However, if the alternate hypothesis is true, then SS(TR) reflects the effects of chance *and* the treatment effects. Because SS(TR) is influenced by two factors and SS(ERROR) by chance alone, we would expect the SS(TR), adjusted for degrees of freedom, to exceed the SS(ERROR), adjusted for degrees of freedom. Thus, we would expect the ratio

$$[SS(TR)/d.f.]/[SS(ERROR)/d.f.]$$

to be much larger than one.

Structural Equations and Tests of Significance: One-Way ANOVA

In the following,

> r represents the sample size (i.e., the number of rows or observations per hospital)
> c corresponds to the number of treatments defined by the number of columns (i.e., the number of hospitals in the example)
> rxc corresponds to the total number of observations
> x_{ij} represents observation i pertaining to treatment j
> $\bar{X}_j$ represents the mean value derived for treatment j
> $\bar{\bar{X}}$ represents a point estimate of the grand mean, μ

The data's total variation is obtained by

$$SS(TOT) = \Sigma\Sigma(x_{ij} - \bar{\bar{X}})^2 \qquad \text{(Equation 8.2)}$$

The expression on the right-hand side of the equation is interpreted as follows: First, we obtain the deviation of each observation relative to the grand mean and square the result. Second, as indicated by the double summation, $\Sigma\Sigma$, we then simply add all of the squared deviations. The grand mean, estimated by $\bar{\bar{X}}$ in Equation 8.2, is given by

$$\bar{\bar{X}} = (3 + 5 + 7 + 10)/4$$

or 6.25 days. Thus, the total variation that the data exhibited is obtained by

$$SS(TOT) = (2 - 6.25)^2 + (3 - 6.25)^2 + (4 - 6.25)^2 + (3 - 6.25)^2 + (4 - 6.25)^2 + (2 - 6.25)^2 + \ldots + (9 - 6.25)^2$$

or 218.5. The first six squared deviations were obtained from the sample selected from hospital A_1, whereas the final value represents the squared deviation derived for the sixth patient in hospital A_4. The dots on the right-hand side of the equation represent the intermediate sums of squared deviations.

Consider next the variation of the column or treatment means relative to the grand mean. In this case, the sum of squares attributable to the treatment effects is given by

$$SS(TR) = \Sigma r_j (\bar{X}_j - \bar{\bar{X}})^2 \qquad \text{(Equation 8.3)}$$

We first calculate the deviation of the mean of column j relative to the grand mean, square the result, and weight the squared deviation by the number of observations, represented by r_j, that were used to calculate $\bar{X}_j$. As before, the summation symbol, Σ, indicates that we then add the weighted squared deviations. We find that the sum of squared deviations of column means relative to the grand mean is obtained by

$$SS(TR) = 6(3 - 6.25)^2 + 6(5 - 6.25)^2 + 6(7 - 6.25)^2 + 6(10 - 6.25)^2$$

The sum of squares attributed to the treatment effects is 160.5.

The final source of variation is related to chance variation and the deviation of each observation in a sample relative to the column or treatment mean. For example, Table 8.1 reveals that several of the patients had a length of stay that differed from the average stay for hospital A_1. The length of stay for each of the patients differed from the average length of stay for hospital A_3. We use these deviations to calculate the within-sample variation, and hence, the sum of squares or variation attributed to chance is given by

$$SS(ERROR) = \Sigma\Sigma(x_{ij} - \bar{X}_j)^2 \qquad \text{(Equation 8.4)}$$

In this case, the within-sample variation is obtained by first calculating the deviation of each observation relative to its column or treatment mean, squaring the results, and then adding all squared deviations. In the example, we see that the within-sample variation is obtained by

$$\begin{aligned} SS(ERROR) = {} & (2 - 3)^2 + (3 - 3)^2 + (4 - 3)^2 + (3 - 3)^2 + (4 - 3)^2 \\ & + (2 - 3)^2 + (3 - 5)^2 + \ldots + (5 - 5)^2 + (5 - 7)^2 + \ldots \\ & + (6 - 7)^2 + (10 - 10)^2 + \ldots + (9 - 10)^2 \end{aligned}$$

After performing these calculations, we find that the sum of within-sample squared deviations is 58.0.

The results obtained thus far are summarized in the second column of Table 8.2. When combined, the sum of squares attributable to treatment effects and the sum of squares due to error or chance variation (i.e., 160.5 + 58) is equal to the total sum of squares represented by 218.5. The third column of the table indicates

Table 8.2 **ANOVA Table**

Source	Sum of Squares (Variation)	Degrees of Freedom	Mean Square (Variance)	Calculated F
Treatment	160.5	3	53.5	18.44
Error	58	20	2.9	
Total	218.5	23		

the degrees of freedom associated with SS(TR), SS(ERROR), and SS(TOT). When a sum of squared deviations listed in column two is divided by degrees of freedom shown in the third column, we obtain a measure of variance, called the mean square in ANOVA. A calculated value of F, defined as MS(TR)/MS(ERROR), appears in the last column of Table 8.2.

A measure of variance, referred to as the mean square, is obtained when variation or the sum of squared deviations is divided by the degrees of freedom. The rationale for the number of degrees of freedom listed in the third column of Table 8.2 is as follows. As indicated, we obtained four deviations of the treatment or column means relative to the grand mean. However, because $\Sigma\Sigma(\bar{X}_j - \bar{\bar{X}})$ must equal zero, the constraint implies that only $4 - 1$ or 3 degrees of freedom are associated with SS(TR). As before, we sacrifice a degree of freedom when $\bar{\bar{X}}$ is used as a point estimate of μ. Because, in general, c differences are required to calculate the sum of squared deviations of treatment means relative to the grand mean, the degrees of freedom assigned to SS(TR) is given by $c - 1$.

Consider next the degrees of freedom that are associated with the variation within samples or the term SS(ERROR); $rc - c$ degrees of freedom are assigned to SS(ERROR). The rationale is as follows:

1. In general, rc squared deviations are required to calculate the value of SS(ERROR).
2. Because the term $\Sigma\Sigma(x_{ij} - \bar{X}_j)$ must equal zero, we sacrifice a degree of freedom on each occasion that $\bar{X}_j$ is used as a point estimate of μ_j. If c treatment means are used to calculate the variation within samples, we sacrifice c degrees of freedom.
3. The number of degrees of freedom assigned to the variation within samples is given by the number of squared deviations, rc, less the number of treatment means, c (i.e., $rc - c$ or $c[r - 1]$).

The degrees of freedom assigned to each sample are $r - 1$, thus supporting the conclusion. Because c treatments are involved in the calculation of the within-sample variation, the degrees of freedom assigned to SS(ERROR) are, as indicated previously here, $rc - c$ or $c(r - 1)$.

In the example, 24 deviations were used to calculate the value of SS(ERROR), and the deviations were calculated relative to the four treatment means. Thus, the degrees of freedom assigned to the within sample variation is 24 less 4 or 4(6 − 1). Both results indicate that (as listed in Table 8.2) 20 degrees of freedom are assigned to the error term.

The total sum of squared deviations, represented by SS(TOT), required the use of 24 or, in general, rc contrasts. Similar to our earlier discussion, we employed $\bar{\bar{X}}$ as a point estimate of μ. Because the value of $\Sigma\Sigma(x_{ij} - \bar{\bar{X}})$ must equal zero, the total number of degrees of freedom is given in general by rc − 1 and in the example by 24 − 1 or 23.

In Table 8.2, when the sum of squares or variation is divided by degrees of freedom, we get a measure of variance that is referred to as a mean square (i.e., the mean of the sum of squared deviations). The value of MS(TR) is obtained by SS(TR)/c − 1. In the example, the MS(TR) is obtained by 160.5/3 or 53.5. Thus, if we divide variation by an appropriate number of degrees of freedom, a measure of the variance exhibited by column or treatment means is obtained. Similarly, the ratio defined as SS(ERROR)/c(r − 1) produces the mean square error (i.e., the mean of the sum of squared errors) and represents the variance existing within the samples.

In general, the F ratio was defined as S_1^2/S_2^2 where it is assumed that S_1^2 exceeds S_2^2. In ANOVA, MS(TR) is the variance that *always* appears in the numerator, and MS(ERROR) is the variance that *always* appears in the denominator. As described previously, we would expect the values of MS(TR) and MS(ERROR) to be similar if the null hypothesis is correct or true. In contrast, if the alternate hypothesis is true, the sum of squared deviations used to calculate MS(TR) is influenced by the treatment effects and chance, whereas the sum of squared deviations used to calculate MS(ERROR) is influenced by chance alone. Thus, if the alternate hypothesis is true, we would expect MS(TR) to exceed MS(ERROR), resulting in a large value of the calculated F ratio.

The discussion in Chapter 6 indicated that we can examine the proposition that the two variances are equal by comparing the calculated value of F with a critical value. The critical value of F, adjusted for degrees of freedom, is based on the assumption that the variances are equal or homoscedastic. If the calculated value of F exceeds the critical value, we reject the null hypothesis of homoscedasticity in favor of the alternate and conclude that the variances differ significantly. After specifying the value of α, the degrees of freedom in the numerator and denominator must be determined. The MS(TR) is listed in the numerator, implying that the corresponding degrees of freedom are c − 1. On the other hand, MS(ERROR) appears in the denominator, suggesting that the corresponding degrees of freedom are given by rc − c. Thus, if the calculated value of F exceeds the critical value, $F_{\alpha,(c-1,rc-c)}$, we reject the null hypothesis that the variances are equal in favor of the alternate, recognizing that the probability of committing a Type I error is α or less.

In Table 8.2, the value of F is given by the ratio 53.5/2.9 or approximately 18.44. Suppose that we let α = 0.05, suggesting that the critical value of F with 3 degrees of freedom in the numerator and 20 degrees of freedom in the denominator is 3.10. We interpret the critical value as follows. If the two variances are equal, the probability of obtaining a calculated value of F that is equal to or greater than 3.10 is 0.05 or less. The calculated value of F greatly exceeds 3.10, and we are forced to conclude that MS(TR) is significantly greater than MS(ERROR). The analysis clearly indicates that at least two of the treatment effects are significant, that at least two of the average lengths of stay among the study hospitals differ, and that the null hypothesis must be rejected.

Hospitals A_1 and A_2 might benefit financially by a relatively long length of stay. Similarly, hospitals A_3 and A_4 might benefit financially by a relatively short length of stay. However, the analysis indicates that the differences among the mean lengths of stay are not attributable to chance and are statistically significant. An inspection of the average lengths of stay suggests that none of the hospitals responded to the financial incentives created by differences in the units of payment. To evaluate the situation further, we might adopt the methods described in Chapter 6 to assess the differences among independent or orthogonal contrasts. In the following, let $\bar{X}_j$ correspond to one of several treatment means. The contrasts are as follows:

$$\bar{X}_1 \text{ versus } \bar{X}_2$$
$$\bar{X}_1 \text{ versus } \bar{X}_3$$
$$\bar{X}_1 \text{ versus } \bar{X}_4$$
$$\bar{X}_2 \text{ versus } \bar{X}_3$$
$$\bar{X}_2 \text{ versus } \bar{X}_4$$
$$\bar{X}_3 \text{ versus } \bar{X}_4$$

When combined with the results from ANOVA, the orthogonal contrasts also allow the organization to assess further the presence of a potential financial weakness.

The discussion of one-way ANOVA is summarized in Table 8.3. The first column lists the sources of variation, and the second summarizes the definitional equations for each source. The third column identifies degrees of freedom, and the fourth indicates the ratios that yield the corresponding mean square terms. The final column defines the calculated value of F.

Table 8.3 **Summary of One-Way ANOVA**

Source	**Sum of Squares**	**Degrees of Freedom**	**Mean Square**	**F Ratio**
Treatment	$\Sigma r_j(\bar{X}_j - \bar{\bar{X}})^2$	$c - 1$	$SS(TR)/c - 1$	$MS(TR)/MS(ERROR)$
Error	$\Sigma\Sigma(x_{ij} - \bar{X}_j)^2$	$rc - c$	$SS(ERROR)/rc - c$	
Total	$\Sigma\Sigma(x_{ij} - \bar{\bar{X}})^2$	$rc - 1$		

An Application of Excel

As described previously, the calculations that are required to perform ANOVA are time consuming and error prone. However, when Excel is used, the calculations are instantaneous, precise, and easy. For example, in Exhibit 8.1, the original data were recorded. The results of ANOVA were obtained as follows:

1. Select "Data Analysis"
2. Select "ANOVA: Single Factor"
3. Highlight the field in which the data appear
4. Indicate the field in which the results will appear
5. Press "OK"

Exhibit 8.1 **Analysis of Variance: One-Way ANOVA**

Patient	Hospital A_1	Hospital A_2	Hospital A_3	Hospital A_4
1	2	3	5	10
2	3	6	8	11
3	4	7	9	13
4	3	5	10	8
5	4	4	4	9
6	2	5	6	9

ANOVA: Single Factor

SUMMARY

Groups	Count	Sum	Average	Variance
Column 1	6	18	3	0.8
Column 2	6	30	5	2
Column 3	6	42	7	5.6
Column 4	6	60	10	3.2

ANOVA

Source of Variation	SS	df	MS	F	P-Value	F crit
Between Groups	160.5	3	53.5	18.44828	5.6E-06	3.098393
Within Groups	58	20	2.9			
Total	218.5	23				

After doing this, the results are reported in two sections. The first is a summary, and the second consists of an ANOVA table that is similar to Table 8.2.

In Exhibit 8.1, the "SUMMARY" section reports the number of observations in each column, the sum of the values in each column, the average value for each column, and the variance exhibited by the data in each column. The "ANOVA" table identifies the source of variation as "between groups," which corresponds to the treatment effects discussed earlier, and "within groups," a designation that refers to the error term identified in this chapter as SS(ERROR). The ANOVA table also contains the sum of squares, represented by SS, the degrees of freedom, df, the mean square, listed in the column identified as MS, and the calculated F ratio. The column identified as "P-value" indicates the probability of obtaining a calculated value of F equal to approximately 18.44 if the mean square treatment is equal to the mean square error. Because the probability represented by the P value is clearly less than 0.05, we reject the assumption of homoscedasticity and conclude that MS(TR) exceeds MS(ERROR). The final column reports the critical value of F. Because the calculated value of F exceeds the critical value, we are forced again to reject the null hypothesis in favor of the alternate and conclude that at least two of the treatment effects (i.e., hospital characteristics) are significant.

Two-Way or Two-Factor ANOVA^R

In the previous section, we examined the effects of differences among groups that were classified in terms of one dimension (e.g., the four hospitals). We referred to the dimension as the treatment effects. The treatment factor might be regarded as the *independent variable*, whereas the variable of administrative interest for which variation is analyzed might be regarded as the *dependent* variable. In the example, we might suppose that the dependent variable, length of stay, depends on the independent variable, which is defined as the treatments and is represented in the example by the four hospitals.

In two-way ANOVA, we introduce a second factor that might "explain" variation in the variable of interest or the dependent variable. For example, refer to the example introduced previously here and assume now that the rows are defined by one of six diagnoses. The mean length of stay associated with each of the six diagnoses can be summarized as follows:

Row	Diagnosis	Length of Stay
1	1	5.00
2	2	7.00
3	3	8.25
4	4	6.50
5	5	5.25
6	6	5.50

After diagnosis is introduced, a new dimension is added to the analysis. The introduction of diagnosis implies that a portion of the term SS(ERROR) calculated previously may be attributable to differences in the diagnoses for which the patients were admitted. The addition of diagnosis also indicates that we should have performed two-way ANOVA instead of one-way ANOVA.

When two-factor or two-way ANOVA is used, the total variation is partitioned into three rather than two components. In this case, the total variation is partitioned first into differences that are attributable to treatment effects, represented by the different hospitals in the example, and into differences that are attributable to the second factor, referred to as the block effects. In the example, the *block effects* refer to the portion of the total variation exhibited by the data that is traced to the diagnoses for which the patients were admitted. The third term consists of unexplained variation and is frequently referred to as experimental error.

Before proceeding, we can identify two approaches to the analysis of experiments involving two factors. The approaches are contingent on our ability to measure the interaction of two variables, A and B. In this section, we assume that we are unable to measure the interaction of A and B. The next section examines two-way or two-factor ANOVA with interaction or replication.

The Basic Model: Two-Way ANOVA Without Interaction

Table 8.4, the focus of this section, illustrates two-factor ANOVA. The inclusion of the mean lengths of stay, grouped by diagnosis, is the only difference between Tables 8.1 and 8.4. As before, we must specify the null hypotheses that we wish to examine. In the following, the focus is on differences among *row* means. We may define the set of row means, represented by μ_i, in terms of the mean, μ, and the

Table 8.4 **Length of Stay and Two-Way ANOVA**

Diagnosis	Hospital				
	A_1	A_2	A_3	A_4	Mean
1	2	3	5	10	5.00
2	3	6	8	11	7.00
3	4	7	9	13	8.25
4	3	5	10	8	6.50
5	4	4	4	9	5.25
6	2	5	6	9	5.50
Total	18	30	42	60	
Mean	3.0	5.0	7.0	10	

block effect, represented in general by θ_i. Similar to our discussion of the treatment effects, we may define the row means by

$$\mu_i = \mu + \theta_i \qquad \text{(Equation 8.5)}$$

for i = 1, . . . , 6. Similar to our discussion of the treatment effects, the null hypothesis presumes that the row means are identical and equal to the mean μ. When viewed from the perspective of Equation 8.5, the null hypothesis with regard to the block effects, H_{ob}, might be expressed as

$$H_{ob}: \theta_1 = \theta_2 = \theta_3 = \theta_4 = \theta_5 = \theta_6 = 0$$

The null hypothesis is equivalent to the assumption that the row means are identical and equal to the common mean μ. Because the sum of the block effects, represented by $\Sigma\theta_i$, must equal zero, the alternate hypothesis states that not all of the block effects are zero, implying that two or more of the θs are nonzero.

As in our discussion of one-way or one-factor ANOVA, we also consider the treatment effects and examine the null hypothesis

$$H_{ot}: \lambda_1 = \lambda_2 = \lambda_3 = \lambda_4 = 0$$

The null hypothesis implies that the treatment effects are zero; thus, the treatment means are identical and equal to the common mean μ. The alternate hypothesis is that not all of the treatment effects are zero and that two or more of the λs are nonzero.

The basic approach in two-factor ANOVA is to partition the total variation exhibited by the data in accordance with

$$SS(TOT) = SS(TR) + SS(B) + SS(ERROR) \qquad \text{(Equation 8.6)}$$

The only difference between one-factor and two-factor ANOVA is the addition of SS(B) to Equation 8.1.

In this case, SS(B) refers to the sum squared deviations that reflect the block effects. Equation 8.2 defines SS(TOT), and Equation 8.3 defines SS(TR). The sum of squared error terms, SS(ERROR), may be treated as a residual as indicated by

$$SS(ERROR) = SS(TOT) - [SS(TR) + SS(B)] \qquad \text{(Equation 8.7)}$$

The definitional formula for the sum of squares that reflect differences among row means is similar to SS(TR). Specifically, we define SS(B) by

$$SS(B) = \Sigma c_i\,(\bar{X}_i - \bar{\bar{X}})^2 \qquad \text{(Equation 8.8)}$$

In this case, $(\bar{X}_i - \bar{\bar{X}})^2$ requires us to find the deviation of the mean for row i relative to the grand mean and square the result. We then weight the squared deviation by the number of observations on which $\bar{X}_i$ was based and then sum over all such weighted squared deviations. We are tempted, as in our previous discussion, to accept the null hypothesis if the value of SS(B) is small or to reject the null hypothesis in favor of the alternate if the value of SS(B) is large.

In the example,

$$SS(TOT) = 218.5$$

a result obtained in the previous section, whereas the sum of square treatment was

$$SS(TR) = 160.5$$

The sum of squared deviations reflecting the block effects is given by

$$SS(B) = 4[(5 - 6.25)^2 + (7 - 6.25)^2 + (8.25 - 6.25)^2 + (6.5 - 6.25)^2 + (5.25 - 6.25)^2 + (5.50 - 6.25)^2]$$

or 31. Finally, the sum of squared error terms, SS(ERROR), is given by

$$SS(ERROR) = 218.5 - (160.5 + 31)$$

or 27. The sum of squared error terms that was calculated when one-way ANOVA was applied to the data exceeds the sum of squared error terms derived from two-factor ANOVA by an amount equal to SS(B). In particular,

SS(ERROR) (one-way)	58
SS(ERROR) (two-way)	− 27
SS(B)	31

Thus, with other factors remaining constant, the two-way ANOVA results in a lower value of SS(ERROR) than one-factor ANOVA.

Thus far this section's discussion has focused on the method of partitioning the total variation in the data into portions representing the treatment effects, the block effects, and the portion of the variation that is unexplained. The assessment of the two null hypotheses, however, requires three measures of variance, represented by MS(TR), MS(B), and MS(ERROR). As demonstrated previously, the variance representing the treatment effects is simply the ratio of SS(TR)/c − 1, where the denominator is the number of degrees of freedom derived by the number of treatments less one. Similarly, we note that the variation derived for the block effects required us to calculate six squared deviations, but we sacrificed one degree of freedom when $\bar{\bar{X}}$ was used as a point estimate of μ. Thus, the degrees of freedom associated with SS(B) is r − 1 (i.e., the number of rows less one), and the corresponding mean square is obtained by

$$MS(B) = SS(B)/r - 1 \qquad \text{(Equation 8.9)}$$

The degrees of freedom assigned to the sum of the squared error term is the product of the number of rows less one and the number of columns less one or alternatively expressed (r − 1)(c − 1).

Using general notation, two-factor ANOVA is summarized in Table 8.5. In this case, the source of variation is identified as the error term, the block effect, and the treatment effect.

The definitional equations for the three components appear in the second column, and the total sum of squares appears in the second column. The third column summarizes the degrees of freedom, and the fourth column defines the ratios that yield the mean square terms or the variances. The final column defines the calculated F ratio used to evaluate the treatment and the block effects. If the ratio of MS(TR)/MS(ERROR) exceeds the critical value of F, represented by $F_{\alpha, c-1, (r-1)(c-1)}$, we are forced to reject the assumption that the two variances are equal and conclude that MS(TR) exceeds MS(ERROR). If the ratio MS(B)/MS(ERROR) exceeds the critical value of F, represented by $F_{\alpha, r-1, (r-1)(c-1)}$, we are forced to conclude that MS(B) is significantly greater than MS(ERROR) and that at least two of the block effects differ from zero.

In the example, the numeric results derived previously here are summarized in Table 8.6. In the final column, the calculated value of F for the treatment effects was 29.72. These results indicate that the value of MS(TR) exceeds the value of MS(ERROR) by a factor of approximately 30. The corresponding critical value of F for $\alpha = 0.05$ with 3 degrees of freedom in the numerator and 15 degrees of freedom in the denominator is 3.29. Because the calculated value of F exceeds the critical value, we are forced to reject the null hypothesis and, as before, conclude that at least two of the treatment effects differ significantly from zero.

The F ratio derived for the block effects was 3.44, whereas the critical value of F for $\alpha = 0.05$ with 5 degrees of freedom in the numerator and 15 degrees of freedom in the denominator is 2.90. In this case, because the calculated value of F ex-

Table 8.5 **Summary of Two-Way ANOVA**

Source	Sum of Squares	Degrees of Freedom	Mean Square	F Ratio
Treatment	$\Sigma r_j (\bar{X}_j - \bar{\bar{X}})^2$	c − 1	SS(TR)/c − 1	MS(TR)/MS(ERROR)
Block	$\Sigma c_i (\bar{X}_i - \bar{\bar{X}})^2$	r − 1	SS(B)/r − 1	MS(B)/MS(ERROR)
Error	Residual	(r − 1)(c − 1)	SS(ERROR)/ (r − 1)(c − 1)	
Total	$\Sigma\Sigma (x_{ij} - \bar{\bar{X}})^2$	rc − 1		

Table 8.6 **Two-Factor ANOVA: Length of Stay**

Source	Sum of Squares	Degrees of Freedom	Mean Square	F Ratio
Treatment	160.5	3	53.5	29.72
Block	31.0	5	6.2	3.44
Error	27.0	15	1.8	
Total	218.5	23		

ceeds the critical value, we are required to reject the null hypothesis and conclude that at least two of the block effects differ significantly from zero.

An Application of Excel

Two-way or two-factor ANOVA is easily calculated with Excel. In Exhibit 8.2, the basic data were entered initially. The results were obtained by

1. Selecting "Data Analysis"
2. Selecting "ANOVA: Two-factor without Replication"
3. Highlighting the field in which the data appear
4. Identifying the field in which the results appear
5. Entering "OK"

The results derived by an application of Excel identify the source of variation by referring to rows, a designation that is identical to the block effects, and to columns, which is a designation that consistently identifies the treatment effects. The results shown in the exhibit agree with those obtained when the definitional equations were applied to the data. In the ANOVA table, we see that, when combined, the calculated value of F, the "P-value" and the critical value of F require us to reject both null hypotheses and conclude that at least two of the treatment effects differ significantly from zero and that at least two of the block effects differ significantly from zero. The "P-value" of 0.0000001 is the likelihood of obtaining a calculated value of F equal to 53.5 if all treatment effects are equal to zero. Similarly, the results indicate that the probability of obtaining a calculated value of F equal to 3.44 is 0.03 if all block effects are equal to zero. Because both probabilities are less 0.05, we must conclude that at least two treatment effects and two block effects differ significantly from zero.

Two-Factor ANOVA: With Interaction or Replication[O]

The methods described in this section are merely an extension of two-factor ANOVA and enable us to examine the main and interactive effects of independent

Exhibit 8.2 **Analysis of Variance; Two-Way ANOVA**

Diagnosis	Hospital A_1	Hospital A_2	Hospital A_3	Hospital A_4
1	2	3	5	10
2	3	6	8	11
3	4	7	9	13
4	3	5	10	8
5	4	4	4	9
6	2	5	6	9

Anova: Two-Factor Without Replication

SUMMARY

Groups	Count	Sum	Average	Variance
Row 1	4	20	5	12.66667
Row 2	4	28	7	11.33333
Row 3	4	33	8.25	14.25
Row 4	4	26	6.5	9.666667
Row 5	4	21	5.25	6.25
Row 6	4	22	5.5	8.333333
Column 1	6	18	3	0.8
Column 2	6	30	5	2
Column 3	6	42	7	5.6
Column 4	6	60	10	3.2

ANOVA

Source of Variation	SS	df	MS	F	P-Value	F crit
Rows	31	5	6.2	3.444444	0.02851	2.901295
Columns	160.5	3	53.5	29.72222	1.48E-06	3.287383
Error	27	15	1.8			
Total	218.5	23				

factors on the dependent variable. For example, consider a situation in which we are interested in the days of delay in transferring older patients, grouped by diagnosis, from each of three hospitals to a source of postdischarge service provided by a long-term care facility. In this case, the length of delay is defined as the number of days that pass between the date that the patient was medically ready for transfer and the date of discharge. In Table 8.7, the three hospitals, A, B, and C, represent the treatment effects, and the diagnoses correspond to the block effect. A sample of four patients was selected for each of the hospitals and each of the

Table 8.7 **Days of Delay in Transferring the Patient to a Long-Term Care Facility**

Diagnosis	Hospital			
	A	B	C	Mean
1	1, 2, 1, 3 **(1.75)**	4, 5, 8, 9 **(6.5)**	3, 6, 10, 12 **(7.75)**	5.33
2	2, 3, 1, 4 **(2.50)**	7, 8, 6, 10 **(7.75)**	6, 4, 3, 5 **(4.50)**	4.92
3	2, 1, 1, 5 **(2.25)**	12, 11, 6, 8 **(9.25)**	7, 4, 3, 2 **(4.00)**	5.17
Mean	2.17	7.83	5.42	5.14

diagnoses. In this case, we are interested in the treatment effects represented by the hospitals, and the block effects, represented by the three diagnoses.

However, the primary focus here is on the interactive effects between the hospitals and diagnoses. It is possible for the hospitals to treat cases of given diagnoses that differ in severity or complexity, a feature that might complicate or facilitate placement and thereby contribute to differences in the length of delay in transferring patients to a source of postdischarge care.

As before, we partition the variation shown by the data into portions that are attributable to the treatment effects (i.e., the hospitals), the block effects (i.e., the diagnostic conditions), and the interactive effects (i.e., between the hospitals and diagnoses). The focus is also on three null hypotheses. Similar to our previous discussion of treatment effects, represented by λ_j, the first of the null hypotheses presumes that the column means are equal. In the example, we may posit the null hypothesis that pertains to the treatment effects as

$$H_{ot}: \lambda_1 = \lambda_2 = \lambda_3 = 0$$

In addition, we examine the null hypothesis that the row means are equal. As before, we represent the block effects by θ_i and express the related null hypothesis as

$$H_{ob}: \theta_1 = \theta_2 = \theta_3 = 0$$

The third of the null hypotheses focuses on the interactive effects, represented by $\theta\lambda_{ij}$, and might be specified as

$$H_{obt}: . \theta\lambda_{11} = \theta\lambda_{12} = \ldots \theta\lambda_{rc}$$

As before, the sum of the treatment effects must equal zero (i.e., $\Sigma\lambda_j = 0$) and the sum of the block effects must equal zero (i.e., $\Sigma\theta_i = 0$). Similarly, the sum of the interactive effects also must equal zero ($\Sigma\Sigma\ \theta\lambda_{ij} = 0$).

The Structural Model

The basic approach to two-factor ANOVA might be expressed as

$$SS(TOT) = SS(TR) + SS(B) + SS(TRB) + SS(ERROR) \qquad \text{(Equation 8.10)}$$

In this case, we let SS(TRB) correspond to the sum of squares that is attributable to the interaction between the treatment and block effects. The definitions of the other terms in the equation are identical to those adopted in previous sections of this chapter. To develop the definitional equations for each of the components identified by Equation 8.10, we let x_{ijk} correspond to one of the observations assigned to block i (diagnosis) and treatment j (hospital). Thus, x_{ijk} is the delay in discharging one of the four patients presenting a given diagnosis and discharged from one of the three hospitals. We also let n represent the size of the sample or the number of observations associated with the cell corresponding to block i and treatment j. In Table 8.5, the sample size, n, consists of four patients that were selected for each diagnosis and treatment.

We may now define the total variation and its components. Specifically, when two-factor ANOVA with interaction is employed, the total sum of squares, representing total variation exhibited by the data, is given by

$$SS(TOT) = \Sigma_k \Sigma_i \Sigma_j (x_{ijk} - \bar{\bar{X}})^2 \qquad \text{(Equation 8.11)}$$

This simply indicates that total variation is obtained by (1) calculating the deviation of each observation relative to the grand mean, (2) squaring the result, and (3) summing all squared deviations. In Equation 8.11, Σ_k indicates that we are required to sum the squared deviations for all observations in a given sample, and Σ_i indicates that we are required to sum over all rows or blocks. Finally, Σ_j indicates that we must sum over all columns or treatments. In the example, we find that the total variation exhibited by the data is given by

$$\begin{aligned} SS(TOT) = {} & (1 - 5.14)^2 + \ldots + (3 - 5.14)^2 + (4 - 5.14)^2 + \ldots + (9 - 5.14)^2 \\ & + (3 - 5.14)^2 + \ldots + (12 - 5.14)^2 + (2 - 5.14)^2 + \ldots + (4 - 5.14)^2 \\ & + (7 - 5.14)^2 + \ldots + (10 - 5.14)^2 + (6 - 5.14)^2 \\ & + \ldots + (5 - 5.14)^2 + (2 - 5.14)^2 + \ldots + (5 - 5.14)^2 + (12 - 5.14)^2 \\ & + \ldots + (8 - 5.14)^2 + (7 - 5.14)^2 + \ldots + (2 - 5.14)^2 \end{aligned}$$

After performing the calculations, we find that the total variation in the data is approximately 378.27 days.

Consider next the portion of the total variation that is attributable to the treatment effects. As before, we measure the treatment effects by the variation exhibited by column or treatment means relative to the grand mean. In two-factor

ANOVA, with repetitions, we calculate the portion of the variation attributable to the treatment effects in accordance with

$$SS(TR) = nr\Sigma(\bar{X}_j - \bar{\bar{X}})^2 \qquad \text{(Equation 8.12)}$$

The product nr is the number of observations on which the value of a given column mean is based. For example, when calculating the average length of delay for hospital A, we used a sample of four patients for each of the three diagnoses, implying that the product of n and r is 12. In the example, the portion of the variation that is attributable to the characteristics of the three hospitals is given by

$$SS(TR) = 12[(2.17 - 5.14)^2 + (7.83 - 5.14)^2 + (5.52 - 5.14)^2]$$

or approximately 194 days.

Similarly, we calculate the portion of the total variation that is attributable to the block effects by

$$SS(B) = nc\Sigma(\bar{X}_i - \bar{\bar{X}})^2 \qquad \text{(Equation 8.13)}$$

Thus, the value of SS(B) is obtained by finding the deviation of each row or block mean from the grand mean, squaring the deviation, summing the results, and weighting the sum of squared deviations by the number of observations on which each row mean is based. In the example,

$$SS(B) = 12[(5.33 - 5.14)^2 + (4.67 - 5.14)^2 + (5.17 - 5.14)^2]$$

After completing the calculations, we find that the portion of the total variation that the data exhibited is approximately 1.03 days.

Consider next the portion of the variation that is attributable to the interactive effects. We define the variation that is attributable to the interaction among the treatment and block effects by

$$(SSTRB) = n\,\Sigma_i\,\Sigma_j\,[\bar{X}_{ij} - (\bar{X}_i + \bar{X}_j - \bar{\bar{X}})]^2 \qquad \text{(Equation 8.14)}$$

In Equation 8.14, $\bar{X}_{ij}$ is the mean of the sample selected for block i and treatment j, whereas $(\bar{X}_i + \bar{X}_j - \bar{\bar{X}})$ is simply the sum of the corresponding block and treatment mean, less the grand mean. As a consequence, the expression

$$[\bar{X}_{ij} - (\bar{X}_i + \bar{X}_j - \bar{\bar{X}})]$$

indicates the magnitude of the deviation of $\bar{X}_{ij}$ relative to the sum of $\bar{X}_i + \bar{X}_j$ less $\bar{\bar{X}}$. Squaring all such deviations, summing the results, and adjusting for the number of observations on which $\overline{X}_{ij}$ is based yield the portion of the variation that is attributable to the interactive effects.

Using Equation 8.14 in the example yields

$$SS(TRB) = 4[(1.75 - (5.33 + 2.17 - 5.14)]^2 + \ldots + [(7.75 - (5.33 + 5.42 - 5.14)]^2 + [2.50 - (4.92 + 2.17 - 5.14)]^2 + \ldots + [(4.50 - (4.92 + 5.42 - 5.14)]^2 + [2.25 - (5.17 + 2.17 - 5.14)]^2 + \ldots + [(4.00 - (5.17 + 5.42 - 5.14)]^2$$

After performing the calculations, we find that the portion of the variation exhibited by the days of delayed transfer amounts to approximately 48.44.

Similar to the discussion in the previous section, we treat the sum of squared error terms as a residual, resulting in

$$SS(ERROR) = SS(TR) - SS(TR) - SS(B) - SS(TRB) \qquad \text{(Equation 8.15)}$$

Using Equation 8.15, the example yields

$$SS(ERROR) = 388.31 - 194 - 1.03 - 1.03 - 48.44$$

or approximately 134.8 days.

Thus far, this discussion has focused on the portion of the variation that is attributable to each of the four components. However, in order to analyze the data, we must transform each measure of variation into the corresponding indicator of variance. In this case, the degrees of freedom associated with the treatment effects are, as before, $c - 1$, whereas the degrees of freedom assigned to the block effects are $r - 1$. The interactive term is assigned $(r - 1)(c - 1)$ degrees of freedom, and the error term is assigned $rc(n - 1)$ degrees of freedom.

The results obtained thus far might be summarized as shown in Table 8.8. The measures of variation summarized in the second column were obtained by applying the definitional equations to the illustrative data. The degrees of freedom in the third column were derived as follows:

Treatment	3 columns or hospitals (i.e., $c - 1 = 3 - 1$)
Block	3 rows or diagnoses (i.e., $r - 1 = 3 - 1$)
Interactive	3 columns and 3 rows [i.e., $(r - 1) * (c - 1) = (3 - 1)(3 - 1)$]
Error	3 rows, 3 columns, and a sample of $n = 4$ [i.e., $rc(n - 1) = 3 * 3 * (4 - 1)$]

When each measure of variation, shown in the second column, is divided by the appropriate number of degrees of freedom, listed in the third column, the mean

Table 8.8 **ANOVA, with Interaction, of the Delay in Transferring Patients**

Source	Variation (SS)	d.f.	Variance (MS)	F
Treatment	194.00	2	97	19.44
Block	1.03	2	0.51	0.10
Interaction	48.44	4	12.11	2.43
Error	134.80	27	4.99	
Total	378.27	35		

square or variance, shown in the fourth column, is obtained. The F ratios that appear in the final column of the table were obtained as follows:

MS(TR)/MS(ERROR) = 97/4.99
MS(B)/MS(ERROR) = 0.51/4.99
MS(TRB)/MS(ERROR) = 12.11/4.99

As before, we examine the assumption of equal variance by comparing the calculated value of F with F_α that is defined for appropriate number of degrees of freedom in the numerator and denominator. If $\alpha = 0.05$, the value of $F_{\alpha,2,27}$ is approximately 3.35. Referring to the F ratio computed for the treatment effects, we observe that the calculated value of F, given by 19.44, exceeds the critical value; thus, we must reject the assumption that MS(TR) is equal to MS(ERROR) and conclude that the two variances differ significantly. The results indicate that hospital characteristics significantly influence the length of delay in transferring patients to a postdischarge source of care.

In contrast, when viewed from the perspective of the block effects or the influence of diagnosis, the calculated value of F, 0.10, is less than 3.35, and thus, we are unable to reject the assumption of homoscedasticity, implying that differences in the medical conditions exert no significant influence on the length of delay. Finally, the value of $F_{\alpha,4,27}$ is approximately 2.73. In this case, the calculated value of F derived for the interactive effects (i.e., 2.43) also is less than the critical value, implying that the interaction between the medical conditions and hospital attributes failed to have a significant influence on the length of delay.

The analysis indicates that the length of delay in transferring patients to a source of postdischarge care is influenced only by differences in the attributes of the three hospitals. The analysis indicates that the administrator should examine the process of discharge planning in Hospitals A, B, and C, an investigation that may result in the implementation of a remedial policy or plan of action.

An Application of Excel

Two-factor ANOVA, with interaction or replication, is easily and accurately performed when Excel is used. The original data are listed in Exhibit 8.3. The hospi-

Exhibit 8.3 **Analysis of Variance with Replication or Interaction**

Diagnosis		**Hospital**	
	A	**B**	**C**
1	**1**	4	3
	2	5	6
	1	8	10
	3	9	12
2	2	**7**	6
	3	**8**	4
	1	**6**	3
	4	**10**	5
3	2	12	7
	1	11	4
	1	6	3
	5	8	2

ANOVA: Two-Factor with Replication

SUMMARY	**A**	**B**	**C**	**Total**
1				
Count	4	4	4	12
Sum	7	26	31	64
Average	**1.75**	**6.5**	**7.75**	**5.333333**
Variance	0.91666667	5.666666667	16.25	13.51515152
2				
Count	4	4	4	12
Sum	10	31	18	59
Average	**2.5**	**7.75**	**4.5**	**4.916667**
Variance	1.666667	2.916667	1.666667	6.810606
3				
Count	4	4	4	12
Sum	9	37	16	62
Average	**2.25**	**9.25**	**4**	**5.166667**
Variance	3.583333	7.583333	4.666667	13.9697
Total				
Count	12	12	12	
Sum	26	94	65	
Average	**2.166667**	**7.833333**	**5.416667**	
Variance	1.787879	5.787879	9.174242	

continues

Exhibit 8.3 **(Continued)**

ANOVA

Source of Variation	**SS**	**df**	**MS**	**F**	**P-Value**	**F crit**
Sample	1.055556	2	0.527778	0.105751	0.900019	3.354131
Columns	194.0556	2	97.02778	19.44156	5.89E-06	3.354131
Interaction	48.44444	4	12.11111	2.426716	0.0723163	2.727766
Within	134.75	27	4.990741			
Total	378.3056	35				

tals and medical conditions are designated, and the data have been arranged in columns. The sample selected for diagnosis 1 and Hospital A and the data derived for diagnosis 2 and Hospital B appear in bold face. The results were obtained by

1. Selecting the "ANOVA: two-factor with replication" function
2. Identifying the field in which the data appear, to include the information that identifies the hospital and the diagnosis
3. Entering a value of 4 to identify the number of rows per sample
4. Identifying the field in which the results will appear
5. Entering "OK"

Excel reports results simultaneously, as shown in the second half of Exhibit 8.3.

The data appearing in the summary section require a brief explanation. The results are reported in four main sections. The first three of these correspond to the mean of each sample, grouped by diagnosis and hospital, and to the mean of each block or treatment. The mean of each sample and row appears in bold face. In the first section, the mean of the samples selected for diagnosis 1 and Hospitals A, B, and C were 1.75, 6.5, and 7.75 days, respectively. The mean delay for all patients hospitalized with diagnosis 1 was 5.33333 days. The fourth section of the summary reports the results that are derived for each column or hospital. In the last row of the summary data, the mean length of delay for Hospitals A, B, and C were 2.166667, 7.83333, and 5.4166667 days, respectively.

The ANOVA table is interpreted as follows. The source of variation identified as "sample" corresponds to the block effects or to the diagnoses, whereas the source identified as "columns" refers to the treatment or hospital effects. The row identified as "interaction" contains results that pertain to the interactive effects, whereas the row identified as "within" refers to the error term. As discussed in the previous section, a comparison of the calculated value of F with the critical value forces us to conclude that MS(B), MS(TRB), and MS(ERROR) do not differ significantly. In contrast, a comparison of the calculated and critical values that enables us to assess the influence of differences among the hospitals on the length of the delay forces us to reject the assumption that the variances are equal and to conclude that MS(TR) is significantly greater than MS(ERROR).

These results are confirmed when we compare the value of α with the exact probability listed in the column identified as "P-value." In this case, approximately 0.9000 is the probability of obtaining a calculated value of F equal to approximately 0.10 if the two variances are equal. Because the "P-value" of 0.90 is much larger than the value of α (0.05), we are unable to reject the null hypothesis and must conclude that MS(B) and MS(ERROR) do not differ significantly. However, if the null hypothesis concerning the treatment effect is true, the probability of getting a calculated value of F equal to 19.44 is 0.000005. Because the probability of 0.000005 is much less than 0.05, these results indicate that the value of MS(TR) is significantly larger than MS(ERROR), and that differences among the hospitals are factors that significantly influence the delay in transferring patients. Finally, minor differences between the values in Table 8.6 and those in Exhibit 8.3 are attributable to rounding errors.

Exercises

1. In a multi-institutional arrangement, we are concerned about the delay in transferring inpatients to an alternate source of care after hospitalization. We measured the delay in transfer by the lapse of time between the date on which the patient was clinically ready for transfer and the date on which the patient was discharged to a long-term care facility. Focusing on three of our hospitals, we randomly selected five patients who were transferred to a nursing home from each hospital and obtained the following data:

	Hospital	
A	B	C
10	8	15
12	6	22
9	5	21
11	10	19
14	9	18

If $\alpha = 0.05$, use these data to determine whether the differences among treatment effects are significant or attributable to chance.

2. A random sample of six employees assigned to each of three departments showed the number of days absence because of illness during the past year:

Radiology	Laboratory	Dietary
9	4	10
6	2	13
7	3	11
5	6	9
8	5	8
7	1	12

If $\alpha = 0.05$, determine whether the differences among the departments are significant or attributable to chance?

3. After selecting six visits from each of four clinics, the amount of time committed to initial visits was as follows:

Clinic			
A	B	C	D
25	20	15	18
30	18	17	21
32	21	17	22
36	19	18	23
31	22	20	19
29	23	21	19

If $\alpha = 0.05$, use these data to determine whether there are significant differences in the amount of time committed to initial visits provided by the four clinics.

4. Referring to the original data in exercise 1, suppose each row is now defined by a different diagnosis:

Diagnosis	Hospital		
	A	B	C
1	10	8	15
2	12	6	22
3	9	5	21
4	11	10	19
5	14	9	18

If $\alpha = 0.05$, determine whether differences among the treatment and block effects are significant.

5. Assume that in an evaluation of the laboratory, we are interested in the efficiency of three technicians when they process four tests. The following data, measured in minutes, represents the time required by each technician to provide each of the services.

	Technician		
Procedure	A	B	C
1	20	18	22
2	35	33	37
3	14	16	18
4	45	47	46

If $\alpha = 0.05$, determine whether the differences among the treatment and block effects are significant.

6. Using the data in exercise 3, assume that each row corresponds to a given time during the day, measured from the physician's initial contact with the patient.

Time	Clinic			
	A	B	C	D
8–9:59	25	20	15	18
10–11:59	30	18	17	21
12–1:59	32	21	17	22
2–3:59	36	19	18	23
4–5:59	31	22	20	19
6 –7:59	29	23	21	19

If $\alpha = 0.05$, determine whether the differences among the treatment and block effects are significant.

7. A large health maintenance organization is interested in the prescribing patterns of physicians. Suppose that we selected a random sample of three patients treated for four diagnoses by three physicians.

	Physician		
Diagnosis	A	B	C
1	11,7,9	8,6,7	5,4,7
2	14,10,11	10,9,8	6,8,7
3	4,5,3	5,5,6	3,4,2
4	10,9,7	6,7,4	5,6,3

If $\alpha = 0.05$, determine whether differences among the treatment, block, and interactive effects are significant.

8. The budgetary request from each of three long-term care facilities operated by our organization was based in part on the case complexity of residents. To assess the situation, suppose that we selected four patients in each of

three age groups from each of the facilities and obtained the number of secondary diagnoses presented by each resident. The results derived from the samples are as follows.

	Facility		
Age Group	A	B	C
65–74	2,4,3,5	7,4,8,9	10,9,7,8
75–84	4,5,5,6	6,8,9,10	11,10,9,12
85+	5,6,7,5	7,9,10,11	13,14,12,12

Let $\alpha = 0.05$ and determine whether differences among the treatment, block, and interactive effects are significant or attributable to chance.

CHAPTER 9 COVARIANCE[R]

OBJECTIVES

1. Describe the role of covariance in measuring the relationship between two variables.
2. Use the data in a graph to show the relationship between two variables.
3. Calculate covariance (x, y).
4. Use Excel to calculate the covariance of x and y.

This chapter focuses on the relationship of one variable with another. The methods introduced here measure the direction of change in one variable as the other variable increases or decreases. For example, it is reasonable to expect that the resource consumption or related costs grow as the volume of care increases. We might speculate that the use of health services increases as the diagnostic condition becomes more complex or severe. In each of these situations, the focus is on the association of one variable with another.

When examining the direction of association in a bivariate analysis, one of the factors is identified as the dependent variable and the other is the independent variable. We focus on paired observations of the dependent and the independent variable represented by the set $\{x_i, y_i\}$. We let y correspond to the dependent variable and x represent the independent variable. The set of paired observations indicates that when x is equal to x_i, y is equal to y_i. Thus, $\{x_i, y_i\}$ enables us to assess the direction of association between the two variables.

In this chapter, a graph of the paired observations is used to see the direction of association between x and y. We also focus on the concept of covariance as an approach that indicates the direction of the relationship. In addition to measuring the association between the two variables, an understanding of covariation and covariance is essential to our consideration of regression analysis, which is discussed in Chapter 10.

A GRAPH OF ASSOCIATION

Suppose that the administrator of a long-term care facility is interested in the association between total costs and the volume of care, measured by the number of bed days of service provided during each month of the past year. Suppose also that the capacity to provide service was constant during the period and was limited to

100 beds. Thus, during a 30-day operating period, the maximum capacity is 3,000 bed days of care. We also suppose that the examination of association between cost and volume is based on the data in Table 9.1.

These data represent paired observations and indicate the cost that was incurred for each volume alternative. For example, during the first period, the organization provided 2,500 bed days of care and incurred costs of $300,000.

Exhibit 9.1 shows that the data might be portrayed as a graph to show the relationship between costs and volume. The scatter gram was prepared by first entering the data and highlighting the field in which they appear. The paired observations were then rearranged in ascending order by employing the "Sort Ascending" function, which is located on the tool bar of the Excel spreadsheet. The rearranged data were then used to construct the scatter gram as follows:

1. Select the "Chart Wizard" function.
2. Select the "XY Scatter" function.
3. Highlight the field in which the data are located, and indicate that the information is arranged in columns.
4. Select next and then finish.

Focusing on the range of volume alternatives that extends from 2,000 to 3,000 bed days of care, the scatter gram indicates that the coordinates form a pattern that rises from left to right, indicating that costs and the volume of care are positively associated (i.e., as volume increases, the costs rise).

In addition to the scatter gram shown in Exhibit 9.1, the distribution of observations among four quadrants might be used to identify direct and inverse asso-

Table 9.1 **The Total Cost and the Corresponding Number of Bed Days of Care**

Period	Cost (y_i) ($)	Volume (x_i)
1	300,000	2,500
2	318,600	2,700
3	294,000	2,800
4	276,000	2,400
5	321,550	2,950
6	322,000	2,875
7	338,100	2,940
8	303,750	2,430
9	286,000	2,200
10	294,900	2,378
11	320,400	2,670
12	308,800	2,552

Exhibit 9.1 **Line Chart Depicting the Relationship of Cost to Volume**

Period	Cost	Volume
4	276,000	2,400
9	286,000	2,200
3	294,000	2,800
10	294,900	2,378
1	300,000	2,500
8	303,750	2,430
12	308,800	2,552
2	318,600	2,700
11	320,400	2,670
5	321,500	2,950
6	322,000	2,875
7	338,100	2,940

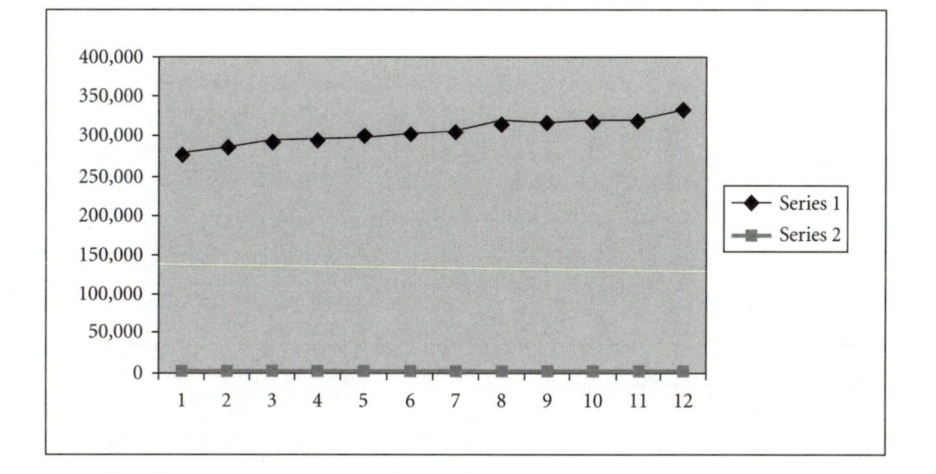

ciations between two variables. We assume that the values of x and y are distributed normally and consider first a positive relationship between x and y. In Figure 9.1, the mean values of y and x were used to divide the graph into four quadrants. The first quadrant, identified by I, consists of observations on x and y that exceed their respective means. The third quadrant, represented by III, consists of values of x and y that are less than their respective means. As a consequence, the distribution shown in Figure 9.1 indicates that relatively high values of y are associated with relatively high values of x and that relatively low values of y are associated with relatively low values of x. Thus, a concentration of observations in the third and first quadrant indicates the presence of a positive association between the two variables of interest.

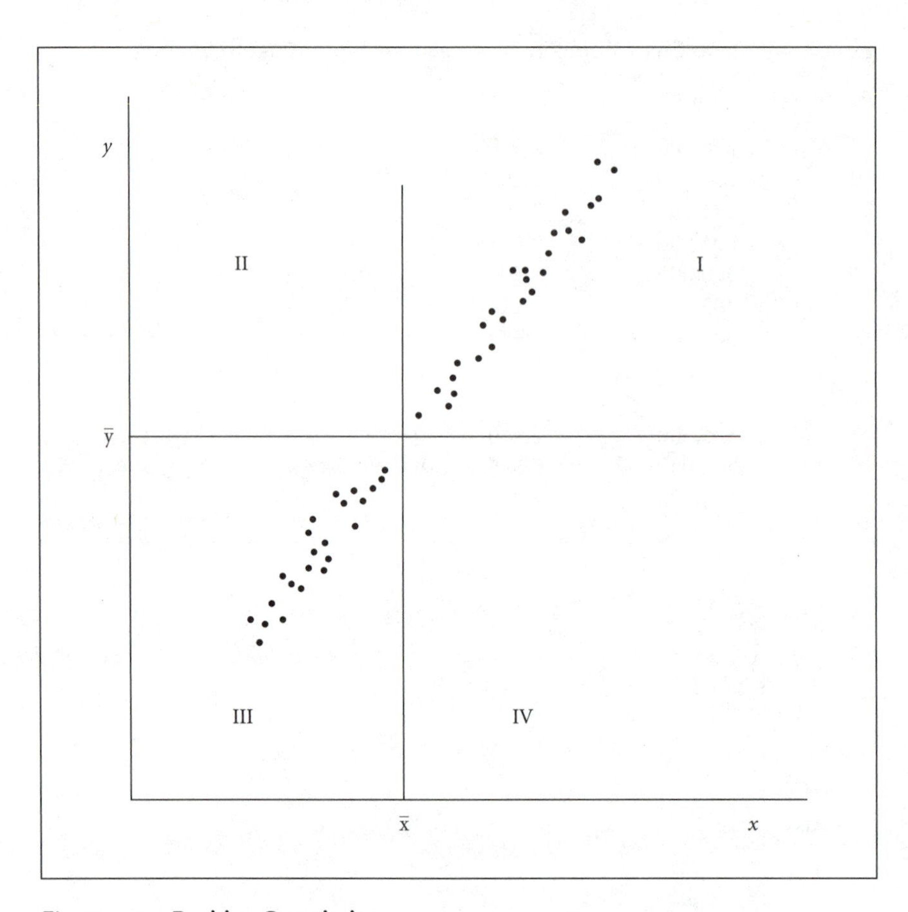

Figure 9.1 **Positive Covariation**

In contrast, the inverse relationship is portrayed in Figure 9.2. An inspection of the figure reveals that the second quadrant, represented by II, consists of values of y that exceed the mean value of y and values of x that are less than the corresponding mean. An inspection of quadrant four, represented by IV, indicates that values of y that are less than the mean value of y and that values of x exceed their corresponding mean. In this case, relatively high values of y are associated with relatively low values of x and vice versa. The distribution of values of x and y shown in Figure 9.2 suggests that a concentration of observations in quadrant two and four indicates an inverse relationship between the two variables.

Covariance

This section focuses on the development of a quantitative measure of association between two variables: x and y. *Covariance* refers to the direction of relationship or the direction in which two variables vary together.

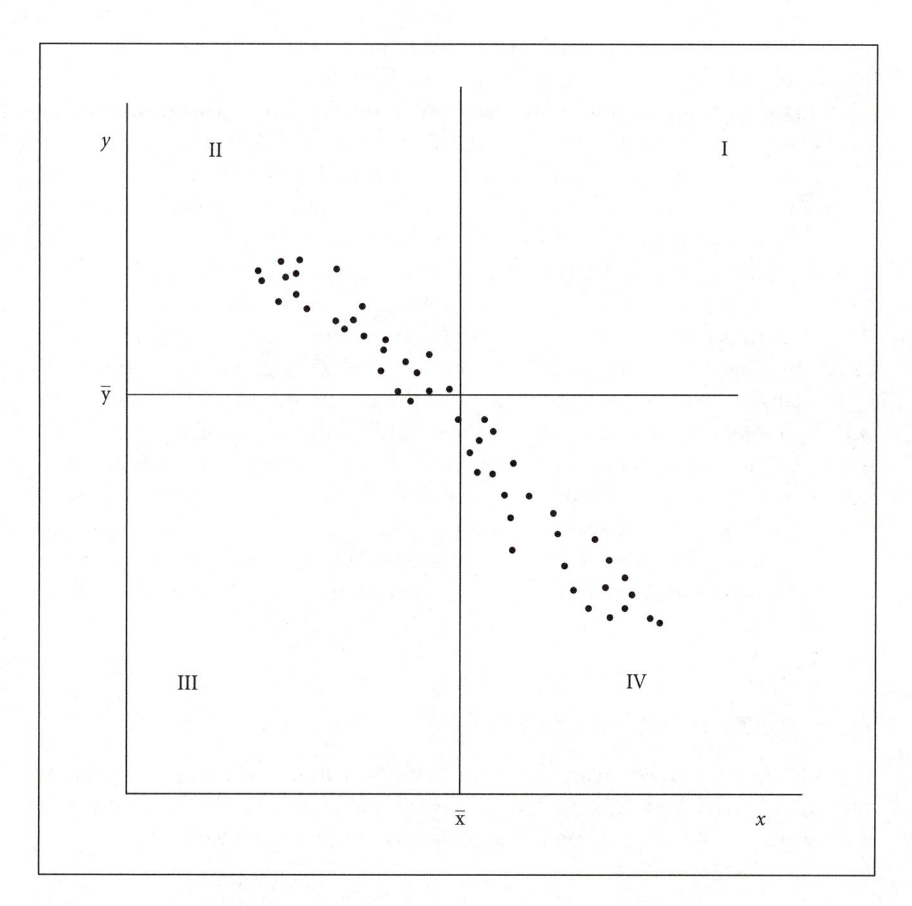

Figure 9.2 **Negative Covariation**

We define the covariance of x and y, represented by Covariance(x,y) by

$$Covariance(x,y) = \Sigma(x_i - \overline{X})(y_i - \overline{Y})/n - 1 \quad \text{(Equation 9.1.1)}$$

Equation 9.1.1 indicates that the covariance of x and y is simply the sum of products among paired deviations divided by the number of observations less one. We now define the numerator of Equation 9.1 as the covariation of x and y, represented by Cov(x,y). Thus, we find that

$$Cov(x,y) = \Sigma(x_i - \overline{X})(y_i - \overline{Y}) \quad \text{(Equation 9.1.2)}$$

After substituting appropriately, Equation 9.1.1 is equivalent to

$$Covariance(x,y) = Cov(x,y)/n - 1 \quad \text{(Equation 9.1.3)}$$

Equation 9.1.3 indicates that if x and y co-vary positively (negatively), the covariance exhibited by the two variables is positive (negative).

In Figure 9.1, the relatively low values of x are associated with relatively low values of y. Thus, limited to the third quadrant of the figure, the deviations $(x_i - \bar{X})$ and $(y_i - \bar{Y})$ are both negative. As a consequence, the product of $(x_i - \bar{X})$ and $(y_i - \bar{Y})$ must be positive. Limited to the first quadrant of the figure, relatively large values of y are associated with relatively large values of x. Thus, the deviations $(x_i - \bar{X})$ and $(y_i - \bar{Y})$ are both positive, suggesting that the product $(x_i - \bar{X})(y_i - \bar{Y})$ appearing in the numerator of Covariance(x,y) also must be positive. If the products among the paired deviations are positive, $\Sigma(x_i - \bar{X})(y_i - \bar{Y})$ must be positive, indicating that the relationship between x and y is direct or positive.

In contrast, the data in Figure 9.2 indicate that low values of x are associated with high values of y and vice versa. In the second quadrant, the deviation $(x_i - \bar{X})$ is negative, and the deviation $(y_i - \bar{Y})$ is positive, indicating that the product $(x_i - \bar{X})(y_i - \bar{Y})$ is negative. The fourth quadrant indicates that the deviation $(x_i - \bar{X})$ is positive and that the deviation $(y_i - \bar{Y})$ is negative. Thus, the deviations are of opposite signs; the sum of products, represented by $\Sigma(x_i - \bar{X})(y_i - \bar{Y})$, will be negative, and we conclude that the relationship between x and y is inverse or negative.

Application of Excel

Consider next the relationship between cost and volume. We anticipate that as volume rises costs increase and that the corresponding measure of covariance will be positive. The corresponding measure of covariance might be expressed as

$$Covariance(v,c) = \Sigma(v_i - \bar{V})(c_i - \bar{C})/n - 1 \qquad \text{(Equation 9.2)}$$

We let c_i represent one of the observations on total cost and $\bar{C}$ correspond to the mean of the cost data. We let v_i represent the volume alternative associated with total cost c_i and $\bar{V}$ represent the mean of the values that depict volume.

After being arranged in ascending order, data have been recorded in the first three columns of Exhibit 9.2. The "AutoSum" function was used to calculate the totals of columns 2 and 3. Based on these results, the average of the cost data, $\bar{C}$, and the average of the volume data, $\bar{V}$, were calculated and appear in cells B18 and C18, respectively. The deviations that were derived from the cost data and appear in column 4 were calculated by

1. Highlighting cell D5
2. Entering the equation = B5 − $B$18
3. Using the "Copy" function to record the equation in the remaining cells of the column

The deviations that were derived from the volume data appear in the fifth column. These deviations were calculated by

1. Highlighting cell E5
2. Entering the equation = C5 – $C$18
3. Using the "Copy" function to record the equation in the remaining cells of the column

An inspection of the deviations $(c_i - \bar{C})$ and $(v_i - \bar{V})$ reveals that, with the exception of the results that were based on activity in the 3rd and 12th periods, the deviations derived for the cost and volume data are of the same sign, suggesting that costs and volume co-vary positively.

To verify these results, the products among the paired deviations that appear in the sixth column were calculated and obtained by

1. Highlighting cell F5
2. Entering the equation = D5*E5
3. Using the "Copy" function to record the equation in the remaining cells of the column

The sum of products among paired deviations that appear in cell F17 (i.e., 37,723,488) was obtained by selecting the "AutoSum" function. Finally, the measure of the covariance between cost and volume that appears in cell B20 was ob-

Exhibit 9.2 **The Covariance of Cost and Volume**

Period	Cost (y)	Volume (x)	Cost Deviations	Volume Deviations	Product
4	276,000	2,400	−31,004.16667	−216.25	6,704,65.042
9	286,000	2,200	−21,004.16667	−416.25	8,742,984.375
3	294,000	2,800	−13,004.16667	183.75	−2,389,515.625
10	294,900	2,378	−12,104.16667	−238.25	2,883,817.708
1	300,000	2,500	−70,04.166667	−116.25	814,234.375
8	303,750	2,430	−32,54.166667	−186.25	606,088.5417
12	308,800	2,552	17,95.833333	−64.25	−115,382.2917
2	318,600	2,700	11,595.83333	83.75	971,151.0417
11	320,400	2,670	13,395.83333	53.75	720,026.0417
5	321,500	2,950	14,495.83333	333.75	4,837,984.375
6	322,000	2,875	14,995.83333	258.75	3,880,171.875
7	338,100	2,940	31,095.83333	323.75	10,067,276.04
Total	3,684,050	31,395			**37,723,47.5**
Mean	**307,004.1667**	**2,616.25**			

Covariance 3,429,407.955

tained by entering the equation = F17/11. As expected, the measure of covariance is positive, indicating that as volume increases the costs incurred by the long-term facility rise.

Exercises

1. Use the data in Exhibit 9.1 to measure the covariance between cost and volume.
2. Suppose that we are interested in the relationship between the age of the individuals who are members of our managed-care organization and the use of physician care, as measured by visits. Suppose also that after selecting 15 members at random we obtained the following paired observations:

   Visits: 3 5 4 2 1 3 6 7 4 5 10 1 2 3 8

   Age 28 45 50 19 16 27 54 63 32 42 68 19 23 30 61

   Use these data to find the covariance between age and the number of visits.
3. Suppose that we are interested in the relationship between the use of physician services and the distance, measured in miles, between the patient's residence and the nearest source of care. The results of a sample survey of 20 patients yielded the following paired observations:

   Visits: 5 6 9 7 1 2 4 3 6 4 2 3 7 10 1 2 5 6 8 4

   Miles: 3 4 6 9 1 1 3 2 5 6 2 5 1 2 9 8 4 3 2 2

   Use these data to find the covariance and covariation between use of care and distance to the nearest source of service.
4. Assume that the nursing unit maintains records that depict the volume of care, measured by days of care, and the number of hours of nursing personnel used during each week. Based on these records, suppose that we got the following set of paired observations:

   Days: 105 147 245 178 210 252 203 154 140 198

   Hours: 300 588 857 525 905 995 709 456 493 903

   Use these data to find the covariation and covariance between the number of days of care and the number of hours of nursing personnel used in the department.
5. Suppose that the administrator of a managed-care organization is interested in the association between the length of stay and the number of secondary conditions. A random sample of 15 patient records yielded the following paired observations:

   Length of stay: 2 5 9 3 7 10 4 5 2 7 8 11 2 5 7

   Number of conditions: 1 3 6 2 5 9 2 4 1 6 5 9 2 4 3

   Use these data to find the covariance and covariation between the length of stay and the number of secondary diagnoses.
6. Assume that the laboratory maintains records showing the number

of procedures performed and the number of technician hours used during the night shift. A review of our performance during the past 10 days yielded the following paired observations:

Procedures: 150 175 200 150 154 250 200 160 120 150

Hours: 24 35 42 22 23 45 23 25 20 23

Use these data to find the covariance and covariation between the number of procedures and the number of hours of technician time used by the laboratory.

7. Suppose that the director of the radiology department assembled data depicting the number of procedures provided and the direct costs of the unit for each month of the past year. The sets of paired observations are as follows:

Costs ($1,000): 12.8 16.1 15.0 12.0 18.3 19.5 19.0 22.0 15.5

Procedures (000): 3.9 4.8 4.7 3.0 6.8 5.5 7.9 6.9 5.3

Costs ($000): 21.0 19.2 16.3

Procedures (000): 7.9 8.1 5.6

Use these data to find the covariance and covariation between costs and the volume of radiologic procedures.

CHAPTER 10 Simple Regression Analysis[R,O]

OBJECTIVES

1. Describe the line of average relationship, the standard error of the estimate, the coefficient of determination, and the coefficient of correlation.
2. Distinguish between a population and a sample regression line.
3. Describe the process of estimating the parameters of the population regression equation.
4. Calculate estimates of the parameters of the population regression equation.
5. Describe the measures of association.
6. Calculate the coefficient of determination and the correlation coefficient.
7. Examine the null and alternate hypotheses concerning the intercept and slope of the population regression equation.
8. Examine the null and alternate hypotheses concerning the correlation coefficient.
9. Develop a confidence and prediction interval for the dependent variable.
10. Use Excel to perform the calculations required in simple regression analysis and interpret related results.

Many of the tasks, problems, or issues that the health administrator must resolve require an understanding and use of simple regression analysis, a technique that enables the administrator to explore the relationship between two variables. For example, the preparation of the budget requires a forecast of the volume of care that the organization expects to provide during the next operating period. The health administrator might be interested in the change in the use of service that is attributable to variation in the economic status or a sociodemographic attribute of an individual or members of an insured population. The administrator might be interested in examining the cost structure of the health service organization, a task that requires an estimate of the relationship between expenses and the volume of service.

In Chapter 9, covariance measures the direction of association between two variables. Covariation and covariance are also the foundations on which the basic concepts of regression analysis are based. In particular, simple regression analysis allows us to examine the general function

$$\hat{y} = f(x)$$

where the y is the dependent variable and x is the independent or predictor variable. Based on a bivariate relationship (i.e., the relationship between two variables), the primary purpose of simple regression analysis is to predict the value of y for a given or assumed value of x and to examine a theory that postulates a positive or negative association between y and x. In this chapter, we assume that the relationship of y to x is linear. The focus is on the methods that enable us to estimate the linear relationship, to predict the value of y for a given or assumed value of x, and to examine hypotheses concerning the relationship of y to x.

The Basic Concepts[R]

Simple regression is based on essentially four basic concepts: the line of average relationship, the standard error of the estimate, the correlation coefficient, and the coefficient of determination. Each is introduced in this section.

The Line of Average Relationship

The line of average relationship portrays the relationship of y to x and is usually expressed as

$$y_i = b_o + b_1 x_i \qquad \text{(Equation 10.1)}$$

Equation 10.1 is expressed in slope-intercept form where b_o is the y intercept (i.e., the value of y when x is equal to zero) and b_1 is the slope of the linear function (i.e., the change in the mean value of y that is associated with a unit change in x); b_o and b_1 are numeric constants and are referred to as regression coefficients or parameter estimates. After the regression coefficients are determined, we may substitute known or assumed values of x for x_i and predict the corresponding value of the dependent variable. The linear equation, when presented as a graph, results in a straight line.

The Standard Error of the Estimate

The standard error of the estimate, $S_{y.x}$, is a standard deviation that is expressed in units that measure the dependent variable. In particular, the standard error of the estimate is a measure of the scatter of observations about the line of average relationship. If the scatter forms a wide band about the line of average relationship, the standard error of the estimate will be large. In contrast, if the scatter of points forms a narrow band, the standard error of the estimate is correspondingly small. In the extreme case, if all observations are on the line of average relationship, the standard error is zero.

The Correlation Coefficient

The correlation coefficient, r, is a measure of the direction and the strength of the relationship between two variables. The correlation coefficient assumes values that range from +1 to −1. The interpretation of r is straightforward. If r is equal to +1, all observations are on the line of average relationship and the function rises from left to right. Thus, in such a situation, the variables are related positively, and the correlation is said to be perfect. In contrast, if r is equal to −1, all observations are on the line of average relationship, and the function falls from left to right. In such a situation, the correlation is perfect, and the two variables are associated negatively. If the correlation coefficient is zero or nearly so, the association between the two variables is nonexistent or weak.

The Coefficient of Determination

The coefficient of determination, R^2, is also a measure of association and indicates the extent to which the line of average relationship fits the data. The coefficient of determination measures the proportion or percentage of the variation exhibited by the dependent variable that is explained or attributed to the regression analysis. Similar to analysis of variance with a single factor, the total variation exhibited by the dependent variable might be expressed by the mathematical identity

$$SS(Y) = SS(REG) + SS(ERROR) \qquad \text{(Equation 10.2)}$$

In this case, SS(Y) represents the sum of squared deviations derived from the distribution of observations concerning the dependent variable (i.e., $\Sigma[y_i - \bar{Y}]^2$). SS(REG) represents the variation that is attributable to or explained by regression, and SS(ERROR) corresponds to the sum of squared error terms (i.e., the sum of the squared differences between an observed value of y and the corresponding point on the line of average relationship).

In Equation 10.2, if the term SS(ERROR) is zero, the variation in the dependent variable is equal to SS(REG). In such a situation, all of the observations are on the line of average relationship, and all of the variation in the dependent variable is explained by the regression analysis. Thus, the value of R^2 is one. The standard error of the estimate is 0, and the correlation coefficient is either +1 or −1. In contrast, if SS(REG) is 0, none of the variation shown by the dependent variable is attributable to the regression analysis, indicating that the value of R^2 is 0. This discussion indicates that the value of the coefficient of determination ranges from 0 to 1.

The Basic Process and the Assumptions[R]

As suggested previously here, regression analysis is a method of estimating an equation that depicts the mean value of y for each value of x and measures the errors that are likely to occur when we use the equation to predict the value of y for a known or assumed value of x. Regression analysis allows us to estimate the change in the mean value of the dependent variable that results from a unit change in the independent variable. Simple regression analysis enables us to estimate the slope of a linear function and to examine expectations concerning the relationship of y to x.

For example, suppose that we are interested in the relationship between an individual's age and the use of health care, as measured by the number of physician–patient contacts. Our focus is on older members of an insured population that reside in a given market or service area. In this case, we posit that

$$Visits = f(Age)$$

where the volume of care consumed, represented by visits, is the dependent variable, and the age of the individual is the independent variable.

Using the previous notation, let $\{x_i, y_i\}$ represent levels of use for each age group. Suppose that we limit the selection of the first observation in our sample to individuals who are 65 years old. After randomly selecting an insured member who was 65 years old, we determine that the individual experienced five physician–patient contacts during the previous year. Similarly, the selection of the second individual might focus on those who are 70 years old, and after selecting one of the many members who are 70 years old, we find that the individual experienced seven physician–patient contacts during the previous year. In this case, the first two selections yielded the paired observations represented by (65,5) and (70,7) where (x_i, y_i) might be represented by (Age, Contacts). Therefore, even though the value of the dependent variable is determined by a process of random selection, the value of the independent variable is known with certainty and is fixed at a given age.

Consider next the conditional probability distribution of y if x is equal to x_i. The conditional probability distribution of y, given x, is determined by the distribution of values of the dependent variable in the population when x is fixed at a known level. We identify the mean of the conditional probability distribution by $\mu_{y.x}$, and we let $\sigma_{y.x}$ correspond to the standard deviation of the distribution of y when x is specified.

Simple regression analysis is based on essentially four assumptions about the conditional probability distribution and its properties. The assumptions concerning the mean, $\mu_{y.x}$, and the standard deviation, $\sigma_{y.x}$, that characterize conditional probability distribution are particularly important. First, simple regression analysis assumes that the mean of the conditional probability distribution is a linear function of the independent variable x. The *population regression equation* is routinely expressed as

$$\mu_{y.x} = \beta_o + \beta_1 x_i \qquad \text{(Equation 10.3)}$$

As before, $\mu_{y.x}$ corresponds to the mean of the conditional probability distribution of y if x is equal to x_i, and β_o is the intercept. The slope of the population regression equation is represented by β_1, a parameter that indicates the change in the mean value of y resulting from a unit change in the value of x. When portrayed graphically, Equation 10.3 forms the *population regression line.*

Second, regression analysis assumes that the variances shown by the family of conditional probability distributions are equal. Thus, the distribution of the dependent variable for each value of x is characterized by the same variance, $\sigma_{x.y}^2$, and the same standard deviation, $\sigma_{x.y}$. In the situation in which we wish to assess the relationship of age to the use of care, it is assumed that the variance associated with each distribution of use by individuals of different ages satisfies the property of homoscedasticity.

Third, when regression analysis is applied, it is necessary to assume that the conditional probability distributions are normal. Finally, we also suppose that a given selection of an observation or case that results in a given value of y is independent of other selections. The fourth assumption implies that the selection of a value of y that lies below the mean of the corresponding conditional probability distribution in no way influences the likelihood of selecting another value that is less than its corresponding mean. Similarly, the selection of a value of y that lies above the mean of the corresponding conditional probability distribution is independent of selecting another value that exceeds its mean value.

Parameter Estimation[R]

As before, we assume that y is equal to y_i when x is equal to x_i, suggesting that $\{x_i, y_i\}$ are paired observations on the dependent and independent variables.

From the discussion in the previous section, we might express y_i as

$$y_i = \mu_{y.x} + e_i \qquad \text{(Equation 10.4.1)}$$

which is equivalent to

$$y_i = \beta_o + \beta_1 x_i + e_i \qquad \text{(Equation 10.4.2)}$$

In Equations 10.4.1 and 10.4.2, e_i is an amount that must be added to the mean of the conditional probability distribution to get the value of y_i. Thus, e_i measures the difference between the value of y_i and the mean of the corresponding conditional probability distribution.

In Figure 10.1, the values of y_i do not coincide or reside on the population regression line, and consistent with Equations 10.4.1 and 10.4.2, e_i measures the deviation of each observation from its respective mean represented by $\mu_{y.x.}$.

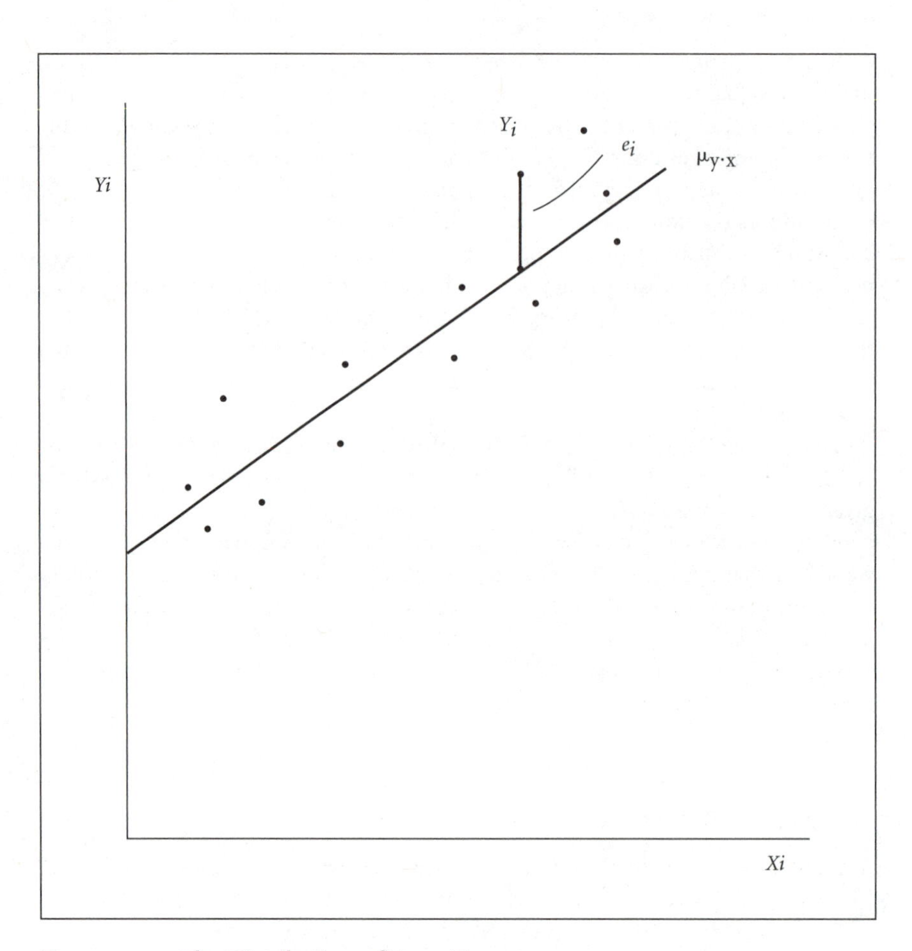

Figure 10.1 **The Distribution of Error Terms**

Figure 10.1 reveals that if y_i is above the population regression line, the value of e_i is positive. If y_i is below the regression line, the value of e_i is negative. We see that the greater are the deviations measured by the values of the error terms, the less precise are the predictions derived from the analysis and vice versa.

The primary purpose of regression analysis is to derive an equation that best describes the relationship between the dependent and independent variables. The sample regression equation is based on a set of paired observations (x_i, y_i) that were derived from a sampling procedure similar to our discussion of the relationship of age to the use of care. The general expression for the sample regression line is

$$\hat{Y}_i = b_o + b_1 x_i \qquad \text{(Equation 10.5)}$$

In Equation 10.5, $\hat{Y}_i$ *is a point estimate of* $\mu_{y.x}$, *and the value of* b_o *is a point estimate of* β_o. *Similarly, the value of* b_1 *is a point estimate of* β_1, *the slope of the population regression equation.* Thus, the discussion indicates that $\hat{Y}_i$ is an estimate of the mean exhibited by the corresponding conditional probability distribution, whereas the values of b_o and b_1 are point estimates of the intercept and slope of the population regression equation, respectively.

Theoretically, it is possible to construct an indefinite number of lines in two space. In Figure 10.2, some of the lines correspond to the scatter of points, whereas others must be disregarded immediately. An indefinite number of lines might be constructed in the space defined by the band formed by the scatter of points. However, when the ordinary least squares approach to regression analysis

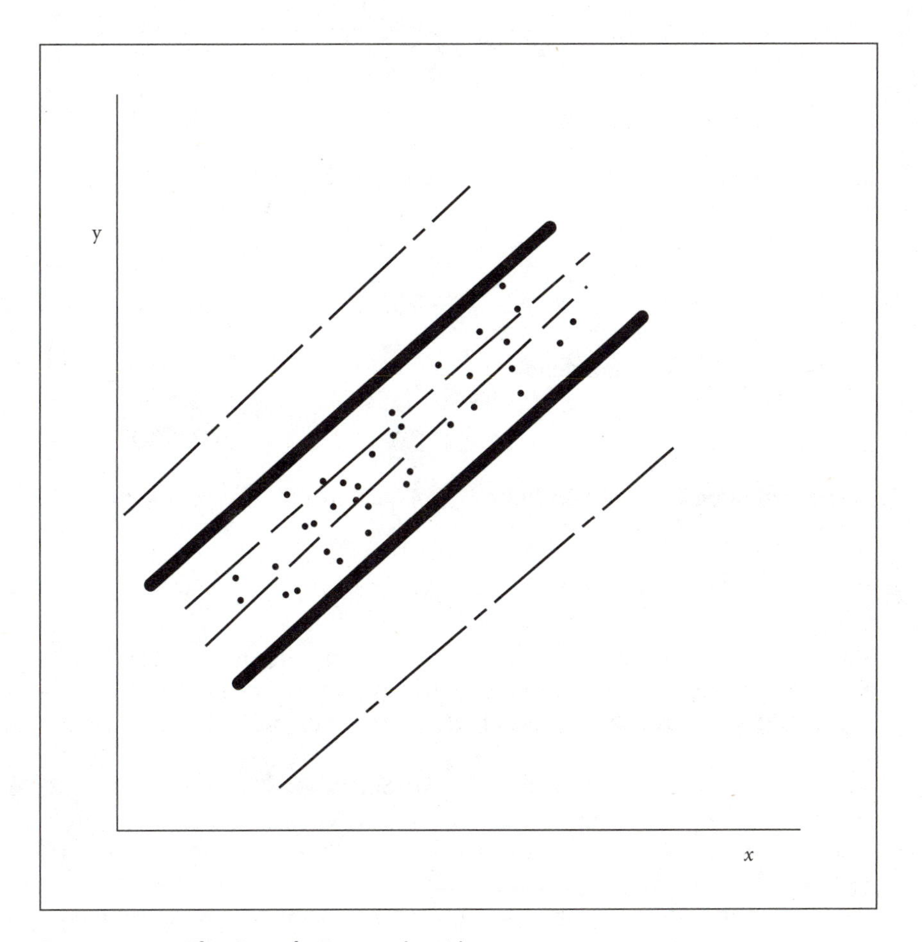

Figure 10.2 **The Sample Regression Line**

is adopted, the parameter estimates b_o and b_1 are calculated so as to *minimize the sum of the squared error terms.*

In Figure 10.1, the error term is defined as the vertical distance between the observed value of the dependent variable and the predicted value, as defined by the line of average relationship. Thus, if we square all such vertical distances and sum the results, the sum of squared error terms is obtained. If the sum of squared error terms is minimized, the line of average relationship that is defined by the values of b_o and b_1 is the best fit to the observed distribution. The greater is the sum of squared error terms, the poorer the line fits the data; the smaller is the sum of squared error terms, the better the line of average relationship fits the data.

The normal equations are derived so as to minimize the sum of squared error terms. Specifically, the normal equations are as follows:

$$nb_o + b_1\Sigma x_i = \Sigma y_i \qquad \text{(Equation 10.5.1)}$$

$$b_o\Sigma x_i + b_1\Sigma x_i^2 = \Sigma x_i y_i \qquad \text{(Equation 10.5.2)}$$

In Equations 10.5.1 and 10.5.2, n, Σx_i, Σy_i, Σx_i^2, and $\Sigma x_i y_i$ are numeric values that are calculated from sample data, represented by $\{x_i, y_i\}$. We may use Equation 10.5.1 to derive

$$b_o = \Sigma y_i/n - b_1\Sigma x_i/n \qquad \text{(Equation 10.6.1)}$$

Equation 10.6.1 also is equivalent to

$$b_o = \overline{Y} - b_1\overline{X} \qquad \text{(Equation 10.6.2)}$$

After substituting $\Sigma y_i/n - b_1\Sigma x_i/n$ for b_o in Equation 10.5.2, we may solve for b_1 and obtain

$$b_1 = [\Sigma(x_i - \overline{X})(y_i - \overline{Y})]/\Sigma(x_i - \overline{X})^2 \qquad \text{(Equation 10.7.1)}$$

Referring to Equation 10.7.1, notice that the numerator of the ratio that defines b_1 is $Cov(x_i,y_i)$ and the denominator is defined by the variation in x which we represent by SS(x), using this notation, observe that Equation 10.7.1 is equivalent to

$$b_1 = Cov(x_i,y_i)/SS(x) \qquad \text{(Equation 10.7.2)}$$

In the following, we use $Cov(x_i,y_i)$ when referring to the covariation of x and y and SS(X) when referring to the variation in x.

Several comments about Equation 10.7.2 are noteworthy. First, the denominator of the ratio that defines b_1 is the variation exhibited by x as defined by the sum of squared deviations of observations on x relative to the mean of the distribution of values for the independent variable. The denominator, represented by SS(x), must be a positive value. On the other hand,

$$\Sigma(x_i - \bar{X})(y_i - \bar{Y})$$

is identical to the numerator of the ratio that defined Covariance (x_i, y_i). Thus, if x and y co-vary positively, the sign attached to b_1 must be positive, and the line of average relationship rises from left to right. In contrast, if x and y co-vary negatively, the sign derived for b_1 must be negative, and the line of average relationship falls from left to right.

To illustrate the definitional equations, return to the situation in which we wished to estimate the relationship between costs and the volume of care provided by the long-term care facility. The original data, the calculation of Cov(v,c), and the total variation exhibited by volume, the independent variable, are listed in Exhibit 10.1. As before, the value of Cov(v,c) is approximately 37,723,488.50, whereas the total variation in the independent variable, shown in the last column of the exhibit, is 655,944.25. As indicated, the slope of the function corresponds to the average variable cost per bed day of care or the change in total costs resulting from varying

Exhibit 10.1 **The Slope and Intercept of the Cost Function**

Period	Cost (y)	Volume (x)	Cost Deviations	Volume Deviations	Covariation	Squared Deviations in Volume
4	276,000	2,400	−31,004.17	−216.25	6,704,651.04	46,764.06
9	286,000	2,200	−21,004.17	−416.25	8,742,984.38	173,264.06
3	294,000	2,800	−13,004.17	183.75	−2,389,515.63	33,764.06
10	294,900	2,378	−12,104.17	−238.25	2,883,817.71	56,763.06
1	300,000	2,500	−7,004.17	−116.25	814,234.38	13,514.06
8	303,750	2,430	−3,254.17	−186.25	606,088.54	34,689.06
12	308,800	2,552	1,795.83	−64.25	−115,382.29	4,128.06
2	318,600	2,700	11,595.83	83.75	971,151.04	7,014.06
11	320,400	2,670	13,395.83	53.75	720,026.04	2,889.06
5	321,500	2,950	14,495.83	333.75	4,837,984.37	111,389.06
6	322,000	2,875	14,995.83	258.75	3,880,171.87	66,951.56
7	338,100	2,940	31,095.83	323.75	10,067,276.04	104,814.06
Total	3,684,050	31,395			**37,723,487.50**	**655,944.25**
Mean	**307,004.1667**	**2,616.25**				

Covariance	**3,429,407.955**
Covariation	**37,723,487.5**
Slope	57.5102038
Intercept	156,543.096

volume by one bed of care. Using Equation 10.7.2, we employ the results in Exhibit 10.1 to find b_1, the slope of the sample regression line, by

$$b_1 = 37{,}723{,}488.50/655{,}944.25$$

The variable cost per bed day of care amounts to approximately \$57.51. This finding allows us to calculate the fixed costs of the facility, represented by the intercept of the line of average relationship. Using Equation 10.6.2, we find that

$$b_o = 307{,}004.167 - 57.51(2{,}616.25)$$

or approximately \$156,543.10.

The calculated values of b_1 and b_o enable us to express the sample regression equation as

$$\hat{Y}_i = \$156{,}543.10 + \$57.51x_i$$

The total cost was identified as the dependent variable, and volume, measured in bed days of care, corresponds to the independent variable. Thus, when expressed in an administratively relevant form, the sample regression line is given by

$$TC_i = \$156{,}543.10 + \$57.51v_i$$

In this case, the intercept of \$156,543.10 corresponds to fixed costs or those expenses that remain constant with respect to changes in volume, whereas the second term, $\$57.51v_i$, is the total variable cost or those expenses that vary proportionately with increases or decreases in the number of bed days of care.

The Standard Error of the Estimate[R]

As indicated previously, regression analysis is a statistical tool that allows us to derive predictions concerning a variable that is of administrative interest and to examine claims or assertions about the relationship of one variable to another. Both purposes require an understanding of the standard error of the estimate. The *standard error of the estimate* is a standard deviation that measures the scatter of points about the line of average relationship. If the observations form a wide band, the standard error of the estimate will be large, and predictions derived from the regression analysis will be correspondingly less precise. In contrast, if the scatter forms a narrow band about the line of average relation, the standard error of the estimate will be small, and estimates derived from the analysis will be correspondingly more precise. In the extreme, if all points reside on the line of average relationship, predictions of the actual values of the dependent variable that are derived from the regression analysis will be perfect.

If the property of homoscedasticity is satisfied, the standard deviation of the conditional probability distribution, $\sigma_{y.x}$, is the same regardless of the value assumed by the independent variable. When sample data are used, we rely on $S_{y.x}$ as an estimate of $\sigma_{y.x}$. In turn, the standard error of the estimate is defined by

$$S_{y.x} = [\Sigma e_i^2/n - (k + 1)]^{1/2} \qquad \text{(Equation 10.8)}$$

The sum of squared errors, Σe_i^2, requires us to measure the vertical distance between the actual value of y and the predicted value, as derived from the line of average relationship.

In Figure 10.3, the line segment ab corresponds to the deviation of observation y_i from the value of $\bar{Y}$, whereas line segment ac corresponds to the error that is committed when $\hat{Y}_i$ is used to predict y_i. Finally, the line segment cb is the portion of the

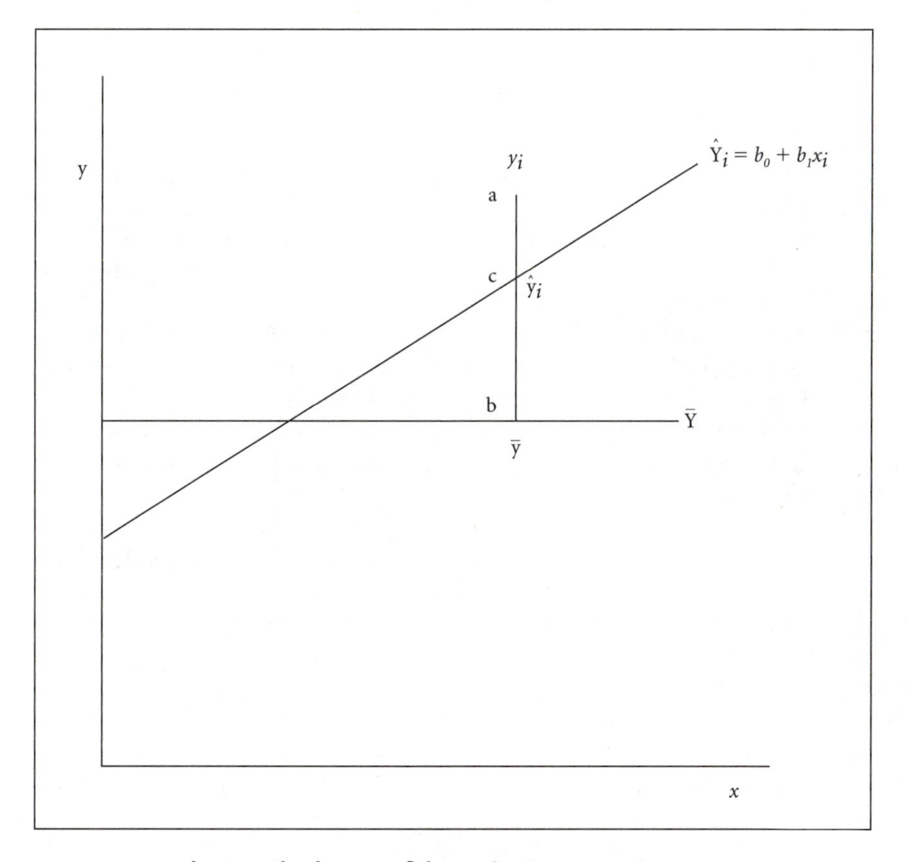

Figure 10.3 **The Standard Error of the Estimate**

deviation ab that measures the distance between the line of average relationship and the mean value of the dependent variable, $\overline{Y}$. These observations suggest that the deviation of the observation y_i from the mean value $\overline{Y}$ might be expressed as

$$ab = ac + cb$$

or by

$$Deviation(y) = Deviation(Error) + Deviation(Regression)$$

The Deviation(y) might be expressed by $(y_i - \overline{Y})$, whereas Deviation(Error) is equivalent to $(y_i - \hat{Y}_i)$. Figure 10.3 also reveals that Deviation(Regression) is given by $(\hat{Y}_i - \overline{Y})$. Thus, we might express the deviation of y relative to its mean value as

$$(y_i - \overline{Y}) = (y_i - \hat{Y}_i) + (\hat{Y}_i - \overline{Y}) \qquad \text{(Equation 10.9)}$$

If we square each term in Equation 10.9 and sum the results, we obtain

$$\Sigma(y_i - \overline{Y})^2 = \Sigma(y_i - \hat{Y}_i)^2 + \Sigma(\hat{Y}_i - \overline{Y})^2 \qquad \text{(Equation 10.10)}$$

Similar to analysis of variance with one factor, $\Sigma(y_i - \overline{Y})^2$ measures the total variation exhibited by the dependent variable, and $\Sigma(\hat{Y}_i - \overline{Y})^2$ indicates the portion of the variation that is attributable or explained by the regression analysis. Finally, $\Sigma(y_i - \hat{Y}_i)^2$ is the sum of squared error terms and measures the portion of the variation that is unexplained.

We now let SS(Y) correspond to the total variation exhibited by the dependent variable and SS(REG) represent the portion of the variation in the dependent variable that is explained by or attributable to the regression analysis. We let SS(ERROR) represent the sum of squared error terms and the portion of the variation in the dependent variable that is unexplained by regression. Equation 10.10 is equivalent to

$$SS(Y) = SS(ERROR) + SS(REG) \qquad \text{(Equation 10.11)}$$

After a slight rearrangement, the sum of the squared error terms might be expressed as

$$SS(ERROR) = SS(Y) - SS(REG) \qquad \text{(Equation 10.12)}$$

The result of Equation 10.12 enables us to express the standard error of the estimate by

$$S_{y.x} = [SS(Y) - SS(REG)/n - (k + 1)]^{1/2} \qquad \text{(Equation 10.13)}$$

As described previously, the standard error of the estimate approaches zero as the value of SS(REG) approaches SS(Y). Similarly, as the value of SS(REG) approaches zero, the standard error of the estimate grows, implying that the predictive ability of the analysis declines.

Equation 10.13 is frequently used to define the standard error of the estimate and to enhance our understanding of the concept. However, the equation is not useful when computing the value of the standard error. The portion of the variation in the dependent variable that is explained by regression might be expressed as

$$SS(REG) = b_1 Cov(x,y) \qquad \text{(Equation 10.14.1)}$$

which, as demonstrated previously, is equivalent to

$$SS(REG) = b_1[\Sigma(x_i - \bar{X})(y_i - \bar{Y})] \qquad \text{(Equation 10.14.2)}$$

Using Equation 10.14.2, we substitute $b_1[\Sigma(x_i - \bar{X})(y_i - \bar{Y})]$ for SS(REG) and $\Sigma(y_i - \bar{Y})^2$ for SS(Y) in Equation 10.13. The standard error of the estimate is given by

$$S_{y.x} = [\Sigma(y_i - \bar{Y})^2 - b_1[\Sigma(x_i - \bar{X})(y_i - \bar{Y})])/n - (k + 1)]^{1/2} \qquad \text{(Equation 10.14.3)}$$

As before, the term $\Sigma(y_i - \bar{Y})^2$ measures the total variation exhibited by the dependent variable; $b_1[\Sigma(x_i - \bar{X})(y_i - \bar{Y})]$ corresponds to the portion of the variation attributed to the regression analysis, and the difference, represented by $\Sigma(y_i - \bar{Y})^2 - b_1[\Sigma(x_i - \bar{X})(y_i - \bar{Y})]$, is the sum of squared error terms.

To illustrate the use of Equation 10.14.3, return to the example that examined the relationship between cost and volume. In Exhibit 10.2, the paired observations about cost and volume are presented in the second and third columns, whereas the variation in cost, represented by SS(Y), and the variation in volume, listed as SS(X), are shown in columns 4 and 5, respectively. Similar to Exhibit 10.1, the sum of products among paired deviations, COV(X,Y), is listed in column 6. The portion of the variation in the dependent variable, SS(REG), is obtained by the product of b_1, 57.51020308, and COV(X,Y), which amounted to 37,723,487.50. In the exhibit, the value of SS(REG) is 2,169,485,454. Because the value of SS(ERROR) is given by SS(Y) − SS(REG), the calculations presented in the exhibit indicate that

$$SS(ERROR) = 3{,}496{,}792{,}291.67 - 2{,}169{,}485{,}454$$

or approximately $1,327,306,837.43. Thus, an application of Equation 10.14.3 to the data yields

$$S_{y.x} = (1{,}327{,}306{,}837.43/10)^{0.5}$$

Exhibit 10.2 **The Standard Error of the Estimate, the Coefficient of Determination, and the Coefficient of Correlation**

Period	Cost (y)	Volume (x)	SS(Y)	SS(X)	COV(X,Y)
4	276,000	2,400	96,125,8350.69	46,764.06	6,704,651.04
9	286,000	2,200	441,175,017.36	173,264.06	8,742,984.38
3	294,000	2,800	169,108,350.69	33,764.06	−2,389,515.63
10	294,900	2378	146,510,850.69	56,763.06	2,883,817.71
1	300,000	2,500	49,058,350.69	13,514.06	814,234.38
8	303,750	2,430	10,589,600.69	34,689.06	606,088.54
12	308,800	2,552	3,225,017.36	4,128.06	−115,382.29
2	318,600	2,700	134,463,350.69	7,014.06	971,151.04
11	320,400	2,670	179,448,350.69	2,889.06	720,026.04
5	321,500	2,950	210,129,184.03	111,389.06	4,837,984.37
6	322,000	2,875	224,875,017.36	66,951.56	3,880,171.87
7	338,100	2,940	966,950,850.69	104,814.06	100,67,276.04
Total	3,684,050	31,395	3,496,792,291.67	655,944.25	37,723,487.50
Mean	**307004.17**	**2616.25**			

SS(Y)	3,496,792,291.67
Slope,b1	57.5102038
SS(REG)	2,169,485,454
SS(ERROR)	1,327,306,837.43
d.f	10
Standard Error	11,520.88034
R Square	0.620421596
Correlation Coefficient, r	0.787668456

After performing the calculations, we find that the standard error of the estimate is $11,520.88034. The standard error is a standard deviation that is expressed in units that measure the dependent variable. As demonstrated later here, the standard error of the estimate plays a crucial role in developing projections of the dependent variable, given a known or assumed value of the independent variable. The standard error of the estimate also plays a key role in testing assertions or hypotheses about the relationship between the dependent and the independent variable.

Measures of Association[R]

In this section, we focus on measures of association or indicators of how well the line of average relationship fits the data. We first consider the coefficient of determination, R^2, as a measure of the strength of association between the dependent and independent variable. We then examine the coefficient of correlation, r, as an indicator of both the strength and direction of relationship in a bivariate analysis.

The Coefficient of Determination

The coefficient of determination, R^2, is a single value that indicates the extent to which the sample regression line coincides with the set of data. As such, the coefficient of determination supplements the information conveyed by the standard error of the estimate. The coefficient of determination measures the proportion or percentage of the variation exhibited by the dependent variable that is attributable to or explained by the regression analysis. The previous notation defines R^2 by

$$R^2 = SS(REG)/SS(Y) \qquad \text{(Equation 10.15)}$$

As indicated previously, the ratio ranges from 0 to 1. If the sum of squares attributed to regression is equal to the variation exhibited by the dependent variable, R^2 is equal to one. If SS(REG) is equal to SS(Y), the standard error of the estimate must equal zero, implying that all of the observations reside on the line of average relationship.

Thus far, we have examined the definitional equation for the coefficient of determination. However, when viewed from a computational perspective, Equation 10.15 requires a slight modification. Specifically, SS(REG) is given by

$$SS(REG) = b_1 Cov(x_i, y_i)$$

In addition, b_1 is given by the ratio $Cov(x_i,y_i)/SS(x_i)$, suggesting that we might express SS(REG) as

$$SS(REG) = [Cov(x_i y_i)]^2/SS(x_i)$$

After substituting appropriately in Equation 10.15, we obtain

$$R^2 = [Cov(x_i, y_i)]^2/SS(x_i)\ SS(y_i) \qquad \text{(Equation 10.16)}$$

Thus, the computational form for R^2 is the square of the covariation between x and y divided by the product of the variation in x and the variation in y.

The use of Equation 10.16 can be shown in Exhibit 10.2 where the covariation of x and y is calculated in the final column. The total in the last column gives the value of $\Sigma(x_i - \bar{X})(y_i - \bar{Y})$. Similarly, the totals of the fourth and fifth columns give the values of SS(Y) and SS(X), respectively. After substituting and performing the calculations, the exhibit indicates that the value of R^2 is 0.620421596. The results suggest that approximately 62% of the variation shown by the cost data is attributable to the regression analysis.

The Coefficient of Correlation

The coefficient of correlation, r, is closely related to the coefficient of determination. The square root of R^2 is given by

$$r = Cov(x_i, y_i)/[SS(X)SS(Y)]^{0.5} \quad \text{(Equation 10.17)}$$

Equation 10.17 indicates that the correlation coefficient is simply the covariation between x and y divided by the square root of the product between the variation in x and the variation in y. The denominator of the ratio is always nonnegative, suggesting that the sign derived for r is determined by the covariation of x and y. Similar to our discussion of b_1, if x and y co-vary positively, the correlation coefficient is positive. In contrast, if x and y co-vary negatively, the coefficient of correlation also must be negative. In Exhibit 10.2, after we perform the required calculations, the correlation coefficient is 0.787668456. Thus, similar to our discussion of the value of b_1, the results suggest that cost and volume are related positively.

At this point, it is useful to describe the relationship among the standard error of the estimate, the coefficient of determination, and the coefficient of correlation. Suppose that SS(REG) is equal to SS(Y), implying that all of the points lie on the line of average relationship. In such a situation, the difference between SS(Y) and SS(REG) is zero, implying that the standard error of the estimate also is zero. Further, the ratio SS(REG)/SS(Y) is one, implying that the coefficient of determination is one, and that the coefficient of correlation is either plus one or minus one. However, as the SS(REG) approaches zero, the difference between SS(Y) and SS(REG) grows, resulting in an increase in the standard error of the estimate. In addition, as the difference between SS(Y) and SS(REG) increases, the coefficient of determination declines, and the coefficient of correlation approaches zero.

An Examination of the Line of Average Relationship[R]

As indicated, simple regression analysis is a statistical method that enables us to examine the relationship between two variables. Specifically, the focus is on a statistical examination of hypotheses concerning β_o and β_1, the intercept and slope of the population regression line, respectively; b_1 and b_o are derived from sample data and used as an estimate of β_1 and β_o, respectively. As indicated by the following discussion, confidence intervals and t ratios are usually used when examining expectations concerning the two parameter estimates.

An Examination of β_o

Consistent with our earlier discussion, the statistical evaluation of β_o, the intercept of the population regression line, requires a specification of the null and alternate hypotheses, a test statistic, and a decision criterion. In this case, the null hypothesis might be expressed as

$$H_o: \beta_{oo} = 0$$

where β_{oo} identifies the value of β_o assumed under the null hypothesis. Specifically, the null hypothesis posits that the line of average relation emanates from the origin. The directional alternate hypotheses assume the form

$$H_a: \beta_o > 0$$

or

$$H_a: \beta_o < 0$$

In most cases, the first of the alternate hypotheses is most appropriate when evaluating or assessing issues that pertain to problems that confront the health administrator.

Two approaches might be employed to assess assertions about the intercept of the population regression line. First, we might rely on a t ratio and the related critical value. It can be shown that the standard error of the intercept, $SE(b_o)$, may be expressed as

$$SE(b_o) = S_{y.x}\{1/n + [\bar{X}^2/\Sigma(x_i - \bar{X})^2]\}^{0.5} \quad \text{(Equation 10.18.1)}$$

Similar to previous discussions, the test statistic is given by

$$t = b_o - \beta_{oo}/SE(b_o) \quad \text{(Equation 10.18.2)}$$

If the null hypothesis is true and the line of average relationship emanates from the origin, we would expect the numerator of the t ratio to be zero or nearly so and the corresponding value of t to be relatively small. If the alternate hypothesis, given by $\beta_o > 0$ is true, we expect to observe a positive value in the numerator and a relatively large computed t ratio.

Returning to the numeric example, the previous discussion shows that b_o is equal to $156,543.10. In addition,

$$\bar{X} = 2{,}616.25$$
$$n = 12$$
$$\Sigma(x_i - \bar{X})^2 = 655{,}944.25$$
$$S_{y.x} = 11{,}520.88034$$

Using these results, we find that the standard error, $SE(b_o)$, is given by

$$SE(b_o) = 11{,}520.88034[1/12 + 2{,}616.25^2/655{,}944.25]^{0.5}$$

or approximately 37,364.45777. Thus, the calculated value of t is simply

$$t = 156{,}453.10/37{,}364.45777$$

or approximately 4.19. If $\alpha = 0.05$, the critical value represented by $t_{0.05,10}$ is 1.812. Because the calculated value of 4.19 greatly exceeds the critical value, we reject the null hypothesis and conclude that the intercept of the population regression line exceeds zero.

The null hypothesis also might be examined by constructing a $1 - \alpha$ confidence interval for β_o. In this case, we adopt an approach that is identical in format to those we used to construct a $1 - \alpha$ confidence interval for μ. The $1 - \alpha$ confidence interval for β_o is

$$b_o \pm t_{\alpha/2,n-(k+1)}\, SE(b_o) \qquad \text{(Equation 10.19)}$$

In the numeric example, the 95% interval is given by

$$156{,}543.10 \pm 2.228\ (37{,}364.45777)$$

where the coefficient 2.228 corresponds to $t_{0.025,10}$. After performing the calculations, we obtain

$$73{,}295.09 \leq \beta_o \leq 239{,}791.10$$

Based on these calculations, we may assert with a probability of 0.95 that the fixed costs, which are measured by the intercept of the population regression equation, range from $73,295.09 to $239,791.10. The confidence interval does not contain zero, a result that also enables us to reject the null hypothesis.

The Examination of β_1

The statistical assessment of β_1 also requires us to specify the null and an alternate hypothesis. Similar to our examination of β_o, we usually specify the null hypothesis as

$$H_o: \beta_1 = \beta_{1o} = 0$$

where β_{1o} corresponds to the value of the slope parameter as specified by the null hypothesis. The null hypothesis presumes that no relationship exists between the dependent and independent variable. In addition to the null hypothesis, it is necessary to construct an alternate hypothesis. The alternate hypothesis might assume one of three forms:

$$H_a: \beta_1 > 0$$
$$H_a: \beta_1 < 0$$
$$H_a: \beta_1 \neq 0$$

The first of the alternate hypotheses suggests that, as the value of the independent variable increases, the mean value of the dependent variable grows. Thus, the first of the alternate hypotheses indicates a positive or direct relationship between the dependent and independent variable. The second alternate hypothesis asserts that as the value of the independent variable increases the mean value of the dependent variable declines. The second alternate hypothesis suggests that the mean value of the dependent variable is inversely related to the independent variable. The third is a nondirectional alternate and the most statistically conservative expression of the alternate hypothesis.

The test statistic is similar to those encountered previously. We define the t ratio by

$$t = b_1/SE(b_1) \qquad \text{(Equation 10.20)}$$

The standard error of the parameter estimate, $SE(B_1)$, measures the variation in b_1 that is attributable to chance or the manner in which the sample was selected. The standard error of b_1 might be expressed as

$$SE(b_1) = S_{y.x}/[SS(x)]^{1/2} \qquad \text{(Equation 10.21)}$$

In the numeric example, it can be verified that

$$SE(b_1) = 11{,}520/(655{,}944.25)^{1/2}$$

or approximately 14.22. Thus, the test statistic is defined as the ratio

$$t = 57.51/14.22$$

or approximately 4.04. In this case, suppose that we rely on the alternate hypothesis, which asserts that β_1 exceeds 0 and let α equal 0.05. The critical value of t for 10 degrees of freedom and α equal 0.05 is approximately 1.81. The calculated value of t (4.04) exceeds the critical value (1.81), an outcome that forces us to reject the null hypothesis and accept the alternate while recognizing that the probability of committing a Type I error is 0.05 or less. Thus, we conclude that, as volume increases, total costs rise.

An Examination of ρ

In this section, we consider the statistical examination of the correlation coefficient, ρ. The *correlation coefficient* measures the direction and strength of relationship in a bivariate analysis. As before, we begin with a specification of the null hypothesis, which is usually expressed as follows:

$$H_o: \rho = 0$$

The null hypothesis specifies that there is no relationship between the two variables, an expectation that is identical to the null hypothesis concerning the slope of the population regression line. Similar to the discussion presented in the previous section, the alternate hypothesis assumes one of the following forms:

$$H_a\text{: } \rho > 0$$
$$H_a\text{: } \rho < 0$$
$$H_a\text{: } \rho \neq 0$$

In the first of these, we presume that the variables are related positively, and an inverse relation is specified by the second of the alternate hypotheses. The third is, of course, a nondirectional or two-tailed hypothesis.

The correlation coefficient r is a point estimate of ρ. When examining assumptions or claims regarding correlation, we rely on the test statistic

$$t = r/SE(r) \qquad \text{(Equation 10.22)}$$

where the corresponding standard error is given by

$$SE(r) = [(1 - R^2)/n - 2]^{1/2} \qquad \text{(Equation 10.23)}$$

R^2 refers to the coefficient of determination, and $n - 2$ represents the number of degrees of freedom available in a bivariate analysis. In the example, we find that the numeric value of the standard error is given by

$$SE(r) = [1 - (0.62042)^2/10]^{1/2}$$

or approximately 0.194828. Thus, the test statistic, t, is simply

$$t = 0.787677/0.194828$$

or 4.04. The test statistics computed when examining b_1 and r are identical, indicating that the result obtained from the statistical assessment of the parameter estimate of β_1 is equivalent to our assessment of ρ. As before, then, the calculated value of t (4.04) exceeds the corresponding critical value (i.e., 1.81). Similar to our assessment of β_1, we are forced to reject the null hypothesis that ρ is equal to zero and conclude that ρ is greater than zero, implying that cost and volume are positively correlated.

An Application of Excel[R]

The previous calculations are easily and precisely performed when Excel is applied to problems requiring regression analysis. In Exhibit 10.3, the original data are listed in Part A. The results of Part B were obtained by

1. Selecting the "Data Analysis" function
2. Selecting "Regression"
3. Highlighting the field in which data depicting the dependent variable appear
4. Highlighting the field in which data depicting the independent variable appear
5. Indicating the area in which the results will appear
6. Selecting "OK"

The computations are instant and are reported in Part B.

The analysis is interpreted as described in the previous section. Refer to the section entitled "SUMMARY OUTPUT," and note that the results of the regression analysis indicate that, as before, the coefficient of determination, identified as "R Square" in the exhibit, is approximately 0.62. In the section "ANOVA," the coefficient of determination might be obtained by the ratio of the sum of squares due

Exhibit 10.3 **Regression Analysis of the Relationship Between Cost and Volume**

PART A

Period	**Cost (y)**	**Volume (x)**
4	276,000	2,400
9	286,000	2,200
3	294,000	2,800
10	294,900	2,378
1	300,000	2,500
8	303,750	2,430
12	308,800	2,552
2	318,600	2,700
11	320,400	2,670
5	321,500	2,950
6	322,000	2,875
7	338,100	2,940

PART B

Summary Output

Regression Statistics	
Multiple R	0.787668456
R Square	0.620421596
Adjusted R Square	0.582463756
Standard Error	11,520.88034
Observations	12

continues

Exhibit 10.3 **(Continued)**

ANOVA

	df	SS	MS	F	Significance F
Regression	1	2,169,485,454	2,169,485,454	16.3450183	0.002350251
Residual	10	1,327,306,837	132,730,683.7		
Total	11	3,496,792,292			

	Coefficients	Standard Error	t Stat	P-Value	Lower 95%	Upper 95%
Intercept	156543.096	37364.45777	4.189625792	0.001859061	73289.88152	239796.3104
X Variable 1	57.5102038	14.22499758	4.042897265	0.002350251	25.81492855	89.20547906

to regression (i.e., 2,169,485,454) relative to the total sum of squared deviations in the dependent variable (i.e., 3,496,792,292). In the example, the results indicate that approximately 62% of the variation in cost is attributable to or explained by the regression analysis. In a bivariate analysis, the square root of the coefficient of determination yields the correlation coefficient. In Exhibit 10.3, the results indicate that r is equal to approximately 0.79, suggesting a positive and relatively strong relationship between costs and volume. The analysis also indicates that, as before, the standard error of the estimate, identified as "Standard Error," is $11,520.88. The standard error of the estimate also might be calculated by first dividing the number of degrees of freedom (i.e., 10) into the sum of the sum of squares due to "Residual" (i.e., 1,327,306,837) and then obtaining the square root of the results.

Consider next the findings that were summarized in the "ANOVA" section of Exhibit 10.3. As in earlier discussions, the F ratio indicates that the variance attributable to regression (i.e., MS, Regression) exceeds the variance due to error (i.e., MS, Residual) by a factor of 16.34502. The final entry in the ANOVA section of Exhibit 10.3 indicates that, if the property of homoscedasticity is satisfied, the probability of obtaining an F ratio equal to approximately 16.34 is 0.002350. Because the reported probability is much less than conventional values of α, we are forced to reject the null hypothesis that the two variances are equal and conclude that the regression analysis absorbed a significant portion of the variance exhibited by the cost data.

The final section of the report summarizes the results derived for estimates of β_o and β_1. The findings reported in the "Intercept" line pertain to b_o, the estimate of β_o. As before, the results indicate that the value of b_o is $156,543.10, an amount that represents the fixed cost component of total expenses. When the value of b_o is divided by the corresponding standard error of approximately 37,364.46, we obtain a calculated value of t equal to 4.19. Because the calculated value of t exceeds the critical value, we reject the presumption that β_o is zero and conclude that fixed costs are positive and significant. Similarly, the "P-value" of approximately 0.002 indicates the likelihood of obtaining a calculated t value equal to 4.19 if the intercept of the population regression equation is zero. Since the exact probability of 0.002 is less than conventional values of α, we reject the presumption that β_o is zero and conclude that fixed costs are positive and differ significantly from zero.

Finally, consider the values appearing in the row entitled "X Variable 1." These results pertain to the slope of the population regression equation, β_1. As before, regression analysis indicates that b_1, a point estimate of the variable cost per patient day of care, is equal to approximately $57.01. Furthermore, the analysis indicates that the standard error $SE(b_1)$ is 14.22, an outcome that results in a computed value of t that is equal to approximately 4.04. Because the calculated value of t exceeds the critical value, we reject the assumption that β_1 is zero and conclude that, as the volume of care increases, variable costs grow. The "P-value" indicates the likelihood of obtaining a computed value of t equal to 4.04 if the slope of the population regression line is zero. Because the probability of approximately 0.002 is less than conventional values of α (i.e., 0.05, 0.02, or 0.01), we reject the assumption that cost is unrelated to volume and conclude that the variable costs per day are positive and significantly different from zero.

PREDICTION[O]

As indicated previously, a primary function of regression analysis is to predict or estimate a value of the dependent variable, if the independent variable assumes a known or assumed value. When deriving a prediction or an estimate of the dependent variable, the administrator must address one of two situations. In the first, it is necessary to derive an estimate of $\mu_{y.x}$, a value representing the mean of the dependent variable, given a known or assumed value of x. In the second situation, the administrator may be interested in predicting or estimating a single or new value of y when x assumes a known or assumed value. Each of these situations is considered in this section.

An Estimate of $\mu_{y.x}$: The Confidence Interval

The standard error of the estimate, $S_{y.x}$, is a standard deviation that measures the width of the band formed by the scatter of observations about the line of average relationship. If the scatter of points forms a narrow band, the standard error will be small. If all observations are on the line, the standard error of the estimate is zero, and predictions of the dependent variable from the regression analysis are identical to the actual values of y. On the other hand, if the scatter of points forms a wide band, the standard error will be large, and as a result, predictions will be less precise. Furthermore, we assume that the property of homoscedasticity is satisfied, implying that the standard deviation of all conditional probability distributions of y given x are equal.

The approach to the construction of a confidence interval for $\mu_{y.x}$ from the line of average relationship is complicated slightly by the tendency of parameter estimates to differ from sample to sample. For example, suppose that we selected the first sample that consisted of the points $\{x_i, y_i\}$ and that these data were used to estimate a sample regression line

$$\hat{Y}_i = b_o + b_1 x_i$$

Limited to the same population, suppose further that we selected a second sample, represented by the set of paired observations $\{x_i^*, y_i^*\}$. Suppose further that these data were used to estimate a second sample regression line given by

$$\hat{Y}_i^* = b_o^* + b_1^* x_i$$

In Figure 10.4, the parameter estimates differ, resulting in two sample regression lines. We wish to estimate $\mu_{y.x}$ from the population regression line, which is in bold. In Figure 10.4, based on the first sample, b_o is less than β_o and b_1 is greater than β_1. In contrast, an inspection of the results obtained from the second sample reveals that b_o^* is greater than β_o and that b_1^* is less than β_1. These observations allow us to assert that when $\bar{X}$ is positive b_o and b_1 co-vary negatively [i.e., $Cov(b_o, b_1) < 0$]. The negative covariation of parameter estimates results in a nonlinear band that forms the confidence interval, as shown by the dotted curve.

To illustrate the need for a nonlinear band that forms the confidence interval, suppose that we adopted the first of the sample regression lines to predict the mean value of y, if x is to equal x_j. An inspection of the figure reveals that the estimate $\hat{Y}_j$ exceeds the corresponding point on the population regression line by the length of line segment ab. On the other hand, if we adopted the analysis derived from the second sample, the corresponding estimate is $\hat{Y}_j^*$, a value that understates the true mean by line segment bc. Thus, depending on the sample, the potential error resulting from the use of the sample regression line to estimate the true mean value of the dependent variable when x is equal to x_j corresponds to line segment ac. The error grows as the distance between x_j and the mean $\bar{X}$ increases. As shown in Figure 10.4, the band that forms the confidence interval for the mean value of y widens as the value of x_j departs from $\bar{X}$.

When constructing a confidence interval for $\mu_{y.x}$, we rely on the standard error of $\hat{Y}_j$, which is defined by

$$SE(\hat{Y}_j) = S_{y.x}[1/n + (x_j - \bar{X})^2/\Sigma(x_i - \bar{X})^2]^{1/2} \quad \text{(Equation 10.24)}$$

Equation 10.24 reveals that as the distance between x_j and $\bar{X}$ increases, the absolute value of $(x_j - \bar{X})$ grows, and as a result, the numerator of the ratio $(x_j - \bar{X})^2/\Sigma(x_i - \bar{X})^2$ must also increase. Because the variation exhibited by the independent variable must remain constant for a given sample, the ratio and thus the standard error $SE(\hat{Y}_j)$ must increase as the distance between x_j and $\bar{X}$ grows.

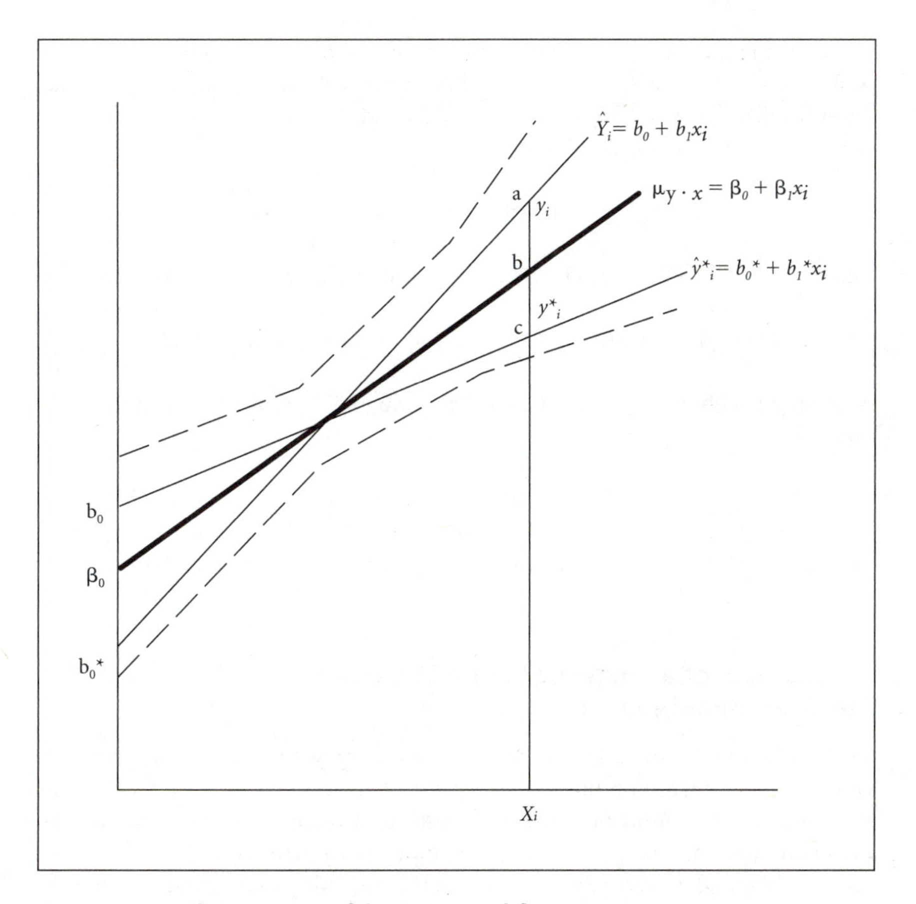

Figure 10.4 **The 1 − α Confidence Interval for μy.x**

We may now construct a $1 - \alpha$ confidence interval for $\mu_{y.x}$ when x is equal to x_j. Because $\hat{Y}_j$ is a point estimate of the mean of the conditional probability distribution when x is x_j, we define the confidence interval for $\mu_{y.x}$ by

$$\hat{Y}_j \pm t_{\alpha,n-(k+1)}[SE(\hat{Y}_j)] \qquad \text{(Equation 10.25)}$$

As the distance between x_j and $\overline{X}$ grows, the standard error $SE(\hat{Y}_j)$ increases, and as a result, the difference between the upper and lower limits of the confidence interval also increases. Thus, the definitional equation for $SE(\hat{Y}_j)$ results in the nonlinear band portrayed in Figure 10.4. If x_j is equal to $\overline{X}$, the ratio

$$[(x_j - \overline{X})^2/\Sigma(x_i - \overline{X})^2]$$

is zero and the standard error is defined by $S_{y.x}/(n)^{.5}$, which is identical to the structure of the standard error of the mean discussed earlier.

Returning to the relationship between cost and volume, suppose that we wished to construct a 95% confidence interval that depicts, on average, the total expenses that we expect to incur when 2,750 bed days of care are provided. The corresponding point estimate of $\mu_{y.x}$ is given by

$$Y_{2,750} = 156{,}543.10 + \$\,57.51(2{,}750)$$

or approximately $314,695.60. The corresponding standard error is obtained by

$$SE(Y_{2,750}) = 11{,}520.88[1/12 + (2{,}750 - 2{,}616.25)^2/655{,}944.25]^{1/2}$$

or approximately $3,831.547. Thus, the resulting 95% confidence interval is obtained by

$$314{,}695.60 \pm 2.228(3{,}831.547)$$

We may assert that, on average, the total cost of providing 2,750 bed days of care ranges from $306,158.90 to $323,232.30.

An Estimate of a Single or Future Value of Y: The Prediction Interval

As described previously, the paired observation (x_q, y_q) indicates that when x is equal to x_q, the corresponding value of y is y_q. This section's focus shifts from the development of a confidence interval for the mean value of y to a description of a prediction interval that pertains to a single value of y, namely y_q. In the previous section, the standard error $SE(\hat{Y}_j)$ expresses the variability that is related to the position of the regression line. However, individual observations, y_q, do not normally reside on the line of average relationship. Thus, it is necessary to add the error variance of the individual observation to the error variance of the mean value, and after a slight rearrangement, we obtain

$$SE(\hat{Y}_q) = S_{y.x}[1 + 1/n + (x_q - \bar{X})^2/\Sigma(x_i - \bar{X})^2]^{1/2} \qquad \text{(Equation 10.26)}$$

The addition of 1 to the expression $1/n + (x_j - \bar{X})^2/\Sigma(x_i - \bar{X})^2$ that appears in Equation 10.4 results in a standard error that exceeds $SE(\hat{Y}_j)$. In our earlier discussion, the $1 - \alpha$ prediction interval is defined by

$$\hat{y}_q \pm t_{\alpha,n-(k+1)}[SE(\hat{Y}_q)] \qquad \text{(Equation 10.27)}$$

As in our discussion of the $1 - \alpha$ confidence interval, the value of y_q is derived from the sample regression equation.

For example, return to the relationship between cost and volume. Suppose that during the next period the administrator expects the facility to provide 2,750 bed days of care. The corresponding cost amounts to \$314,695.10, and the related standard error is given by

$$SE(y_{2,750}) = 11{,}520.88[1 + 1/12 + (2{,}750 - 2{,}616.25)^2/655{,}944.25]^{1/2}$$

or approximately \$12,141.31. If, as before, we let $1 - \alpha$ equal 0.95, the corresponding prediction interval is obtained by

$$\$\,314{,}695.60 \pm 2.228(12{,}141.31)$$

After performing the required calculations, we may assert with a probability of 0.95 that the costs of the next period should be no more than \$341,746.40 and no less than \$287,644.80.

Suppose now that 2,750 bed days of care were provided during the period and that the actual costs amounted to \$350,567. A comparison of the actual expenses with the upper limit of the prediction interval suggests that costs were higher than anticipated, an outcome that might compromise the fiscal performance of the organization and impede the accumulation of the internally generated funding required to implement the organization's strategic plan.

Exercises

1. Use the "Regression" function in Excel and the data presented in Exercise 2 of Chapter 9 to estimate the linear relation between the number of visits and the age of the patient. Examine the results of the analysis by
   1. Interpreting the coefficient of determination
   2. Interpreting the square root of the coefficient of determination
   3. Interpreting findings presented in the ANOVA table
   4. Determining whether the intercept and slope of the sample regression line are significant

   In your evaluation, let $\alpha = 0.05$.
2. Use the "Regression" function in Excel and the data presented in Exercise 3 of Chapter 9 to estimate the linear relation between the number of visits and the distance to the nearest source of care. Examine the results of the analysis by
   1. Interpreting the coefficient of determination
   2. Interpreting the square root of the coefficient of determination
   3. Interpreting findings presented in the ANOVA table
   4. Determining whether the intercept and slope of the sample regression line are significant

   In your evaluation, let $\alpha = 0.05$.
3. Use the "Regression" function in Excel and the data presented in Exercise 4 of Chapter 9 to estimate the linear relation between

the number of days of care and the number of hours of nursing hours used in the unit. Examine the results of the analysis by

1. Interpreting the coefficient of determination
2. Interpreting the square root of the coefficient of determination
3. Interpreting findings presented in the ANOVA table
4. Determining whether the intercept and slope of the sample regression line are significant

In your evaluation, let $\alpha = 0.05$.

4. Use the "Regression" function in Excel and the data presented in Exercise 5 of Chapter 9 to estimate the linear relationship between the length of stay and the number of secondary conditions presented by the patient. Examine the results of the analysis by
   1. Interpreting the coefficient of determination
   2. Interpreting the square root of the coefficient of determination
   3. Interpreting findings presented in the ANOVA table
   4. Determining whether the intercept and slope of the sample regression line are significant

   In your evaluation of the regression results, let $\alpha = 0.05$.
5. Use the "Regression" function in Excel and the data presented in Exercise 6 of Chapter 9 to estimate the linear relationship between the number of procedures provided and the hours of technician time used in the laboratory. Examine the results of the analysis by
   1. Interpreting the coefficient of determination
   2. Interpreting the square root of the coefficient of determination
   3. Interpreting findings presented in the ANOVA table
   4. Determining whether the intercept and slope of the sample regression line are significant

   In your evaluation of the regression results, let $\alpha = 0.05$.
6. Use the "Regression" function in Excel and the data presented in Exercise 7 of Chapter 9 to estimate the linear relation between the direct costs of radiology and the number of procedures. Examine the results of the analysis by
   1. Interpreting the coefficient of determination
   2. Interpreting the square root of the coefficient of determination
   3. Interpreting findings presented in the ANOVA table
   4. Determining whether the intercept and slope of the sample regression line are significant

   In your evaluation of the results, let $\alpha = 0.05$. In addition, construct a 0.95 confidence interval and a 0.95 prediction interval. Interpret a finding that indicates the direct costs exceed the upper limit of the interval.
7. The following observations were assembled to assess the relationship between costs and volume. Use the "Regression" function in

Excel to estimate a linear cost function that relates cost to volume.

Costs ($000)	Volume
150	110
158	120
162	126
169	130
174	150
178	150
183	165
187	170
193	176
198	180
201	181

In your evaluation, let $\alpha = 0.05$. Construct a 0.95 prediction interval, and use the results to assess a situation in which the actual costs of providing 190 units of service were $232,000.

CHAPTER 11

Multiple Regression Analysis°

OBJECTIVES

1. Distinguish between multiple and simple regression analysis.
2. Describe the need for multiple regression.
3. Describe the multiple regression model.
4. Calculate, describe, and interpret parameter estimates derived for each independent variable included in the analysis.
5. Calculate, describe, and interpret the coefficient of multiple determination and the standard error of the estimate.
6. Perform the tests required to examine hypotheses concerning the parameters of the population regression equation.
7. Calculate, describe, and interpret the adjusted R^2.
8. Estimate nonlinear relationships.
9. Define and use binary and interactive terms in multiple regression analysis.
10. Use Excel to perform the calculations required by multiple regression analysis and to interpret the results when viewed from a statistical and administrative perspective.

Simple linear regression (described in Chapter 10) enables us to examine a bivariate relationship that might be expressed by

$$y = f(x)$$

where only one independent variable is included in the analysis. Multiple linear regression is an extension of simple regression analysis. It can be used to examine the influence of two or more independent variables on the dependent variable. In particular, multiple regression analysis allows the administrator to examine the functional relation

$$y = f(x_1, \ldots, x_k) \qquad \text{(Equation 11.1)}$$

In Equation 11.1, $(x_1, \ldots, x_k)$ corresponds to the set of independent variables that is examined in the regression model.

In many situations, the variable of interest is influenced by several factors; thus, simple regression analysis may result in biased estimates of the relationship of y to x. For example, the influence on use exerted by market pressures and the demographic or economic characteristics of potential patients in the service area is important to any health administrator. In particular, we might suggest that the use of service, U, is a function of several variables that are specified by

$$U = f(HS, R, E, D, M)$$

In this case, HS corresponds to a set of variables that depicts the individual's health status. R represents a set of factors depicting the individual's exposure to health risks. E corresponds to a set of variables depicting the individual's economic status, to include insurance coverage, and D is a set of demographic characteristics, such as the individual's age, gender, and marital status. Finally, M is a set of variables that measures market conditions such as the number of rivals and the distance to the nearest competitor.

The health administrator might be interested in the variation in the rate of activity that results from changes in the use of resources. For example, we might suggest that

$$V = f(L, K, S)$$

where V is an indicator of volume of care provided, measured by the days of care or number of physician visits that the organization provided. L corresponds to the consumption of labor and S to the use of consumable supplies. Finally, the K represents the consumption of capital equipment, as indicated by the hours of operation. In each example, the analysis requires an examination of several independent variables and the use of regression analysis to examine the administrative issue of interest.

The General Model

As indicated in the previous section, we might suppose that

$$y = f(x_1, \ldots, x_k)$$

We might estimate a linear relationship by the sample regression equation that is specified by

$$\hat{Y}_i = b_o + b_1x_{i1} + \ldots + b_kx_{ik} \qquad \text{(Equation 11.2)}$$

Similar to our discussion of simple regression, b_o is a point estimate of β_o, and b_1 and b_k are point estimates of β_1 and β_k, respectively. In contrast to the sample regression equation, $\mu_{y(i)}$ corresponds to the mean value of the probability distribution of y when x_1 is equal to x_{1i}, x_2 is equal to x_{2i}, and similarly for all other independent variables.

Using the notation introduced in the previous chapter, we may specify the population regression equation by

$$\mu_{y(i)} = \beta_o + \beta_1 x_{i1} + \ldots + \beta_k x_{ik} \qquad \text{(Equation 11.3)}$$

The parameters in Equation 11.3 are interpreted as follows:

β_o *is the mean of the distribution of y when all independent variables are equal to zero.*

β_1 *indicates the change in the mean value of y when independent variable* x_1 *is varied by one unit, holding all other independent variables constant.*

β_k *indicates the change in the mean value of y when independent variable* x_k *is varied by one unit, holding all other independent variables constant.*

These observations suggest that a given parameter estimate indicates the direction of relationship between the mean value of the dependent variable and the corresponding independent variable. For example, suppose that the coefficient β_1 is positive, implying that when all other factors included in the regression analysis are held constant the mean value of the dependent variable y increases or decreases as the value of the independent variable x_1 increases or decreases.

Equation 11.3 also enables us to express the actual or observed value of y in a convenient form. In the following, ϵ_i corresponds to the error term associated with the value of the ith observation on y. Using Equation 11.3,

$$y_i = [\beta_o + \beta_1 x_{i1} + \ldots + \beta_k x_{ik}] + \epsilon_i \qquad \text{(Equation 11.4.1)}$$

Thus, ϵ_i when added to $\mu_{y(i)}$ yields the response or value associated with the ith case. In simple regression analysis, we assume that the values of y were selected independently and that the property of homoscedasticity is satisfied. Similarly, multiple regression assumes that the error terms are statistically independent. We also assume that ϵ_i is a normally distributed random variable, with a mean equal to zero and common variance, σ^2.

Parameter Estimation

As before, the parameters of the population regression equation must be estimated. For example, we focus on the simplest case of multiple regression and posit that

$$y = f(x_1, x_2)$$

The population regression equation is expressed as

$$\mu_{y(i)} = \beta_o + \beta_1 x_{i1} + \beta_2 x_{i2} \qquad \text{(Equation 11.4.2)}$$

where β_o is the intercept of the plane formed by the regression equation (i.e., the mean value of y when both x_1 and x_2 equal zero). As discussed previously, β_1 indicates the change in the mean value of the dependent variable when x_1 is varied by one unit, holding x_2 constant; β_2 indicates the change in the mean value of the dependent variable when the variable x_2 is varied by one unit, holding the value of x_1 constant.

When two independent variables are included in the analysis, the sample regression equation is expressed as

$$\hat{Y}_i = b_o + b_1 x_{1i} + b_2 x_{2i}$$

As discussed previously, b_o is an estimate of β_o; b_1 is an estimate of β_1, and b_2 is an estimate of parameter β_2. In multiple linear regression, the values of b_o, b_1, and b_2 are selected so as to minimize the sum of squared error terms, Σe_i^2. After an appropriate mathematical derivation is performed, the normal equations that minimize the sum of squared error terms may be expressed as

$$\begin{aligned} nb_o + b_1\Sigma x_1 + b_2\Sigma x_2 &= \Sigma y \\ b_o\Sigma x_1 + b_1\Sigma x_1^2 + b_2\Sigma x_1 x_2 &= \Sigma x_1 y \\ b_o\Sigma x_2 + b_1\Sigma x_1 x_2 + b_2\Sigma x_2^2 &= \Sigma x_2 y \end{aligned}$$

After solving the system of normal equations and rearranging slightly,

$$b_o = Y - b_1\bar{X}_1 - b_2\bar{X}_2 \qquad \text{(Equation 11.5.1)}$$

$$b_1 = \frac{SS(x_2)Cov(x_1,y) - Cov(x_1,x_2)Cov(x_2,y)}{SS(x_1)SS(x_2) - Cov(x_1,x_2)^2} \qquad \text{(Equation 11.5.2)}$$

$$b_2 = \frac{SS(x_1)Cov(x_2,y) - Cov(x_1,x_2)Cov(x_1,y)}{SS(x_1)SS(x_2) - Cov(x_1,x_2)^2} \qquad \text{(Equation 11.5.3)}$$

In Equations 11.5.2 and 11.5.3, $SS(x_1)$ and $SS(x_2)$ represent the sum of squared deviations of x_1 and x_2 relative to their respective means. $SS(x_1)$ and $SS(x_2)$ are identical to $Var(x_1)$ and $Var(x_2)$, respectively. The components that are used to determine the values of the parameter estimates may be expressed as

$$\begin{aligned} SS(x_1) &= \Sigma(x_{1i} - \bar{X}_1)^2 \\ SS(x_2) &= \Sigma(x_{2i} - \bar{X}_2)^2 \\ Cov(x_1,y) &= \Sigma(x_{1i} - \bar{X}_1)(y_i - \bar{Y}) \\ Cov(x_2,y) &= \Sigma(x_{2i} - \bar{X}_2)(y_i - \bar{Y}) \\ Cov(x_1,x_2) &= \Sigma(x_{1i} - \bar{X}_1)(x_{2i} - \bar{X}_2) \end{aligned}$$

These expressions have the same format as the definitional equations for variation and covariation presented previously.

For example, consider a situation in which the administrator is interested in the variation in the volume of care consumed by members of the insured population during the past year. Suppose also that we decide to use the individual as the unit of analysis and wish to examine the expectation that as the individual's ability to pay increases the average volume of care consumed grows. For example, the individual's ability to pay is defined by a ratio in which disposable family income is the numerator and the family size is the denominator. We also posit that a growing distance from the individual's residence to the site of care reduces access and impedes the use of service. Thus, we might expect that as the distance between the individual's residence and the source of care increases the number of visits consumed will on average decline.

To examine the situation, suppose that the administrator gathered data depicting the amount of care, measured by visits, used by 15 individuals during the past year. Suppose also that we obtained the adjusted income of each individual and the number of miles from the individual's residence to the usual source of care. With an Excel spreadsheet, the results are presented in the second, third, and fourth columns of Exhibit 11.1. The variation in income [i.e., $SS(x_1)$] is shown in the fifth column, and the sixth column displays the variation in the number of miles separating the individual's residence from the source of care [i.e., $SS(x_2)$]. The covariation between the number of visits and income [i.e., $Cov(x_1,y)$] and the covariation between the number of visits and distance to the source of care [i.e., $Cov\ (x_2,y)$] are listed in the seventh and eighth columns, respectively. The final column measures the covariation between the individual's income and the distance separating the individual's place of residence and the source of care [i.e., $Cov(x_1,x_2)$].

These data enable us to calculate the values of the parameter estimates as follows:

$$b_1 = \frac{(269.6)(288.4) - (-492.2)(-113.2)}{(1{,}774.4)(269.6) - (-492.2)^2}$$

$$= 0.093325$$

$$b_2 = \frac{(1{,}774.4)(-113.2) - (-492.2)(288.4)}{(1{,}774.4)(269.6) - (-492.2)^2}$$

$$= -\ 0.249501$$

$$b_o = 3.8 - [(0.093325)(17.8) + (-0.249501)(6.6)]$$

$$= 3.785528$$

When distance to the source of care is constant, the numeric value calculated for b_1 indicates that income and the average use of care per year are positively related.

Exhibit 11.1 **Parameter Estimates: Multiple Regression**

Observation	Visits per Year	Income (in $1,000)	Distance (Miles)	Variation (Income)	Variation (Miles)	COV (Visits and Income)	COV (Visits and Miles)	COV (Income and Miles)
1	1	4	10	190.44	11.56	38.64	−9.52	−46.92
2	3	6	6	139.24	0.36	9.44	0.48	7.08
3	4	8	3	96.04	12.96	−1.96	−0.72	35.28
4	2	9	9	77.44	5.76	15.84	−4.32	−21.12
5	5	21	4	10.24	6.76	3.84	−3.12	−8.32
6	5	22	2	17.64	21.16	5.04	−5.52	−19.32
7	6	34	1	262.44	31.36	35.64	−12.32	−90.72
8	3	17	9	0.64	5.76	0.64	−1.92	−1.92
9	7	35	2	295.84	21.16	55.04	−14.72	−79.12
10	3	12	12	33.64	29.16	4.64	−4.32	−31.32
11	2	8	11	96.04	19.36	17.64	−7.92	−43.12
12	7	29	3	125.44	12.96	35.84	−11.52	−40.32
13	1	11	13	46.24	40.96	19.04	−17.92	−43.52
14	2	14	12	14.44	29.16	6.84	−9.72	−20.52
15	6	37	2	368.64	21.16	42.24	−10.12	−88.32
Total	57	267	99	**1,774.40**	**269.60**	**288.40**	**−113.20**	**−492.20**
Mean	3.80	17.80	6.60					
b(1)	0.093324761							
b(2)	−0.249501307							
b(0)	3.785527877							

If the income of the individual is increased by $1,000, the annual use of service grows on average by approximately 0.09 visits per person per year.

On the other hand, if income is held constant, the coefficient for b_2 indicates that the use of physician care and the distance from the usual source of service are inversely related. In particular, the results suggest that as the distance between the individual's residence and the source of care increases by 1 mile, the use of service declines, on average, by approximately 0.25 visits per person per year.

The Standard Error of the Estimate

Similar to our discussion of simple linear regression, the standard error of the estimate that is derived in multiple linear regression analysis is a standard deviation that is expressed in units that measure the dependent variable. In simple regression analysis, the standard error of the estimate measures the width of the band formed by the scatter of points around the line of average relationship. In a multiple regression analysis that involves only two independent variables, the standard error measures the scatter of points about the plane formed by the regression equation. The greater is the standard error of the estimate, the wider is the scatter about the plane. In contrast, the lower is the value of the standard error, the narrower is the scatter of points about the plane formed by the regression equation.

Based on these observations, the standard error of the estimate in Chapter 10 must be modified only slightly to accommodate the inclusion of two or more independent variables. In both simple and multiple regression analysis, the standard error of the estimate, SE(EST) might be defined by

$$SE(EST) = [SS(ERROR)/n - (k + 1)]^{1/2}$$

As before, the term SS(ERROR) represents the sum of squared error terms, and the denominator corresponds to the number of degrees of freedom, represented by the number of cases less the sum of the number of independent variables, k, and one.

The sum of squared error terms might be expressed as

$$SS(ERROR) = SS(Y) - SS(REG)$$

where SS(Y) is the total variation in the dependent variable and SS(REG) is the portion of the variation in the dependent variable that is attributable to the regression analysis. In simple regression analysis, the sum of squared error terms is defined by

$$SS(ERROR) = \Sigma(y_i - \overline{Y})^2 - b_1 Cov(x,y)$$

However, when a second independent variable is included in the regression analysis, the sum of squared error terms is given by

$$SS(ERROR) = \Sigma(y_i - \overline{Y})^2 - [b_1 Cov(x_1,y) + b_2 Cov(x_2,y)]$$

Relative to the case of simple regression analysis, the addition of a second significant variable increases the value of SS(REG) and for a given sample reduces the value of SS(ERROR). As a consequence, the inclusion of an additional independent variable reduces the standard error of the estimate, an outcome that enhances the predictive and explanatory power of the model.

Based on these results, we now express the standard error of the estimate for a multiple regression analysis that involves two independent variables in the form

$$SE(EST) = \{\Sigma(y_i - \overline{Y})^2 - [b_1 Cov(x_1,y) + b_2 Cov(x_2,y)]\}/n - (k + 1)]^{1/2} \quad \text{(Equation 11.6)}$$

For a given sample, the dependent variable exhibits a fixed variation. Thus, if the portion of the variation in the dependent variable that is attributable to the regression analysis grows, the standard error of the estimate declines. In the extreme, when SS(REG) is equal to SS(Y), the standard error of the estimate is zero, implying that the results enable us to predict the dependent variable with precision.

In the example, when Excel is used, the components that combine to determine the standard error of the estimate are easily calculated. In Exhibit 11.2, the methods described previously are used to calculate the variation in the dependent variable (60.40). The covariation between the individual's income and the use of service and between the use of service and distance is also presented. The numeric value of SS(REG) was obtained by

$$SS(REG) = 0.093325(288.4) + [-0.249501(-113.2)]$$

Exhibit 11.2 **The Standard Error of the Estimate and the Coefficient of Multiple Determination**

Observation	Visits per Year	Income (in $1,000)	Distance (Miles)	Variation Visits	COV (Visits and Income)	COV (Visits and Miles)
1	1	4	10	7.84	38.64	−9.52
2	3	6	6	0.64	9.44	0.48
3	4	8	3	0.04	−1.96	−0.72
4	2	9	9	3.24	15.84	−4.32
5	5	21	4	1.44	3.84	−3.12
6	5	22	2	1.44	5.04	−5.52
7	6	34	1	4.84	35.64	−12.32
8	3	17	9	0.64	0.64	−1.92
9	7	35	2	10.24	55.04	−14.72
10	3	12	12	0.64	4.64	−4.32
11	2	8	11	3.24	17.64	−7.92
12	7	29	3	10.24	35.84	−11.52
13	1	11	13	7.84	19.04	−17.92
14	2	14	12	3.24	6.84	−9.72
15	6	37	2	4.84	42.24	−10.12
Total	57	267	99	**60.40**	**288.40**	**−113.20**
Mean	3.80	17.80	6.60			

SS(Y)	60.40
SS(REG)	55.15840902
SS(ERROR)	5.241590975
VARIANCE	0.436799248
STANDARD ERROR	0.660907897
R Square	0.913218692

or 55.15841. The sum of squared error terms was treated as a residual and was found by

$$SS(ERROR) = 60.40 - 55.15841$$

or 5.241591. As described previously, the variance of 0.436799 was obtained by a ratio in which SS(ERROR) (i.e., 5.241591) is in the numerator and the degrees of freedom (i.e., 15 − 3 or 12) are the denominator. Finally, the standard error of the estimate (i.e., 660908) is simply the square root of the variance (i.e., 436799). The standard error of the estimate is a point estimate of the common standard deviation of the probability distribution of y, given values of x_1 and x_2.

The Coefficient of Multiple Determination: R^2

As in our discussion of the coefficient of determination, the coefficient of multiple determination measures the proportion or percentage of the variation exhibited by the dependent variable that is attributable to the regression analysis. As before, then, we conceptually define the coefficient of multiple determination, R^2, by

$$R^2 = SS(REG)/SS(Y)$$

In simple regression analysis, the sum of squared deviations that are attributable to the regression analysis was given by

$$SS(REG) = b_1 Cov(x,y)$$

However, as indicated previously here, the value of SS(REG) in a multiple regression analysis involving two independent variables is

$$SS(REG) = b_1 Cov(x_1,y) + b_2 Cov(x_2,y)$$

In such a situation, we define the coefficient of multiple determination by

$$R^2 = [b_1 Cov(x_1,y) + b_2 Cov(x_2,y)]/\Sigma(y_i - \bar{Y})^2 \quad \text{(Equation 11.7)}$$

In terms of the example,

$$R^2 = 55.15841/60.40$$

or approximately 0.91. Similar to our interpretation of the coefficient of determination, these results indicate that approximately 0.91 or 91% of the variation exhibited by the dependent variable is attributable to the regression equation.

Evaluation of the Parameter Estimates

A primary purpose of multiple regression analysis is to assess the direction of relationship between the dependent variable and each of the independent variables, holding all others constant. In the following, let the subscript k identify one of several independent variables that is examined in the regression analysis and, as before, the subscript o identify the intercept of the regression equation. When specifying the null and alternate hypotheses about the intercept β_o, we identify the null hypothesis as

$$H_o\text{: } \beta_{oo} = 0$$

The null hypothesis assumes that the intercept is zero. In contrast, the alternate hypothesis that the health administrator usually examines is given by

$$H_a\text{: } \beta_o > 0$$

which posits that the intercept is a positive value.

When the focus is on the relationship of a given independent variable to the dependent variable, we posit that

$$H_o\text{: } \beta_k = 0$$

In this case, the null hypothesis indicates that with other factors held constant the mean value of the dependent variable is unrelated to changes in the corresponding independent variable. The alternate hypothesis might be directional or nondirectional. We might specify the alternate hypothesis concerning β_k as

$$H_a\text{: } \beta_k > 0$$

With all other independent variables held constant, the alternate hypothesis indicates that the mean value of the dependent variable increases when the value of the independent variable grows by one unit. In contrast, we might form the alternate hypothesis represented by

$$H_a\text{: } \beta_k < 0$$

In this case, the alternate hypothesis indicates that with all other variables in the analysis held constant the mean value of the dependent variable decreases as the value of the independent variable grows by one unit. Finally, we might posit that

$$H_a\text{: } \beta_k \neq 0$$

which is a nondirectional or two-tailed alternative.

Returning to a regression analysis involving two independent variables, we evaluate each of the three null hypotheses that are specified here:

$$H_{oo}: \beta_{oo} = 0$$
$$H_{10}: \beta_{10} = 0$$
$$H_{20}: \beta_{20} = 0$$

In contrast, the alternate hypothesis may be directional or nondirectional. In terms of the example, each of the alternate hypotheses might be specified as follows:

$$H_a: \beta_o > 0$$
$$H_{10}: \beta_1 > 0$$
$$H_{20}: \beta_2 < 0$$

In general, the test statistic is similar to those encountered previously. If b_k corresponds to one of several parameter estimates, we rely on

$$t = b_k/SE(b_k) \qquad \text{(Equation 11.8.1)}$$

to evaluate the null and alternate hypotheses.

In Equation 11.8, , the denominator of the ratio, $SE(b_k)$, is the standard error of the parameter estimate and measures chance variation in its value. With the parameter estimates b_1 and b_2, the corresponding standard error is given by

$$SE(b_1) = SE(EST)/[SS(x_1)(1 - R_{1,2}{}^2)]^{1/2} \qquad \text{(Equation 11.8.2)}$$

and by

$$SE(b_2) = SE(EST)/[SS(x_2)(1 - R_{1,2}{}^2)]^{1/2} \qquad \text{(Equation 11.8.3)}$$

respectively. In this formula, $R_{1,2}{}^2$ is a coefficient of determination that indicates the proportion of the variation in x_1 that is attributable to its relationship with x_2 and vice versa. The complement of $R_{1,2}{}^2$, measured by $1 - R_{1,2}{}^2$, measures the proportion of the variation in x_1 that is unrelated to x_2. We simply modify Equation 10.16 slightly and obtain

$$R_{1,2}{}^2 = Cov(x_1,x_2)^2/SS(x_1)SS(x_2)$$

In the example, data from Exhibit 11.1 show that

$$R_{1,2}{}^2 = (-492.2)^2/(1,774.4)(269.6)$$

or approximately 0.50642. Thus, the standard error of b_1 is given by

$$SE(b_1) = 0.660908/[1{,}774.4(1 - 0.50642)]^{1/2}$$

or approximately 0.02233. Similarly, the standard error of b_2 is obtained by

$$SE(b_2) = 0.660908/[269.6(1 - 0.50462)]^{1/2}$$

or approximately 0.05729.

Based on these results, the test statistics are calculated as follows: Concerning the null and alternate hypothesis about b_1, the t ratio is given by

$$t = 0.093325/0.02233$$

or approximately 4.18. If we wish to be 95% certain of avoiding a Type I error, we observe that the calculated value of t exceeds the critical value of 1.782. Based on these findings, we are forced to reject the null hypothesis and conclude that the individual's income is positively associated with the use of care, recognizing that the probability of committing a Type I error is 0.05 or less.

Similarly, the test concerning the relationship between use and distance from the individual's residence to a usual source of care is given by

$$t = -0.24/0.05729$$

or approximately −4.35. Because the calculated value of t is less than the critical value of −1.782, we reject the null hypothesis and accept the alternate, recognizing that the probability of committing a Type I error is 0.05 or less. The results of the regression analysis indicate that with the measure of income held constant the distance traveled to a usual source of care is inversely related to use and represents an impediment to the consumption of care.

The Use of Excel to Perform the Analysis

The use of Excel makes multiple regression analysis quick and precise. In Exhibit 11.3, the data are simply recorded in the spreadsheet. The results from the multiple regression analysis were obtained by

1. Selecting "Data Analysis"
2. Selecting the "Regression" function
3. Identifying the field in which the data that are related to the dependent variable appear

4. Identifying the field in which the data that are related to the independent variables appear
5. Identifying the field in which the results will appear
6. Selecting "OK"

Exhibit 11.3 **Analysis of Physician Use**

Observation	Visits	Income (in $1000)	Distance (Miles)
1	1	4	10
2	3	6	6
3	4	8	3
4	2	9	9
5	5	21	4
6	5	22	2
7	6	34	1
8	3	17	9
9	7	35	2
10	3	12	12
11	2	8	11
12	7	29	3
13	1	11	13
14	2	14	12
15	6	37	2

SUMMARY OUTPUT

Regression Statistics	
Multiple R	0.955624767
R Square	0.913218695
Adjusted R Square	0.898755144
Standard Error	0.660907888
Observations	15

ANOVA

	df	SS	MS	F	Significance F
Regression	2	55.15840916	27.57920458	63.13932	4.271E−07
Residual	12	5.241590836	0.436799236		
Total	14	60.4			

	Coefficients	Standard Error	t Stat	P-Value	Lower 95%	Upper 95%
Intercept	3.785527877	0.737607773	5.132169174	0.000248202	2.178418625	5.39263713
X Variable 1	0.093324761	0.022332476	4.178881008	0.001279055	0.044666476	0.141983047
X Variable 2	−0.249501307	0.05729315	−4.354819132	0.000936862	−0.374332356	−0.124670258

The results listed as "SUMMARY OUTPUT" are similar to those described previously. Specifically, the coefficient of multiple determination represented by "R Square" may be obtained from the data presented in the "ANOVA" table. As indicated, the sum of squared deviations due to regression equaled 55.15840916, whereas the total variation in the use of physician care was 60.4. Thus, the ratio given by 55.15840916/60.4 indicates that 91.3218695% of the variation in the dependent variable is explained by the regression analysis.

As discussed previously, the standard error of the estimate requires the sum of squared error terms that appear in the row identified by the caption "Residual." Consistent with the discussion presented in the previous section, the estimate of the common variance is given by MS(ERROR) [i.e., SS(ERROR)/n − (k + 1) or 5.241590836/12]. The square root of the MS(ERROR), 0.436799236, yields a standard error of the estimate that amounts to 0.660907888.

The value of the "Adjusted R Square" modifies the coefficient of determination to reflect the number of independent variables in the analysis. If the total variation in the dependent variable is fixed for a given sample, then the addition of independent variables increases the value of SS(REG), lowers the value of SS(ERROR), and increases the value of R^2. If the ratio SS(ERROR)/SS(Y) is the proportion of the variation in the dependent variable that is unexplained by the regression analysis, then we may define the coefficient of determination by

$$R^2 = 1 - \text{SS(ERROR)/SS(Y)} \qquad \text{(Equation 11.9.1)}$$

Using this approach, the adjusted R^2 may be defined by

$$ADJ\ R^2 = 1 - (n - 1/n - \text{k})[\text{SS(ERROR)}]/\text{SS(Y)} \qquad \text{(Equation 11.9.2)}$$

In Equation 11.9.2, the proportion of the variation of the dependent variable that is not explained by the regression analysis is adjusted by the ratio n − 1/n − k. As the number of independent variables grows, the value of the expression n − k decreases, implying that the ratio n − 1/n − k must increase. With additional independent variables, the value of SS(ERROR) declines. Thus, if the increase in the ratio n − 1/n − k is not offset by a corresponding decrease in the value of SS(ERROR), the adjusted R^2 may decline.

As discussed in Chapter 10, the results in the "ANOVA" table allow us to determine whether there is a relationship between the dependent variable and the independent variables. The null hypothesis is that β_1 and β_2 are both zero, implying that the mean value of y is equal to β_o. In contrast, the alternate hypothesis is that β_1 and β_2 are not both equal to zero, implying that the mean value of y differs for various combinations of x_1 and x_2. If the ratio of F, MS(REG)/MS(ERROR), is significant, we reject the assumption of homoscedasticity and conclude that a regression relationship exists. In Exhibit 11.3, MS(REG) exceeds MS(ERROR) by a factor of 63.13932. If the presumption of homoscedasticity is true, the probability of obtaining an F ratio equal to approximately 63.14 is 0.0000004, which is much less than conventional levels of avoiding a Type I error. Thus, the results from the "ANOVA" table clearly support the proposition that use is related to income and distance.

The final section of Exhibit 11.3 is similar to the results obtained from a simple regression anasis. The findings indicate that if $\beta_o = 0$ is true, the probability of obtaining a t ratio of approximately 5.13 is 0.0002. Because $p = 0.0002$ is much less than $\alpha = 0.05, 0.02$, or 0.01, the intercept of the plane formed by the regression equation exceeds zero. Similarly, if β_1 is zero, the probability of obtaining a calculated value of t equaling 4.178881008 is 0.001. Again, the results indicate that we must reject the null hypothesis and accept the alternate. If the distance between the place of residence and the usual source of care is held constant, the average number of visits consumed per person per year is positively related to the individual's income. Finally, the results indicate that if β_2 is zero, the probability of obtaining a calculated value of t equaling -4.354819132 is 0.000937. The probability $p = 0.000937$ is much less than commonly used values of α. Thus, we are required to reject the null hypothesis in favor of the alternate, implying that with income held constant, the average number of visits used per person per year is inversely related to the distance that separates the individual's residence and the usual source of care.

Nonlinear Relationships

A number of situations require the health administrator to estimate a nonlinear relationship. For example, it is possible that profitability and volume exhibit a nonlinear relationship. If the capacity to provide service is held constant, we might suppose that as volume is initially increased the net surplus of the organization grows, reaches a maximum, and, after a point, declines. In this situation, the relationship between the organization's net surplus and volume forms a parabola that opens downward and is approximated by a quadratic equation

$$y = b_o + b_1x + b_2x^2$$

Because the parabola opens downward, we expect that the value of b_1 will be positive and that the value of the parameter estimate b_2 will be negative.

For example, suppose that the administrator of a long-term, 90-bed care facility assembled information showing monthly profits and the number of bed days of care provided during the corresponding month of the previous year (Part A of Exhibit 11.4). An inspection of the second and third columns reveals that the net surplus grows from \$34,500 to \$60,480 as the volume is increased from 1,150 to 1,440 bed days of care. The maximum net surplus earned by the facility was when approximately 1,500 bed days of care were provided. However, when the volume of service exceeded 1,500 bed days of care, the net surplus of the organization declined.

As described previously, the relationship between the organization's net surplus and the volume of service is nonlinear and may be approximated by a quadratic expression that might be expressed as

$$\mu_{y(i)} = \beta_o + \beta_1 x + \beta_2 x^2$$

Exhibit 11.4 **Estimation of Nonlinear Function**

Part A: The Data

Observation	Profit	Days of Care	Days of Care Squared
1	34,500	1,150	1,322,500
2	38,400	1,200	1,440,000
3	46,620	1,260	1,587,600
4	60,480	1,440	2,073,600
5	72,000	1,500	2,250,000
6	68,370	1,590	2,528,100
7	68,400	1,710	2,924,100
8	66,960	1,860	3,459,600
9	60,450	1,950	3,802,500
10	62,640	2,160	4,665,600
11	58,590	2,170	4,708,900
12	55,000	2,500	6,250,000

Part B: Statistical Results

SUMMARY OUTPUT

Regression Statistics	
Multiple R	0.882898379
R Square	0.779509547
Adjusted R Square	0.730511669
Standard Error	6260.560309
Observations	12

ANOVA

	df	SS	MS	F	Significance F
Regression	2	1247097953	623548976.6	15.90904696	0.001109824
Residual	9	352751538.4	39194615.38		
Total	11	1599849492			

	Coefficients	Standard Error	t Stat	P-Value	Lower 95%	Upper 95%
Intercept	−126029.7884	34213.58828	−3.683617963	0.005047072	−203426.3612	−48633.21559
X Variable 1	205.8320639	39.92597442	5.155342277	0.000598834	115.513166	296.1509617
X Variable 2	−0.054379778	0.011162241	−4.871761627	0.000881366	−0.079630541	−0.029129015

As indicated previously, the linear coefficient β_1 would be expected to exceed zero and the nonlinear coefficient, β_2, less than zero.

In the previous section, the sample regression equation is defined by

$$\hat{Y}_i = b_o + b_1 x_{1i} + b_2 x_{2i}$$

When we examine the case of a nonlinear expression, we simply substitute x_i^2 for x_{2i} and obtain

$$\hat{Y}_i = b_o + b_1 x_{1i} + b_2 x_i^2$$

Thus, the multiple regression techniques described in the previous section may be used appropriately when examining nonlinear relationships.

To examine expectations concerning β_1 and β_2 in the nonlinear case, we simply create a second independent variable by squaring the bed days of care that appear in the second column. In Exhibit 11.4, the square of the bed days of care provided each month was calculated by

1. Locating the cursor in cell D8
2. Entering the equation = C8^2
3. Using the "Copy" function to transfer the equation to the remaining cells of the column

The results from the "Regression" function were obtained by using the instructions described in the previous section.

Consider next the results in the section entitled "Summary Output." As in our earlier interpretation, the coefficient of multiple determination indicates that approximately 78% of the variation in the profitability of the organization is explained by the regression analysis. Similarly, the findings in the ANOVA table indicate that the value of MS(REG) exceeds that of MS(ERROR) by a factor of approximately 16. Because the probability that the two variances are equal is 0.001, we reject the null hypothesis that the property of homoscedasticity is satisfied and conclude that at least one of the parameter estimates is significant.

The results that pertain to the parameter estimates of β_o, β_1, and β_2 support the conclusion. The results summarized in the row identified by "Intercept" related to the null and alternate hypotheses are summarized here:

$$H_o\colon \beta_o = 0$$
$$H_a\colon \beta_o \neq 0$$

The findings indicate that if the null hypothesis is true the probability of obtaining a calculated value of t equal to approximately −3.68 is 0.005. We reject the null hypothesis and accept the proposition that the intercept is negative and significant. Similarly, the results also examine the null and alternate hypotheses about the linear parameter β_1.

$$H_o: \beta_1 = 0$$
$$H_a: \beta_1 > 0$$

An inspection of the results ($t = 5.15$, $p = 0.0006$) leads us to reject the null hypothesis and accept the proposition that the linear coefficient is positive. The findings in the last row of the exhibit are related to the nonlinear coefficient β_2. If the relationship between profitability and bed days of care is nonlinear and forms a parabola that opens downward, the null and alternate hypotheses are

$$H_o: \beta_2 = 0$$
$$H_a: \beta_2 < 0$$

If the null hypothesis is true, the probability of obtaining a calculated value of t equal to approximately −4.87 is 0.0008. Thus, we reject the null hypothesis and conclude that the nonlinear coefficient is negative and significant. The multiple regression analysis clearly indicates that the relationship between profitability and the monthly volume of care is nonlinear and forms a parabola that opens downward. Using the previously developed methods, the results are valuable to the health administrator when evaluating or forecasting profitability for a given volume alternative.

Binary Variables

Thus far, the analysis has focused on variables that are measured in quantitative terms, such as income, age, or distance. In this section, we introduce methods of capturing the effects of qualitative variables. There are occasions in which it is useful to develop an independent variable that refers to a qualitative characteristic such as the gender of respondents, insurance status (insured or uninsured), residence of the individual (rural or urban), or socioeconomic status (high, medium, or low). In each of these cases, a binary or dummy variable is used to measure the qualitative factor or dimension in the analysis. A binary variable assumes the value of 0 or 1 where the value of 1 is used to identify cases exhibiting the attribute of interest. As illustrated later here, a qualitative characteristic that has m mutually exclusive and collectively exhaustive classes or categories requires $m - 1$ binary variables.

For example, suppose that we are interested in examining factors that influence the use of service, as measured by the number of days of delay in the patient's transfer from the hospital to a long-term care facility. Limited to those who required posthospital care, suppose that we measured the length of delay as the span of time between the date of transfer and the date that the patient was ready for discharge. Suppose also that we believe the patient's age and gender are primary factors that influence the length of delay. We posit that the length of delay is a function of income and gender, implying that we must estimate the parameters of the linear relationship:

$$\textit{Days Delay} = b_0 + b_1\,\textit{Age} + b_2\,\textit{Male}$$

We now employ a binary variable to separate male from female patients as follows:

1. If the patient is a male, we assign a value of one to the variable Male.
2. If the patient is a female, we assign a a value of zero to the variable Male.

The binary variable separates males from females, and only one binary variable is required to capture the two domains of gender. Because we assigned a zero to each female patient, we implicitly identified women as the reference category.

After collecting and analyzing the data, we obtained the following regression equation:

$$\textit{Days Delay} = 4.2 + 0.3\,\textit{Age} + 0.5\,\textit{Male}$$

Consider first the equation that is derived for males. After substituting one for the variable Male, we obtain

$$\textit{Days Delay} = 4.7 + 0.3\,\textit{Age} \qquad \text{(Equation 11.10.1)}$$

When the focus is on females, we simply substitute a zero for Male and obtain

$$\textit{Days Delay} = 4.2 + 0.3\,\textit{Age} \qquad \text{(Equation 11.10.2)}$$

The value of the intercept is the only difference between Equations 11.10.1 and 11.10.2. The results show that for a given age the delay in transferring males to a postdischarge source of care is 0.5 days longer than for females. The use of a binary variable compresses two equations into one and enables us to evaluate the parameter estimate of 0.5 as the additional delay in transferring male patients relative to female patients.

The method of including a binary variable in the regression model is shown in Exhibit 11.5. Using the medical records of 15 patients who were hospitalized with the same condition, we assembled and recorded the number of laboratory procedures used during the hospital episode in the column identified as "Procedures." We also assembled data depicting the number of procedures provided before admission, the income of each patient, and the insurance status of each individual.

As implied in Exhibit 11.5, the administrator is interested in examining the use of laboratory procedures during the hospital episode. The administrator believes

Exhibit 11.5 **The Use of Binary Variables in Regression Analysis**

Patient	Procedures	Income (in $1,000)	Preadmission Tests	Insured	Insurance Status
1	7	4	10	0	ni
2	4	6	6	0	ni
3	8	8	3	1	i
4	3	9	9	0	ni
5	9	21	4	1	i
6	5	22	2	0	ni
7	7	34	1	1	i
8	2	17	9	0	ni
9	7	35	2	1	i
10	3	12	12	0	ni
11	2	8	11	0	ni
12	6	29	3	1	i
13	3	11	13	0	ni
14	2	14	12	0	ni
15	6	37	2	1	i

SUMMARY OUTPUT

Regression Statistics	
Multiple R	0.873964208
R Square	0.763813438
Adjusted R Square	0.699398921
Standard Error	1.301851571
Observations	15

ANOVA

	df	SS	MS	F	Significance F
Regression	3	60.29034069	20.09678023	11.85778414	0.000901523
Residual	11	18.64299265	1.694817513		
Total	14	78.93333333			

	Coefficients	Standard Error	t Stat	P-Value	Lower 95%	Upper 95%
Intercept	7.016817062	1.612038111	4.352761275	0.001150076	3.468743309	10.56489082
X Variable 1	−0.101935644	0.047087363	−2.16481956	0.053255509	−0.205574283	0.001702995
X Variable 2	−0.257761694	0.137505104	−1.874560912	0.087637399	−0.56040854	0.044885153
X Variable 3	3.580494766	1.196972275	2.991292982	0.012269308	0.945975219	6.215014314

that the use of the laboratory care during the hospital episode is reduced by the number of procedures performed before the patient's admission. Thus, it is possible to expect that the number of procedures used during the hospital episode will be inversely related to prior use. The administrator also believes that health needs are inversely related to the patient's socioeconomic status, measured by income. It is possible that those who are wealthy enjoy a good health status and will consume fewer units of laboratory care during hospitalization. In contrast, those who are less wealthy suffer from a poor health status and will require additional units of service. Thus, the administrator believes that the individual's income is negatively related to the use of laboratory care.

Finally, the administrator wishes to examine the role of the individual's insurance status on the use of care. In the exhibit, the effects of the individual's insurance status are captured by the binary variable "Insured." Using the notation in cells F5 to F19, we see that "i" identifies a patient who was insured and "ni" identifies those who were not insured; the 0 and 1 that appear in cells E 5 to E19 were entered using an IF statement as follows:

1. Locate the cursor in cell F5.
2. Enter = IF(F5 = "i", 1,0).
3. Press enter.
4. Use the "Copy" function to record the IF statement in the remaining cells of the column.

In this case, the IF statement automatically records a value of 1 if the letter i appears in one of the cells F5 to F9. If ni appears, Excel automatically enters a zero. The first two patients were uninsured, as evidenced by the assignment of a zero to the binary variable. In contrast, the third and fifth patients were insured, and as a result, a value of one was assigned to the binary variable Insured. Obviously, the uninsured patients represent the reference group, and the administrator expects insured patients to use more care than their uninsured counterparts.

It is necessary to estimate the parameters of the linear equation.

$$Procedures = \beta_o + \beta_1 Income + \beta_2 Preadmission\ Tests + \beta_3 Insured$$

As before, the null hypotheses specify that $\beta_o = \beta_1 = \beta_2 = \beta_3 = 0$. The alternate hypotheses are as follows:

$$H_{a1}: \beta_1 < 0$$
$$H_{a2}: \beta_2 < 0$$
$$H_{a3}: \beta_3 > 0$$

In Exhibit 11.5, each of the alternate hypotheses was examined by applying multiple regression analysis to the data.

Referring to the value of R^2, the coefficient of multiple determination indicates that approximately 87% of the variation exhibited by the dependent variable is attributable to the regression analysis. Similarly, the results in the ANOVA table indicate that at least one parameter estimate is significant. If $\alpha = 0.05$, b_1 differs significantly from zero (i.e., directional alternate hypothesis with $p = 0.0532/2$ or approximately 0.03) and indicates that as the use of laboratory care before admission increases the volume of service consumed during the hospital episode declines. Similarly, the coefficient derived for the amount of income per family member differs significantly from zero (i.e., directional alternate hypothesis with $p = 0.09/2$ or approximately 0.045). This result indicates that as the amount of income per family member grows, the volume of ancillary care consumed during the hospital episode declines.

Finally and important to the discussion in this section, the coefficient derived for the binary variable "Insured" is approximately 3.58 and is significantly different from zero. Thus, for a given level of income per family member and use of laboratory care before the hospital episode, insured patients used approximately 3.58 more procedures than their uninsured counterparts. The binary variable enabled us to capture the qualitative aspects of insurance status and to estimate the numeric difference in the use of laboratory care by insured and uninsured patients.

Interactive Variables^O

Occasionally, a health administrator is required to examine the interactive effects of independent variables on the dependent variable. For example, suppose that we are interested in the cost per case associated with three hospitals that are in a multi-institutional arrangement. We might posit that the cost per case is related to the attributes of the hospital and to the severity of cases treated in each. It also is possible that one of the hospitals treats a more severe mix of cases, implying that the interaction between the hospital and type of patients may contribute to our understanding of the variation in the cost per case. Similarly, the administrator might believe that the distribution of ambulatory care is inconsistent with the health needs of an insured population and that the distance to nearest source of care is an impediment to the appropriate use of service. In this case, the interactive influence of health needs and distance to the nearest source of care is important in assessing the organization's ability to address the health needs of the population at risk.

In the simplest case, an assessment of interactive effects requires a focus on a model similar to

$$\mu_{y(i)} = \beta_o + \beta_1 x_1 + \beta_2 x_2 + \beta_3 x_1 x_2 \qquad \text{(Equation 11.11)}$$

The introduction of the interactive or multiplicative term, represented by x_1x_2 in Equation 11.11, implies that the effect of x_1 on the dependent variable depends on the value of x_2 and that the effect of x_2 on the dependent variable also depends on the value of x_1. For example, we might rearrange Equation 11.11 slightly and obtain

$$\mu_{y(i)} = (\beta_o + \beta_2 x_2) + (\beta_1 + \beta_3 x_2)x_1 \qquad \text{(Equation 11.12)}$$

Suppose now that we assign a fixed value to variable x_2. The sum of β_o and $\beta_2 x_2$ is a constant and represents the intercept of Equation 11.12. After substituting the fixed value for x_2, $(\beta_1 + \beta_3 x_2)$ is the slope coefficient for variable x_1. Thus, when the focus is on independent variable x_1, the intercept and slope of the function are contingent on the value assigned to x_2.

Similarly, Equation 11.11 might be slightly rearranged to obtain

$$\mu_{y(i)} = (\beta_o + \beta_1 x_1) + (\beta_2 + \beta_3 x_1)x_2 \qquad \text{(Equation 11.13)}$$

In this case, we find the slope coefficient for variable x_2 by assigning a fixed value to x_1, implying that the sum of β_o and $\beta_1 x_1$ corresponds to the intercept of the function. After substituting a given value for x_1, $(\beta_2 + \beta_3 x_1)$ is the slope coefficient for variable x_2. Hence, when the focus is on x_2, the intercept and the value of the slope coefficient depend on the value of independent variable x_1.

For example, consider a health service organization that is dedicated to the proposition that the provision of service should be congruent with the health needs of the insured population. In this case, the administrator believes that with advancing age health needs increase, and as a result, older members of the population at risk should use more physician services than their younger counterparts. Suppose also that the organization is committed to ensuring that members of the insured population are guaranteed equal access to physician services. Based on previous experience, assume the administrator suspects that the geographic distribution of clinics is less than desirable, implying that distance to the nearest source of care is an impediment to use.

Suppose that we surveyed 17 members of the insured population that reside in our market area (Exhibit 11.6). The second column lists the number of visits for each individual during the past year, and the third column represents the distance from the respondent's home to the nearest source of care. The data in the fourth column depict the individual's age. The values in the final column comprise the multiplicative or interactive term and were derived by the product of the individual's age and the distance from the individual's residence to the nearest clinic.

The results of the regression analysis also are presented in Exhibit 11.6. The coefficients derived for distance to the nearest clinic were significant and negative. These findings suggest that as the distance between the respondent's home and the source of care increases the average number of visits during the year declined. Similarly, the coefficient derived for the age of the individual was significant and positive, implying that older individuals consume, on average, a greater number

Exhibit 11.6 **The Use of Interactive Terms in Regression Analysis**

Patient	Visits	Age	Distance	Age and Distance
1	7	45	2.0	90.0
2	6	54	1.0	54.0
3	1	23	5.0	115.0
4	4	33	2.0	66.0
5	6	61	0.1	6.1
6	1	30	6.0	180.0
7	2	28	8.0	224.0
8	9	59	1.0	59.0
9	6	42	2.0	84.0
10	2	28	5.0	140.0
11	6	53	0.2	10.6
12	7	56	1.0	56.0
13	2	31	7.0	217.0
14	1	24	6.0	144.0
15	8	59	1.0	59.0
16	4	40	1.0	40.0
17	6	62	1.0	62.0

SUMMARY OUTPUT

Regression Statistics	
Multiple R	0.940466076
R Square	0.88447644
Adjusted R Square	0.857817157
Standard Error	0.998160989
Observations	17

ANOVA

	df	SS	MS	F	Significance F
Regression	3	99.16541737	33.05513912	33.17705283	2.32912E−06
Residual	13	12.95222969	0.99632536		
Total	16	112.1176471			

	Coefficients	Standard Error	t Stat	P-Value	Lower 95%	Upper 95%
Intercept	1.60331294	2.042858452	0.784837999	0.446615827	−2.8100133577	6.016639458
X Variable 1	0.079288797	0.039554461	2.004547542	0.066298095	−0.006163401	0.164740998
X Variable 2	−1.504531408	0.583335786	−2.579185857	0.022891906	−2.764751512	−0.244311304
X Variable 3	0.041821643	0.018691393	2.237481382	0.0433984392	0.001441352	0.082201935

of visits than younger members of the insured population. The estimate of β_3 is clearly positive and differs significantly from zero, suggesting that the interaction between the two variables is significant.

To interpret these results, suppose that we let the distance to the nearest clinic equal 2 miles. In this case, the slope coefficient for the age of the individual is given by

$$[0.08 + 0.04(2)]$$

or 0.16. Thus, the administrator estimates that for those respondents who must travel 2 miles for care an increase in age of 1 year increases the use of service, on average, by 0.16 visit. Similarly, suppose that the age of the individual is 30 years. The slope coefficient for the distance to the nearest clinic is given as

$$[-1.50 + 0.04(30)]$$

or approximately -0.30. If the age of the individual is held constant and equal to 30 years, the results indicate that on average an increase in the distance to the nearest clinic of 1 mile reduces the use of physician services by 0.30 visit per year. The interactive effects augmented or reinforced the influence of age on use. In contrast, the interactive term dampened or lowered the slope coefficient derived for the distance separating the individual's residence and the nearest source of care.

Exercises

1. Suppose that the administrator of a managed-care organization is interested in the relationship of the number of visits to the number of disability days reported by the patient and the distance from the residence of the member to the nearest source of care. The results of a random survey yielded these results:

Patient	Visits	Distance	Disability Days
1	7	1	8
2	7	1	9
3	2	10	1
4	4	4	3
5	5	2	5
6	3	9	2
7	2	10	1
8	9	2	10
9	6	3	7
10	2	11	2

11	4	2	3
12	7	2	8
13	3	14	2
14	2	16	1
15	8	2	9
16	4	4	2
17	6	2	5

Use Excel's "Regression" function to estimate the linear relationship between use and the number of disability days and distance to the nearest source of care. Examine your results by

1. Interpreting the coefficient of multiple determination
2. Interpreting the results reported in the ANOVA table
3. Determining whether the intercept and the slope coefficients are significant
4. Interpreting the direction of association between each independent variable and related administrative implications

Let $\alpha = 0.05$.

2. Using the data in Exercise 1, include an independent variable depicting the interactive effects of distance and disability days in the analysis. Examine your results by
   1. Interpreting the coefficient of multiple determination
   2. Interpreting the results reported in the ANOVA table
   3. Determining whether the intercept and the slope coefficients are significant
   4. Interpreting the direction of association between each independent variable and related administrative implications

   Let $\alpha = 0.05$.

3. During an evaluation of internal operations, the administrator is concerned that the use of labor and consumable supplies fail to vary directly with the volume of service. To examine the situation, the following data were assembled:

Volume (000 visits)	Labor (000 hours)	Supplies (000 units)
7	4	1
8	4	1
12	7	2
11	7	2
17	9	5
20	12	8
22	13	9
24	14	9

Use multiple regression analysis to examine the relationship between volume and the use of labor and consumable supplies. Assess your results from a statistical and administrative perspective. Let $\alpha = 0.05$.

4. The director of human resources is concerned that the salary policy of the organization contributes to an excessive turnover rate. To assess the situation, the following data were assembled:

Salary ($000)	Years of Experience	Education	Position
24	10	Undergraduate	Director
32	8	Undergraduate	Technician
42	15	High School	Staff
18	7	High School	Staff
38	11	Graduate School	Director
54	17	High School	Staff
44	3	Undergraduate	Technician
35	7	Undergraduate	Technician
43	2	High School	Director
65	12	Graduate School	Technician
51	6	High School	Staff
22	14	Undergraduate	Technician
37	9	Graduate School	Staff
48	22	High School	Technician
73	4	Undergraduate	Technician
81	17	Undergraduate	Director
40	15	Graduate	Technician
19	13	High School	Staff
47	1	Undergraduate	Technician
52	7	Undergraduate	Technician

In this case, the categories in the "Education" column represent the highest educational attainment of the individual. Specifically, "Undergraduate" refers to an individual who completed college; "High School" refers to an individual who completed high school, and "Graduate" identifies an individual who completed a graduate program leading to a master's degree. Use "High School" as the reference category for the educational attainment of the individual and "Staff" as the reference category for the position of the individual. Use multiple regression analysis to assess the salary policy of the organization. In your evaluation, let $\alpha = 0.05$.

5. The director of a long-term care facility is interested in the relationship between the cost per day and the number of days of care provided during each month of the last year. The following data were assembled by the administrator:

Cost Per Day	Days of Care
65	1,190
68	1,200
63	1,260
58	1,440
52	1,500
57	1,590
60	1,710
64	1,860
69	1,950
71	2,160
73	2,250
74	2,300

Use the "Regression" function in Excel to estimate the relationship between the cost per day and the volume of care provided by the facility. Interpret your results when viewed from a statistical and administrative perspective. Let $\alpha = 0.05$.

6. Assume that the administrator of a short-term acute hospital wishes to examine factors that influence the length of stay. The administrator is interested in the influence of age and insurance status on the use of care. It is expected that the use of care increases with advancing age and that the insured use more care than the uninsured. After selecting a random sample of 15 patients who were treated for a disease of the digestive system, we obtained the following information:

Length of Stay	Age	Insurance Status
5	18	Uninsured
10	54	Insured
6	32	Insured
9	61	Insured
11	58	Insured
3	24	Uninsured
6	34	Insured
15	64	Insured
12	58	Insured
4	43	Uninsured
3	52	Uninsured
15	49	Insured
4	29	Uninsured
2	24	Insured
3	28	Uninsured

Use the "Uninsured" as the reference category and the "Regression" function to estimate the linear function relating the length of stay to age and insurance status. Interpret your results when viewed from a statistical and administrative perspective. Let $\alpha = 0.05$.

7. The hospital administrator is interested in examining the use of laboratory services and believes that the number of comorbidities and the age of the patient are factors that influence volume. Limited to inpatients with an eye disease, a random sample of 15 live discharges yielded the following results:

Number of Procedures	Number of Comorbidities	Age
15	5	23
8	2	27
23	10	45
19	8	39
25	14	55
27	13	62
16	7	31
10	6	30
9	2	19
31	15	67
29	14	59
22	10	44
14	7	32
25	14	37
11	5	29

Use the "Regression" function in Excel to estimate the relationship of the number of laboratory procedures to the age of the individual and number of comorbidities presented by the patient. Interpret your results when viewed from a statistical and administrative perspective. Let $\alpha = 0.05$.

8. Using the data in Exercise 7, estimate the relationship of laboratory use to age, the number of comorbidities, and a variable that captures the interactive effects of age and the number of comorbidities. Interpret the results from a statistical and administrative perspective. Let $\alpha = 0.05$.

CHAPTER 12 INTRODUCTION TO FORECASTING[O]

OBJECTIVES

1. Describe the importance of forecasts.
2. Describe trend, seasonal, cyclical, and irregular variation as components that combine to determine the value of the time series in a given period.
3. Compute and identify the advantages or disadvantages of using the mean absolute deviation and the mean square error as measures of errors present in a set of predictions.
4. Use exponential smoothing to derive projections for a horizontal time series.
5. Use the average periodic rate of change and regression analysis to estimate the effects of trend.
6. Use regression analysis to estimate a nonlinear trend.
7. Define autocorrelation and use the autocorrelation coefficient to measure the relationship of the time series in one period with one or more antecedent values.
8. Estimate an autoregressive model and use the results to derive projections.
9. Use seasonal decomposition as a method to estimate trend and projections for each of four seasons.

This chapter focuses on the use of statistical methods to derive forecasts of the volume of care, production coefficients that represent the amount of resources required to provide a unit of service, the mix of resources required, and the costs of care. A health service administrator's primary function is to prepare an annual budget showing anticipated costs, revenues, and the related net surplus or loss. Obviously, the anticipated volume of care, resource requirements, and costs are essential items when preparing the expense budget. The costs that the health service organization expects to incur also play a role in preparing charges and developing the fee schedule, which is essential when preparing the revenue budget.

The need to develop accurate estimates of cost and revenue is enhanced by the reliance on prospective payment systems to finance the use of care in the American health industry. *Prospective payment* refers to any system in which the rate or level of compensation is predetermined and the health service organization receives the rate or amount irrespective of the costs that are incurred. Thus, before negotiating a payment rate, the administrator needs to have an accurate estimate of related costs. Similarly, the costs of providing care to patients whose use is financed by a prospective payment system need to be monitored and controlled. The effectiveness of systems that are designed to monitor and control costs depends on the accuracy of related estimates.

The development of accurate projections also stems from the inherent need to reduce the uncertainty and the risks that exist in the environment of the typical health care organization. Most health administrators prefer to manage their organizations when conditions are certain. In a world of certainty, the values of administratively relevant factors are known with certainty and show no variation. However, the administrator must manage the affairs of the organization in a world of uncertainty, one in which administratively relevant variables exhibit variability. A primary purpose of the forecasting methods described here is to reduce the variation in projections and thereby minimize the a priori uncertainty and related risks for the health organization.

The Data

This chapter is limited to the process of developing forecasts for an established program or health service organization. The typical health service organization records and retains data that show financial and operational activity. The sets of information that the health organization maintains might be regarded as time series data. A *time series* is a set of observations that is reported at or during successive times. For example, the average daily census, the annual number of admissions or discharges, the number of patient days of care, the number of visits to the emergency department, and the occupancy rate per month or year are time series data. The purpose of time series analysis is to examine variation in the processes that generate the data and to enhance the administrator's ability to understand, control, and predict the performance of the health service organization.

In the following we let Y_t correspond to the value of the time series during a specific period, which is identified by the subscript t. Trend, seasonal, cyclical, and irregular variations combine to determine the value Y_t. Each of the components that combine to determine the value of the time series is considered next.

Trend is the component of a time series that refers to the increase or decrease in the time series during a prolonged period of time. In turn, trend is usually attributable to long-term changes in the size of the population, the demographic attributes of the population, the prevalence or incidence of illness, technology, or preferences for health care. As indicated later here, the trend component of a time series may be linear or nonlinear.

In Figure 12.1, the value of the time series is measured on the vertical axis, and units of time are recorded on the horizontal axis. In Figure 12.1.a, the trend component may increase, rising from left to right with the passage of time. An example of the trend (shown in Figure 12.1) is the long-term growth in spending on health care. In Figure 12.1.b, the trend component also may fall from left to right.

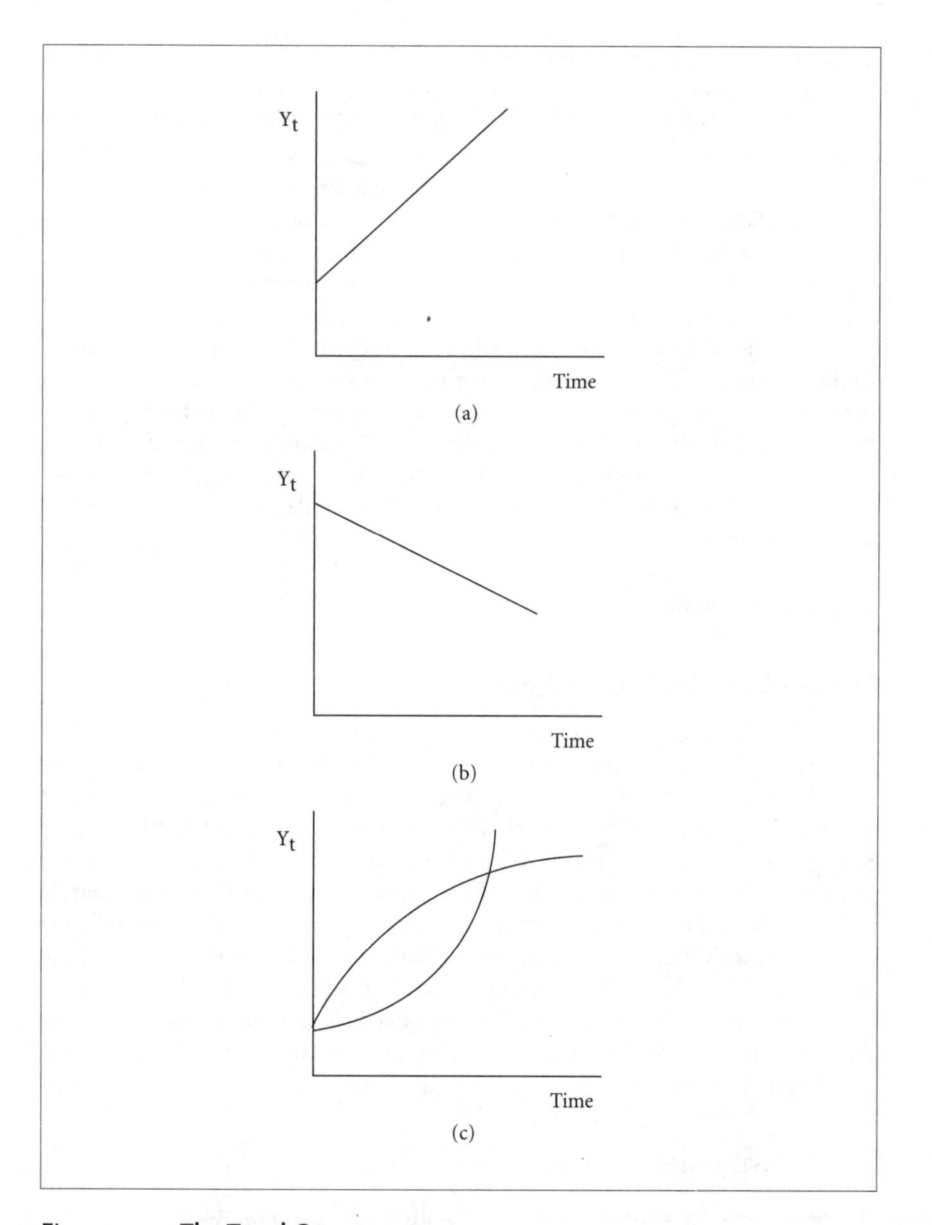

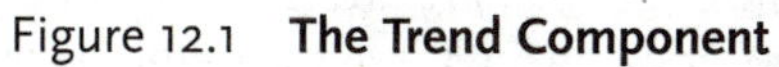
Figure 12.1 **The Trend Component**

Similar to the trend illustrated in the figure, many analysts contend that the reliance on prospective payment systems and the proliferation of managed-care organizations contributed to a long-term decline in the number of admissions, the length of stay, the number of patient days of care, and the occupancy rate of hospitals. In Figure 12.1.c, the trend component may rise or fall nonlinearly. Because the trend component refers to long periods of time, we usually represent gradual changes in the data by a continuous function that spans the entire period.

In addition to the trend component, projections derived by the health administrator are frequently based on data that are influenced by seasonal variation. Seasonal variation is a recurring pattern exhibited by the data that occur within the span of 1 year. Obvious examples of seasonal variation include variation in the occupancy rate during weekends or holiday seasons, emergency room visits, particularly on Friday or Saturday, and utility expenses during the year.

Time series data also reflect the influence of cyclical and irregular variation. Cyclical variation is characterized by periods of recession and expansion and by peaks and troughs. Cyclical variation is attributable to volatility in business activity that might result from unintended changes in inventory, changes in fiscal policy, and shifts in the rate of capital accumulation. After measuring the influence of the trend, cyclical, and seasonal components, the irregular component consists of the residual movement or change in time series data. The irregular component may reflect the effects of unique events or nonrecurring factors such as strikes, epidemics, or the weather.

Horizontal or Stable Time Series

In this section, we consider a set of data that exhibits no trend, cyclical, or seasonal variation. For example, consider the volume of care that a long-term care facility provides. Suppose that the bed capacity has remained constant during the recent past and that the annual occupancy rate varied between 0.90 and 0.98 during the study period. Given a fixed capacity to provide care, differences in the occupancy rate dictate variation in the number of patient days of care provided each year. In this case, the set of data might form a pattern similar to the distribution in Figure 12.2. The distribution showing the days of care provided each year forms a band that is parallel to the x-axis, suggesting that trend and cyclical variations are absent from the data. Thus, the administrator needs to develop a forecast that reduces or eliminates the irregular variation and thereby minimizes the error in the projection of future use.

The Measurement of Residuals

In this section, our focus is on measuring the errors that are present in the forecasts derived from a horizontal or stable time series. Again, Y_t represents the value of the time series in period t, and F_t represents the corresponding forecast. If Y_t differs from F_t, an error is present in the forecast, an error that is measured by the difference $Y_t - F_t$. If the actual value of the time series, Y_t, exceeds the corresponding forecast, the difference is positive, and the projection underestimated the actual volume. In contrast, if the actual value is less than the corresponding projection, the forecast overestimated Y_t and the error term is negative.

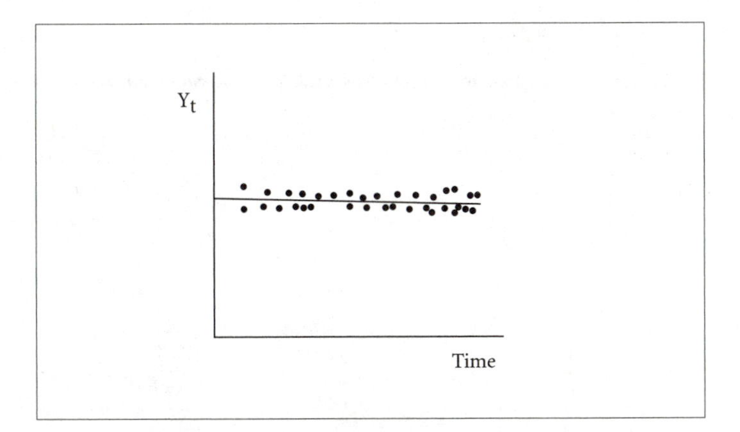

Figure 12.2 **Horizontal Time Series**

Essentially, two methods of measuring residual or error terms might be used when the data form a band that is horizontal to the x-axis. The first, the mean absolute deviation (MAD), is defined by

$$MAD = \Sigma|Y_t - F_t|/n \qquad \text{(Equation 12.1)}$$

The sum of the absolute deviations between the actual and predicted value of the time series is in the numerator of Equation 12.1. The absolute value of −3, represented by |−3| is 3. The denominator, n, refers to the number of error or residual terms that appears in the numerator. For example, in Table 12.1, the number of visits during each of the five periods is listed in the second column, and the corresponding projections are in the third column. The absolute values of the differences between the actual and projected number of visits are shown in the fourth column.

The sum of the absolute deviations is 18 visits. Recognizing that five error terms were used to calculate the sum, the value of MAD is given by

$$MAD = 18/5$$

or 3.6 visits. The greater is the differences between each of the actual and predicted values, the larger is the value of the absolute deviations and, hence, the greater is the value of MAD. The analyst's object is to select an approach that results in a minimum value of the MAD.

A second and perhaps preferred approach for measuring the errors that are present in a set of projections is the mean square error (MSE). The MSE may be defined by

$$MSE = \Sigma(Y_t - F_t)^2/n \qquad \text{(Equation 12.2)}$$

Table 12.1 **The MAD and the Mean Square Error**

Period	Visits (in 1,000s)	Projection (in 1,000s)	Absolute Deviation	Squared Error
	(Y_t)	(F_t)		
1	22	25	3	9
2	25	27	2	4
3	21	24	3	9
4	22	26	4	16
5	19	25	6	36
Total			18	74
Mean			3.6	14.8

The sum of squared error terms is in the numerator of Equation 12.2, and as before, the number of error or residual terms is in the denominator. The square of the deviations between the actual and predicted values is shown in the fifth column of Table 12.1. When divided by 5, the sum of the squared error terms yields an MSE of 14.8 visits. Similar to the discussion of MAD, the greater is the difference between each of the actual and predicted values, represented by $(Y_t - F_t)$, the greater is the sum of the squared error terms and thus the larger is the value of MSE. Because the square of the deviations is the cornerstone of Equation 12.2, the MSE is more sensitive to large deviations and thus is frequently preferred to MAD as an indicator of the errors that are present in the set of projections.

Exponential Smoothing

In this section, the band that the set of time series data formed is parallel to the x-axis. We presume that the effects of the trend, seasonal, and cyclical components are negligible, implying that the accuracy of our projections is contingent on reducing or eliminating the influence of irregular variation. In this section, we employ exponential smoothing to derive projections and an Excel spreadsheet to perform the required calculations.

Exponential smoothing is a relatively simple and administratively efficient method of deriving projections. We may express the exponential smoothing as a method for deriving a forecast for the next period, represented by F_{t+1} in the following

$$F_{t+1} = F_t + \lambda(Y_t - F_t) \qquad \text{(Equation 12.3)}$$

In this formula, F_t represents the forecast for the current period, and Y_t corresponds to the actual value of the time series during the current period; λ represents the smoothing constant that ranges from zero to one. The forecast for the next period, F_{t+1}, is simply the forecast for the current period, F_t, plus a fraction, λ, of the error in the current forecast represented by $(Y_t - F_t)$.

When applying exponential smoothing to the general problem of deriving a projection for the next period, the first task is to select a value of λ. To illustrate the influence of different values of λ, suppose that our focus is on developing a projection of visits. Suppose also that the current forecast is 100 visits and that the current volume is 120 visits. If λ equals 0.2, a forecast for the next period is

$$F_{t+1} = 100 + 0.2(120 - 100)$$

The error in the current forecast is 20 visits, implying that the forecast for the next period is 104 visits. Now, suppose that λ is equal to 0.8. The corresponding forecast is given by

$$F_{t+1} = 100 + 0.8(120 - 100)$$

As before, the error in the current forecast is 20 visits, but after performing the calculations, we find that the forecast is 116 visits. The illustration indicates that the greater is the value of λ, the more sensitive is the forecast for the next period to errors in the current projection. In contrast, the lower is the value of λ, the less sensitive is the forecast to errors in the current projection. Thus, it is customary to recommend the assignment of a low value to λ if the irregular variation is relatively large and a high value if the irregular variation is relatively small.

As indicated, however, the value assigned to λ should reduce or minimize the MSE, thereby assuring that the forecast uncertainty is at a minimum. For example, assume that the focus of the analysis is on a long-term care facility that operates 70 beds. Suppose further that the capacity to provide care remains constant during the study period and that the administrator assembled data that depict the actual and predicted volume of care for the first year of operation as follows:

Year	Days	Forecast
1	23,500	23,500

Because the forecast is developed during the first year of operation, the actual volume is assumed to be equal to the projected number of patient days of service. If λ equal 0.2, we now develop a projection at the end of the first year for the second year of operation by computing

$$F_2 = 23{,}500 + 0.2(23{,}500 - 23{,}500)$$

Thus, for the second year, the administrator expects to provide 23,500 bed days of care during the second year. Suppose, however, that the facility actually provided 25,000 bed days of care. Based on these data, we are able to develop a projection for the third year of operation by

$$F_3 = 23{,}500 + 0.2(25{,}000 - 23{,}500)$$

Thus, these calculations suggest that the organization expects to provide 23,800 bed days of care.

An application of exponential smoothing when developing a projection of volume for each year in a 12-year period is shown in Exhibit 12.1. Three sets of pro-

Exhibit 12.1 **Exponential Smoothing**

Part A				**Part B**			
Smoothing Constant	**0.2**				**0.3**		
Year	**Bed Days of Care**	**Forecast**	**Error Squared**	**Year**	**Bed Days of Care**	**Forecast**	**Error Squared**
1	23,500	23,500.0	0	1	23,500	23,500.0	0.0
2	25,000	23,500.0	2,250,000.0	2	25,000	23,500.0	2,250000.0
3	24,000	23,800.0	40,000.0	3	24,000	23,950.0	2,500.0
4	21,000	23,840.0	8,065,600.0	4	21,000	23,965.0	8,791,225.0
5	23,700	23,272.0	183,184.0	5	23,700	23,075.5	390,000.3
6	22,900	23,357.6	209,397.8	6	22,900	23,262.9	131,660.1
7	22,500	23,266.1	586,878.6	7	22,500	23,154.0	427,709.5
8	23,800	23,112.9	472,155.9	8	23,800	22,957.8	709,306.7
9	23,900	23,250.3	422,121.5	9	23,900	23,210.5	475,468.8
10	22,500	23,380.2	774,810.1	10	22,500	23,417.3	841,476.5
11	24,000	23,204.2	633,319.3	11	24,000	23,142.1	735,950.9
12	23,900	23,363.3	287,994.2	12	23,900	23,399.5	250,513.3
Total			13,925,461.3	Total			15,005,811.1
MSE			**11,604,55.1**	MSE			**1,250,484.3**

Part C			
Smoothing Constant	**0.4**		
Year	**Bed Days of Care**	**Forecast**	**Error Squared**
1	23,500	23,500.0	0.0
2	25,000	23,500.0	2,250,000.0
3	24,000	24,100.0	10,000.0
4	21,000	24,060.0	9,363,600.0
5	23,700	22,836.0	746,496.0
6	22,900	23,181.6	79,298.6
7	22,500	23,069.0	323,715.5
8	23,800	22,841.4	918,960.0
9	23,900	23,224.8	455,860.5
10	22,500	23,494.9	989,816.8
11	24,000	23,096.9	815,522.4
12	23,900	23,458.2	195,220.5
Total			16,148,490.2
MSE			**1,345,707.5**

jections were derived and the MSE was calculated for each set of forecasts. In Part A, let λ equal 0.2, and in Part B, the smoothing constant is 0.3. Part C of the exhibit lists projections and the MSE when λ is equal to 0.4. In Part A, the projections were based on the following observations:

1. The current volume and the current forecast for the first period are located in cells B10 and C10, respectively.
2. The forecast for period two was obtained by entering =C10 + 0.2*(B10 − C10) in cell C11.
3. The remaining forecasts were obtained by copying the expression residing in C11 to the remainder of the column.
4. The squared error terms were obtained by entering =(B10 − C10)^2 in cell D11.
5. The sum of the squared error terms was obtained by using the "AutoSum" function.
6. The mean of the sum of squared error terms was obtained by entering = D22/12 in cell D23.

The projections, squared error terms, and MSEs in Parts B and C were calculated similarly.

As indicated, the object of the analysis is to select the value of λ that minimizes variation or uncertainty as measured by the MSE. In this case, it is necessary to compare the computed values of the MSE terms and to select the value of λ that minimizes the sum of the squared residuals. Based on the results in Exhibit 12.1, the MSE is lowest when λ is equal to 0.2. The calculations are so easily performed that it is a relatively simple matter to replicate the analysis presented in Exhibit 12.1 for other values of λ and select the value of λ that minimizes the MSE.

The Estimation of Trend

This section focuses on several methods of estimating the trend component of time series data. *Trend* refers to the long-term or gradual movement in the data, and the pattern formed by the data may be linear or nonlinear.To accommodate the usual situations encountered in health administration, we examine the average rate of periodic change and regression analysis as methods of measuring trend and deriving predictions.

Average Rate of Periodic Change

The average rate of periodic change is a numeric value that enables us to summarize the movement shown by the time series data. For example, the number of admissions and the number of days of care provided by our hospital might decline on average by 6% and 7% per year during the last decade. Similarly, inpatient costs might have risen, on average, by 10% per year during the study period.

For example, suppose that our focus is on a single diagnosis and that we assembled the following data that measure the cost per case during each year of a 5-year period.

Year	Cost Per Case
1	$2,800
2	$3,200
3	$3,500
4	$3,750
5	$4,000

The set of information reveals that the cost per case increased during each year of the study period. Furthermore, we might express the factor by which the value in 1 year exceeds that of the previous year by Y_t/Y_{t-1}. Thus, in the illustration involving the cost per case, the corresponding ratios are

$4,000/$3,750, $3,750/$3,500, $3,500/$3,200, $3,200/$2,800

Let g correspond to the average rate of periodic change and apply the geometric mean to obtain

$$g = [(Y_n/Y_{n-1})\,(Y_{n-1}/Y_{n-2}) \ldots (Y_3/Y_2)(Y_2/Y_1)]^{1/(n-1)} - 1 \qquad \text{(Equation 12.4)}$$

In this case, we assume the time series consists of n observations on the item of interest. Equation 12.4 also reveals that the expression

$$[(Y_n/Y_{n-1})(Y_{n-1}/Y_{n-2}) \ldots (Y_3/Y_2)(Y_2/Y_1)]^{1/(n-1)}$$

reduces to $[Y_n/Y_1]^{1/(n-1)}$ and, thus,

$$g = [Y_n/Y_1]^{1/(n-1)} - 1 \qquad \text{(Equation 12.5)}$$

In the problem involving the cost per case, the average periodic rate of change is simply

$$g = [\$4{,}000/\$2{,}800]^{0.25} - 1$$

After calculating, we find that g is approximately 0.0932 per year. The results indicate that, on average, the cost per case increased by approximately 9% per year during the period. If the processes that produced the time series remain relatively invariant during the planning period, a projection for the sixth year might be obtained by the product of \$4,000 and 1.0932 or \$4,372.80.

Consider next a situation in which we wish to examine a time series showing a long-term decline in the days of care that our hospital provided. In this instance, suppose the administrator assembled this information:

Year	Days
1	36,000
2	35,400
3	35,000
4	34,200
5	33,800
6	33,000

With these data, we might calculate the average rate of annual change as follows:

$$g = (33{,}000/36{,}000)^{0.2} - 1$$

or −0.017252. These calculations indicate that the volume of care that the hospital provided declined by approximately 1.7% per year during the period. If the processes or factors contributing to the decline remain relatively invariant, the projected volume is the product of 0.9827 and 33,000 or approximately 32,429 days of care.

Regression Analysis and the Estimation of a Linear Trend

As described previously, regression analysis requires only a slight modification that allows the administrator to apply the approach to the problem of developing a forecast. Parameter estimates are given by

$$b_o = \bar{Y} - b_1\bar{X}$$

and by

$$b_1 = Cov(x,y)/Var(x)$$

When we focus on the use of regression analysis to estimate trend, the independent variable is time, t. After substituting $\bar{T}$ for $\bar{X}$ and t for x, we obtain

$$b_o = \bar{Y}_t - b_1\bar{T}$$
$$b_1 = Cov(t,y_t)/Var(t)$$

Thus, the line of average relationship is given by

$$\hat{Y}_t = b_o + b_1 t \qquad \text{(Equation 12.6)}$$

The line of average relationship, as indicated by Equation 12.6, suggests that the dependent variable is a function of t rather than x.

For example, suppose that we wish to develop a line of average relationship that describes the relationship between the number of visits provided by a clinic and time, measured in years. Suppose also that we collected the data in Exhibit 12.2. In this case, the number of visits, representing the dependent variable, appears in the first column, and the corresponding time period, representing the in-

Exhibit 12.2 **Estimation of Trend Using Regression Analysis**

Visits	Year
1,147	1
1,175	2
1,150	3
1,191	4
1,188	5
1,179	6
1,200	7
1,220	8
1,208	9
1,230	10

SUMMARY OUTPUT

Regression Statistics	
Multiple R	0.90456499
R Square	0.818237821
Adjusted R Square	0.795517549
Standard Error	12.346819
Observations	10

ANOVA

	df	SS	MS	F	Significance F
Regression	1	5490.048485	5490.048485	36.0135569	0.000322986
Residual	8	1219.551515	152.4439394		
Total	9	6709.6			

	Coefficients	Standard Error	t Stat	P-Value	Lower 95%	Upper 95%
Intercept	1143.933333	8.434483093	135.6257782	9.76788E-15	1124.483368	1163.383299
X Variable 1	8.157575758	1.359340033	6.001129635	0.000322986	5.022929993	11.29222152

dependent variable, appears in the second column. The regression results were obtained using the methods described previously.

As indicated, the coefficient of determination is approximately 0.82, implying that 82% of the variation exhibited by the number of visits is attributable to the regression analysis and the trend component. The value of MS(REG) exceeds the value of MS(ERROR) by a factor of approximately 36, implying that a parameter estimate is significant. An inspection of the t ratios and "P-values" reveals that both parameter estimates are significant at conventional levels. Thus, the equation relating visits to time is expressed by

$$\hat{Y}_t = 1{,}143.9 + 8.16t$$

These results indicate that the volume of care increased, on average, by 8.16 visits per year. If the processes and factors that produced the time series remain relatively invariant during the next period, period 11, the corresponding projection is

$$\hat{Y}_{11} = 1{,}143.9 + 8.16(11)$$

or approximately 1,234 visits.

Estimation of an Exponential Trend

Occasionally, the health administrator must base projections on a set of data that increases or decreases at a given rate per period rather than by a given amount per period.

Equal distances on an arithmetic scale represent equal amounts of increase or decrease. On the other hand, equal distances on a ratio or logarithmic scale represent equal rates of increase or decrease. For example, when portrayed on a ratio scale, the distances between 20 and 40, 40 and 80, or 80 and 160 scale are all equal because each represents an increase of 100%.

When portrayed in original units, an exponential trend that rises from left to right may bend backward, forming a nonlinear pattern. However, when displayed using a semilogarithmic scale, the observations will form a long-term pattern that is linear or nearly so. Thus, when estimating an exponential trend, we first determine the logarithm that corresponds to each observation and then use the logarithms of the time series to estimate the trend component. For example, consider

$$100 = 10^2$$

In this case, 2 is the exponent or logarithm of 100 when 10 is adopted as the base. When examining an exponential trend, the logarithm rather than the original value is used in the estimation process. The task is to estimate the parameters of

$$Log(Y_t) = b_o + b_1 t \qquad \text{(Equation 12.7.1)}$$

Forecasts are obtained in natural units by a slight transformation represented by

$$\hat{Y}_t = 10^{b_o + b_1 t} \quad \text{(Equation 12.7.2)}$$

where we use base 10 to calculate the logarithms of the values comprising the original time series.

For example, suppose that the administrator focuses on the costs of providing outpatient care in a given clinic and that the data appearing in Exhibit 12.3.a are

Exhibit 12.3.a **Estimation of Exponential Trend: The Basic Data**

Costs (in Millions)	Logcosts	Time
37	1.568201724	1
38	1.579783597	2
41	1.612783857	3
52	1.716003344	4
60	1.77815125	5
55	1.740362689	6
79	1.897627091	7
78	1.892094603	8
84	1.924279286	9
86	1.934498451	10
90	1.954242509	11
102	2.008600172	12
101	2.004321374	13
102	2.008600172	14
106	2.025305865	15
103	2.012837225	16
110	2.041392685	17
124	2.093421685	18
160	2.204119983	19
191	2.281033367	20
208	2.318063335	21
222	2.346352974	22
277	2.442479769	23
319	2.503790683	24
332	2.521138084	25
338	2.5289167	26
339	2.530199698	27
379	2.57863921	28
427	2.630427875	29

Exhibit 12.3.b **Regression Results: Exponential Trend**

SUMMARY OUTPUT

Regression Statistics	
Multiple R	0.984467079
R Square	0.96917543
Adjusted R Square	0.968033779
Standard Error	0.057188584
Observations	29

ANOVA

	df	SS	MS	F	Significance F
Regression	1	2.776436919	2.776436919	848.9246135	6.14712E-22
Residual	27	0.088304421	0.003270534		
Total	28	2.86474134			

	Coefficients	Standard Error	t Stat	P-Value	Lower 95%	Upper 95%
Intercept	1.537596407	0.021800795	70.52937317	3.70694E-32	1.492864901	1.582327914
X Variable 1	0.036982468	0.001269291	29.13631091	6.14712E-22	0.034378099	0.039586837

available. Costs grew from $37 million to $427 million during the study period. The logarithms of each value in the time series are listed in the second column. These values were obtained by

1. Highlighting cell B6
2. Selecting the "Insert" function
3. Selecting the "Log" function
4. Entering cell A6 in the window identified as "number"
5. Entering 10 in the window identified as "base"
6. Using the "Copy" function to transfer the equation in cell B6 to the remainder of the column identified by the title Logcost

In this example, we use the information listed in the column identified as "Logcost" as the dependent variable and the time intervals listed in the column identified as "Time" as the independent variable. The regression results in Exhibit 12.3.b were obtained using the previously described methods.

As before, we interpret the computed value of R^2 to imply that approximately 97% of the variation in spending is explained by the regression analysis and that the ratio defined by MS(REG)/MS(ERROR) is significant ($P < 0.01$). The parameter estimates b_o and b_1 differ significantly from zero ($P < 0.05$). Thus, the predictive model is given by

$$Log(Y_t) = 1.537 + 0.037t$$

Using Equation 12.7.2, the values of the time series, expressed in original units, are given by

$$\hat{Y}_t = 10^{1.537 + 0.037t}$$

We may now use the result to derive a forecast for period t = 30 by simply substituting the result of 1.537 + 0.037(30) as the exponent. Thus, the projected amount of cost associated with the provision of outpatient care during the next period is given by

$$\hat{Y}_{30} = 10^{2.647}$$

or approximately $443.61 million.

The average periodic rate of change in the costs of care also might be derived from the regression results. As before, let g correspond to the average rate of periodic change. In the example, it can be shown that

$$g = 10^{0.037} - 1$$

or approximately 9% per year. If the administrator also knows that related revenues grew, on average, by 6% per year, the results of the regression analysis suggest a financial weakness and a potential inability to generate the internal funding required to implement longer term plans.

An Autoregressive Approach to Forecasting

Thus far we have ignored the likely possibility that the value of the time series in a given period may be correlated with the value of the time series in one or more preceding periods. For example, the value of the time series in period t may be correlated with the value in the preceding period, represented by y_{t-1}. In such a situation, it is possible to construct a model that allows us to predict the value y_t from y_{t-1}. This approach might be extended by supposing the volume of ancillary services provided by the organization is related to (1) the volume 2 months ago, (2) the volume of care provided 4 months ago, and (3) the volume provided 8 months ago. In such a situation, we might use

$$\hat{Y}_t = b_o + b_1 y_{t-2} + b_2 y_{t-4} + b_3 y_{t-8}$$

to derive an accurate forecast from the time series. In this case, the subscripts indicate the number of time lags presumed by the model.

Before a consideration of the model, however, we must consider an approach that enables us to examine the autocorrelation or the association of a value of the time series in a given period with the value in one or more previous periods. We consider a first-order autocorrelation that is based on the paired observations $[(y_1,y_2), (y_2,y_3), (y_3,y_4), \ldots (y_{n-1},y_n)]$. Similarly, the paired observations that enable us to assess a second-order autocorrelation are represented by $[(y_1,y_3), (y_2,y_4), \ldots (y_{n-2},y_n)]$.

In the following, r_k represents the kth order autocorrelation coefficient, implying that r_1 is the first-order autocorrelation coefficient and r_2 is the second-order autocorrelation coefficient. Autocorrelation, in turn, is measured by the correlation coefficient that was introduced initially in Chapter 10. In this case, we define the kth order autocorrelation coefficient by

$$r_k = Cov(y_t,y_{t+k})/[var(y_t)var(y_{t+k})]^{1/2} \qquad \text{(Equation 12.8)}$$

which is identical in structure to the correlation coefficient defined by Equation 10.17 that was discussed in Chapter 10.

For example, suppose that we are interested in the number of physician–patient contacts and assembled the data in Exhibit 12.4. In Part A of Exhibit 12.4, the focus is on the first-order autocorrelation coefficient. In this case, the value adjacent to the observation for period 2 is 24,589, the number of contacts in period 1. Similarly, the value adjacent to the observation for period 3 is 24,879, the number of contacts in period 2. The other observations in Part A form a similar pattern. The first-order autocorrelation coefficient of approximately 0.9795 was obtained by

1. Selecting "Data Analysis"
2. Selecting the "Correlation" function
3. Ignoring the 24,589 contacts appearing in the second column and highlighting the field in which the paired observations appear
4. Indicating the field in which the results appear
5. Selecting "OK"

Part B of Exhibit 12.4 shows the second-order autocorrelation coefficient. In this case, in period 3, the value adjacent to 25,416 is 24,589, the number of contacts during period 1. Similarly, in period 4, the value adjacent to 26,000 is 24,879, the number of contacts in period 2. The other paired observations form a similar pattern. The autocorrelation coefficient of approximately 0.9612 was obtained by

1. Selecting "Data Analysis"
2. Selecting the "Correlation" function
3. Ignoring the 24,589 contacts and the 24,879 contacts that occurred in periods 1 and 2, highlighting the field in which the paired observations appear
4. Indicating the field in which the results appear
5. Selecting "OK"

Exhibit 12.4 **The Calculation of Autocorrelation Coefficients**

Part A: First-Order Autocorrelation			**Part B: Second-Order Autocorrelation**		
Period	**Contacts**		**Period**	**Contacts**	
1	24589		1	24589	
2	24879	24589	2	24879	
3	26416	24879	3	26416	24589
4	26000	26416	4	26000	24879
5	26120	26000	5	26120	26416
6	26500	26120	6	26500	26000
7	26884	26500	7	26884	26120
8	26900	26884	8	26900	26500
9	27100	26900	9	27100	26884
10	27778	27100	10	27778	26900
11	28700	27778	11	28700	27100
12	29954	28700	12	29954	27778
13	29264	29954	13	29264	28700
14	29300	29264	14	29300	29954
15	30000	29300	15	30000	29264
16	30500	30000	16	30500	29300
17	30474	30500	17	30474	30000
18	30620	30474	18	30620	30500
19	30740	30620	19	30740	30474
20	30800	30740	20	30800	30620
21	31000	30800	21	31000	30740
22	31200	31000	22	31200	30800
23	31250	31200	23	31250	31000
24	31330	31250	24	31330	31200
25	31400	31330	25	31400	31250
26	31252	31400	26	31252	31330
27	31300	31252	27	31300	31400
28	31500	31300	28	31500	31252

	Column 1	**Column 2**		**Column 1**	**Column 2**
Column 1	1		Column 1	1	
Column 2	0.979580441	1	Column 2	0.961210778	1

Both coefficients indicate a high degree of autocorrelation in the data, suggesting that an autoregressive model will enable us to derive accurate forecasts.

To illustrate the usefulness of the autocorrelation coefficient, suppose we derived the following results:

Time Lag	r_k
1	0.89
2	−0.12
3	0.16
4	0.53
5	0.01

The coefficients indicate that a lag of one and four periods should be incorporated in the autoregressive model.

In general, it is possible to employ a kth order autoregressive model of the general form

$$\hat{Y}_t = b_o + b_1 y_{t-1} + \ldots + b_k y_{t-k} \qquad \text{(Equation 12.9)}$$

where k time lags are included in the predictive model. However, for example, we focus our attention on a first-order autoregressive model as

$$\hat{Y}_t = b_o + b_1 y_{t-1} + \epsilon$$

As before, b_o and b_1 correspond to estimates of β_o and β_1, respectively, suggesting that the first-order autoregressive model is

$$\hat{Y}_t = b_o + b_1 y_{t-1}$$

where b_o and b_1 are derived by ordinary least squares regression analysis.

In Exhibit 12.5, the data are arranged so that the contacts in period t serve as the dependent variable and the number of contacts in the preceding period represents the independent variable. After regression analysis, the results indicate that the coefficient of determination is approximately 0.96. The parameter estimates b_o and b_1 differ significantly from zero ($P < 0.05$). The forecasting equation may be expressed as

$$Y_t = 2467.74 + 0.92 y_{t-1}$$

These results enable us to construct a forecast for period 29 by

$$Y_{29} = 2467.74 + 0.92(31{,}500)$$

or 31,373 patient−physician contacts.

An attribute of the autoregressive approach is noteworthy. When we derived a first-order autoregressive model, one observation was eliminated from the analysis. Similarly, when a second-order autoregressive model is used to develop projections, two observations are eliminated. In general, an increase of one in the

Exhibit 12.5 **First Order Autoregressive Model**

Period	Contacts	
1	24,589	
2	24,879	24,589
3	26,416	24,879
4	26,000	26,416
5	26,120	26,000
6	26,500	26,120
7	26,884	26,500
8	26,900	26,884
9	27,100	26,900
10	27,778	27,100
11	28,700	27,778
12	29,954	28,700
13	29,264	29,954
14	29,300	29,264
15	30,000	29,300
16	30,500	30,000
17	30,474	30,500
18	30,620	30,474
19	30,740	30,620
20	30,800	30,740
21	31,000	30,800
22	31,200	31,000
23	31,250	31,200
24	31,330	31,250
25	31,400	31,330
26	31,252	31,400
27	31,300	31,252
28	31,500	31,300

SUMMARY OUTPUT

Regression Statistics	
Multiple R	0.979580441
R Square	0.95957784
Adjusted R Square	0.957960953
Standard Error	434.880846
Observations	27

ANOVA

	df	SS	MS	F	Significance F
Regression	1	112238346.3	112238346.3	593.4726364	6.16108E-19
Residual	25	4728033.756	189121.3502		
Total	26	116966380.1			

continues

Exhibit 12.5 **(Continued)**

	Coefficients	Standard Error	t Stat	P-Value	Lower 95%	Upper 95%
Intercept	2467.743123	1101.665619	2.240011016	0.034221326	198.8218979	4736.664348
X Variable 1	0.923658595	0.037915006	24.36129382	6.16108E-19	0.845571233	1.001745956

autoregressive order eliminates an additional observation from the analysis. When viewed from a practical perspective, the order of the autoregressive model might be limited by the volume of data that is available for the analysis.

Estimating Seasonal Variation

Thus far, the estimation of seasonal effects has not been addressed. Seasonal variation might be defined as recurring patterns in the time series that occur within a period of 1 year. In this section, an approach is introduced that is frequently referred to as seasonal decomposition. For example, the administrator is interested in developing a forecast of the number of operative procedures that the hospital will perform. The data in Exhibit 12.6 are available. In this case, the focus is on seasonal variation represented in Exhibit 12.6 by winter, spring, and summer. Specifically, winter consists of December, January, and February, whereas spring is March, April, and May. Summer consists of June, July, and August.

In Exhibit 12.6, the dependent variable is defined as the number of procedures performed during the 3 months that define each season. For example, focusing on the first two values that appear in the column identified as "Procedures," an analysis of the data revealed that a total of 4,621 procedures were performed during the winter months of December, January, and February and that 3,575 were performed during the spring months of March, April, and May. The independent variables consist of the variable Time and the binary variables represented by Winter, Spring, and Summer. The binary variables were constructed as follows:

1. If the observation represents the sum of procedures provided during December, January, and February, the binary variable Winter is equal to 1 and 0 otherwise.
2. If the observation represents the sum of the procedures performed during March, April, and May, the binary variable Spring is equal to 1 and 0 otherwise.
3. If the observation represents the sum of procedures performed in June, July, and August, the binary variable Summer is equal to 1 and 0 otherwise.

In the discussion of binary variables, these definitions indicate that fall, consisting of the months September, October, and November, represents the reference category.

Exhibit 12.6 **The Estimation of Seasonal Variation**

Procedures	Time	Winter	Spring	Summer	Season
4621	1	1	0	0	Winter
3575	2	0	1	0	Spring
2092	3	0	0	1	Summer
4970	4	0	0	0	Fall
6103	5	1	0	0	Winter
5231	6	0	1	0	Spring
3575	7	0	0	1	Summer
6714	8	0	0	0	Fall
7062	9	1	0	0	Winter
6103	10	0	1	0	Spring
4359	11	0	0	1	Summer
7585	12	0	0	0	Fall
8196	13	1	0	0	Winter
7498	14	0	1	0	Spring
5580	15	0	0	1	Summer
8632	16	0	0	0	Fall
9504	17	1	0	0	Winter
8806	18	0	1	0	Spring
6714	19	0	0	1	Summer
9590	20	0	0	0	Fall
10724	21	1	0	0	Winter
10463	22	0	1	0	Spring
8283	23	0	0	1	Summer
10986	24	0	0	0	Fall

SUMMARY OUTPUT

Regression Statistics	
Multiple R	0.99626205
R Square	0.992538073
Adjusted R Square	0.990967141
Standard Error	230.6858739
Observations	24

ANOVA

	df	SS	MS	F	Significance F
Regression	4	134490550.4	33622637.59	631.8147739	6.46148E-20
Residual	19	1011103.476	53215.97243		
Total	23	135501653.8			

continues

Exhibit 12.6 **(Continued)**

	Coefficients	Standard Error	t Stat	P-Value	Lower 95%	Upper 95%
Intercept	3835.5	134.8411062	28.44459015	4.87311E-17	3553.274234	4117.725766
X Variable 1	303.1428571	6.893058907	43.97798731	1.39677E-20	288.7155146	317.5701997
X Variable 2	531.5952381	134.7823647	3.944100843	0.000870548	249.4924191	813.6980571
X Variable 3	−527.2142857	133.8981498	−3.937427713	0.00088392	−807.4664212	−246.9621503
X Variable 4	−2675.857143	133.364807	−20.06419237	3.00451E-14	−2954.992979	−2396.721307

The values assigned to the binary variables Winter, Spring, and Summer were entered by using an IF statement. Specifically, the season to which each observation corresponds appears in cells F4 to F27. The binary variable Winter was created by

1. Locating the cursor in cell C4
2. Entering the equation = IF(F4 = "Winter",1,0)
3. Using the "Copy" function to record the IF statement to the remaining cells in the column

Similarly, the binary variable Spring was created by

1. Locating the cursor in cell D4
2. Entering = IF(F4 = "Spring," 1,0)
3. Using the "Copy" function to transfer the IF statement to the other cells of the column

Finally, the binary variable Summer was created by

1. Locating the cursor in cell E4
2. Entering = IF(F4 = "Summer," 1,0)
3. Using the "Copy" function to transfer the IF statement to the other cells of the column

As before, then, the IF statement determines whether the condition is true or false and assigns a value of 1 to cases that satisfy the condition and a 0 to all others.

Employing the variable names appearing in the exhibit, the predictive model may be specified as follows:

$$Procedures = [b_0 + b_1 Time] + b_2 Winter + b_3 Spring + b_4 Summer \quad \text{(Equation 12.10)}$$

The sum $b_0 + b_1$Time is identical in form to the line of average relationship that was used to estimate a linear trend previously here and in particular Equation

12.6. The parameter estimates derived for the binary variables are interpreted relative to the reference group, which in this case is the fall season.

After performing the regression analysis, the results indicate that the coefficient of multiple determination is 0.99, indicating that the model yields an accurate forecast of the number of operative procedures provided by the organization. The results of the analysis also enable us to express the forecasting model as

$$Procedures = 3{,}835 + 303Time + 532Winter - 527Spring - 2{,}676Summer$$

The forecasting model indicates that with the passage of one period consisting of 3 months, the volume of operative care grows, on average, by 303 procedures. Similarly, the coefficient derived for the variable Winter indicates that the volume of operative care during December, January, and February is greater than during the fall season by 532 procedures. On the other hand, the results also indicate that 527 fewer operative procedures are provided during the spring than in the fall and that 2,676 fewer procedures are provided in the summer than in the fall.

In the exhibit, we may use the model to forecast the number of procedures for the next period. After substituting 25 for the variable Time, a value of 1 for Winter, and a 0 for the other binary variables, we obtain

$$Procedures = 3{,}835 + 303(25) + 532(1)$$

Thus, the organization expects to provide 11,942 operative procedures during the next 3 months. Similarly, the projection for the next period might be obtained by substituting 26 for the variable Time, a value of 1 for Spring, and 0 for the other binary variables. In this case, the projection is given by

$$Procedures = 3{,}835 + 303(26) - 527(1)$$

After performing the calculations, we find that the organization might expect to provide 11,186 operative procedures during the next spring season. This illustration indicates that the use of seasonal decomposition as a forecasting method enables the administrator to incorporate both the trend component and seasonal variation in projections of the organization's future activity.

Exercises

1. Measured in 1,000s, the following represent the number of visits to our emergency department:

Period	Visits
1	8.2
2	7.9
3	10.1
4	6.9
5	11.4
6	5.9
7	8.6
8	9.2

Use exponential smoothing, and let λ = 0.1, 0.5, and 0.9 to calculate projections for periods 2 through 8. Calculate the MSE for each set of projections, and determine the value of λ that results in the most accurate set of forecasts.

2. Measured in 1,000s of days, the following represents the volume of care provided by a long-term care facility:

Period	Days
1	17.3
2	21.2
3	19.5
4	23.6
5	18.5
6	16.4
7	20.9
8	18.6
9	22.9
10	15.7
11	22.1
12	18.6

Use exponential smoothing, and let λ = 0.1, 0.3, and 0.6 to construct forecasts for periods 2 through 12. Calculate the MSE for each of the three sets of forecasts, and determine the value of λ that results in the most accurate set of projections.

3. The following represents the trend in the number of admissions to our hospital during the past 8 years:

Year	Admissions
1	11,680
2	11,654
3	11,540
4	11,420
5	11,400
6	11,320
7	11,290
8	11,150

Calculate the average periodic rate of change, and use the results to develop a projection for year 9.

4. Referring to the data in Exercise 3, use the "Regression" function and a 0.95 prediction interval to develop a forecast for period 9.

5. Assume that the organization collected a time series depicting the annual number of visits, measured in 1,000s, to the emergency department as follows:

Year:	1	2	3	4	5	6	7	8	9	10
Visits:	4.1	4.3	4.4	4.5	4.7	4.6	4.8	4.9	5.1	5.2

Use these data to calculate the average periodic rate of change and develop a forecast of visits for year 11.

6. Use the data in Exercise 5 and the "Regression" function in Excel to estimate the trend in the annual number of visits. Construct a 0.98 prediction interval and estimate the number of visits for year 11.

7. The following data represent the costs of operating two of our outpatient clinics during each of the past 10 years: Use the "Regression" function in Excel to estimate the trend in the costs of operating the clinics, and use the results to develop a forecast for year 11.

Year:	1	2	3	4	5	6	7	8	9	10
Costs:	126.0	136.1	144.2	154.3	160.5	171.8	180.3	187.6	198.8	216.7

8. The following data represent the amount of gross revenue, measured in $1,000, earned by our managed-care organization during each of the past 10 years: Use the "Regression" function in Excel to estimate the trend in gross patient revenue, and use the results to develop a forecast for year 11.

Year:	1	2	3	4	5	6	7	8	9	10
Revenue:	548.8	532.3	537.7	516.1	500.7	490.6	485.7	466.3	457.0	434.1

9. The following data represent the number of patient–physician contacts, measured in 1,000, during the past 27 months. Patient–physician contacts: 23.7, 24.9, 25.4, 24.7, 25.8, 25.4, 26.8, 26.1, 27.1, 26.6, 28.7, 30.0, 29.2, 29.2, 30.2, 29.7, 30.6, 30.7, 30.7, 31.5, 31.9, 32.3, 32.2, 33.5, 33.9, 34.3, 34.5
   1. Use these data to calculate a first- and second-order autocorrelation coefficient.
   2. Use the "Regression" function in Excel to estimate a first-order autoregressive model and develop a forecast for the 28th month.

10. The administrator of a hospital is interested in predicting the amount of gross patient revenue that the organization expects to earn during the winter, spring, summer, and fall of next year. The following data represent the gross patient revenue earned during the past 6 years:

Season	Time	Gross Revenue (in Millions)
Winter	1	36.0
Spring	2	27.0
Summer	3	15.1
Fall	4	37.8
Winter	5	47.6
Spring	6	41.4
Summer	7	26.9

Fall	8	51.7
Winter	9	53.3
Spring	10	44.7
Summer	11	31.3
Fall	12	57.0
Winter	13	62.7
Spring	14	54.5
Summer	15	39.3
Fall	16	64.0
Winter	17	69.8
Spring	18	62.1
Summer	19	44.1
Fall	20	67.0
Winter	21	77.1
Spring	22	62.4
Summer	23	47.4
Fall	24	70.2

If fall represents the reference category, use the "Regression" function, seasonal decomposition, and "IF" statements to develop forecasts for each quarter of the next year.

APPENDIX A GLOSSARY OF TERMS

A

Alpha (α): Represents the probability of committing a Type I error, which occurs when a true claim or assertion is rejected.

Alpha-Four (α_4): A measure of kurtosis, which refers to the relative peakedness or flatness of a distribution. The measure is given by $\alpha_4 = \Sigma(x_i - \mu)^4/\sigma^4$. If α_4 is less than 3, the distribution is platykurtic or broad humped and less peaked than the normal distribution. Platykurtic distributions are also characterized by tails that are wider than the normal distribution. If α_4 is greater than 3, the distribution is leptokurtic, implying that the distribution is more peaked and has wider tails than the normal distribution.

Alpha-Three (α_3): A measure of symmetry or skewness. It is given by $\alpha_3 = \Sigma(x_i - \mu)^3/\sigma^3$. If α_3 is zero, the distribution is symmetrical. If α_3 is positive, the distribution is positively skewed (i.e., a long thin tail appears on the right of the distribution), and if α_3 is negative, the distribution is negatively skewed (i.e., a long thin tail appears on the left of the distribution).

Alternate Hypothesis: The assumption, claim, or hypothesis that one accepts when the null hypothesis is rejected. H_a or H_1 usually represents the alternate hypothesis.

Analysis of Variance (ANOVA): A method of assessing the difference among three or more means. ANOVA partitions the total variability shown by the data into components that are attributable to different sources of variation. The ANOVA table lists the sources of variation, the sum of squares for each, the related degrees of freedom, the corresponding mean square or variance, and values of F. In this text, the F ratio is used to determine whether the treatment, block, or interactive effects are significant or attributable to chance.

Arithmetic Line Chart: A graph obtained by plotting values of a time series on arithmetic paper and connecting successive points with a straight line.

Arithmetic Mean: The arithmetic mean, or more commonly the mean of n values, is given by their sum, divided by n.

Arithmetic Paper: A graph paper with uniform subdivisions for both scales. On both scales, equal distances represent equal amounts.

Autoregression: A forecasting method in which the value of a time series in a given period is related to the value of the time series in one or more previous periods.

B

Bar Chart: A chart that is used to present frequency distributions or time series data. A bar chart consists of rectangles of equal width and heights that are proportional to the frequencies or values they represent.

Base Year: In index construction, the base year is the period that serves as a reference to which subsequent years or periods are compared. Subscript "o" usually represents the base period. For example, q_o represents a base year quantity.

Bell-Shaped Distribution: A distribution characterized by the shape of a vertical cross-section of a bell. Normal distributions are among those characterized by a bell shape.

Beta (β): The probability of committing a Type II error, which occurs when a false claim, assertion, or null hypothesis is accepted as true.

Bias: (1) In problems of estimation, a statistic is biased if its expected value is not equal to the corresponding parameter. (2) In index construction, the bias of the index is a systematic tendency to overestimate or underestimate changes. (3) In sampling, a bias is a systematic error resulting from selecting items from the wrong population or favoring some items in the selection of the sample.

Binary Variable: A variable that assumes the values of 0 or 1 and separates cases or items exhibiting an attribute of interest from those that fail to exhibit the characteristic. In regression analysis, binary variables are used to capture the effects of qualitative factors, such as gender or occupational category, on the dependent variable or item of administrative interest.

Binomial Coefficient: The number of ways an event can occur x times in n trials. Using factorial notation, the binomial coefficient is given by $n!/x!(n - x)!$.

Binomial Distribution: The distribution of the number of successes, x, that can occur in n trials when the characteristic of interest is binary. The probability of a success remains constant from trial to trial, and trials are independent.

Block Effect: In analysis of variance, the amount or quantity that represents the change in response produced by a given block. The block effects are represented in this text by θ_i.

Business Cycle: Recurring patterns of expansion, peak, recession, and trough, lasting for a period of more than 1 year.

C

Categorical or Qualitative Distribution: A frequency distribution in which the categories are defined as categorical terms. A categorical distribution might be defined as occupational groups such as physicians, nurses, and staff.

Cell Frequency: In the analysis of frequency data or counts, the number of items assigned to a given category. It is frequently used when referring to a contingency table.

Census: A complete enumeration of a population.

Central Limit Theorem: For random variables from a population with a finite variance, the sampling distribution of the sample mean approaches the standard normal distribution as the sample size becomes indefinite.

Central Tendency: Refers to statistics such as the mean, the mode, and the median.

Chi-Square Distribution (χ^2 Distribution): A family of probability distributions each defined by a single parameter represented by degrees of freedom. In general, the χ^2 distribution is unimodal and asymmetrical. In this text, the χ^2 distribution is applied to problems that require an examination of k proportions, where $k > 2$, and the hypothesis that two variables are independent.

Chi-Square Statistic: A statistic that is given by $\Sigma(o - e)^2/e$ where o and e refer to an observed and expected frequency, respectively. The calculated value of χ^2 is compared with a critical value to determine whether observed and expected frequencies differ significantly.

Class Boundary: A class boundary is the dividing line that separates successive categories in a quantitative frequency distribution. To avoid ambiguities, class boundaries are assigned values that cannot occur in the set of data that are to be grouped.

Class Frequency: The number of items or observations assigned to a given category of a frequency distribution.

Class Interval: The length of a class or the range of values that might be assigned to a class or category of a frequency distribution. The class interval is given by the difference between the upper and lower boundaries of the category.

Class Limit: The upper and lower limits of a class are, respectively, the largest and smallest values it can contain.

Class Mark: The midpoint of a class, calculated by the mean of its boundaries or the mean of its limits.

Coefficient of Determination: Represented by R^2, the coefficient of determination is a statistical measure of the proportion or percentage of the variation exhibited by the dependent variable that is explained by or is attributable to the regression analysis.

Collectively Exhaustive: A situation in which all observations are accommodated by the categories that characterize a frequency distribution.

Combination: The selection of one or more objects from a set of distinct objects without regard for order. The number of possible combinations of x objects that may be formed from a collection of n distinct objects is given by $n!/x!(n - x)!$. See binomial coefficient.

Complement: The complement of set A, represented by A′, is the set of elements in the sample space that does not belong to A.

Components of a Time Series: The components that combine to determine the movement of a time series are trend, seasonal variation, cyclical variation, and irregular variation.

Conditional Distribution: The distribution of a random variable or the joint distribution of several random variables when the values of one or more other random variables are held fixed or some other event has occurred.

Conditional Probability: If A and B are two events and the probability of B is greater than zero, the conditional probability of A, given B, is given by $P(A \mid B) = P(A \cap B)/P(B)$. The conditional probability is the likelihood that A will occur if B has occurred or will occur.

Confidence Interval: An interval for which we are able to assert with a given probability, represented by $1 - \alpha$ and called the degree of confidence, that it will contain the parameter it is intended to estimate. The end points of the confidence interval are referred to as the upper and lower confidence limits. A confidence interval is routinely estimated using sample data.

Contingency Table: A table consisting of two or more rows and two or more columns. A contingency table consisting of r rows and k columns is characterized by $r \times k$ cells into which individuals or items are grouped. The simplest form is a 2×2 table and results when both variables are dichotomized or binary.

Continuous Random Variable: A random variable that assumes values defined as an interval on the real or the entire real axis and that possesses a probability density function.

Correlation: In general, it refers to the relationship between two variables. Given a set of paired observations, (x_i, y_i), the correlation coefficient is given by the ratio of their covariance to the product of their standard deviations. The Pearson correlation coefficient assumes a value extending from −1 to +1, where 0 indicates the absence of a linear relationship. A value of 1 indicates that the linear relation between the two variables is positive and perfect. A value of −1 indicates that the linear relationship between the two variables is negative and perfect.

Covariation: Indicates the direction of linear relationship between two variables and is given by the sum of products among paired deviations $(x_i - X)$ and $(y_i - Y)$. If the covariation of x and y is positive, the two variables exhibit a positive linear relationship. If the covariation of x and y is negative, the two variables exhibit a negative linear relation. Covariance is defined as the ratio of covariation divided by degrees of freedom.

Critical or Rejection Region: For a given test, the proportion of the sample space that contains all outcomes for which the null hypothesis is rejected. The size of the critical region is the probability of obtaining an outcome residing in the critical region and, thus, is the probability of committing a Type I error, α.

Critical Values: The dividing lines of a test criterion or the boundary of a critical region.

Cumulative Distribution: For grouped data, a distribution showing the number of items that are "more than" or "less than" given values, usually defined by class limits or class boundaries.

Cyclical Variation: In time series analysis, the variation that is attributable to expansion, recession, the peak, and the trough of the business cycle.

D

Deciles: A fractile, represented by $D_1, \ldots, D_9$. The deciles indicate the value below which lie 10%, 20%, . . . , and 90% of the data.

Degrees of Freedom: A random sample of size n is said to have n − 1 degrees of freedom available for estimating the population variance, in the sense that there are only n − 1 independent deviations from the mean on which to base the estimate. In a contingency table consisting of r rows and k columns, degrees of freedom are given by $rk - (r + k - 1)$ or $(r - 1)(k - 1)$ degrees of freedom. The F distribution is characterized by degrees of freedom in the numerator ($n_1 - 1$ or $n_2 - 1$) and degrees of freedom in the denominator ($n_2 - 1$ or $n_1 - 1$).

Dependent Variable: If the values of a function f is given by $y = f(x_1, \ldots, x_k)$, y is the dependent variable, and $(x_1, \ldots, x_k)$ is referred to collectively as the set of independent variables. The object of many statistical investigations is to predict the value of the dependent variable in terms of known or assumed values of the independent variables.

Descriptive Statistics: Refers to the graph or table portrayal of data and the treatment of data that does not involve generalizations or inferences.

Determination, Coefficient of: Coefficient of determination measures the proportion or percentage of the variation exhibited by the dependent variable that is attributable to regression analysis.

Deviation from the Mean: For a given set of data, the amount by which an individual observation differs from the mean (i.e., $x_i - \bar{X}$). An important characteristic of deviations from the mean is that $\Sigma(x_i - \bar{X})$ must equal zero. The absolute value of $x_i - \bar{X}$, represented by $|x_i - \bar{X}|$, is called an absolute deviation from the mean.

Dichotomy: A classification scheme that divides the elements of a population or sample into two categories. For example, we might characterize the results of a set of laboratory procedures as correct or defective.

Difference Between Proportions, Standard Error of: The standard deviation of the difference between two proportions.

Discrete Random Variable: Random variables that are measured by integer values and having the binomial or the Poisson distribution are referred to as discrete.

Dispersion: The extent of scatter or variation among elements of a population or sample.

Distribution: For observed data, it is used to refer to their overall variation or scatter. The distribution of a random variable is its probability structure as described, for example, the binomial distribution or the normal distribution.

E

Error Mean Square: In analysis of variance, the sum of squared deviations within samples divided by degrees of freedom. Represented in ANOVA by MS(E), the error mean square is an estimate of the common error variance of the populations.

Error Sum of Squares: In analysis of variance, the portion of total variation that is attributable to experimental error.

Estimate: A single value or interval based on a sample that is intended to match a parameter.

Event: Consists of one or more outcomes that result from a given random experiment.

Expected Frequency: In the analysis of frequencies or counts, a cell frequency that is calculated on the basis of a theory or an assumption.

Experimental Sampling Distribution: A distribution of values of a statistic obtained by means of random numbers or repeated samples. For example, if the means of repeated samples from a given population are grouped, the resulting distribution is called an experimental sampling distribution of the mean.

Exponential Smoothing: A method of developing forecasts that is based on exponentially weighted moving averages. It continuously corrects for the differences between actual and predicted values that occur in a just completed period.

Exponential Trend: A secular movement in the time series that rises or falls at an increasing or decreasing rate.

F

F Distribution: A distribution that is of fundamental importance to the analysis of variance. In this text, the F distribution is the ratio of two variances of two random samples from a normal population. The parameters, represented by υ_1 and υ_2, are the numerator and denominator degrees of freedom. Based on the assumption that the two variances are equal, the appendix of this text contains critical values of F, represented generally by F_α for appropriate degrees of freedom in the numerator and denominator that enable us to evaluate the assumption of homoscedasticity.

F Test: A test based on sample variances, which on the assumption that the property of homoscedasticity is satisfied is the F distribution. The F test is used in ANOVA, regression analysis, and the general assessment of the equality of two variances.

Factor: A variable or quantity under investigation.

Factorial Notation: The product of all positive integers less than or equal to the integer n. For example, 3! is given by the product $3 \times 2 \times 1$. By definition, 0! is one.

Finite Population: A well-defined set of a finite number of elements or observations.

Forecasting: Predictions of events or values that will occur during a future period are called forecasts. The process of deriving the forecast and related explanation is called forecasting. Predictions of future values may be based on their past values, a feature that allows us to apply standard statistical techniques in a time series analysis.

Fractile: A value below which lies a given proportion or percentage of the data. The median, the decile, the quartile, and the percentile are the mostly commonly used fractiles.

Frequency: The number of items, observations, or cases falling or expecting to fall in a given category or classification.

Frequency Distribution: A table displaying the classes into which a set of data have been grouped and the corresponding frequencies or number of items falling into each category.

Frequency Interpretation of Probability: A theory in which the probability of an event occurring is interpreted as the proportion or percentage of the time the event will occur in the long run or in a repeated series of trials.

G

Geometric Mean: Given a set of n positive numbers, the geometric mean is given by the nth root of their product. The geometric mean is applied routinely to ratios, rates of change, or indices.

Given Year: In index construction, the year or period we wish to compare with a base period and usually represented by the subscript "n."

Goodness of Fit: In the comparison of actual and expected frequencies, goodness of fit refers to closeness of agreement between the two sets of frequencies. In regression analysis, it is the closeness of points to the line, curve, or plane formed by the regression equation.

Grand Mean: In ANOVA, the grand mean is estimated by the mean of all observations available for analysis.

Graphic Presentation: The graphic presentation in a graph form such as a bar chart, a line chart, or a pie chart.

H

Histogram: A graph of a frequency distribution consisting of rectangles whose bases correspond to class intervals and heights determined by class frequencies. When the bases of the rectangles are equal, the areas and heights of the rectangles are proportional to the class frequencies.

Homoscedasticity: In regression analysis, the property that the conditional probability distributions of Y for fixed values of the independent variable have the same variance.

Hypothesis: An assertion or claim about one or more parameters.

I

Independent Events: Two events are independent if the probability that they will both occur is equal to the product of the probabilities that each one individually will occur.

Infinite Population: The set of infinite values that may be assumed by a continuous random variable.

Interaction: The joint effects of several factors or variables.

Internal Data: Information derived from an organization's private records and used for statistical analyses.

Intersection: The intersection of two events A and B is the set that consists of all elements or outcomes that belong to both A and B.

Interval Estimation: See confidence interval.

Irregular Variation: In time series analysis, the variation that is not attributable to trend, cyclical, or seasonal variation.

K

Kurtosis: The relative peakedness or flatness of a distribution. See Alpha four or peakedness.

L

Laspeyres Index: A weighted aggregate index in which prices (quantities) are weighted by the corresponding quantities (prices) that prevailed in the base year.

Least Squares, Method of: A method of deriving parameter estimates of a population regression equation that minimizes the sum of squared deviations between predicted and the corresponding values calculated from the regression equation.

Leptokurtic: See kurtosis.

Level of Significance: The probability of erroneously rejecting a true null hypothesis; the probability of committing a type I error.

Line of Average Relation: Represented by the general linear equation $y = a + bx$ and describes the relationship between the dependent variable y and the independent variable x.

Linear Trend: In time series analysis, a secular trend that might be represented reasonably by a straight line.

Location, Measures of: Statistical descriptions such as the mean, the mode, the median, and the quartile.

M

Mean: The mean of n values is their sum divided by n. The mean of a finite population, μ, is given by the sum of its elements divided by N.

Mean Absolute Deviation: A measure of variation exhibited by a set of data and given by the sum of the absolute deviations of observations relative to the mean divided by the number of observations.

Mean Square: In ANOVA, the sum of squared deviations divided by corresponding degrees of freedom.

Mean Square Error: A measure of the error present in forecasts. The greater is the value of the mean square error the less accurate is the forecast. The smaller is the value of the mean square error the more accurate is the forecast.

Median: A fractile that identifies the value in a distribution below which lies 50% of the observations.

Mode: The value or values that occurs with greatest frequency. For a distribution, a mode is the value of a random variable for which the probability function has a relative maximum.

Multiple Correlation Coefficient: A measure of the goodness of the fit of a regression plane and hence an indication of how well one variable can be predicted from a linear combination of the others.

Multiple Regression Analysis: A linear regression involving two or more independent variables.

Mutually Exclusive Events: Two events are mutually exclusive if they share no outcomes or elements in common.

N

Negative Correlation or Covariation: Two variables are negatively correlated or covary negatively when large values of one are associated with small values of the other.

Normal Distribution: A distribution that is unimodal, symmetrical, and asymptotic with respect to the x-axis. The normal distribution has two parameters, μ and σ. When $\mu = 0$ and $\sigma = 1$, it is referred to as the standard normal distribution.

Normal Equations: In least squares regression, a system of equations whose solutions result in parameter estimates that minimize the sum of squared error terms.

Null Hypothesis: A hypothesis, represented by H_o, that is examined relative to the alternate hypothesis H_a. The erroneous rejection of a true null hypothesis results in a type I error.

O

Observed Frequency: The actual number of sample items or observations assigned to a class or category of a distribution or into a cell of a contingency table.

Observed Probability: In contrast to subjective probability, observed probability is interpreted in terms of frequencies.

One-Sided or Directional Alternate Hypothesis: A one-sided or directional alternate hypothesis assumes that the value or values of a parameter are larger or smaller than the value or values assumed under the null hypothesis. For example, if the null hypothesis specifies that $\mu - \mu_o = 0$, the alternate hypotheses $\mu - \mu_o > 0$ and $\mu - \mu_o < 0$ are one-sided or directional, whereas the alternate $\mu - \mu_o \neq 0$ is a two-sided or nondirectional alternative hypothesis.

One-Sided or Directional Test: A statistical test of a hypothesis in which the rejection region resides in the right-hand tail or the left-hand tail of the sampling distribution of the statistic. A test is two-sided or nondirectional if the rejection region is in both tails of the sampling distribution of the statistic.

One-Way ANOVA: An analysis of variance in which the total sum of squares is expressed as the sum of the treatment sum of squares and the error sum of squares and no others.

Outliers: Observations that are much larger or smaller than the main body of data, suggesting that the appropriateness of including them in the analysis is questionable.

P

Paasche Index: A weighted aggregate index in which prices (quantities) are weighted by quantities (prices) that prevailed in the given year.

Parabolic Function: A relationship that is best expressed by $y = b_o + b_1x + b_2x^2$.

Parameter: In statistics, a value, such as the mean or standard deviation, that characterizes a population and is represented by a Greek letter.

Peakedness: Refers to the kurtosis exhibited by a distribution. A platykurtic or broad-humped distribution is characterized by a flat middle. A leptokurtic distribution is narrow-humped or very peaked.

Pearsonian Coefficient of Skewness: A measure of symmetry or skewness and is given by 3(mean − median)/standard deviation. If the Pearsonian coefficient is positive, the tail appears on the right of the distribution. If the coefficient is negative, the tail appears on the left of the distribution. If the coefficient is zero, the distribution is symmetrical.

Percentiles: The percentiles $P_1, P_2, \ldots, P_{99}$ indicate the values below which lie 1%, 2%, . . . , 99% of the observations.

Point Estimation: The estimation of a parameter with a single value or point estimate.

Poisson Distribution: A special form of the binomial distribution. It is usually applied when n is large, the probability of a success on any given trial approaches zero, and the product of the two remains constant.

Pooled Estimate: An estimate of a parameter that is obtained by combining two or more sets of data. For example, in a two-sample t test, the sum of the squared deviations from the means of the two samples are combined to obtain an estimate of the common population variance.

Population Size: The number of elements or observations in a finite population, usually represented by N.

Positive Correlation: Two variables are said to be positively correlated if large values of one variable are associated with large values of the other and smaller values of the variable are associated with smaller values of the other.

Power: For a given alternative, the probability of $1 - \beta$ of not committing a type II error. The probability of committing a Type II error or accepting a false null hypothesis is represented by β.

Prediction Interval: In regression analysis, the pair of values for which we can assert with a given probability that they will contain a future observation of the dependent variable for a given value of the independent variable.

Primary Data: Information that is collected and reported by the same entity.

Probability: A proportion, percentage, or relative frequency that indicates the likelihood that an outcome or event will occur.

Probability Function: A function that assigns a probability to each value within the range of a discrete random variable.

Probability Sample: A sample obtained by a method in which every element of a finite population has a known probability of being included in the sample.

Q

Quartiles: The quartiles Q_1, Q_2 and Q_3 are values below which lie 25%, 50%, and 75% of the data, respectively.

Questionnaire: A list or set of questions sent or given to a subject. It is hoped that respondents will complete each question truthfully and return the results promptly.

R

Random Experiment: Any process leading to one of several results for which the concepts of probability might be applied.

Random Sample: A sample of size n from a finite population is said to be a simple random sample if each of the possible samples has the same probability of being selected.

Range: A measure of variation that is given by the difference between the maximum and minimum values that appear in a set of data.

Regression Analysis: The analysis of paired observations (x_i,y_i) where the x's are constants or known values and the y's are the values of a random variable. It is customary to assume that the y's are values of independent random variables having normal distributions with the respective means $\beta_o + \beta_1 x$ and a common variance σ^2.

Regression Coefficient: A coefficient in a regression equation.

Rejection Region: The area of a probability distribution that requires the analyst to reject the null hypothesis in favor of the alternate.

Relative Frequency: If an event occurs on x occasions in n trials, the relative frequency of its occurrence is x/n.

Rules of Addition: In probability theory, formulae for calculating the probability that at least one of two events occurs. The probability is given by $P(A \cup B) = P(A) + P(B) - P(A \cap B)$. When the two events are mutually exclusive, the special rule of addition is given by $P(A \cup B) = P(A) + P(B)$.

Rules of Multiplication: In probability theory, formulae for calculating the probability those two events will both occur. The general rule of multiplication specifies that $P(A \cap B) = P(A \mid B)P(B)$. If the two events are independent, the special rule of multiplication specifies that $P(A \cap B) = P(A)P(B)$.

S

Sample Size: The number of observations in a sample, usually represented by n.

Sample Space: In probability, a set of points or elements that represent all possible outcomes of an experiment.

Sampling: The process of selecting a sample.

Sampling Distribution: The distribution of a statistic; for example, the distribution of means for random samples from a normal population.

Scatter Diagram: A set of points obtained by plotting paired measurements of two variables represented by (x_i,y_i); the resulting diagram provides a visual image of the relationship, if any, between the two variables.

Seasonal Decomposition: A forecasting method that isolates the effects of seasonal variation in time series data.

Seasonal Variation: Recurring patterns in a time series that occur within a period of 1 year or less.

Secondary Data: Information that is published by an organization other than the one that collected the data.

Secular Trend: The gradual or long-term movement in a time series.

Semilogarithmic Graph: Graph paper on which equal intervals on the vertical scale correspond to equal rates of change (e.g., 1, 2, 4, 8, 16). Equal intervals on the horizontal scale represent equal amounts of change.

Significance Test: In the examination of hypotheses, a criterion for deciding if the difference between an observation and an expectation or the difference between an observed statistic and an assumed value of a parameter can be attributed to chance.

Size of Critical Region: The probability of committing a Type I error.

Skewness: A distribution is skewed if it is not possible to construct a perpendicular line that divides it into two identical halves. A distribution is positively skewed if a tail appears on the right of the distribution. A distribution is negatively skewed if a tail appears on the left of the distribution.

Standard Deviation: A measure of dispersion or scatter. For a sample of size n, the standard deviation, S, is the square root of the sum of squared deviations divided by $n - 1$. For a finite population of size N, the standard, σ, is the square root of the sum of squared deviations divided by N.

Standard Error of the Estimate: In regression analysis, it is the square root of the sum of squared error terms divided by degrees of freedom, $n - (k + 1)$. The standard error is a standard deviation that is measured in units that describe the dependent variable. The greater is the standard error the less precise are the estimates derived from the regression analysis and vice versa.

Standard Error of the Mean: A measure of the variation in a distribution of means derived from several sets of sample data.

Statistic: A quantity, such as the mean or standard deviation, derived from sample data.

Statistical Inference: A form of reasoning from sample data to population parameters. Statistical inference involves generalizations, predictions estimation, and decisions based on sample data.

Subjective Probability: A probability related to single events or events that are nonrecurring. Subjective probability is based on the strength of an individual's belief concerning the occurrence or nonoccurrence of the event.

Symmetry: A property of a distribution. The distribution is symmetrical if it is possible to construct a perpendicular line that divides the distribution into two identical halves.

T

t-Distribution: A unimodal and symmetric distribution, with degrees of freedom as its parameter. As degrees of freedom increase indefinitely, the t distribution approaches the standard normal distribution.

Test Statistic: A statistic on which the decision to accept or reject a given hypothesis is based.

t Tests: Tests based on statistics having the t-distribution and used when the standard deviation of the population is unknown.

Theoretical Distribution: A term used to denote the distribution of a random variable as contrasted with a distribution of observed data.

Time Series: Any series of data observed, collected, or recorded at regular intervals of time.

Total Sum of Squares: In analysis of variance, the sum of squared deviations of all observations in a given experiment relative to the grand mean.

Treatment Effect: In analysis of variance, a quantity that represents the change in response resulting from a given treatment.

Treatment Sum of Squares: In analysis of variance, that component of total variation or sum of squared deviations that is attributed to possible differences among the treatments.

Two-Way Analysis of Variance: An analysis of variance in which total sum of squared deviations is expressed as the sum of the treatment sum of squared deviations, the block sum of squared deviations, and the error sum of squared deviations.

Type I Error: In hypothesis testing, the erroneous rejection of a true null hypothesis. The probability of committing a Type I error is represented by α.

Type II Error: In hypothesis testing, the erroneous acceptance of a false null hypothesis. The probability of committing a Type II error is represented by β.

U

Unimodal: A set of data or distribution is unimodal if it has one mode or one modal class.

Union of Two Sets: The union of two sets, A and B, is the set that consists of all elements that belong to A, to B, or to both A and B.

Universe: A synonym for a population.

V

Variation: The extent to which observations are dispersed.

Venn Diagram: A diagram that may be used to represent the sample space for a given experiment. Sets are represented by circular regions or parts of circular regions or their complements.

W

Weighted Mean: The average of a set of numbers obtained by the sum of products between each value and a weight depicting its relative importance. The sum of products is then divided by the sum of the weights to obtain the weighted mean.

Within Samples Variation: Another name for the error sum of squares in one-way analysis of variance.

APPENDIX B An Introduction to Excel

This appendix familiarizes the student with the basics of Excel. Specifically, the focus is on (1) the characteristics of the spreadsheet, (2) data entry, (3) the use of mathematical operations, and (4) statistical functions that are available. In addition, the appendix also focuses on methods of performing mathematical operations and entering equations. Those who are familiar with Excel may disregard Appendix B; however, discussion about the statistical functions forms the foundation for much of the text.

The Spreadsheet

Rows and columns form an Excel spreadsheet. Letters of the alphabet identify the columns, and the integer values such as 1 or 2 identify the rows. The rows and columns identify the cell address. For example, the cell address A1 appears in the column designated by the letter A and row 1 of the spreadsheet. Similarly, the cell address C3 appears in row 3 and the column identified by the letter C. The current cell address is listed in the window that appears in the fourth row of the toolbar on the left side of the spreadsheet.

Navigation in the spreadsheet is simple. Four arrows—up, down, left, and right—appear on the keypad. If, for example, the current cell address is C3, movement to C4 requires the use of the down arrow, whereas a movement to C2 requires the use of the up arrow. Similarly, movement to B4 requires the use of the left arrow, and movement to D4 requires the use of the right arrow.

The words File, Edit, Insert, Format, Tools, Data, Window, and Help appear in the first row of the menu bar. The novice uses File, Insert, and Tools the most frequently. When File is selected, the user may open a previously prepared file, close the current file, save the current file, and using the Save As function, save the current file with a different name or in a different drive. The "Page Setup" function allows the user to alter margins, insert a header or footer, and select portrait or landscape as a printing format.

The insert function allows the user to insert another worksheet in the current worksheet and to insert a column or row in the current worksheet. To insert a column, simply locate the black down arrow on the appropriate letter. Select insert and then column. Similarly, to insert a row, locate the black arrow on the appropriate row number; select insert and then row. For this text, the functions in "Tools" are the most important. When Tools is selected, the set of statistical analyses and methods is immediately available in Data Analysis. Thus, selecting Tools and then Data Analysis allows the user to select statistical methods such as "Correlation," "Covariance," "Descriptive Statistics," "Exponential Smoothing," and various approaches to analysis of variance.

The second row of the menu bar contains a set of icons that are shortcuts to commonly used functions. The monitor icon allows the user to save the current worksheet, and the printer icon enables the user to print the current worksheet. The page and magnifying glass icon serves as a print preview, showing the page as it would appear in hard copy. When you return to the worksheet, the page preview is closed; dotted lines appear on the worksheet and show the boundaries of the page, a feature that facilitates the process of preparing the page or pages for presentation. The icon with a check and the letters ABC checks the spelling and grammar in the current worksheet. The scissors icon allows you to cut a field and move it to another location. To use the Cut function, highlight the field that you wish to move; locate the cursor in the cell in which the first observation will appear, and press the Enter key. For example, suppose that you want to move a column of data from one location in the spreadsheet to another. Highlight the column by placing the cursor in the cell with the first observation and then simultaneously selecting Control/Shift and the down arrow appearing on the keypad located at the lower left of the keyboard.

The Copy icon, identified by two pages, is used extensively when preparing a spreadsheet. This function enables you to transfer data or equations from one location in the spreadsheet to another. Simply highlight the data or material that you wish to copy (e.g., shift/control and down arrow). Select the Copy function. Move the cursor to the cell in which the first item will appear, and press Enter.

The AutoSum function, identified by the Greek letter Σ, is particularly valuable when preparing a spreadsheet and performing statistical calculations. It calculates the sum of data in the contiguous cells of a row or column. Simply locate the cursor in the cell in which you wish the summation to appear. Select the Auto Sum function, and press the Enter key.

It is sometimes useful or necessary to sort data in ascending or descending order. After entering the data, simply highlight the field in which the observations appear, and select the icon that has the letter A that appears above the letter Z. A down arrow also appears on the right side of the icon. Similarly, to arrange the data in descending order, highlight the field in which the data appear, and select the icon that has the letter Z appearing above the letter A. A down arrow also identifies the icon. In both cases, the data are automatically sorted in ascending or descending order.

As described in Chapter 2, the Chart Wizard function is invaluable when presenting data in graphic form. The Chart Wizard is identified by a multicolored bar chart and appears to the left of the icon that enables you to sort data in descending order. Chapter 2 provides details about this important function.

The Entry of Equations

Throughout this text, Excel is used to perform calculations after the equations have been entered in a worksheet. In general, when we enter an equation, common notation is used to identify the mathematical operations of addition, subtraction, multiplication, division, and exponentiation. Specifically, Excel recognizes the following notation when performing calculations:

1. Addition uses the plus (+) sign.
2. Subtraction uses the minus (−) sign.
3. Multiplication uses a star (*).
4. Division uses the slash (/).
5. Exponentiation uses a caret (^).

The ease with which equations are entered in a spreadsheet is shown in Exhibit B.1. Beginning in cells A6 to A10 is one series of data and in cells B6 to B10 is another. Suppose that we want to add the values comprising series 1 to those that comprise series 2. In this case, we simply

1. Locate the cursor on cell C6.
2. Enter the equation = A1 + B1.
3. Press enter.
4. Locate the cursor on the cell in which the equation resides.
5. Select the "Copy" function.
6. Highlight the remaining cells in column C (i.e., C2 to C10).
7. Press the enter key.

Exhibit B.1 **The Use of Excel to Perform Mathematical Operations**

Data Series 1	Data Series 2	Addition	Subtraction	Multiplication	Division	Exponentiation
4	1	5	3	4	4	16
6	2	8	4	12	3	36
8	2	10	6	16	4	64
10	4	14	6	40	2.5	100
12	5	17	7	60	2.4	144

In this example, subtraction simply requires us to

1. Locate the cursor on cell D6.
2. Enter the equation = A1 − B1.
3. Press enter.
4. Locate the cursor on the cell in which the equation resides.
5. Select the "Copy" function.
6. Highlight the remaining cells in column D (i.e., D2 to D10).
7. Press the enter key.

For multiplication, division, and exponentiation, simply substitute a star (*), a slash (/), and a caret (^) as the mathematical operator.

In our discussion of chi-square and the assessment of multiple proportions, it is useful to limit the operation of multiplication to a given row or column. If we wish to limit a set of calculations to the data appearing in column C and allow the rows to vary, we use $C1. Similarly, if we wish to limit calculations to the fifth row and allow the columns to vary, we use A$5. Finally, we frequently require calculations that involve a fixed value appearing in a given cell, for example, B6. In this instance, when we enter $B$6, the calculations are limited to the value in cell B6.

The IF Statement

We frequently use an IF statement as a method of making decisions in the context of a spreadsheet. The IF function tests a condition and results in one outcome if it is true and another if it is false. For example, consider Exhibit B.2 where we wish to consider the gender of eight patients. The letters M and F, representing a male or a female patient, respectively, are located in cells C17 to C24. Suppose also that we wish to assign a value of 1 to each of the male patients and a value of 0 to each of the female patients. In cell B17, we enter an IF statement as follows:

= IF(C17 = "M",1,0)

Exhibit B.2 **The IF Statement**

ID	Male	Gender
1	1	M
2	1	M
3	0	F
4	1	M
5	0	F
6	0	F
7	0	F
8	1	M

Excel interprets the IF statement as follows: If the entry in cell C17 is the letter "M," a 1 is recorded in cell B17. If the entry is not the letter "M," 0 is recorded. The other values in column B of Exhibit B.2 were obtained by using the "Copy" function as described previously.

APPENDIX C Solutions to Selected Exercises

Chapter 2

EXERCISE 1

Visits	Frequency Patients	Relative frequency	Visits or More Than	Visits or Frequency	Less Than	Frequency
0 to 3	13	0.52	0	25	3	13
4 to 7	9	0.36	4	12	7	22
8 to 11	3	0.12	8	3	11	25
	25	1				

EXERCISE 2

Bar Charts

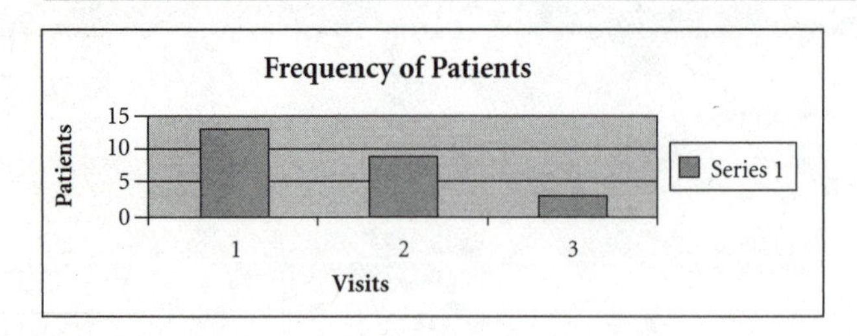

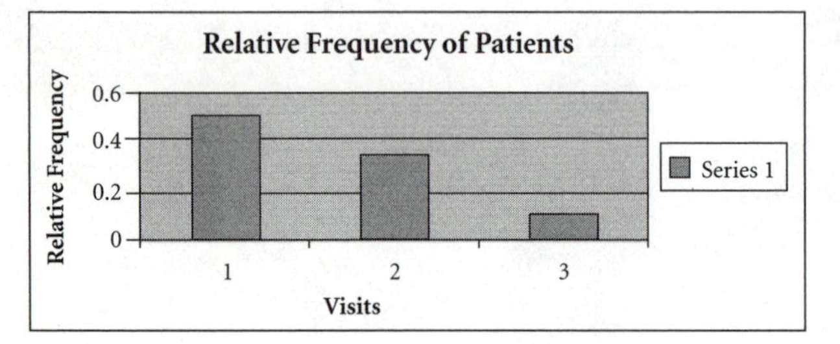

Pie Charts

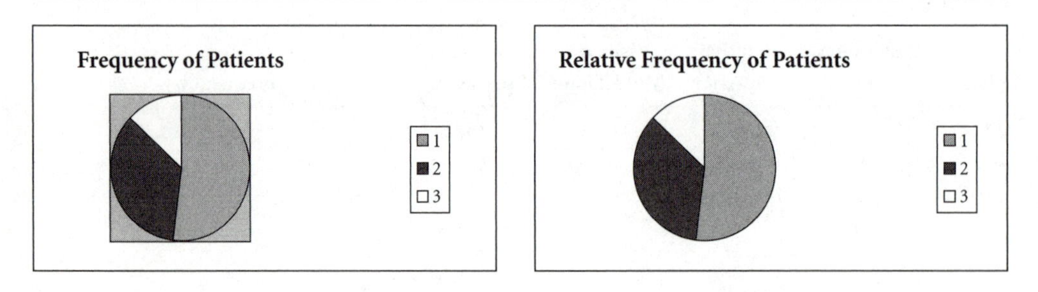

EXERCISE 5

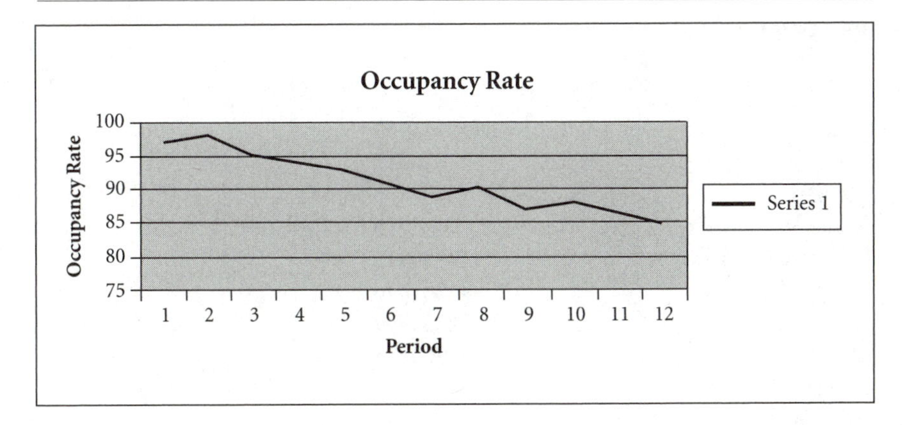

EXERCISE 7

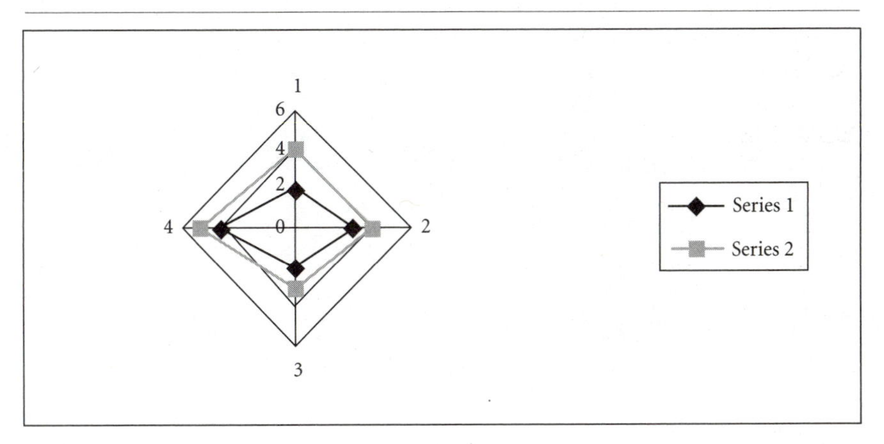

Chapter 3

EXERCISE 2

Column1	
Mean	5.111111111
Standard Error	0.571026417
Median	5
Mode	5
Standard Deviation	2.422659911
Sample Variance	5.869281046
Kurtosis	−0.352254949
Skewness	0.384960373
Range	9
Minimum	1
Maximum	10
Sum	92
Count	18

First Quartile	3.25
Sixth Decile	5.2
25th Percentile	3.25

EXERCISE 3

Average	
Wage Rate	16.7540107

EXERCISE 7

GM	1.033949796

EXERCISE 9

Column1	
Mean	88.26666667
Standard Error	9.83020935
Median	89
Mode	67
Standard Deviation	38.0722371
Sample Variance	1449.495238
Kurtosis	−0.362934648
Skewness	0.192844056
Range	133
Minimum	23
Maximum	156
Sum	1324
Count	15

3rd Decile	69.2
15th Percentile	57.1

EXERCISE 12

LI	1.173726332
PI	1.176041999

Chapter 4

EXERCISE 1

$P(A \cup B)$	0.64
$P(A \cap B)$	0.01
$P(A \mid B)$	0.04

A is negatively associated with B

EXERCISE 3

P(A1)	0.65
P(A2)	0.35
P(B1)	0.3
P(B2)	0.45
P(B3)	0.25
$P(A1 \cap B3)$	0.2
$P(A1 \cap B2)$	0.25
$P(A2 \cap B1)$	0.1
$P(A2 \cap B3)$	0.05
$P(A1 \cup B1)$	0.75
$P(B1 \cup B2)$	0.75
$P(B2 \cup B3)$	0.7
$P(A1 \mid B1)$	0.67
$P(A2 \mid B1)$	0.33
$P(A1 \mid B2)$	0.56
$P(A2 \mid B2)$	0.44
$P(A1 \mid B3)$	0.8
$P(A2 \mid B3)$	0.2

EXERCISE 4

$P(A1 \cap B1)$	0.6
$P(A2 \cap B2)$	0.15
$P(A1 \cup B2)$	0.85
$P(PA1 \mid B1)$	0.8
$P(A1 \mid B2)$	0.4

EXERCISE 7

P(A2)	0.68
P(B2)	0.565
P(B3 ∩ A3)	0.09
Royer	
0 to 19	0.250
20 to 25	0.083
25+	0.667
Peak	1
0 to 19	0.118
20 to 25	0.735
25+	0.147
Uinta	1
0 to 19	0.275
20 to 25	0.275
25+	0.450
	1

EXERCISE 8

P(A)	0.4
P(B)	0.3
P(A ∩ B)	0.2
P(B I A)	0.4

Chapter 5

EXERCISE 1

f(4)	0.13824

EXERCISE 3

f(0)	0.000104858
f(5)	0.200658125
f(7)	0.214990848

EXERCISE 5

f(0)	0.060810063
f(4)	0.155738624
f(2)	0.238375445

EXERCISE 9

$P(0 \leq Z \leq 2.51)$	0.494
$P(-1.69 \leq Z \leq 0)$	0.4545
$P(1.69 \leq Z \leq 1.84)$	0.0126
$P(Z \geq .87)$	0.1922
$P(Z \leq .87)$	0.8078
$P(Z \leq -1.23)$	0.1093
$P(-1.72 \leq Z \leq -.69)$	0.2024
$P(Z \geq -.69)$	0.7549
$P(-.75 \leq Z \leq 1.83)$	0.7398
$P(.23 \leq Z \leq 2.58)$	0.3681

EXERCISE 11

a	0.1357
b	0.8944
c	0.383
d	0.3721

Chapter 6

EXERCISE 1 0.97 minutes

EXERCISE 2 $19.17 \leq \mu \leq 21.47$

EXERCISE 5 $3.01 \leq \mu \leq 3.99$

EXERCISE 10

Column1	
Mean	17.4444444
Standard Error	0.52921692
Median	17
Mode	18
Standard Deviation	3.17530151
Sample Variance	10.0825397
Kurtosis	−0.9355557
Skewness	0.25921472
Range	11
Minimum	12
Maximum	23
Sum	628
Count	36

$Z = (17.44–20)/0.53$
−4.830188679 The calculated value of Z is much less than −1.96.
Reject union claim: Procedure requires less than 20 minutes to perform.

EXERCISE 12

1. Examine the assumption of equal variances

F-Test Two-Sample for Variances

	Variable 1	Variable 2
Mean	29.5	30
Variance	2.05555556	1.5555556
Observations	10	10
df	9	9
F	1.32142857	
$P(F \le f)$ one-tail	0.34236996	
F Critical one-tail	3.17889715	

continues

EXERCISE 12 (Continued)

t-Test: Two-Sample Assuming Equal Variances

	Variable 1	Variable 2
Mean	29.5	30
Variance	2.05555556	1.5555556
Observations	10	10
Pooled Variance	1.80555556	
Hypothesized Mean	0	
df	18	
t Stat	−0.8320503	
P(T ≤ t) one-tail	0.20814164	
t Critical one-tail	1.73406306	
P(T ≤ t) two-tail	0.41628327	
t Critical two-tail	2.10092367	

There is no difference in the mean time required to complete the procedure by the two technicians.

EXERCISE 14 2,213 observations

Chapter 7

EXERCISE 1 $.22 \leq \Pi \leq .28$

EXERCISE 3 $.309 \leq \Pi \leq .368$

EXERCISE 5 $Z = -9.24 < -1.96$

Null hypothesis must be rejected.

EXERCISE 7

$Z = 5 > 1.96$ or 1.64

The defective rate significantly exceeds the standard.

EXERCISE 9

$Z = 1.674395 > 1.64$

Therefore, we conclude that the rate is greater at the Tejon Hospital exceeds that at the Memorial Hospital.

EXERCISE 12

Chi square = $144.89 > 9.488$

There is a significant relation between SES and the use of prenatal care.

Chapter 8

EXERCISE 2

ANOVA: Single Factor

SUMMARY

Groups	Count	Sum	Average	Variance
Column 1	6	42	7	2
Column 2	6	21	3.5	3.5
Column 3	6	63	10.5	3.5

ANOVA

Source of Variation	SS	df	MS	F	P-Value	F Crit
Between Groups	147	2	73.5	24.5	1.88077E-05	3.6823167
Within Groups	45	15	3			
Total	192	17				

At least two of the treatment effects are significant.

EXERCISE 5

Anova: Two-Factor Without Replication

SUMMARY	Count	Sum	Average	Variance
Row 1	3	60	20	4
Row 2	3	105	35	4
Row 3	3	48	16	4
Row 4	3	138	46	1
Column 1	4	114	28.5	199
Column 2	4	114	28.5	209.6667
Column 3	4	123	30.75	170.25

ANOVA

Source of Variation	SS	df	MS	F	P-Value	F Crit
Rows	1,724.25	3	574.75	275.88	8.13375E-07	4.7570552
Columns	13.5	2	6.75	3.24	0.111124545	5.1432494
Error	12.5	6	2.0833333			
Total	1,750.25	11				

At least two of the block effects are significant.

Differences among the technicians were not significant.

EXERCISE 7

ANOVA: Two-Factor with Replication

SUMMARY	**A**	**B**	**C**	**Total**
1				
Count	3	3	3	9
Sum	27	21	16	64
Average	9	7	5.3333333	7.1111111
Variance	4	1	2.3333333	4.3611111
2				
Count	3	3	3	9
Sum	35	27	21	83
Average	11.66666667	9	7	9.222222
Variance	4.333333333	1	1	5.694444
3				
Count	3	3	3	9
Sum	12	16	9	37
Average	4	5.33333333	3	4.1111111
Variance	1	0.33333333	1	1.6111111
4				
Count	3	3	3	9
Sum	26	17	14	57
Average	8.666666667	5.66666667	4.66666667	6.333333
Variance	2.333333333	2.33333333	2.3333333	5
Total				
Count	12	12	12	
Sum	100	81	60	
Average	8.333333333	6.75	5	
Variance	10.42424242	3.11363636	3.45454555	

continues

EXERCISE 7 (Continued)

ANOVA

Source of Variation	SS	df	MS	F	P-Value	F Crit
Sample	120.3055556	3	40.101852	20.922701	6.97287E-07	3.0087861
Columns	66.72222222	2	33.361111	17.4058	2.13294E-05	3.4028318
Interaction	20.61111111	6	3.4351852	1.7922761	0.143291356	2.5081874
Within	46	24	1.9166667			
Total	253.6388889	35				

Only the block and treatment effects are significant.

The interactive effects are not significant.

Chapter 9

EXERCISE 2

Covariation	608.1333333
Covariance	43.43809524

The age and the number of visits covary positively.

EXERCISE 4

Covariation	90986.8
Covariance	10109.64444

The days of care and hours covary positively.

EXERCISE 6

Covariation	2473.2
Covariance	274.8

The number of procedures and hours covary positively.

Chapter 10

EXERCISE 1

SUMMARY OUTPUT

Regression Statistics	
Multiple R	0.955412252
R Square	0.912812571
Adjusted R Square	0.906105846
Standard Error	0.797929689
Observations	15

ANOVA

	df	SS	MS	F	Significance F
Regression	1	86.6563401	86.65634	136.1041	2.92857E-08
Residual	13	8.27699325	0.6366918		
Total	14	94.9333333			

	Coefficients	Standard Error	t Stat	P-Value	Lower 95%	Upper 95%
Intercept	−1.214665084	0.51302661	−2.3676454	0.034085	−2.322991488	−0.1063387
X Variable 1	0.142495626	0.01221423	11.666365	2.93E-08	0.116108398	0.1688829

R square indicates that approximately 91% of the variation in visits is attributable to the regression analysis.

The F ratio is significant, indicating that MS(REG) is greater than MS(ERROR).

The intercept and slope coefficient are both significant; as age increases by 1 year, the average use of service increases by approximately 0.14 visits.

EXERCISE 3

SUMMARY OUTPUT

Regression Statistics	
Multiple R	0.914794663
R Square	0.836849275
Adjusted R Square	0.816455435
Standard Error	20.22300477
Observations	10

ANOVA

	df	SS	MS	F	Significance F
Regression	1	16781.8406	16781.841	41.03441	0.000207842
Residual	8	3271.75938	408.96992		
Total	9	20053.6			

	Coefficients	Standard Error	t Stat	P-Value	Lower 95%	Upper 95%
Intercept	59.05169581	20.4084227	2.8934963	0.020091	11.98975821	106.11363
X Variable 1	0.184442585	0.02879301	6.4058109	0.000208	0.118045739	0.2508394

R square indicates that approximately 84% of the variation in days of care is explained by regression.

The F ratio is significant, implying that MS(REG) is significantly greater than MS(ERROR).

The intercept and the slope coefficient are both significantly greater than zero. The coefficient slope coefficient indicates that an increase of 1 hour in the use of nursing personnel increases the volume of stay specific services by approximately 0.03 patient days of care.

EXERCISE 5

SUMMARY OUTPUT

Regression Statistics	
Multiple R	0.82424435
R Square	0.679378748
Adjusted R Square	0.639301092
Standard Error	22.17812143
Observations	10

ANOVA

	df	SS	MS	F	Significance F
Regression	1	8337.94744	8337.9474	16.951556	0.003357009
Residual	8	3934.95256	491.86907		
Total	9	12272.9			

	Coefficients	Standard Error	t Stat	P-Value	Lower 95%	Upper 95%
Intercept	75.82878953	24.1326497	3.1421659	0.01376	20.17876362	131.47882
X Variable 1	3.37131952	0.81883255	4.1172271	0.003357	1.483087064	5.259552

R square indicates that approximately 68% of the variation in the number of procedures is explained by the regression analysis.

The F ratio is significant, indicating that MS(REG) is greater than MS(ERROR).

The intercept and slope coefficient are both significantly different from zero.

The slope coefficient indicates that an increase of one hour in the use of technicians on average increases the volume of ancillary care by approximately 3.37 procedures.

Chapter 11

EXERCISE 1

SUMMARY OUTPUT

Regression Statistics	
Multiple R	0.979549288
R Square	0.959516808
Adjusted R Square	0.953733495
Standard Error	0.495944458
Observations	17

ANOVA

	df	SS	MS	F	Significance F
Regression	2	81.61537085	40.80768542	165.9112666	1.78206E-10
Residual	14	3.443452681	0.245960906		
Total	16	85.05882353			

	Coefficients	Standard Error	t Stat	P-Value	Lower 95%	Upper 95%
Intercept	2.468793074	0.469148904	5.26228038	0.00012013	1.462567855	3.475018294
X Variable 1	−0.08084552	0.038432371	−2.103578794	0.053974508	−0.163274831	0.00158379
X Variable 2	0.598856951	0.058544799	10.22903753	7.05148E-08	0.473290733	0.724423169

R square indicates that approximately 96% of the variation exhibited by the number of visits is attributable to the regression analysis.

The F ratio is significant, indicating that MS(REG) exceeds MS(ERROR).
All coefficients are significant ($P < 0.05$).
The number of visits is negatively related to distance and positively related to disability days.

EXERCISE 2

SUMMARY OUTPUT

Regression Statistics	
Multiple R	0.98020536
R Square	0.960802547
Adjusted R Square	0.951756981
Standard Error	0.506427094
Observations	17

ANOVA

	df	SS	MS	F	Significance F
Regression	3	81.7247343	27.241578	106.2181	2.14498E-09
Residual	13	3.33408922	0.2564684		
Total	16	85.0588235			

	Coefficients	Standard Error	t Stat	P-Value	Lower 95%	Upper 95%
Intercept	2.498794898	0.48126322	5.1921585	0.000173	1.459089128	3.5385007
X Variable 1	−0.108820375	0.05809824	−1.8730408	0.08372	−0.234333969	0.0166932
X Variable 2	0.564988319	0.07914509	7.1386401	7.6E-06	0.394005779	0.7359709
X Variable 3	0.019790634	0.03030683	0.653009	0.525131	−0.045683279	0.0852645

R square indicates that approximately 96% of the variation in the number of visits is attributable to the regression analysis.

The F ratio is significant, indicating that MS(REG) exceeds MS(ERROR).

All slope coefficients are significant, ($P < 0.05$, directional alternate hypothesis).

The interactive term is not significant.

EXERCISE 5

SUMMARY OUTPUT

Regression Statistics	
Multiple R	0.930040846
R Square	0.864975976
Adjusted R Square	0.834970637
Standard Error	2.913161504
Observations	12

ANOVA

	df	SS	MS	F	Significance F
Regression	2	489.288077	244.64404	28.8274	0.000122138
Residual	9	76.3785895	8.4865099		
Total	11	565.666667			

	Coefficients	Standard Error	t Stat	P-Value	Lower 95%	Upper 95%
Intercept	187.3678619	20.6163378	9.0883194	7.88E-06	140.7304301	234.00529
X Variable 1	−0.157896667	0.02466537	−6.4015532	0.000125	−0.213693649	−0.1020997
X Variable 2	4.76787E-05	7.0767E-06	6.7374162	8.4E-05	3.167E-05	6.36E-05

R square indicates that approximately 86% of the variation in the cost per day is attributable to regression.

The F ratio is significant, implying that MS(REG) > MS(ERROR).

All coefficients are significantly different from zero (P > 0.05).

The regression equation forms a parabola that opens upward.

EXERCISE 6

SUMMARY OUTPUT

Regression Statistics	
Multiple R	0.819407544
R Square	0.671428723
Adjusted R Square	0.616666843
Standard Error	2.760951582
Observations	15

ANOVA

	df	SS	MS	F	Significance F
Regression	2	186.925756	93.462878	12.26088	0.001258281
Residual	12	91.4742436	7.6228536		
Total	14	278.4			

	Coefficients	Standard Error	t Stat	P-Value	Lower 95%	Upper 95%
Intercept	−1.433746029	2.112987	−0.6785399	0.510304	−6.037549125	3.1700571
X Variable 1	0.157744723	0.05527556	2.8537876	0.014520	0.037309616	0.2781798
X Variable 2	3.38250052	1.69965079	1.990115	0.069855	−0.320720357	7.0857214

The F ratio is significant, implying that MS(REG) is greater than MS(ERROR).

The slope coefficient derived for the age of the patient is significant and indicates that with an increase in age of 1 year, on average use increases by approximately 0.16 days. The coefficient derived for insurance status is significant ($P < 0.05$, directional alternate) and indicates the insured use approximately 3.38 more days of care than the uninsured.

Chapter 12

EXERCISE 1

Smoothing Constant		0.1
Visits	Projection	MSE
8.2	8.2	0
7.9	8.2	0.09
10.1	8.17	3.7249
6.9	8.363	2.140369
11.4	8.2167	10.13339889
5.9	8.53503	6.9433831
8.6	8.271527	0.10789451
9.2	8.3043743	0.80214539
		23.9420909
		2.99276136

Smoothing Constant		0.5
Visits	Projection	MSE
8.2	8.2	0
7.9	8.2	0.09
10.1	8.05	4.2025
6.9	9.075	4.730625
11.4	7.9875	11.6451563
5.9	9.69375	14.3925391
8.6	7.796875	0.64500977
9.2	8.1984375	1.00312744
		36.7089575
		4.58861969

Smoothing Constant		0.9
Visits	Projection	MSE
8.2	8.2	0
7.9	8.2	0.09
10.1	7.93	4.7089
6.9	9.883	8.898289
11.4	7.1983	17.6542829
5.9	10.97983	25.8046728
8.6	6.407983	4.80493853
9.2	8.3807983	0.67109143
		62.6321747
		7.82902183

EXERCISE 5

Rate of Change	0.02675703
Projection	5.339136555

EXERCISE 7

SUMMARY OUTPUT

Regression Statistics	
Multiple R	0.995155909
R Square	0.990335284
Adjusted R Square	0.989127195
Standard Error	3.002226447
Observations	10

ANOVA

	df	SS	MS	F	Significance F	
Regression	1	7388.73409	7388.7341	819.7532	2.39497E-09	
Residual	8	72.1069091	9.0133636			
Total	9	7460.841				
	Coefficients	**Standard Error**	**t Stat**	**P-Value**	**Lower 95%**	**Upper 95%**
Intercept	115.58	2.05091111	56.355441	1.09E-11	110.8505875	120.30941
X Variable 1	9.463636364	0.33053425	28.631333	2.39E-09	8.701422516	10.22585
Projection	219.68					

EXERCISE 9

First Order Correlation	0.969628798
Second Order Correlation	0.965935856

SUMMARY OUTPUT

Regression Statistics	
Multiple R	0.969628798
R Square	0.940180005
Adjusted R Square	0.937687505
Standard Error	3.770954037
Observations	26

ANOVA

	df	SS	MS	F	Significance F
Regression	1	224.198578	224.19858	377.2036	3.48182E-16
Residual	24	14.2648831	0.5943701		
Total	25	238.463462			

	Coefficients	Standard Error	t Stat	P-Value	Lower 95%	Upper 95%
Intercept	1.486813307	1.44809951	1.0267342	0.314783	−1.501916568	4.4755432
X Variable 1	0.963108004	0.04958919	19.421731	3.48E-16	0.860760959	1.065455
Projection	34.71403945					

APPENDIX D Statistical Tables

Table D.1 **The Standard Normal Distribution***

z	.00	.01	.02	.03	.04	.05	.06	.07	.08	.09
0.0	.0000	.0040	.0080	.0120	.0160	.0199	.0239	.0279	.0319	.0359
0.1	.0398	.0438	.0478	.0517	.0557	.0596	.0636	.0675	.0714	.0753
0.2	.0793	.0832	.0871	.0910	.0948	.0987	.1026	.1064	.1103	.1141
0.3	.1179	.1217	.1255	.1293	.1331	.1368	.1406	.1443	.1480	.1517
0.4	.1554	.1591	.1628	.1664	.1700	.1736	.1772	.1808	.1844	.1879
0.5	.1915	.1950	.1985	.2019	.2054	.2088	.2123	.2157	.2190	.2224
0.6	.2257	.2291	.2324	.2357	.2389	.2422	.2454	.2486	.2517	.2549
0.7	.2580	.2611	.2642	.2673	.2704	.2734	.2764	.2794	.2823	.2852
0.8	.2881	.2910	.2939	.2967	.2995	.3023	.3051	.3078	.3106	.3133
0.9	.3159	.3186	.3212	.3238	.3264	.3289	.3315	.3340	.3365	.3389
1.0	.3413	.3438	.3461	.3485	.3508	.3531	.3554	.3577	.3599	.3621
1.1	.3643	.3665	.3686	.3708	.3729	.3749	.3770	.3790	.3810	.3830
1.2	.3849	.3869	.3888	.3907	.3925	.3944	.3962	.3980	.3997	.4015
1.3	.4032	.4049	.4066	.4082	.4099	.4115	.4131	.4147	.4162	.4177
1.4	.4192	.4207	.4222	.4236	.4251	.4265	.4279	.4292	.4306	.4319
1.5	.4332	.4345	.4357	.4370	.4382	.4394	.4406	.4418	.4429	.4441
1.6	.4452	.4463	.4474	.4484	.4495	.4505	.4515	.4525	.4535	.4545
1.7	.4554	.4564	.4573	.4582	.4591	.4599	.4608	.4616	.4625	.4633
1.8	.4641	.4649	.4656	.4664	.4671	.4678	.4686	.4693	.4699	.4706
1.9	.4713	.4719	.4726	.4732	.4738	.4744	.4750	.4756	.4761	.4767
2.0	.4772	.4778	.4783	.4788	.4793	.4798	.4803	.4808	.4812	.4817
2.1	.4821	.4826	.4830	.4834	.4838	.4842	.4846	.4850	.4854	.4857
2.2	.4861	.4864	.4868	.4871	.4875	.4878	.4881	.4884	.4887	.4890
2.3	.4893	.4896	.4898	.4901	.4904	.4906	.4909	.4911	.4913	.4916
2.4	.4918	.4920	.4922	.4925	.4927	.4929	.4931	.4932	.4934	.4936
2.5	.4938	.4940	.4941	.4943	.4945	.4946	.4948	.4949	.4951	.4952
2.6	.4953	.4955	.4956	.4957	.4959	.4960	.4961	.4962	.4963	.4964
2.7	.4965	.4966	.4967	.4968	.4969	.4970	.4971	.4972	.4973	.4974
2.8	.4974	.4975	.4976	.4977	.4977	.4978	.4979	.4979	.4980	.4981
2.9	.4981	.4982	.4982	.4983	.4984	.4984	.4985	.4985	.4986	.4986
3.0	.4987	.4987	.4987	.4988	.4988	.4989	.4989	.4989	.4990	.4990

*This table is based on Table 1 of *Biometrika Tables for Statisticians. Volume I*, 3rd ed., Cambridge University Press. 1966, by permission of the *Biometrika* trustees.

Table D.2 **The *t* Distribution (Values of t_α—One-Tailed Test)***

d.f.	$t_{.100}$	$t_{.050}$	$t_{.025}$	$t_{.010}$	$t_{.005}$	*d.f.*
1	3.078	6.314	12.706	31.821	63.657	1
2	1.886	2.920	4.303	6.965	9.925	2
3	1.638	2.353	3.182	4.541	5.841	3
4	1.533	2.132	2.776	3.747	4.604	4
5	1.476	2.015	2.571	3.365	4.032	5
6	1.440	1.943	2.447	3.143	3.707	6
7	1.415	1.895	2.365	2.998	3.499	7
8	1.397	1.860	2.306	2.896	3.355	8
9	1.383	1.833	2.262	2.821	3.250	9
10	1.372	1.812	2.228	2.764	3.169	10
11	1.363	1.796	2.201	2.718	3.106	11
12	1.356	1.782	2.179	2.681	3.055	12
13	1.350	1.771	2.160	2.650	3.012	13
14	1.345	1.761	2.145	2.624	2.977	14
15	1.341	1.753	2.131	2.602	2.947	15
16	1.337	1.746	2.120	2.583	2.921	16
17	1.333	1.740	2.110	2.567	2.898	17
18	1.330	1.734	2.101	2.552	2.878	18
19	1.328	1.729	2.093	2.539	2.861	19
20	1.325	1.725	2.086	2.528	2.845	20
21	1.323	1.721	2.080	2.518	2.831	21
22	1.321	1.717	2.074	2.508	2.819	22
23	1.319	1.714	2.069	2.500	2.807	23
24	1.318	1.711	2.064	2.492	2.797	24
25	1.316	1.708	2.060	2.485	2.787	25
26	1.315	1.706	2.056	2.479	2.779	26
27	1.314	1.703	2.052	2.473	2.771	27
28	1.313	1.701	2.048	2.467	2.763	28
29	1.311	1.699	2.045	2.462	2.756	29
inf.	1.282	1.645	1.960	2.326	2.576	inf.

*This table is from Table IV of R. A. Fisher, *Statistical Methods for Research Workers*, published by Hafner Press, A Division of Macmillan Publishing Co., Inc. and *Biometrika Tables for Statisticians, Volume I*, 3rd ed., Cambridge University Press. 1966, by permission of *Biometrika* trustees.

Table D.3 **The *F* Distribution (Values of $F_{.05}$)***

Degrees of freedom for denominator	Degrees of freedom for numerator																		
	1	**2**	**3**	**4**	**5**	**6**	**7**	**8**	**9**	**10**	**12**	**15**	**20**	**24**	**30**	**40**	**60**	**120**	**∞**
1	161	200	216	225	230	234	237	239	241	242	244	246	248	249	250	251	252	253	254
2	18.5	19.0	19.2	19.2	19.3	19.3	19.4	19.4	19.4	19.4	19.4	19.4	19.4	19.5	19.5	19.5	19.5	19.5	19.5
3	10.1	9.55	9.28	9.12	9.01	8.94	8.89	8.85	8.81	8.79	8.74	8.70	8.66	8.64	8.62	8.59	8.57	8.55	8.53
4	7.71	6.94	6.59	6.39	6.26	6.16	6.09	6.04	6.00	5.96	5.91	5.86	5.80	5.77	5.75	5.72	5.69	5.66	5.63
5	6.61	5.79	5.41	5.19	5.05	4.95	4.88	4.82	4.77	4.74	4.68	4.62	4.56	4.53	4.50	4.46	4.43	4.40	4.37
6	5.99	5.14	4.76	4.53	4.39	4.28	4.21	4.15	4.10	4.06	4.00	3.94	3.87	3.84	3.81	3.77	3.74	3.70	3.67
7	5.59	4.74	4.35	4.12	3.97	3.87	3.79	3.73	3.68	3.64	3.57	3.51	3.44	3.41	3.38	3.34	3.30	3.27	3.23
8	5.32	4.46	4.07	3.84	3.69	3.58	3.50	3.44	3.39	3.35	3.28	3.22	3.15	3.12	3.08	3.04	3.01	2.97	2.93
9	5.12	4.26	3.86	3.63	3.48	3.37	3.29	3.23	3.18	3.14	3.07	3.01	2.94	2.90	2.86	2.83	2.79	2.75	2.71
10	4.96	4.10	3.71	3.48	3.33	3.22	3.14	3.07	3.02	2.98	2.91	2.85	2.77	2.74	2.70	2.66	2.62	2.58	2.54
11	4.84	3.98	3.59	3.36	3.20	3.09	3.01	2.95	2.90	2.85	2.79	2.72	2.65	2.61	2.57	2.53	2.49	2.45	2.40
12	4.75	3.89	3.49	3.26	3.11	3.00	2.91	2.85	2.80	2.75	2.69	2.62	2.54	2.51	2.47	2.43	2.38	2.34	2.30
13	4.67	3.81	3.41	3.18	3.03	2.92	2.83	2.77	2.71	2.67	2.60	2.53	2.46	2.42	2.38	2.34	2.30	2.25	2.21
14	4.60	3.74	3.34	3.11	2.96	2.85	2.76	2.70	2.65	2.60	2.53	2.46	2.39	2.35	2.31	2.27	2.22	2.18	2.13
15	4.54	3.68	3.29	3.06	2.90	2.79	2.71	2.64	2.59	2.54	2.48	2.40	2.33	2.29	2.25	2.20	2.16	2.11	2.07
16	4.49	3.63	3.24	3.01	2.85	2.74	2.66	2.59	2.54	2.49	2.42	2.35	2.28	2.24	2.19	2.15	2.11	2.06	2.01
17	4.45	3.59	3.20	2.96	2.81	2.70	2.61	2.55	2.49	2.45	2.38	2.31	2.23	2.19	2.15	2.10	2.06	2.01	1.96
18	4.41	3.55	3.16	2.93	2.77	2.66	2.58	2.51	2.46	2.41	2.34	2.27	2.19	2.15	2.11	2.06	2.02	1.97	1.92
19	4.38	3.52	3.13	2.90	2.74	2.63	2.54	2.48	2.42	2.38	2.31	2.23	2.16	2.11	2.07	2.03	1.98	1.93	1.88
20	4.35	3.49	3.10	2.87	2.71	2.60	2.51	2.45	2.39	2.35	2.28	2.20	2.12	2.08	2.04	1.99	1.95	1.90	1.84
21	4.32	3.47	3.07	2.84	2.68	2.57	2.49	2.42	2.37	2.32	2.25	2.18	2.10	2.05	2.01	1.96	1.92	1.87	1.81
22	4.30	3.44	3.05	2.82	2.66	2.55	2.46	2.40	2.34	2.30	2.23	2.15	2.07	2.03	1.98	1.94	1.89	1.84	1.78

Degrees of freedom for denominator																			
23	4.28	3.42	3.03	2.80	2.64	2.53	2.44	2.37	2.32	2.27	2.20	2.13	2.05	2.01	1.96	1.91	1.86	1.81	1.76
24	4.26	3.40	3.01	2.78	2.62	2.51	2.42	2.36	2.30	2.25	2.18	2.11	2.03	1.98	1.94	1.89	1.84	1.79	1.73
25	4.24	3.39	2.99	2.76	2.60	2.49	2.40	2.34	2.28	2.24	2.16	2.09	2.01	1.96	1.92	1.87	1.82	1.77	1.71
30	4.17	3.32	2.92	2.69	2.53	2.42	2.33	2.27	2.21	2.16	2.09	2.01	1.93	1.89	1.84	1.79	1.74	1.68	1.62
40	4.08	3.23	2.84	2.61	2.45	2.34	2.25	2.18	2.12	2.08	2.00	1.92	1.84	1.79	1.74	1.69	1.64	1.58	1.51
60	4.00	3.15	2.76	2.53	2.37	2.25	2.17	2.10	2.04	1.99	1.92	1.84	1.75	1.70	1.65	1.59	1.53	1.47	1.39
120	3.92	3.07	2.68	2.45	2.29	2.18	2.09	2.02	1.96	1.91	1.83	1.75	1.66	1.61	1.55	1.50	1.43	1.35	1.25
∞	3.84	3.00	2.60	2.37	2.21	2.10	2.01	1.94	1.88	1.83	1.75	1.67	1.57	1.52	1.46	1.39	1.32	1.22	1.00

*This table is reproduced from M. Merrington and C. M. Thompson. "Tables of percentage points of the inverted beta (F) distribution," *Biometrika*, Vol. 33 (1943), by permission of the *Biometrika* Trustees.

Table D.4 **The *F* Distribution (Values of $F_{.01}$)***

Degrees of freedom for denominator	Degrees of freedom for numerator																		
	1	2	3	4	5	6	7	8	9	10	12	15	20	24	30	40	60	120	∞
1	4,052	5,000	5,403	5,625	5,764	5,859	5,928	5,982	6,023	6,056	6,106	6,157	6,209	6,235	6,261	6,287	6,313	6,339	6,366
2	98.5	99.0	99.2	99.2	99.3	99.3	99.4	99.4	99.4	99.4	99.4	99.4	99.4	99.5	99.5	99.5	99.5	99.5	99.5
3	34.1	30.8	29.5	28.7	28.2	27.9	27.7	27.5	27.3	27.2	27.1	26.9	26.7	26.6	26.5	26.4	26.3	26.2	26.1
4	21.2	18.0	16.7	16.0	15.5	15.2	15.0	14.8	14.7	14.5	14.4	14.2	14.0	13.9	13.8	13.7	13.7	13.6	13.5
5	16.3	13.3	12.1	11.4	11.0	10.7	10.5	10.3	10.2	10.1	9.89	9.72	9.55	9.47	9.38	9.29	9.20	9.11	9.02
6	13.7	10.9	9.78	9.15	8.75	8.47	8.26	8.10	7.98	7.87	7.72	7.56	7.40	7.31	7.23	7.14	7.06	6.97	6.88
7	12.2	9.55	8.45	7.85	7.46	7.19	6.99	6.84	6.72	6.62	6.47	6.31	6.16	6.07	5.99	5.91	5.82	5.74	5.65
8	11.3	8.65	7.59	7.01	6.63	6.37	6.18	6.03	5.91	5.81	5.67	5.52	5.36	5.28	5.20	5.12	5.03	4.95	4.86
9	10.6	8.02	6.99	6.42	6.06	5.80	5.61	5.47	5.35	5.26	5.11	4.96	4.81	4.73	4.65	4.57	4.48	4.40	4.31
10	10.0	7.56	6.55	5.99	5.64	5.39	5.20	5.06	4.94	4.85	4.71	4.56	4.41	4.33	4.25	4.17	4.08	4.00	3.91
11	9.65	7.21	6.22	5.67	5.32	5.07	4.89	4.74	4.63	4.54	4.40	4.25	4.10	4.02	3.94	3.86	3.78	3.69	3.60
12	9.33	6.93	5.95	5.41	5.06	4.82	4.64	4.50	4.39	4.30	4.16	4.01	3.86	3.78	3.70	3.62	3.54	3.45	3.36
13	9.07	6.70	5.74	5.21	4.86	4.62	4.44	4.30	4.19	4.10	3.96	3.82	3.66	3.59	3.51	3.43	3.34	3.25	3.17
14	8.86	6.51	5.56	5.04	4.70	4.46	4.28	4.14	4.03	3.94	3.80	3.66	3.51	3.43	3.35	3.27	3.18	3.09	3.00
15	8.68	6.36	5.42	4.89	4.56	4.32	4.14	4.00	3.89	3.80	3.67	3.52	3.37	3.29	3.21	3.13	3.05	2.96	2.87
16	8.53	6.23	5.29	4.77	4.44	4.20	4.03	3.89	3.78	3.69	3.55	3.41	3.26	3.18	3.10	3.02	2.93	2.84	2.75
17	8.40	6.11	5.19	4.67	4.34	4.10	3.93	3.79	3.68	3.59	3.46	3.31	3.16	3.08	3.00	2.92	2.83	2.75	2.65
18	8.29	6.01	5.09	4.58	4.25	4.01	3.84	3.71	3.60	3.51	3.37	3.23	3.08	3.00	2.92	2.84	2.75	2.66	2.57
19	8.19	5.93	5.01	4.50	4.17	3.94	3.77	3.63	3.52	3.43	3.30	3.15	3.00	2.92	2.84	2.76	2.67	2.58	2.49
20	8.10	5.85	4.94	4.43	4.10	3.87	3.70	3.56	3.46	3.37	3.23	3.09	2.94	2.86	2.78	2.69	2.61	2.52	2.42

Degrees of freedom for denominator																			
21	8.02	5.78	4.87	4.37	4.04	3.81	3.64	3.51	3.40	3.31	3.17	3.03	2.88	2.80	2.72	2.64	2.55	2.46	2.36
22	7.95	5.72	4.82	4.31	3.99	3.76	3.59	3.45	3.35	3.26	3.12	2.98	2.83	2.75	2.67	2.58	2.50	2.40	2.31
23	7.88	5.66	4.76	4.26	3.94	3.71	3.54	3.41	3.30	3.21	3.07	2.93	2.78	2.70	2.62	2.54	2.45	2.35	2.26
24	7.82	5.61	4.72	4.22	3.90	3.67	3.50	3.36	3.26	3.17	3.03	2.89	2.74	2.66	2.58	2.49	2.40	2.31	2.21
25	7.77	5.57	4.68	4.18	3.86	3.63	3.46	3.32	3.22	3.13	2.99	2.85	2.70	2.62	2.53	2.45	2.36	2.27	2.17
30	7.56	5.39	4.51	4.02	3.70	3.47	3.30	3.17	3.07	2.98	2.84	2.70	2.55	2.47	2.39	2.30	2.21	2.11	2.01
40	7.31	5.18	4.31	3.83	3.51	3.29	3.12	2.99	2.89	2.80	2.66	2.52	2.37	2.29	2.20	2.11	2.02	1.92	1.80
60	7.08	4.98	4.13	3.65	3.34	3.12	2.95	2.82	2.72	2.63	2.50	2.35	2.20	2.12	2.03	1.94	1.84	1.73	1.60
120	6.85	4.79	3.95	3.48	3.17	2.96	2.79	2.66	2.56	2.47	2.34	2.19	2.03	1.95	1.86	1.76	1.66	1.53	1.38
∞	6.63	4.61	3.78	3.32	3.02	2.80	2.64	2.51	2.41	2.32	2.18	2.04	1.88	1.79	1.70	1.59	1.47	1.32	1.00

*This table is reproduced from M. Merrington and C. M. Thompson. "Tables of percentage points of the inverted beta (F) distribution," *Biometrika*, Vol. 33 (1943), by permission of the *Biometrika* Trustees.

Table D.5 **The Chi-Square Distribution (Values of χ_{α}^{2})***

d.f.	$\chi^2_{.995}$	$\chi^2_{.99}$	$\chi^2_{.975}$	$\chi^2_{.95}$	$\chi^2_{.05}$	$\chi^2_{.025}$	$\chi^2_{.01}$	$\chi^2_{.005}$	d.f.
1	.0000393	.000157	.000982	.00393	3.841	5.024	6.635	7.879	1
2	.0100	.0201	.0506	.103	5.991	7.378	9.210	10.597	2
3	.0717	.115	.216	.352	7.815	9.348	11.345	12.838	3
4	.207	.297	.484	.711	9.488	11.143	13.277	14.860	4
5	.412	.554	.831	1.145	11.070	12.832	15.086	16.750	5
6	.676	.872	1.237	1.635	12.592	14.449	16.812	18.548	6
7	.989	1.239	1.690	2.167	14.067	16.013	18.475	20.278	7
8	1.344	1.646	2.180	2.733	15.507	17.535	20.090	21.955	8
9	1.735	2.088	2.700	3.325	16.919	19.023	21.666	23.589	9
10	2.156	2.558	3.247	3.940	18.307	20.483	23.209	25.188	10
11	2.603	3.053	3.816	4.575	19.675	21.920	24.725	26.757	11
12	3.074	3.571	4.404	5.226	21.026	23.337	26.217	28.300	12
13	3.565	4.107	5.009	5.892	22.362	24.736	27.688	29.819	13
14	4.075	4.660	5.629	6.571	23.685	26.119	29.141	31.319	14
15	4.601	5.229	6.262	7.261	24.996	27.488	30.578	32.801	15
16	5.142	5.812	6.908	7.962	26.296	28.845	32.000	34.267	16
17	5.697	6.408	7.564	8.672	27.587	30.191	33.409	35.718	17
18	6.265	7.015	8.231	9.390	28.869	31.526	34.805	37.156	18
19	6.844	7.633	8.907	10.117	30.144	32.852	36.191	38.582	19
20	7.434	8.260	9.591	10.851	31.410	34.170	37.566	39.997	20

21	8.034	8.897	10.283	11.591	32.671	35.479	38.932	41.401	21
22	8.643	9.542	10.982	12.338	33.924	36.781	40.289	42.796	22
23	9.260	10.196	11.689	13.091	35.172	38.076	41.638	44.181	23
24	9.886	10.856	12.401	13.848	36.415	39.364	42.980	45.558	24
25	10.520	11.524	13.120	14.611	37.652	40.646	44.314	46.928	25
26	11.160	12.198	13.844	15.379	38.885	41.923	45.642	48.290	26
27	11.808	12.879	14.573	16.151	40.113	43.194	46.963	49.645	27
28	12.461	13.565	15.308	16.928	41.337	44.461	48.278	50.993	28
29	13.121	14.256	16.047	17.708	42.557	45.722	49.588	52.336	29
30	13.787	14.953	16.791	18.493	43.773	46.979	50.892	53.672	30

*This table is based on Table 8 of *Biometrika Tables for Statisticians, Volume I*, 3rd ed., Cambridge University Press, 1966, by permission of the *Biometrika* trustees.

INDEX

Page numbers in *italics* indicate figures. Those ending with *t* indicate tables. Those ending with **E** indicate exhibits.

C

D

E

F

Q

R

S